Retiring to the seaside

International Library of Social Policy

General Editor   Kathleen Jones
Professor of Social Administration
University of York

Arbor Scientiæ
Arbor Vitæ

A catalogue of the books available in the **International Library of Social Policy** and other series of Social Science books published by Routledge & Kegan Paul will be found at the end of this volume

Retiring to the seaside

Valerie A. Karn
*Centre for Urban and Regional Studies,
University of Birmingham*

Routledge & Kegan Paul
London Henley and Boston

*First published in 1977
by Routledge & Kegan Paul Ltd
39 Store Street,
London WC1E 7DD,
Broadway House,
Newtown Road,
Henley-on-Thames,
Oxon RG9 1EN and
9 Park Street,
Boston, Mass. 02108, USA
Printed in Great Britain
by Redwood Burn Limited
Trowbridge and Esher
© Valerie A. Karn 1977
No part of this book may be reproduced in
any form without permission from the
publisher, except for the quotation of brief
passages in criticism*

ISBN 0 7100 8418 8

If ever I become a rich man,
Or if ever I grow to be old,
I will build a house with deep thatch,
To shelter me from the cold,
And there shall the Sussex songs be sung,
And the story of Sussex told.
I will hold my house in the high wood,
Within a walk of the sea,
And the men that were boys when I was a boy,
Shall sit and drink with me.

    Hilaire Belloc: The South Country

Contents

	Acknowledgments	xii
	Introduction	1
Part one	**The retirement move**	
1	From inland spas to seaside resorts	11
2	The scale of the movement to the coast	24
3	Who are the movers?	33
4	The movers' homes in the cities and suburbs	43
5	The move itself: motives and choices	49
Part two	**Life in the seaside resorts**	
6	The retired population of Bexhill and Clacton	65
7	Family life and friends	80
8	In case of emergency	99
9	Leisure	107
10	The financial position of retired people	120
11	The present retirement home	129
12	Moving from one retirement home to another	156
13	Satisfaction with the retirement move	169

Part three Some policy implications of retirement migration

	Introduction to Part three	183
14	Hospital facilities in the retirement areas	186
15	Housing and residential homes: public versus private provision	194
16	Community health and domiciliary services	203
17	Paying for services for the elderly	215
	Conclusions to Part three	231
18	Retirement to the seaside: success or failure?	238
	Appendix 1: supplementary tables	250
	Appendix 2: definitions	307
	Appendix 3: the sampling method and response	309
	Appendix 4: questionnaire	318
	Appendix 5: list of resorts used for analysis of local authority finance	350
	Notes	352
	Bibliography	374
	Index	378

Tables

1.1	Proportions of people of pensionable age: inland spas and Sussex resorts, 1901–71	14
1.2	Retirement counties	16
3.1	Social class and previous employment status	35
3.2	Retirement age	36
3.3	Reasons for retiring from work	37
5.1	Main reasons for retirement move	50
5.2	Ideas about retirement	53
6.1	Age and sex of head of retired household	66
6.2	Proportion of widows, by age group	68
6.3	Distance from nearest child	72
7.1	Contact with children, brothers and sisters and close friends after the move	82
7.2	Opinions about making friends, by marital status	85
7.3	Loneliness, by marital status	91
8.1	The use of health and social services	102
9.1	Number of clubs, by type	113
10.1	Weekly net incomes, by marital status and sex	121
11.1	Tenure of dwelling, by marital status	135
12.1	Reasons for wanting to move to another town	167
13.1	Considered views about the retirement move, by marital status	172
17.1	Estimated expenditure per head of population in retirement areas on Local Authority Health, Social and Housing Services	219
17.2	Total net rate and grant-borne expenditure per head in the retirement areas	223
17.3	Rate Support Grant per head of population, 1974–5	227
A1.1	Larger local authorities (more than 15,000 inhabitants) with the highest proportions of elderly residents	250
A1.2	Smaller local authorities (less than 15,000 inhabitants) with the highest proportions of elderly residents	254
A1.3	In-migrants of pensionable age in some retirement resorts and counties	258

A1.4	Main areas of origin of retirement movers	260
A1.5	Destinations of retirement movers	262
A1.6	Areas of origin of people who had moved to Bexhill and Clacton to retire	264
A1.7	Migration by people of 65 and over, from the conurbations and to the retirement regions	265
A1.8	Movers of pensionable age, 1961–6	267
A1.9	Social class characteristics of some retirement resorts, 1966	268
A1.10	Age at retirement move	270
A1.11	Surviving children	270
A1.12	Likes and dislikes about the pre-retirement house	271
A1.13	Likes and dislikes about the pre-retirement area	272
A1.14	Consideration of other retirement areas	273
A1.15	Main reason for choosing Bexhill and Clacton	273
A1.16	Date of move to Bexhill and Clacton	274
A1.17	Age, by sex and marital status: people of 65 and over, Bexhill, Clacton and England and Wales	275
A1.18	Proportions of women in each age group who were widowed – some seaside resorts and inland cities, 1971	277
A1.19	Main reasons for finding it easier to make friends	278
A1.20	Main reasons for finding it more difficult to make friends	278
A1.21	The number of services received	279
A1.22	Ways of spending most of the time	280
A1.23	Use of leisure facilities	281
A1.24	Social class and weekly net income of retirement units, by sex of head of retirement unit	282
A1.25	Weekly gross income of elderly households in Great Britain and average tax paid, 1968	284
A1.26	Savings and their current use	285
A1.27	Sources of income	286
A1.28	Type of dwelling	287
A1.29	Price of house, by weekly net income of retired household	287
A1.30	Rates as a percentage of income of head of retired household	288
A1.31	Gross rents in Bexhill and Clacton	289
A1.32	Resident guests of pensionable age in hotels, 1971	290
A1.33	Number of moves since retirement	291

A1.34 Reasons for last retirement move: people with more than one retirement move — 292
A1.35 Reasons for expecting or wanting to move to a different house in the same town — 293
A1.36 Immigrants and emigrants of pensionable age, Bexhill and Clacton, 1965–6 and 1961–6 — 294
A1.37 Reasons for moving to the coast again — 294
A1.38 Reasons for NOT moving to the coast again — 295
A1.39 Geriatric beds per 1,000 of the population aged 65 and over in retirement areas — 295
A1.40 Local authority housing, in resort county boroughs, 1971 — 296
A1.41 Residents in residential homes in retirement areas, 1974 — 297
A1.42 Residents in residential homes in retirement areas, 1970 — 299
A1.43 Principal medical practitioners: analysis by list size, 1973 — 301
A1.44 The home help service in retirement areas, 1973 — 303
A1.45 Meals services in retirement areas, 1973 — 304
A1.46 Home nurses in retirement areas, 1973 — 305
A1.47 Health visitors in retirement areas, 1973 — 306
A3.1 Response to Bexhill and Clacton survey — 315
A3.2 Non-respondents compared with respondents, by sex and household type — 316

Maps

Map A The distribution of the elderly in England and Wales, by county, 1971 — 18
Map B The location of retirement towns in England and Wales — 20

Acknowledgments

I wish to thank all the people who so kindly co-operated in providing material for this survey, in particular the retired people of Bexhill and Clacton. The others are too numerous to mention but include local authority officials of numerous resorts and from many different departments, doctors, home nurses, health visitors, the secretaries of Hospital Management Committees and Executive Councils, officials of the Department of Health and Social Security, and the Department of the Environment, voluntary workers and hotel owners.

In addition, I would like to thank John Edwards who worked with me on this project for the first year. I am also very grateful to other members of the staff of the Centre for Urban and Regional Studies, particularly Professor J. B. Cullingworth and Miss Greta Summer, for their advice and criticism.

Finally, I would like to express special gratitude to the National Corporation for the Care of Old People for financing the project, and to Mr Hugh Mellor of that organization for his help and encouragement.

Introduction

THE BACKGROUND TO THE STUDY

Retirement communities are not an innovation of modern industrial societies. The Roman government built retirement villages for military officers who retired from active duty with distinguished service records. These villages were located on the outskirts of large cities and were equipped with gymnasia, baths and other recreational facilities. In medieval England, the guilds constructed villages, again located on the outskirts of cities, especially for retired craftsmen. (1)

Although the movement of elderly people to the seaside is a matter of common knowledge (the bungalow-by-the-sea is almost folklore), it had, until recently, received scarcely any attention in social research in this country. However, interest in such moves at retirement has increased for a number of reasons. First, there are signs that movement to certain retirement areas, particularly those on the coast, is growing. Second, the cumulative effect of this movement is quite noticeably altering the character of large stretches of the coast, particularly the South Coast. Third, a number of seaside towns have about one-third of their population aged 65 and over, nearly three times the average for England and Wales (13 per cent in 1971). (2) With the decline of the traditional holiday hotel trade, many towns have begun to acknowledge that their central role is now that of a 'retirement resort' and the character of the town's commercial and social life begins to reflect this role.

Over the years, retirement to coastal resorts has come within the scope of a larger number of people than formerly. People of only medium incomes are selling houses in the city and with the proceeds moving to those resorts where property is cheapest. Also efforts are being made to extend the possibility of moving to people who would not otherwise be able to afford it, for example, through the Greater London Council's scheme to provide bungalows by the sea for their retired tenants and by certain housing associations who build flats and bungalows in resorts. These efforts are as yet, however, very limited in size compared with the movement of owner-occupiers. This has reached such a large scale that some estate agents and building firms organise 'retirement specials' - coach trips from the cities to seaside areas to look at property being built. Some of these are provided free by the building firms. (3)

Yet while all this is happening, serious doubts have begun to be felt about the desirability of retirement migration. The fear is expressed that large concentrations of elderly people may be socially undesirable, that elderly people may experience social isolation and that social services may be overstrained. (4) The GLC has experienced antagonism to its bungalows-by-the-sea scheme and resorts such as Worthing have made strenuous efforts to attract more industrial and commercial employment. (5)

RETIREMENT RESORTS: AN INTERNATIONAL PHENOMENON

Neither retirement resorts, nor discussions of the problems said to be associated with them, are unique to Britain. They are a common feature of the whole of North America, Western Europe, Australia and New Zealand, in fact, all the highly developed capitalist countries. It is, therefore, worthwhile mentioning here some parallel developments abroad.

In the USA there have been retirement resorts for about one hundred years, particularly in Florida, Arizona and California. These resorts grew up by an unplanned movement of elderly people towards mild climates. The cumulative effect was to produce such 'retirement cities' as Palm Springs, Carmel and Santa Cruz. These resorts are the equivalent of those in Britain. However, in the last fifteen years there has been a new development, the creation of self-contained, 'planned-package retirement communities', (6) often called 'retirement villages'. They are devoted entirely to retired people and often have minimum age limits to prevent anyone younger, apart from staff, living there. Some are built by private enterprise, others by organizations such as the Moose. (Moosehaven is one of the best-known 'villages'.) In 1966 in California there were thirty-five of these 'villages' with a total of 54,000 elderly inhabitants. In 1956 there had been none. So far, in Britain, there have been no such developments on a similar scale. The only rough equivalents are the groups of flats or bungalows built by professional or commercial associations for their retired members. These are dotted round the seaside resorts but are small and are an integral part of the privately developed resort, not a separate community.

In France the Côte d'Azur is the retirement area par excellence, but it is strongly rivalled by Brittany, the East and West Pyrenees and the Atlantic coast. In 1968, Nice which had 322,000 inhabitants had 24.5 per cent of its population of pensionable age. (7) Along the same strip of coast Cannes (67,000) had 25.2 per cent and Menton (58,000) 30.0 per cent. They are the largest towns on a strip of coast which is almost totally built up with resorts with similar proportions of elderly people. On the coast of the Eastern Pyrenees, on the Atlantic Coast and in Brittany the resorts are more widely spaced but individual towns such as Dinard, Douarnenez, Pornic, Arcachon, Soulez, Biarritz, Angetes and Banyuls rival the Côte d'Azur's percentages of elderly people. Even on the Channel coast, Cayeux, St Valery, Deauville and others had over 20 per cent of people of retirement age in 1968. The percentages are not as high as those in the British resorts but then France as a whole has a smaller percentage of people of retirement age. The scale of retirement migration is certainly comparable.

On the Mediterranean coast and islands, and on the Atlantic coasts of Portugal and France, retirement resorts have the additional feature that they have an international clientele. To them come retired people from England, Germany, Sweden and elsewhere, as well as the elderly French or Italians. In some countries, particularly the poorer ones, the retirement resorts have been developed specifically for retired people from abroad, not for local elderly people at all.

For those who wish to retire abroad there are grander equivalents of the 'retirement special' coach. Organisations will search out property for prospective buyers, run cut-rate inspection flights, give legal and financial advice and, if the owner has bought prior to retirement, arrange private air holidays to the villa when the owner is not using it, and thus bring him income. (8)

Despite all the obstacles of currency controls, retirement resorts have been booming in Southern Europe. International development companies have been investing in the construction of retirement settlements. Majorca and the

Bahamas have experienced a property boom and Cyprus until recently had been following suit. In Malta, which, like Cyprus, benefited from the British currency restrictions on the 'non-scheduled territories', the government, in 1972, set a minimum value for the property that a foreigner could buy in the country and a minimum amount of capital, £20,000, which would entitle them to become resident there. The aim was to bring in the most wealthy residents and discourage cut-price retirement packages. In Portugal, the change in government has presented a quite different set of problems for the property developers, who have invested heavily and led elderly people to invest heavily in retirement settlements on the Algarve coast.

For those who cannot afford or do not want to buy a villa, or to move permanently to another country, there is the alternative of spending the winter months in a holiday hotel. These charge reduced rates out of the summer season. Many Germans, in particular, have taken to this seasonal migration - for instance to Majorca and the Canary Islands, and previously to Portugal. (9)

Whatever the arrangement, for the affluent retired person, particularly one from a country where the currency is strong, horizons have widened. Provision for retirement migration has become big business and so, too, unfortunately, has the provision of health and other services for those who become sick or infirm. It is all part of the retirement 'industry'.

This study, of British retirement migration has, therefore, wider implications than those just for British resorts or the British government. Retirement resorts are a truly international phenomenon about which the exchange of knowledge and ideas should be of great value.

AIMS OF THE STUDY

The main aim of the study was to find out more about the process of retirement to the coast from the point of view of the retired people themselves. Of course not every aspect of retirement migration could be examined. Attention was therefore concentrated on a series of selected but interrelated questions, which seemed to be of most relevance to the people who had already retired to seaside resorts or to those who were perhaps considering such a move.

First, the study was concerned with the characteristics of the people who move to resorts. Do they have, for instance, characteristics which help to explain their willingness and ability to move in old age, such as lack of family ties or a history of mobility?

Second, the timing of the move was of interest, both in relation to retirement from work and the age of the person moving. Did most moves take place at the point of retirement from work, or had people moved after they had been retired some time? Had they already experienced what it was like to be a retired person in the community in which they had been working?

Third, there was the whole question of motivation for the move. Were the movers leaving because they were attracted to the resorts or repelled by the area in which they had worked most of their lives? Or was there a combination of the two? Were they seeking to fulfil some ideal about retirement? Why had they chosen the particular resort to which they had moved?

Fourth, after the move had taken place, how did retired people fare in terms of expenditure, housing, social relationships and activities? How did they themselves see the success of their move?

However, there are other matters to be taken into consideration. What, for instance, are the implications for retirement migration of the situation of the health and social services in the seaside resorts and counties? Or more generally, are concentrations of elderly people undesirable on social or economic grounds? Even if one is concentrating upon the views of the elderly people themselves about retirement resorts it is important to know whether they are misguided or unrealistic in relation to the ability of the authorities to plan and provide adequate facilities for large numbers of elderly people. The fifth group of questions is therefore concerned with the provision of services for elderly people in resorts and the financial implications of making such provisions.

From a study of these questions it was hoped to derive a better understanding of the processes involved in retirement migration and, in particular, its consequences for the elderly people themselves.

METHODS

Several sources of data were used. The most important, however, was a questionnaire survey of about 1,000 elderly people who had moved to two coastal resorts, Bexhill and Clacton. This was carried out in the winter of 1968. A full account of the grounds upon which Bexhill and Clacton were chosen, the methods of sampling and the response rate obtained, is given in Appendix 3. There were also numerous interviews with officials of health, social and voluntary services, councillors, clergymen and other relevant people and statistical data were collected concerning the provision of services in a large number of retirement resorts and counties.

As a separate exercise published and unpublished Census material was examined to obtain a picture of the directions and scale of retirement migration nationally and to locate the main retirement areas and resorts.

Other than that in the Social Survey, all material is now based on the latest information available at January 1976.

BEXHILL AND CLACTON

Though this study is concerned with the elderly people themselves rather than with the resorts to which they retire, it is inevitable that the characteristics of the two towns selected for the social survey should have distinct effects on the results. For this reason, it may be useful to give a short description of their location and character for the benefit of readers who are not familiar with them.

Bexhill is about fifty miles south of Central London, on the Sussex coast between Eastbourne and Hastings. Rail and road links are not, however, direct, because they have to skirt round the ridge of the South Downs. The rail link to London is either via Lewes or from Hastings. This lack of a direct rail link has been an obstacle to the development of Bexhill as a commuter settlement for London.

Clacton is also about fifty miles from London, but to the north-east, on the Essex coast about fifteen miles south of Harwich. Again rail and road links are indirect, but this time because of the indented coastline to the south.

In 1901, Bexhill and Clacton were small towns with populations of 12,213 and 7,456 respectively. Bexhill had only the same proportion of people of pensionable age as did England and Wales (6.3 per cent). Clacton's was even slightly less (5.7 per cent). However, by 1921, when the pensionable age population of England and Wales had risen to only 7.8 per cent, Bexhill's and Clacton's had nearly doubled to 11.8 per cent and 10.2 per cent respectively. In each, also, the total population of the town had risen by about 10,000. In the next ten years, the proportion of elderly people continued to rise rapidly, reaching 15.0 per cent in Bexhill and 13.3 per cent in Clacton, compared with 9.6 per cent nationally. However, Bexhill's total population grew by less than 1,000 between

1921 and 1931 and Clacton's actually decreased. Between 1931 and 1951 both towns grew to about 25,000, with Clacton growing more rapidly than Bexhill. However, it was Bexhill which had most elderly people - 28.0 per cent, double the national average, compared with 23.6 per cent in Clacton. Remarkable though this increase was, the next twenty years were to see an even bigger increase. Bexhill's development as a retirement resort has, until the last five years, been the more spectacular. The proportion of people of pensionable age rose from 28.0 per cent in 1951, to 37.0 per cent in 1961, to 41.2 per cent in 1966 and to 44.2 per cent in 1971. In 1966, Bexhill had the largest proportion of elderly people of any town in Britain with more than 20,000 population. Clacton's proportions rose from 23.6 per cent in 1951, to 29.2 per cent in 1961, to 32.0 per cent in 1966 and then leapt to 39.0 per cent in 1971. Between 1966 and 1971, Bexhill's total population rose by only 740 while Clacton's rose by 5,030. The recent difference in the rates of expansion of the two towns is probably explained by the greater availability of building land in Clacton. So, recently, increases in the retired population of Bexhill have meant the displacement of younger people, whilst Clacton's increase has been achieved more by new house building.

As their full names suggest, both Bexhill on Sea and Clacton on Sea were nineteenth- and early twentieth-century seaward expansions of small villages which were originally situated slightly inland. They developed when seaside holidays became popular. The old village centres remain with their church and cottages but now the focus of each town has completely shifted to the sea-front area of boarding houses, hotels and shops. More recently in both towns, there has been, in association with the growth of the retired population, a massive spread of low density residential development enveloping both the old village and seaside resort. In both towns the main development has been bungalow building since the last war but Bexhill also has, in the direction of Cooden, a vast area of large and expensive houses with big gardens.

Property in Bexhill is much more expensive than that in Clacton and the area attracts more wealthy people. In 1966, 31.4 per cent of Bexhill's male population were or had been professional workers, employers or managers. In Clacton the comparable proportion was 17.8 per cent.

Clacton still maintains its tourism on a much larger scale than Bexhill does. In 1969 there were 104 hotels and boarding houses in Clacton, compared with 45 in Bexhill. In addition the Clacton hotels were larger than those in Bexhill. However, Bexhill like Clacton, still receives a large number of day-trippers during summer weekends. Bexhill's holiday image has always been much quieter and more 'genteel' than Clacton's. Its holiday facilities, catering mostly for middle-aged and elderly people, consist of accommodation, parks, bowls, the sea front but little else. There is no pier, but a pavilion with a theatre, cafe and band. The tourist image is not at all incompatible with the environment preferred by retired residents. Neither town has the facilities, such as Eastbourne has, to develop a conference trade, and in both, because of the decline in the popularity of seaside hotels in favour of caravans, camping and holiday flats, the largest hotels have been forced to close. In both cases the very largest have been converted into residential accommodation for old people.

OUTLINE

This book is in three sections. The first contains a short description of the growth and location of the main retirement areas and of the main directions and scale of retirement migration in England and Wales. It then goes on to consider the characteristics of retired people at the time of their move to Bexhill and Clacton, the reasons they had for moving and the nature of the move itself. The second describes the population of retired people in Bexhill and Clacton at the time of the survey, their family and household structure, social contacts and leisure activities, financial situation and accommodation, and their level of satisfaction with the retirement move. The third part considers the situation of the health and social services in retirement areas and the financial position of the resort authorities. Finally an attempt is made to assess, from the point of view of the elderly people themselves, whether or not retirement migration works and in what ways it could be made to work better.

Part one

The retirement move

1 From inland spas to seaside resorts

'One would think that the English were ducks; they are for ever waddling to the waters.'
                                        Horace Walpole (1)

THE RISE OF THE COASTAL RESORTS

The development of coastal resorts in Britain dates roughly from the mid-eighteenth century, when doctors began to write about the health-giving qualities of the seaside and particularly of sea-bathing. (2) Before that, the inland spas had been the dominant health resorts. Bath, which had been so flourishing in Roman times, again became a great centre in the seventeenth century and its success led to a proliferation of inland spas Clifton, Epsom, Tunbridge Wells, Cheltenham, Harrogate and later Leamington.

With the exception of Scarborough all the popular spas were inland. The revolution which switched the fashion from inland spas to seaside resorts was triggered off by the publication in 1750, of a book by Dr Richard Russell of Lewes and Brighton about the health-giving properties of sea water.

Dr. Russell was the instigator of the seaside mania; in the words of George Roberts, 'he was to seaside visitors what Peter the Hermit was to the crusades - the genius that raised the latent spirit'. The effect of his work was such that the fashionable world began to desert Bath, Tunbridge Wells, Epsom and other inland watering-places for the newly discovered coastal resorts. (3)

Health resorts in England could then be classified into three types, the inland spas, the old ports or fishing harbours and the entirely newly built seaside resorts. (4) The old harbours which were expanded into resorts were, for example, Hastings, Scarborough, Brighton and Margate. The totally new resorts were places such as Bournemouth, Hove, St Leonards, Southport, Blackpool, Clacton on Sea and Bexhill on Sea.

Particular seaside resorts came into prominence either because a doctor wrote a paper about the superior qualities of the local climate or the place was patronised by some eminent person, particularly royalty. Sometimes both happened. The effects on the size of a resort's population and the price of land could be dramatic. For instance, the price of building land at the village of Ventnor, Isle of Wight, rose from £100 per acre to £800 or £1,000 in a very few years after the publication in 1829 of a book called 'The Influence of Climate in the Prevention and Cure of Chronic Diseases', later republished as 'The Sanative Influence of Climate: with an account of the best places or Resorts in England, the South of Europe etc.' (5) The patronage of royalty had much the same effect. Weymouth which was visited by George III in the 1780s was the first to benefit in this way. The Isle of Wight's popularity owed much to Queen Victoria's partiality for it, Southend's to the visits of Queen Charlotte. This pattern continued well into the twentieth century, with Bognor being renamed 'Bognor Regis' to celebrate George V's successful convelescence there in 1929. (It is interesting to see this pattern continued with the new elite in present-day holiday resorts, for instance the effect on St Tropez of Brigitte Bardot's visits, and the way in which each rising Mediterranean resort cherishes its pop star.)

The quite unprecedented scale of growth of the seaside resorts round the coast of Britain can be attributed initially to their reputation as health resorts, but then to the growing fashionability and then popularity of sea-bathing, originally for health reasons but later for recreation. Rail services from the cities allowed larger numbers of people to go for day-trips or longer visits to the seaside and in the 1920s and 1930s the paid holiday (6) and, later, the general rise in living standards of the working classes, meant that it was no longer just the middle classes or, even, skilled working classes who could have a week or a fortnight's holiday. Previously, a day-trip had been all that they could afford. Now such vast numbers were going off to the coast that the resorts could scarcely accommodate them. As motor cars and coaches came into their own, people were able to go farther afield and to spread out from the more established resorts. In particular the tourist trade of Devon and Cornwall expanded rapidly.

But the heyday of the Victorian seaside holiday hotel has now passed. Although people still go to the coast for holidays in large numbers the style has changed. There is a greater emphasis on holiday camps, caravaning, or short 'second' holidays and on day-trips rather than staying visits. Cheap holidays abroad have been eating into the hotel trade.

The impact of these changes has been to close many of the largest hotels in the South Coast resorts. They have either been converted into flats or old people's homes or have been demolished to make way for new blocks of flats. In Bexhill, for instance, the largest hotel is now converted into eighty flats for elderly people, one of a chain of such buildings all along the South Coast, owned by the same organisation. In Clacton, the largest hotel is now a home for elderly people, owned by the Social Services Department. Such changes are symptomatic of the shift of emphasis from the hotel trade to other types of holiday accommodation and to residential accommodation for elderly people.

This has not been a sudden process or even a new role. The resorts inherited from the inland spas a role as residential resorts for the sick and elderly. Some of the more wealthy people had seaside as well as town houses. Some of the less wealthy also moved there more or less permanently, apparently for a variety of motives.

> It has been suggested that the needs of health, the edicts of fashion, and the slavish copying of Royalty were not the only factors to stimulate the custom of going to the seaside; and that some members of the upper classes were actually drawn to the coast by the peremptory necessity for retrenchment.... It was believed that some people went to inconvenient lodgings at a watering-place under the plea of health, but that their real purpose was to save money. Whether they succeeded in doing so is another matter. (7)

In 1901 the inland spas still had larger proportions of people of pensionable age than the coastal resorts did, mainly between 9 per cent and 10 per cent compared with 8-9 per cent, but the total numbers of old people in the spas at that time were smaller because the spas were relatively few and the seaside resorts were already numerous. By 1921 some of the coastal resorts, notably Worthing, Hastings and Hove with about 14 per cent of people of pensionable age were ranking with the most popular inland spas in their proportions of elderly people and by 1931 these three seaside resorts with over 18 per cent had overtaken the inland towns though other resorts were about level. It was in the period from 1931 to 1951 that the proportions of elderly people in seaside resorts expanded most dramatically to between 25 per cent and 30 per cent, and this rapid expansion has been kept up. The only areas in which the proportions of elderly people have levelled off are those, such as Hove, Hastings and Brighton, which have developed commuting or new industry or are running out of building land. By 1971 the inland resorts had been left far behind in their proportions of elderly people, most of them having developed other functions and industries. Only Harrogate rivalled the less popular seaside resorts in their proportions of elderly people.

TABLE 1.1 Proportions of people of pensionable age:*
inland spas and Sussex resorts, 1901-71

	1901	1921	1931	1951	1961	1966	1971
SPAS							
Cheltenham	9.5	12.8	15.4	16.7	16.1	17.8	17.7
Royal Leamington Spa	10.6	12.0	14.2	15.5	11.4	13.6	14.8
Bath	10.6	12.8	16.0	17.6	18.5	19.0	20.4
Royal Tunbridge Wells	8.6	13.6	16.4	22.4	22.8	22.6	19.8
Epsom	7.9	10.1	12.7	15.4	17.2	17.5	19.6
Wells	9.2	14.3	14.6	15.6	19.3	N/A	19.9
Droitwich	9.8	14.6	15.7	15.7	12.3	N/A	12.2
Malvern	8.6	12.0	18.9	18.4	15.0	17.7	18.3
Harrogate	7.2	11.2	14.2	19.9	20.5	20.7	22.1
SUSSEX RESORTS							
Bexhill	6.3	11.8	15.0	28.0	37.0	41.2	44.2
Brighton	7.7	10.6	13.7	19.0	21.4	22.8	23.0
Eastbourne	6.3	10.7	15.5	23.2	29.8	33.7	33.4
Hastings	8.7	13.9	18.2	23.9	28.7	28.9	29.5
Hove	8.3	14.0	18.1	26.2	30.8	31.1	33.6
Bognor	8.2	9.6	14.5	22.4	28.4	31.4	33.9
Worthing	9.2	14.4	18.7	29.7	36.3	38.0	38.8
CLACTON	5.7	10.2	13.3	23.6	29.2	32.0	39.0
ENGLAND & WALES	6.1	7.8	9.6	13.8	14.9	15.5	16.1

Source: Census, England and Wales, County Reports, 1901-71.
* Men of 65 and over and women of 60 and over.

So, compared with the present day, the movement of elderly people to inland spas and seaside resorts in the nineteenth century was on a relatively small scale. There are a number of reasons why the scale of movement has escalated so dramatically. First, throughout the second half of the nineteenth century the proportion of people of pensionable age in England and Wales had remained relatively steady at about 6.1 per cent but in the twentieth century improved survival rates and a falling birth rate brought dramatic changes. (8) The proportion of people of pensionable age more than doubled between 1901 and 1951 and in fact will soon have trebled. In addition the total population of England and Wales in 1971 was 48.5 million compared with only 32.5 million in 1901, which meant that there were about 7,813,300 people of pensionable age in 1971 compared with only 1,998,000 in 1901. In these circumstances, the present-day fashion for retirement to the coast has a much greater impact upon the resorts than a similar fashion for moving either to inland or coastal resorts had in the nineteenth century.

Of course, if retirement to resorts had been open only to the wealthy, the size of the movement would have remained quite small, but simultaneously with this increase in the size of the elderly population, there have been changes which have increased the economic independence of elderly people from their children. Retirement pensions supplemented by occupational pensions and savings have allowed more old people to maintain a separate household in old age. At the same time the introduction of compulsory retirement ages in many occupations, has, along with increased life expectancy, brought much longer periods of retirement than were common in the nineteenth century. Fifty years age retirement was not a norm. Many people did not retire at all, and others only did so when overtaken by bad health.

To sum up, there are not only more old people now, there are also more of them in a financial position to live separately from their families. Also a longer period of retirement provides more incentive to make special plans not just for a few 'winding down' years of relatively poor health but for a substantial period of one's active lifetime.

For all these reasons the proportions of old people in seaside resorts in the twentieth century are of a totally different order from those in inland or coastal resorts in the nineteenth century.

THE PRESENT DISTRIBUTION OF RETIREMENT AREAS

Of all the counties in England and Wales, those with the largest percentage of elderly people in 1971 were East and West Sussex and the Isle of Wight. After these three,

TABLE 1.2 Retirement counties

Geographical counties in descending order of proportion of people aged 65 and over in 1971	Percentage of population aged 65 and over*		Men aged 65* and women 60* (Pensionable age population)*		Net migration rate (1961-6 of people of pensionable age per 1,000 resident population 1966)**
	Col.1	Col.2	Col.3	Col.4	Col.5
	1966	1971	1966	1971	1961-6
ENGLAND					
East Sussex	21.3	22.3	25.8	26.7	23.05
West Sussex	19.8	20.9	23.8	24.8	30.04
Isle of Wight	19.1	20.7	23.2	25.1	20.35
Devon	17.1	18.6	20.9	22.5	11.60
Dorset	16.1	17.7	19.8	21.5	10.95
Cornwall and Scilly Isles	16.5	17.6	20.3	21.5	10.70
(Westmorland)	(15.0)	NA	(18.5)	NA	NA
Somerset	14.9	16.1	18.3	19.5	10.52
Norfolk	14.6	15.8	17.9	19.1	10.07
East Suffolk	14.3	15.3	17.4	18.6	9.12
Kent	14.3	14.9	17.5	18.0	10.42
Hampshire	13.9	14.2	17.0	17.3	8.47

WALES				
Caernarvonshire	18.0	19.4	22.2	23.5	8.17
Merionethshire	15.3	17.9	19.0	21.9	1.40
Radnorshire	15.4	17.4	18.8	20.8	1.13
Cardiganshire	17.1	17.2	20.8	20.9	6.73
Denbighshire	15.3	16.6	18.8	20.2	8.90
Montgomeryshire	13.5	16.1	17.2	19.1	2.80
Caermarthenshire	13.8	15.3	17.4	19.0	0.12
Breconshire	14.5	14.9	17.6	18.3	2.56
Flintshire	13.9	14.5	17.3	17.8	12.09
Anglesey	13.4	14.0	16.6	17.1	1.95
England and Wales	12.5	13.3	15.5	16.1	-

* Sample Census 1966 and Census 1971 County Reports. Both the percentage aged 65 and over and the percentage of pensionable age are given because the Census migration data are given for people of pensionable age but standards for social services are based on the percentage aged 65 and over.

** Sample Census 1966 Regional Migration Reports. Net migration rate is defined as the balance of immigration and emigration of people of pensionable age expressed per 1,000 of the total resident population of all ages in 1966. At the time of publication only a few of the Migration Reports for the 1971 Census had been published.

Note: Parentheses around figures in Tables mean that percentages are based on a total sample of less than 50; * = less than 0.5 per cent; - = nil.

18 Chapter 1

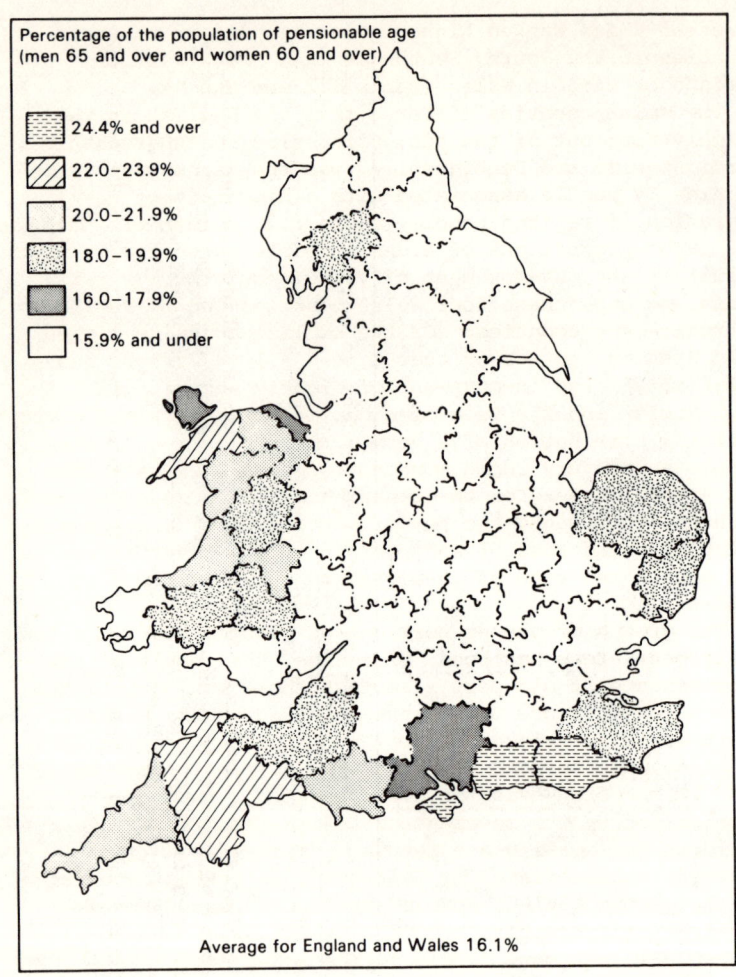

MAP A The distribution of the elderly in England and Wales by county, 1971 (1971 Census, Great Britain, County Reports)

nineteen which ranked highest were all either coastal counties in the South, South-East and South-West of England or were in Wales (Table 1.2 and Map A).

The Welsh counties differed from the English in that in only four out of the ten, Flintshire, Caernarvonshire, Cardiganshire and Denbighshire, was the large proportion of elderly people associated with a high rate of in-migration of retired people (Table 1.2, column 5). Instead the large proportions of elderly people were largely the result of the out-movement of young people from rural areas, so only these four Welsh counties can be regarded as retirement counties. Of the English counties listed only Westmorland was of that type. All the others had a relatively large in-movement of elderly people. East and West Sussex and the Isle of Wight in particular had a very striking combination of a very large proportion of elderly people and a very rapid movement of elderly people into the area. Essex, on the other hand, which does not rank with the top twenty-two for proportion of elderly people (12.9 per cent aged 65 and over in 1971), nevertheless had a high net rate of in-migration (9.80 per 1000 in 1961-6).

The growth of the proportions of elderly people in the retirement areas has been, of course, the result of the predominance of old people amongst those moving into the area. For instance of all the women moving to Bexhill, Eastbourne, Worthing, Clacton and Herne Bay between 1961 and 1966 more than 40 per cent were of pensionable age. (9) It is often said, however, that the trend is accelerated by the movement out of the resorts of children and working-age people. This view was not, however, substantiated by 1961 and 1966 census material. In the period 1961-6, none of the South Coast, Devon, Somerset or Lancashire resorts (except Brighton and Blackpool) lost more people in the age groups 5-14 or 15-45 than they gained. (10) The balance was very small but there was no actual net loss. This means that the change in the age structure of the population in this period must be explained only by the large numbers of elderly people moving in, plus the fact that natural increase is low because of the age structure of the population. The numbers of children born in these towns are small relative to the size of the population and will decline further as the proportion of elderly people rises, but the numbers of young people moving out have been balanced by those moving in. The 1971 census may, however, show different results, particularly in places such as Bexhill where there has been little growth in population between 1966 and 1971, but a continuing growth in the proportion of people of retirement age.

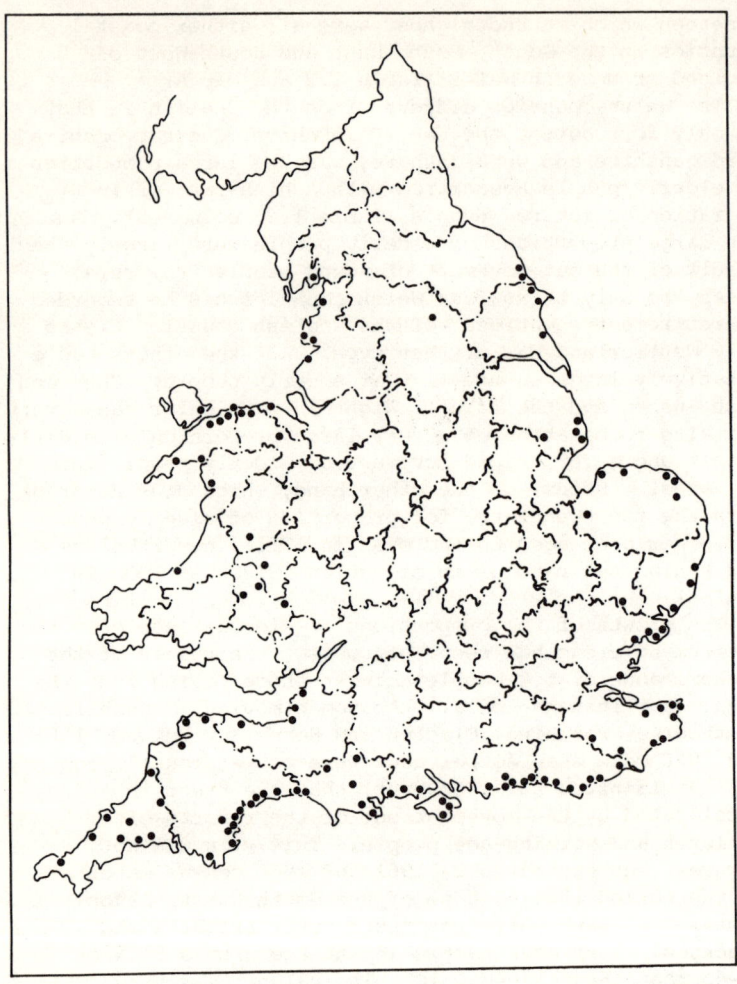

MAP B The location of retirement towns in England and Wales

To describe the distribution of retirement resorts, it is necessary to use more detailed census material than statistics for counties, because retirement migration tends to be very localised in its destination and individual resorts can be lost in the county totals. If a county is large or heterogeneous the effect of retirement resorts on the total population may be small. The best examples of this are Lancashire, with resorts such as Blackpool and Lytham St Annes; Yorkshire, with Scarborough and Bridlington; Essex, with Clacton, Frinton, Walton and Southend; and Kent with Herne Bay, Margate and Whitstable. In order to get a true picture of the distribution of retirement resorts it is necessary to examine census data for all the coastal authorities within the counties listed in Table 1.2 and to look at coastal authorities in all other counties, notable Lancashire, Yorkshire, Essex and Lincolnshire.

Taking as an arbitrary definition of a retirement town one with 20 per cent or more of its population of pensionable age (that is, 40 per cent above the national average for 1971) then a map of the distribution of these resorts shows up a very clear pattern (Map B). The most striking point is that the concentration at the coast is indisputable, with the largest number of resorts being along the South Coast. The industrial area around Southampton is the only major gap. The number of resort towns noticeably thins out towards Cornwall as the distance from the major centres of population increases. With the exception of the South-West the concentration of resorts on coasts within from fifty to seventy-five miles of the major population centres is very conspicuous. It is interesting too that the West Midlands conurbation, with no coast within fifty miles, has some development of retirement in the nearby Welsh border country, but the resorts are very small and the proportions of elderly people lower than on the coast. Seen in this way the South-West region retirement area appears to be the only one which is not obviously linked in location to a particular population centre. We will see in Chapter 2 whether the data on directions of movement to particular resort areas support this view.

The Sussex coast has more and larger resorts than other parts of England and Wales. In addition the proportions of elderly people in these resorts are on average higher than those in resorts on other parts of the English coast. However, Herne Bay, and other resorts in Kent, Clacton and Frinton in Essex, and the string of resorts along the South Devon coast are growing rapidly in their proportions of elderly people. Devon, in particular, has several small resorts with exceptionally large proportions of old people, larger even than Bexhill's.

There is a close relationship between climate and the distribution of resorts. The most popular retirement resorts are concentrated in that part of England, the South Coast, which is both not much more than fifty miles from London and has the highest winter temperatures, the least fog and air pollution and the most sunshine. (11) The South Devon and Cornwall coasts share the climatic advantages but are much more remote. The North Wales, Lancashire, Yorkshire, Norfolk and Essex coasts do not have such climatic advantages but are more accessible from the Northern and Midland industrial cities.

The link between low temperatures, particularly sharp falls in temperature, and mortality amongst the elderly has been well documented. (12) So, too, has the relationship between deaths from bronchitis and air pollution in the cities. (13) In fact bronchitis is the most usual ailment for which doctors recommend a move to the coast. So the climatic features which elderly people are most likely to be recommended to seek are high temperatures in winter, long hours of sunshine and clean air. It is interesting to recall George Cheyne's advice to the sick and elderly of the eighteenth century on this score:

> From the beginning of November till towards the beginning of February, London is cover'd over with one universal nitreus and sulphurous Smoak, from the Multitude of Coal Fires, the absence of that material Divinity the Sun and the Consequences thereof, the falling of the Dews, the Vapours of the Night. In such a Season weak and tender People, and those that are subject to nervous or pulmonick Distempers, ought either to go into the Country, or to be at home soon after Sun-set, and to dispel the Damps with clear, warm Fires and chearful Conversation. (14)
>
> Or, if they would lengthen on their days, to remove to a warmer climate, by which they may live as long as the Crow. (15)

As a final observation on the distribution of retirement areas, and perhaps this is the most interesting feature, there is a remarkable similarity between the distribution of retirement areas and the areas that school leavers in Britain said they would prefer to live in, according to a survey published in 1968. (16) The school leavers particularly favoured the South and South-West coasts, with the southern part of the East Coast closely following. Next come the Welsh borders and the Lake District and the Welsh coast. Clearly then a preference for the South Coast is shared right down the age scale. The preference of American students for Florida and California, (17) two retirement areas of the

USA, adds weight to this, but also suggests that ideas about climate or possibly the image of holiday areas may be important in area preferences at all ages. It has been suggested that such research on residential preferences can help towards an understanding of migration patterns. (18) It seems likely that this may be the case in relation to the movement of elderly people on retirement.

2 The scale of the movement to the coast

Solihull, Headingley and Golders Green
Preston and Swindon, Manchester and Leeds,
Braintree and Bocking, hear the sea! the sea!
    John Betjeman: Beside the Seaside

The location of the main retirement areas is relatively easy to establish. One can also discover the main directions of retirement migration and whether there are any strong connections between particular resorts and particular areas of origin. However, it is less easy, because of the nature of census data, to give an estimate of what proportion of all elderly people move to retirement areas. Because of this difficulty, the question of the scale of movement is left to the end of the chapter, after all the material on the distance and directions of movement has been discussed.

THE GENERAL CHARACTER OF MOVES BY ELDERLY PEOPLE

The 1961 Census provided more detailed analyses of moves by elderly people than did the 1966 Census so the general observations about moves by elderly people are based on this material. (1)
 The first point which emerged from the 1961 analysis was that people of 65 and over moved less often than younger people. In 1960-1 some 317,730 people aged 65 and over moved, that is 5.8 per cent of all people of that age, compared with 10.5 per cent of people of all ages. (2) Second, when elderly people did move they were more likely to do so only within a local authority area; 53.7 per cent of all their moves were of this type compared with 48.3 per cent of the moves of all age groups. (3)
 Third, when they moved from one area to another, they

were more likely than other age groups to move forty miles
or more; 31.7 per cent of their moves from one area to
another, were of this distance, compared with 25.3 per
cent of the moves of all age groups. Fourth, when moving
from one area to another, elderly people were only slightly
more likely than all movers to be moving to a rural area.
About 72.4 per cent of moves by elderly people, which were
from one area to another, were to or between urban areas.
This compared with 73.6 per cent for all movers. This is
an important point, namely that retirement migration does
not usually involve a move to a rural area. As we saw in
the preceding chapter the largest proportions of elderly
people are found in resort towns, usually by the seaside.
These seaside towns can be regarded as a compromise between
urban and country living. They have the openness and clean
air of the country, combined with urban shopping facilities,
transport and entertainment. This compromise nicely solves
the dilemma of the English, who romanticize the country but
do not really want to live there permanently: 'Townsmen
though they are, they still think of rural England as home,
the countryside as the essential nation.' (4) The actual
resorts may be far from qualifying as countryside; Brighton,
Bournemouth and Blackpool, the three largest resorts, are
the centres of urban areas each containing about 250,000
people.

DIRECTIONS OF RETIREMENT MIGRATION

We have seen the areas which now have the largest proportions of elderly people. But from which areas do people
come to these resorts, and do people from the same cities
tend to move to the same resort areas?
   The 1966 Census provides data from which it is possible
to establish the origins of people of pensionable age in
1966 who moved between 1961 and 1966 into the five regions
of England and Wales which contain most of the retirement
resorts. (5) These are the South-West, East Anglia, the
South-East Remainder Sub-Region (that is the South-East
outside London and the Outer Metropolitan Area), the
Wales Remainder Sub-Region, which excludes South Wales
and the North-West Remainder Sub-Region - that is the area
outside the Lancashire and Merseyside Conurbations. (6)
The census data reveal that, as suggested earlier, retirement areas did tend to attract people from their geographically closest region of dense population. Thus East Anglia
and the South-East attracted overwhelmingly from London
and the Outer Metropolitan Area; 55 per cent of people of
pensionable age moving into East Anglia between 1961 and

1966 and 74 per cent moving into the South-East Remainder Sub-Region, came from these two regions. On the other hand, the Wales Remainder and North-West Remainder Regions received few people from the South; the largest proportions of elderly people moving there came from the North-West Region (45 per cent and 48 per cent respectively) particularly from the North-West Conurbation. However, Wales had a second major source in the West Midlands: 19 per cent of all elderly movers came from there and the North-West received 14 per cent of its elderly movers from the Yorkshire and Humberside Region. The South-West Region is about equidistant from the Midlands and London and though London and the Metropolitan Region dominated as areas of origin, partly because of the size of their populations, the Midlands and even the North-West played a proportionately greater role than they did in the South-East and East Anglia.

It is also interesting to know what share particular retirement areas received of all the elderly people moving out of particular urban areas in the same period 1961-6. This approach shows up the links between certain areas of origin and destination even more clearly. For instance, 29 per cent of the people of pensionable age who left the West Midlands went to the South-West, which emerged as the main retirement area for that region, followed by the South-East Remainder with 18 per cent, Wales with 13 per cent and the North-West with 10 per cent. (7) Elderly people from the East Midlands were much less likely to go to the South-West, tending instead to go to the Yorkshire and Humberside Region (22 per cent) with the South-East (18 per cent) and the South-West (13 per cent) next most popular. For the North-West, Wales was the major retirement region, with 23 per cent of the elderly people who left the region going there. People from Yorkshire and Humberside, however, went mainly to the North and North-West Regions. Over 40 per cent of elderly movers from London and the Outer Metropolitan Area went to the remainder of the South-East Region but there was a substantial movement from London itself to the Outer Metropolitan Area and, to a lesser extent, in the opposite direction. If elderly people moved out of the remainder of the South-East Region, they tended to move to London or the Outer Metropolitan Area or to the South-West. The movement to London and the Outer Metropolitan Area may, to some extent, consist of returning migrants.

Although the regional breakdown is not fine enough to give anything but the most general impression, it is apparent from these data that migration out of the major population centres in old age is distinctly concentrated

Chapter 2

in certain directions, namely into adjoining regions, and particularly towards the nearest 'retirement region'.

However, the fact remains that most moves are not across the boundaries of regions or sub-regions, so they do not appear in the regional migration data. The importance of this omission is particularly apparent in the South-East where moves from Surrey and Kent, outside the Metropolitan area, to the Sussex and Kent coasts are treated as internal moves and ignored in the migration statistics.

To obtain a better idea of the origins of people moving to resorts and in particular the proportion of shorter distance moves, one can use the Census migration statistics for individual local authority areas. Unfortunately, in these the origins of movers are not differentiated according to the age of the movers. However, as in many resorts a very large proportion of people moving into the area are elderly, the statistics are worth examining for a number of different parts of the coast of England and Wales.

According to the Census, (8) Bexhill, Worthing and Eastbourne, on the Sussex coast, received a large proportion of their movers between 1961 and 1966 from Sussex, Kent and Surrey. Bexhill received 33 per cent of its movers from those three counties, Eastbourne 30 per cent and Worthing 37 per cent. Most of the rest came from Greater London, that is 37 per cent of those who moved to Bexhill, 34 per cent to Eastbourne and 34 per cent to Worthing.

In Kent, Herne Bay also received many people from Kent itself; 19 per cent of all movers came from Kent, but the majority, 57 per cent, came from Greater London. Clacton, in Essex, received 21 per cent of its movers from Essex and 48 per cent from Greater London. In Devon, Paignton, Exmouth, Sidmouth, Torquay and Teignmouth all received between a quarter and a third of their movers from Devon itself and 15-17 per cent from Greater London. Weymouth in Dorset received 30 per cent from Dorset and Hampshire compared with 8 per cent from Greater London. Weston-Super-Mare in Somerset, received 35 per cent from Somerset and Gloucester, compared with 15 per cent from Warwickshire (including Birmingham), and 7 per cent from Greater London. In the North-West, the same feature of a local catchment area is also apparent. Forty per cent of the people moving to Lytham St Annes in Lancashire came from Lancashire itself. So did 48 per cent and 44 per cent respectively of those moving to Blackpool and Southport.

The local movers are, perhaps, likely to include larger proportions of younger age groups than the long distance movers but still it is important to recognise that elderly people from geographically adjacent areas are more likely to move to a particular resort than are people from more remote places. The same feature is found in relation to the origins of holiday-makers to the same resorts. For instance, 56 per cent of holiday makers in Bexhill come from London and the South-East, compared with only 7 per cent from the Midlands. On the other hand, 46 per cent of holiday-makers to Weston-Super-Mare come from the Midlands and only 6 per cent from London and the South-East. Of those who go to Whitby, 72 per cent are from the North and North-East and only 2 per cent from London and the South-East. (9) It is frequently suggested that there is a close causal link between holiday-making and the choice of retirement resorts. However, this similarity of area of origin is no proof of this link; it just suggests that geographical location affects holiday-making and retirement migration in much the same way. (10)

ORIGINS OF MOVERS TO BEXHILL AND CLACTON

In the social survey of Bexhill and Clacton, it was, of course, possible to obtain much more detailed material about the origins of movers. People aged 55 and over were asked to say where they lived before their first retirement move (11) that is the last place they lived in when they were working. Some people (11 per cent in Bexhill and 7 per cent in Clacton) had had an intervening retirement move before coming to Bexhill or Clacton. The majority of them had lived in other retirement resorts. This had a bearing on the census results which also showed considerable movement between resorts on the South Coast. For instance, 10 per cent of people who moved into Bexhill between 1961 and 1966 came from Eastbourne and Hastings and 5 per cent of those who moved to Eastbourne came from Brighton, Hastings, Bexhill and Hove. (12)

By far the largest proportion of people who retired to Bexhill (45 per cent) and, even more so, Clacton, (63 per cent) came from Greater London. (13) Those moving to Clacton came mainly from north and east London but those moving to Bexhill came from south London, particularly the outer suburbs. Similarly, the Home Counties from which Bexhill people came were mostly Kent, Surrey and Sussex itself (24 per cent). People moving to Clacton from the Home Counties came mainly from the Metropolitan end of Essex and, to a much lesser extent, from Bedfordshire and Hertfordshire (25 per cent).

The rest of the movers to the two towns came from a variety of regions. Those who moved to Bexhill were more likely to come from the South and Midlands (12 per cent) than were those moving to Clacton (5 per cent). A number of the retired Bexhill people (5 per cent) came from abroad. They had usually been executives of international firms, notably oil and mining companies, managers of overseas branches of banks or in the higher ranks of the forces.

The information obtained about the origins of retired people who moved to Bexhill and Clacton clearly tied in very closely with that provided by the census. The proportion of retired people coming from the adjoining county or counties was, as expected, large, but it was right to assume that younger people would be disproportionately numerous amongst local movers. Thus the census found 33 per cent of all movers coming to Bexhill from Kent, Surrey and Sussex, whereas this study found 24 per cent of elderly people. Similarly in Clacton, 21 per cent of all movers came from Essex whereas according to the social survey data, 16 per cent of elderly people did. The difference in the last case is, however, scarcely significant. (14)

A more striking difference from the census was the much larger proportion of elderly people who moved from Greater London to Clacton than the census showed for all movers; 63 per cent of retired movers came from Greater London compared with 48 per cent of all movers according to the census. In Bexhill there was also a difference, but much smaller; 45 per cent of retired movers came from London compared with 37 per cent of all movers.

CONCLUSIONS ON DIRECTIONS OF RETIREMENT MIGRATION

It is apparent, both from the census and the social surveys of Bexhill and Clacton, that there are certain well-marked directions of retirement migration and clear links between particular areas of origin and destination. The movement is usually from a city to the nearest coastal area, preferably one to the south or west. In addition, there is a large volume of relatively local migration to resorts, from the county or counties immediately inland, and a small, but interesting, movement from one resort to another. Retirement migration is, essentially, to urban areas. Though these resort towns are away from the major industrial centres, several are now situated in urbanised areas containing a quarter of a million people.

TRENDS IN THE SCALE OF RETIREMENT TO THE COAST (15)

As mentioned earlier, in the period 1960-1, some 5.8 per cent of all people aged 65 and over moved either within a local authority area or from one to another. Of these, 14.7 per cent or 46,700 moved from one region to another. They represented 0.85 per cent of all people aged 65 and over in that year.

In 1965-6 there were 36,800 inter-regional migrants aged 65 and over, which represented 0.63 per cent of all people aged 65 and over in that year. However, the regions had been redefined between 1961 and 1966, so that it is not possible to use this regional migration data for a comparison of the scale of movement in 1961 and 1966.

In addition, inter-regional movement is, for the reasons mentioned earlier, not a good measure of the size of retirement migration. Movement of elderly people out of the conurbations gives a better idea of the scale of the exodus from the cities. In 1960-1, 29,070 people aged 65 and over moved out of the Greater London, West Midlands, West Yorkshire, Tyneside, South-East Lancashire and Merseyside Conurbations. (16) Of these, 2,080 moved into another conurbation, so the total number that moved out was 26,990. In 1965-6 the number that moved out was 31,190 with 1,250 moving to another conurbation, so the total who moved out was 29,940. In 1960-1 the total who moved out represented 1.4 per cent of thos aged 65 and over who lived in the conurbations in 1961 and in 1965-6 they represented 1.6 per cent of those who lived in the conurbations in 1966. There was, therefore, a slight increase in the proportion moving out.

However, at the same time there was a movement of elderly people into the conurbations. In 1960-1 they totalled 9,590 and in 1965-6 11,800, excluding again those who moved into one conurbation from another. So the net loss of elderly people in each period was much smaller than the number moving out. The net loss was 17,400 in 1960-1 and 18,140 in 1965-6. These net losses represented 0.91 per cent of the population of those aged 65 and over in 1961 and 0.94 per cent in 1966. So, because of the greater numbers coming in in 1965-6, there was no increase in the rate of net loss in the five years.

In the period from 1961 to 1966, the population aged 65 and over in the conurbations rose from 1,899,325 to 1,926,860, an increase of only 27,535. On the other hand, the net loss by migration in this age group in the same period was approaching 90,000. The effect on the cities of the emigration of elderly people was, therefore, very substantial. The five-year natural increase of people aged

65 and over was cut by about three-quarters. Of course, much of this movement can be explained by movement to more suburban areas round the conurbations; not all can be attributed to moves to retirement resorts.

Because of changes in the definitions of the retirement regions between 1961 and 1966, it is not possible to trace trends of movement into those areas as easily. However, the regions can be looked at individually. In the South-West, where there was no change of definition, there was a clear increase in the scale of movement into the region, from a net figure of 3,520 in 1960-1 to 5,060 in 1965-6. The North-West also increased its balance of elderly immigrants from 830 in 1960-1 to 1,860 in 1965-6.

One further feature which emerges is the relatively large scale of movement out of retirement regions as well as into them. In 1965-6 some 34,450 elderly people moved out of the five individual retirement regions, of whom 17 per cent (5,730) moved to one of the other four. Of these, 2,180 moved to the South-East Remainder Region and 2,210 to the South-West. There was a very large exchange between the two regions; the South-East Remainder received 1,400 from the South-West and the South-West 1,770 from the South-East.

After this movement between retirement regions has been taken into account, there were still 12,730 elderly people who moved out of the retirement regions altogether in 1965-6. Of these 4,480 moved into the six conurbations. Part of this movement is accounted for by the unsatisfactory use of the South-East and North-West Remainder Regions as substitutes for retirement areas; 1,770 of the moves were from the South-East Remainder into Greater London and 910 were from the North-West Remainder Region into the Merseyside and South-East Lancashire Conurbations. There is no means of knowing how many of these were from retirement areas and how many from the inland areas.

However, whatever the actual scale of movement, there is clearly a substantial element of 'return-migration' from the resorts to the cities, and, probably on a larger scale, from one resort area to another.

So what is the closest we can get to an estimate of how many elderly people currently move to seaside resorts? In 1961-6, 217,770 people of pensionable age moved into 16 retirement counties, and into 6 resorts in Lancashire and Yorkshire. (17) These 217,770 represented 3.0 per cent of people of pensionable age in 1966 and 4.0 per cent in 1961, so it seems as if about 3.5 per cent of elderly people currently move to retirement areas in a five-year period. Though this estimate is exceedingly rough, omitting retirement moves before the statutory retirement age, and those within counties and including moves to inland areas of heterogeneous counties such as Kent and Essex, it is as near an estimate as seems possible. If correct it means that roughly an eighth of all moves by elderly people are to retirement areas.

3   Who are the movers?

>   Mr. and Mrs. Stephen Grosvenor Smith
>   (He manages a Bank in Nottingham)
>   Have come to Sandy Cove for thirty years
>   And now they think the place is going down.
>   'Not what it was, I'm very much afraid.'
>   John Betjeman: Beside the Seaside

Though people who move to retire in resorts are very numerous, they are still only a tiny minority of all retired people. In what ways, if any, does this minority differ from the rest of the elderly population?

Even a superficial inspection of census data suggests that in one respect at least there is a very marked distinction, namely in the social class composition of the movers. In the majority of resorts the proportions of the professional and managerial classes are well above the national average. Bexhill had 41.1 per cent of retired men in Classes I and II in 1966, which was well above the national average, but there were some resorts with over 50 per cent.

Though this is the general conclusion, there are big differences between individual resorts. Resorts seem, in fact, to specialize in provision for different social classes in retirement in much the same way that they do for different classes of holiday-makers. Contrasting resorts may often be close neighbours; thus Budleigh Salterton, Sidmouth and Seaton may be considered 'upper-class' resorts on the South Devon coast while Teignmouth and Dawlish have less people in Social Classes I and II. (1) Similarly, on the Sussex coast, Eastbourne and Bexhill are the 'upper-class' resorts, Hastings and Bognor, far less exalted. On the East coast, West Mersea and Southwold are 'upper-class', Clacton and Cromer much less so with Frinton and Walton somewhere between. These differences are well known locally. They are also reflected in the image that each town has for holidaymakers. This image is maintained partly through the price of property but partly, too, through the type of people who take their holidays there and through the class similarity of people who come to join friends and relatives. The holiday brochures that the resorts send out are quite a good guide to the 'class' of the resort both in the design of the cover and in the entertainments and facilities described.

There is usually a big difference between the social class of retired and working people in these towns. In the vast majority of resorts the proportions of economically active males in Classes I and II are much lower than the proportions of retired males in Classes I and II. In a few cases the difference is so great that it must create a considerable social gulf between the retired and working population. Budleigh Salterton, Seaton, Sidmouth and Southwold are the most extreme examples, closely followed by Swanage, West Mersea, Bexhill and Worthing. It is noteworthy that these places are almost invariably those with the largest proportions of elderly people. (2)

Such a social gulf could greatly exacerbate any difficulties of communication which may already exist between the young and old because of the lack of shared experiences. Several of the officers in resort authorities mentioned reactions of 'upper-class' old people to, for instance, home helps or nurses whom they regard as 'lackeys'. Such difficulties of communication must sometimes be likely to result in isolation from younger people and an unwillingness to seek help from them.

One of the reasons for choosing Bexhill and Clacton for the social surveys was that they had contrasting social class characteristics, Bexhill with a very large proportion of Classes I and II and Clacton with a proportion nearer the national average. The results of the social surveys in the two towns confirmed the census findings (Table 3.1). Bexhill had quite a different social class pattern from the national average; semi-skilled and unskilled workers were very unlikely to move there. Clacton's social class pattern was, however, not so different from the national average. In Clacton the professional classes were not over-represented as they were in Bexhill and whereas half the elderly people in Bexhill were from the managerial class only 22 per cent were so in Clacton. The largest proportion (41 per cent) of the Clacton retired people had been skilled manual workers and there was a much larger proportion of semi-skilled and unskilled workers in Clacton (15 per cent) than

Chapter 3

TABLE 3.1 Social class and previous employment status (%)

	Bexhill All respondents	Clacton All respondents	England and Wales All economically active and retired males (1966)*
Sample no.	501	497	–
SOCIAL CLASS			
Professional	10	3	4
Managerial	50	22	15
Skilled non-manual	24	18	} 49
Skilled manual	9	41	
Semi-skilled and unskilled	2	15	29
Armed forces and indefinite	4	1	3
PREVIOUS EMPLOYMENT STATUS*			
Self-employed	14	11	8**
Employee	85	88	92**

* Registrar General, 1966 Sample Census, Great Britain Economic Activity Tables, Part III, Table 30 and Part I, Table 13.
** Economically active only.
*** For married and widowed women, other than widowed women with life-long employment, the data are for their husbands.

in Bexhill (2 per cent). The Clacton proportion was still, however, well below the national average of 29 per cent for semi-skilled and unskilled workers.

The proportions of self-employed people were not significantly different from the national average. In Clacton they tended to be shopkeepers and small traders, in Bexhill professionals and owners of larger businesses.

The people interviewed in the social survey were, of course, only those who had moved to the two towns to retire. The census figures for all retired males included local people as well. It is therefore interesting to see if the general population had, as one would expect, a greater proportion of the semi-skilled and unskilled. This was in fact the case; of the movers 2 per cent in Bexhill and 15 per cent in Clacton were in Classes IV and V while the census gave figures of 8 per cent and 22 per cent respectively for all retired males, movers and local residents together.

The social surveys of Bexhill and Clacton revealed a number of other characteristics of movers about which the census provides no information. There were, in particular, several features of the circumstances in which they retired from work which are interesting. First, the age at which the movers retired from work was lower than the national average (Table 3.2). Fifty-seven per cent of men of 65 and over in Bexhill and 34 per cent in Clacton had retired before they were 65, compared with 21 per cent nationally. The difference lay not in the proportion who retired before they were 60 but in the extraordinarily large proportion in Bexhill and Clacton who had retired between the ages of 60 and 64, and the small proportion who had retired at 70 or over. The latter was only 20-5 per cent of the national proportion. In fact, of the Bexhill and Clacton men of 65 and over, 87 per cent and 89 per cent respectively had retired between the ages of 60 and 69, compared with 68 per cent nationally. (3)

TABLE 3.2 Retirement age

	Retired men 65 and over				All retired men	
	Bexhill	Clacton		Britain 1962*	Bexhill	Clacton
Sample no.	316	337		719	392	399
AGE	%	%		%	%	%
59 and under	9	6	60 and under	10	13	9
60-4	48	28	61-4	11	47	29
65-9	39	61		57	34	57
70 and over	4	5		23	5	5

* E. Shanas et al., 'Old People in Three Industrial Societies', London, Routledge & Kegan Paul, 1968, p.325, Table XI-2.

A likely explanation of the earlier retirement age might seem to be social class differences in the usual age of retirement. In particular, Bexhill's population contained a large number of retired civil servants for whom 'the age of retirement is regarded as normally being between 60 and 65, with retention beyond 65 only in suitable cases'. (4) An analysis of retirement age by social

class did reveal that the managerial class, which includes
senior civil servants, bankers and so on, was particularly
likely to retire between the ages of 60 and 65 and so were
skilled non-manual workers in Bexhill, who included many
junior grade civil servants. However, the fact remains
that the other classes were also more likely than the
national average to retire at this age and the discrepancy
in the proportions who retired at 70 and over is left
unaffected. In the cross-national survey, it was found
that:

> the great majority of men ... who stopped working
> before reaching the 66th year did so owing to a reason
> that in one way or another implies "bad health". This
> simply serves to underline that the standard (in the
> USA, Denmark and Britain) is that a healthy man goes
> on working until about 65 years of age. (5)

TABLE 3.3 Reasons for retiring from work

	Bexhill	Clacton	Britain*
Sample no.	459	429	772
REASON	%	%	%
Ill-health	18	26	44
Compulsory retirement age	33	30	26
Redundant	2	2	6
Voluntary	44	38	16
Other	3	4	7

* Shanas et al., op. cit., p.315, Table X-21.

In the present survey it also emerged that younger men
were more likely to retire for health reasons, but in
contrast to the national findings, it was only the under
60s in Bexhill, not the under 65s who stressed health
reasons. Only 17 per cent of those in the 60-4 age group
mentioned their health compared with 42 per cent of the
under 60s. In Clacton, too, the under 60s mentioned
health most frequently (56 per cent). A substantial
proportion (35 per cent) of the 60-4 group also did, but
this was significantly lower than the national figure of
50 per cent for the 60-4 age group.

Even more striking was the very large proportion of
elderly people in Bexhill and Clacton who said they had
retired voluntarily (Table 3.3). There may be some

problems of interpretation here, in that the cross-national survey may have, by additional probing, included under health, answers which have been coded under voluntary retirement in this study. However, in this survey, bad health, old age and finding the job too tiring were included under health, so that the difference arising from interpretations should not be very great. (6) Certainly, they cannot explain the difference between 16 per cent of voluntary retirement in the cross-national survey and 44 per cent and 38 per cent in Bexhill and Clacton. It seems more logical to explain this difference, and the difference in retirement age, in terms of the attitudes of the Bexhill and Clacton residents towards retirement. The combination of the reasons they gave for retiring and the way in which they mostly anticipated the usual retirement age by a few years, suggests that many were looking forward to retirement, or were, at least, keen to leave their work.

Discussion of the images movers had of the ideal retirement must be left until a later chapter but it is relevant to consider here their attitudes towards continuing work. Those who had ever worked full-time were asked 'Would you have preferred to continue working?' Thirty-five per cent in Clacton and 27 per cent in Bexhill said they would have, 2 per cent and 3 per cent had no preference and all the others said they would not.

The proportions who said they did not want to continue work were larger than the proportions who said they retired voluntarily; so, many who had to retire compulsorily or because of ill-health, must have done so quite willingly. In Bexhill, of those who said they would have liked to continue work, 45 per cent were people who gave health reasons for retiring and 28 per cent were people who had reached compulsory retirement age. The proportions in Clacton were 46 per cent and 36 per cent. A few of the people who said they retired voluntarily, also said they would have preferred to work in other circumstances. Some of these referred to the fact that they moved to Bexhill or Clacton before retirement and found the burden of commuting forced them to give up their job.

Some clearly felt they would have preferred to work in their new place of residence, though how much effort they had made to do so is quite another question. Of all the heads of retirement units only 12 per cent in Bexhill and 15 per cent in Clacton said they had worked at all after their retirement move. In Bexhill 34 per cent of the people who continued work, and in Clacton 36 per cent, commuted back up to London or to the place they came from; most of these continued working for a relatively short time. Most found travelling a strain. The rest took up employment locally. In Bexhill 21 per cent compared with only 3 per cent in Clacton bought a business or hotel locally or set up in a professional practice of some kind; four-fifths of those who did this in Bexhill were in the professional and managerial classes and most of the others had been in the armed forces. In Clacton those who went into business usually bought a hotel or boarding house. (7)

These were all the people who worked after their retirement move; there were far fewer who were still working full- or even part-time at the time of the survey. The numbers were particularly small in Bexhill, only 5 per cent of all respondents and 6 per cent of the men, compared with 10 per cent of all respondents in Clacton or 12 per cent of the men. In addition, two-thirds of the people still working in Bexhill were only part-time compared with 44 per cent in Clacton. Those still working full-time were naturally concentrated in the younger age groups, under 65, but part-time workers were frequently in their late 60s and early 70s. The national proportion of men over 65 who were working in 1971 was 19 per cent. (8) In both Bexhill and Clacton only 5 per cent of men of 65 and over were still working, and four-fifths of them worked only part-time.

Retirement from work was very closely linked in timing with the retirement move. For Bexhill 45 per cent and for Clacton 40 per cent of the people moved in their year of retirement, and a further 12 per cent in Bexhill and 14 per cent in Clacton moved within a year after it. Thirteen per cent in Bexhill and 18 per cent in Clacton moved before their retirement from work, but usually only shortly before. After the concentration of moves in the first year of retirement, there was a rapid drop; only 6 per cent in Bexhill and 4 per cent in Clacton moved two years after their retirement. In fact they were just as likely to move five years after it, as two years after it. People who retired voluntarily were more likely to have moved immediately than were the people who retired for other reasons. These people probably left work in order to move or at least had the two carefully synchronised.

It appears, then, that the people who moved to Bexhill and Clacton were mainly those who were quite eager to give up work, rather than those who were forced to do so by bad health. The majority timed their move to the seaside to coincide with or very rapidly follow their retirement from work. A minority moved slightly earlier and commuted for a time. So they were not usually people who had experienced a lengthy period of retirement in the place in which they had worked. For this reason any views most of them may have had on the satisfactoriness of being retired in cities and suburbs must have been largely based on others' experiences or on their own predictions.

A national survey of migration (9) has shown that the maximum amount of movement amongst elderly people occurs round about the statutory retirement age, that is in the 65-9 age group. This is particularly the case for long distance movers. (10) The people who moved to Bexhill and Clacton had also usually made their retirement move between the ages of 60 and 69; (11) 71 per cent in Bexhill and 74 per cent in Clacton had moved at that age. This was to be expected in view of the close relationship in time between retirement from work and the move away. (12)

The people who lived in Bexhill appeared to have moved when they were a little younger than those who went to Clacton. Just as Bexhill men retired from work earlier than Clacton men did, so they tended to move in their early 60s rather than in their late 60s. Bexhill women who were heads of retirement units were much more likely to have moved in their late 50s than were the Clacton women, and seemed slightly less likely to have moved when they were over 70. (13) This is partly linked with the fact that the Bexhill women were often single, whereas the Clacton women were mainly widows who came to join relatives and friends. (14) Widowed people in both towns were generally older than others when they made their retirement move, and those who came to Clacton moved at a later age than those who came to Bexhill.

Most elderly people made their retirement move with their husband or wife; in other words as a married couple. Taking all the heads of moving households, males and females, of those who moved to Bexhill 79 per cent were married, 15 per cent were single and 6 per cent were widowed at the time of their move to Bexhill. Of those who moved to Clacton 86 per cent were married, 5 per cent were single and 9 per cent widowed. Hardly any of the men (2 per cent in each town) were widowed or single at the time of their move; the single and widowed people were almost invariably women. The two towns differed, however, in that in Bexhill most of these women were single, whereas in Clacton, most (63 per cent) were widowed. Most of the married couples moved alone but surprisingly large numbers (15-20 per cent) were accompanied by one or more of their children. Most of these no longer lived with their parents at the time of the survey.

However, an even more striking number of people had no

surviving children at all. In Bexhill 47 per cent of
the retired households had no children at the time of the
survey and so did 30 per cent in Clacton. (15) In
addition those who did have children had relatively few;
of those who had children, 40 per cent in Bexhill and
35 per cent in Clacton had only one child; 42 per cent
and 40 per cent had two. Comparison of the family
structure of these households in Bexhill and Clacton
with that of elderly people nationally is rather difficult
because of the differences in the data available. (16)
However, it is possible to compare male heads of retired
households in our sample with men respondents of 65 and
over in the cross-national survey and to separate married
and widowed men. The conclusion is that both towns had
more childless people than the national average. Whereas
16 per cent of married and widowed men of 65 and over in
Britain were childless, in Clacton the proportion was 25
per cent and in Bexhill 36 per cent. (17)

There was, in Bexhill and Clacton, no relationship
between social class and childlessness. The cross-
national survey also found that 'no straightforward case
can be made from our findings that class position affects
the probability of both older men and older women being
childless'. (18) However, the cross-national survey did
find that the number of children of those who had them
was 'clearly related to class position'. This was also
true in Bexhill and Clacton, where the professional and
intermediate classes were more likely to have only one
child than were manual workers.

The conclusion is then that the people who moved on
retirement, particularly to Bexhill, were less likely to
have children than were elderly people nationally and
that those with children had less than the national
average. (19) This result was not unexpected. In
considering what sort of people might decide to move on
retirement, it seemed likely that those who had no
surviving children might have the least ties and so be
more willing to move away from the town in which they
had spent their working life. In addition, however, it
should be remembered that the interviews were with only
those people who had stayed in the retirement towns not
those who had left or died. Later we will see that there
seems some likelihood that those who are widowed after
their retirement move may frequently return to their
children, if they have any. This would mean that childless people would be more likely to stay on in retirement
towns once they had moved there.

This discussion of the household characteristics of
movers can therefore be summarized as follows:

Retirement to resorts such as Bexhill and Clacton is very much a feature of the middle-class married couple in their 60s. The husband has typically just retired from full-time work and has not worked again, even part-time. Nearly half the heads of retirement units in Bexhill and nearly a third in Clacton have no surviving children, which may well have been a factor in their willingness to move. But about a fifth of all married couples moved with an unmarried child, or children. The ability to take these children with them may also have made them more willing to move. However, nearly all these children had moved away from their parents by the time the survey was undertaken.

4   The movers' homes in the cities and suburbs

'No Sir, when a man is tired of London, he is tired of life; for there is in London all that life can afford.'

Dr Johnson (1)

'Hell is a city much like London
A populous and smoky city'
      Shelley: 'Peter Bell the Third', Part 3: Hell

Discussions about the problems of moving in retirement often concentrate upon the strain caused by wrenching up deep roots. This assumes that movers have lived a long time in the place they left on retirement. To check on this assumption, the retired people in Bexhill and Clacton were asked how long they had lived in their last home town before their retirement move. The largest proportion of people had lived at least twenty years in this town; for Bexhill residents the figure was 55 per cent and for Clacton residents, 69 per cent. The Bexhill movers had clearly stayed a shorter period but in both cases the majority were moving at the end of a long period of residence in the same place. In fact 26 per cent of the elderly people in Bexhill and 38 per cent in Clacton had lived in no place since they were 20 other than that from which they retired. Again the greater mobility of Bexhill movers is apparent. A third of the Bexhill respondents had lived in five or more places since they were 20, compared with 17 per cent of the Clacton respondents. It seems that in Bexhill there is some evidence that retired people had, in their working life, been more mobile than the national average but the same is probably not true for Clacton. (2)

One of the problems which frequently distresses elderly people and may even prompt them to move is that of maintenance of a large house. This is a general problem, but it seemed possible that it might be one of the 'push' factors which caused retired people to move in retirement, even if it were an inadequate explanation of why they chose to go to seaside resorts. The type of accommodation that elderly people had in their pre-retirement home was therefore relevant to the study.

The vast majority of elderly people had in fact been owner-occupiers in their previous home. Of the Bexhill respondents, 72 per cent had been owner-occupiers in their pre-retirement home and in Clacton the figure was 77 per cent. Compared with this, the proportion of owner-occupied dwellings in 1971 was 52 per cent for England and Wales and 43 per cent for Greater London. (3) Clearly the movers were a very atypical group in this respect. But the difference from the national average does not end there. In England and Wales in 1971, 28 per cent of households lived in local authority housing; in Greater London the proportion was 24 per cent. Only 1 per cent of those who moved to Bexhill had moved from local authority housing and in Clacton only 2 per cent. Most of these had bought houses in the resorts. Several in Clacton had saved throughout the period of their tenancy and could buy a house outright from savings. One or two others had cashed in their superannuation, and one man in Bexhill had won £70,000 on the football pools and had felt that it was wrong to continue living in a GLC flat.

The proportions who had been living in privately rented housing were also small, 16 per cent in Bexhill and 13 per cent in Clacton, compared with 21 per cent in England and Wales and 32 per cent in Greater London in 1971. (4) There was however a stronger than average representation of tied housing, particularly amongst those moving to Bexhill. For those who moved to Bexhill this had been mainly hospital, school or vicarage accommodation and for those who moved to Clacton, accommodation attached to shops and pubs.

Since the people who retired to seaside resorts were often from the more affluent social classes, it was not surprising to find that they were also mainly owner-occupiers. However, manual workers who moved were almost as likely as the others to have been owner-occupiers, whereas nationally they are far less likely to own their houses. In Bexhill 70 per cent and in Clacton 83 per cent of skilled manual workers had been owner-occupiers before their move, compared with 45 per cent of all skilled manual workers in England and Wales in 1971 (5) Similarly 84 per cent of semi-skilled and unskilled workers in Clacton had been owner-occupiers compared with 29 per cent for these classes nationally. (6)

What explanations can be offered for this great predominance of owner-occupiers? The social class composition of the towns is not sufficient explanation. Two other explanations might be given, one that owner-occupiers have more motive for moving, the other that, though many want to move, the owner-occupiers find it much easier to do so.

In the first case, it might be suggested that owner-occupiers may be more status conscious than others and that moving to the seaside on retirement is one of the high-status actions to take. There is no proof of this but it is a possibility, because of the social class composition of the most popular resorts.

Another reason why owner-occupiers might have more motive for moving is that in old age they frequently find themselves with large houses which are expensive to maintain. Council and private tenants may also have houses which are too large for them but at least they are not responsible for external decoration and repairs.

The other explanation, that mobility is easier for owner-occupiers, seems however to have more validity. Someone who wants to move needs both to be able to leave their present house, and to be able to find and afford another. Owner-occupiers have the most trouble in leaving their house because of the need to sell it, instead of just giving a month's notice to the landlord. However, they have a great advantage over tenants in their ability to find another house, especially if they own enough of the equity in their house to be able to buy the next one outright. Then they will not have the trouble of obtaining a mortgage. It is difficult for an elderly person who has not previously owned a house to buy one for the first time when they are over 60, unless they have savings to cover the whole price of the house or superannuation to cash in to cover it. Mortgages are not usually given for a period beyond the borrower's 65th birthday. For these reasons it is extremely likely that an elderly person who is buying a house will have had one to sell.

But what are the prospects of being able to rent accommodation in the resorts? Local authority housing is not an immediate possibility for an elderly person moving to a resort. In the first place there are residential qualifications which make them ineligible. Second, there is a shortage of council housing suitable for old people, and long waiting lists. Private rented accommodation is more plentiful but it is either very expensive or of poor quality. Also much of the property such as flats in converted houses that one might expect to be let, is sold leasehold. Thus the private rented property available is either suitable only for the well-to-do or consists of poor quality rooms and converted flats. This would deter rather than attract the average council or private tenant from moving out of London.

Looking at the pre-retirement home in more detail, the elderly people were asked to say what they had liked and disliked about it at the time of their move. They were not asked if the dislikes caused them to move; there was a quite separate question about reasons for moving. In fact, the replies about likes and dislikes included as many factors which would have deterred a person from moving as encouraged them to do so: the desire to move, or the need to do so, often over-rode a lifelong attachment to the house or area.

The most immediately striking fact was that 61 per cent of the Bexhill people and 48 per cent in Clacton said they could think of nothing they disliked about their previous house. Furthermore 48 per cent in Bexhill and 55 per cent in Clacton said they disliked nothing about the area in which they had lived. (7)

The features about their house which people most disliked were to do with problems of maintenance and standards of comfort for an older person. Three quarters were living in houses, rather than flats or bungalows which are often more convenient for older people. The most common complaint was that the house was too large; together with the problems of excessive housework and gardening, this constituted more than half of the dislikes mentioned. Many also remarked on heating problems and the inadequacies and inconvenience of an old house. Of the other dislikes, the location of the house was the most frequently mentioned. Considering that 29 per cent of the Bexhill people and 12 per cent of those who moved to Clacton (8) had had four or more bedrooms it is rather surprising that not more people said their house had been too large. In fact the Clacton respondents were more likely to mention size and housework, whereas the Bexhill people more frequently complained of the problems of managing their gardens. Perhaps Bexhill people more often had domestic help before retirement. This suggests that size in itself is not the problem, but rather cost and inconvenience of upkeep.

The features which people particularly liked about their houses were suitable size, a nice garden, good quality building and attractive appearance, but many were very vague, replying that they 'just liked it'.

Apart from the problems of size and maintenance, which were mentioned by a quarter of respondents, these replies would certainly not lead to the conclusion that housing conditions were a primary reason for the majority of retirement moves. They would not have been an adequate 'push'.

Reactions to the area seem to give more clues about motives for moving. For one thing, the features which were liked were mainly expressed in terms of a working situation. Thus a third of the respondents said they liked the convenience of their area for getting to the city, to their work and for transport. Another quarter mentioned convenience for shopping. These features were particularly stressed by the people from Greater London. During their working life, proximity to work, or to transport had to take priority, but, given that it was necessary for them to live in the city, they seem to have particularly appreciated living in a part of the city which gave access to open space and where also the neighbours were congenial. The Bexhill people, who usually came from suburban South London, were more likely to say they had these assets than were the Clacton people who came from North East London and nearer the centre of London.

But, living near to one's work in a city usually brings environmental disadvantages, particularly noisy traffic and lack of open space. Also people who have lived a long time in a city, or in any place for that matter, tend to become very aware of changes taking place, in their opinion usually for the worse. Thus more than a tenth of the respondents mentioned that their area had in their opinion deteriorated socially. Particularly in Greater London, coloured immigrants were mentioned and a few people from the suburbs regretted the arrival of Jews, whom some called 'the Hebrews'. Particularly in the suburbs too, many people deplored the way in which former open space was getting very built up. However, the growth in traffic was the major problem. Old people not only dislike the noise and dirt of traffic but they find difficulty in coping with its speed and the complexity of traffic management. Many people flee from the worst of the inner city problems into suburbia, but there were some of our respondents who found the suburban environment dull and characterless. It was only made supportable for these people by leaving it for work every day; the prospect of staying in the suburbs in retirement appalled them.

So it is possible that while people found the cities and suburbs convenient during their working life, when retirement approached they asked themselves why they should continue to accept the second best in terms of open space, put up with heavy traffic, stay to watch the area change its social character, or accept what they felt to be the tedium of suburban life?

At this point one can see the significance of so many of the movers having no children. If a person wants to move, it is easier to do so if there are no social ties, particularly if there are no members of the family living nearby. The same point can be made about retired people who moved with their unmarried children. In this case there was no need to leave them behind.

As far as the movers' pre-retirement home is concerned, it appears then that there was a certain amount of dissatisfaction with large old houses that were unsuitable and expensive for elderly people to maintain and a dislike of the inescapable features of the city environment, traffic, noise, dirt and lack of open space. However, the fact remains that at least half the people questioned had nothing to say about disliking the area. And yet they moved. Why?

5 The move itself: motives and choices

> To one who has been long in city pent;
> 'Tis very sweet to look into the fair
> And open face of heaven.
> > Keats, Sonnet: To One Who Has
> > Been Long in City Pent

The remarkable similarity between the distribution of retirement areas in Britain and the areas selected by school leavers as the most desirable in which to live, was mentioned in Chapter 1. Clearly the desire for improved surroundings (in whatever way improved surroundings are perceived) may be expected to be amongst the reasons elderly people give for moving in retirement. (1)

But 'improvement in surroundings' is too loose a term to be useful. What were the movers looking for? The answer to this question was sought by asking them what had been their main reason for moving (Table 5.1).

By far the largest proportion of people said they moved to live by the sea, usually linking this with a better climate and cleaner air, or said they had health reasons. Some of these people had been specifically advised to move by their doctors but most had made the decision of their own accord. Some were really ill, but the majority merely wanted to improve or maintain their health by getting away from the effects of air pollution and by living in a warmer place. It seems that the traditional reasons for moving to resorts are still the major ones, climate and health, a motive justified in that the major resort areas do in fact have more sunshine, warmer winters, less fog and less air pollution than the cities from which the migrants came. Even many of the people who said that there was nothing they disliked about the actual area in which they had previously lived criticized its environment by implication in their reasons for moving.

After climate and health reasons, the largest number of people in Bexhill (16 per cent) mentioned the desire to get away from towns and live in a quiet place. This reaction, like the desire for a more healthy environment, was linked with the features which many people had said they had particularly disliked about their previous home, namely smoke and dirt, the heavy traffic and the lack of open space. In addition there was a desire to change to a more relaxed way of life. One very old lady, explaining her move at the age of 84, said: 'The pace was too hot up there.' The chance to pass the time of day with other people was cherished by many old people. 'What is this life if, full of care, We have no time to stand and stare', they quoted.

TABLE 5.1 Main reasons for retirement move

	Bexhill	Clacton
Sample number	503	487
REASONS FOR MOVING	%	%
Better climate; cleaner air; sea air	33	19
Health reasons	11	18
Flat country	1	1
To get away from town or live in a quiet place	16	10
To live in a bungalow	4	9
Having to leave a tied house	5	5
The expense of living in the previous place	5	9
To have a change	7	9
To join friends or relations	10	15
Other	7	6

Housing was also a motive for moving for 14 per cent of people in Bexhill and 23 per cent in Clacton. There were three aspects. First, some people particularly wanted a bungalow, to avoid climbing stairs and to reduce housework. Second, many found their existing house too expensive; sometimes the rent was too high but more often, because the majority were owner-occupiers, it was the rates and maintenance which were worrying them. Some who had previously said they had no complaints about their house said they foresaw the problem arising in retirement when there would be a reduction in their income. Others had discovered it already after being retired for a time. Third, 5 per cent of the respondents in each town had lived in tied accommodation and had to move from it when they retired from work. On the face of it none of these reasons need have involved anything more than a local move but most of these people came from London and the housing market there is such that for a number of reasons they had little choice but to move some distance. Bungalows are almost non-existent except in the outer suburbs and there the cost is high relative to other property. Bungalows at a reasonable price are also scarce in other parts of the country, particularly near the centres of towns. For instance one respondent claimed that he had wanted a bungalow in Warwick and that if he could have got one he would not have moved to Bexhill. In addition, the cost of a smaller house in London is often greater than the proceeds of selling an older, larger house. Also the rates would be just as high if not higher. Last, most people from tied rented accommodation would find it hard to afford decent rented accommodation in London or to buy a house. So all these people would in fact be facing a move of some distance. Probably they felt they might as well move to an attractive place if they were going to move at all. It is interesting that housing reasons for moving were mentioned more frequently in Clacton than in Bexhill, and it was the retired people in Clacton who were the more dissatisfied with their pre-retirement housing conditions. This is not surprising, since they were mainly working class, with lower incomes than people who moved to Bexhill. They must have had much greater difficulty in finding satisfactory housing in London.

The next largest group of reasons for moving was to do with joining friends or relations. These were more numerous in Clacton (15 per cent of all respondents) than in Bexhill (10 per cent). Those who had no complaints about their previous house or area were likely to be joining friends or relatives, and so were those who moved some years after their retirement from work. Also, of those who had been widowed before their retirement move 43 per cent in Clacton and 30 per cent in Bexhill said this was their reason for moving, compared with 15 per cent and 10 per cent of all respondents. So the desire to join friends and relations is unlikely to be the reason for a move to the seaside at the time of retirement from work, which is the typical time for such a move, but it is the typical motive for a person who moves at some later point during their retirement. Most men who move at the time of their retirement from work come with their wife and at that time are probably unaware of the problem of loneliness. It is those men, or more frequently, women, who have already been widowed who are hit by this, and so are more likely to move to the resorts to join friends or relatives.

One interesting group of respondents (9 per cent in the Clacton sample and 7 per cent in Bexhill) said they moved in order to have a complete change. They felt they were starting a new phase of their life and they wanted a change of surroundings to match it. For some this was a long-awaited fresh start, and they had built up great ideas over the years of how they were going to spend their retirement. For others the change of surroundings was needed because they did not want to be retired in the area in which they had worked. One woman said that her husband had moved 'to get away from the sight of Hoover's factory which he loved so much'. There were references to the unsatisfactory character of suburbs for retirement, the draining away of everyone in the day time, the predominance of mothers and babies, the self-absorption of young families at the weekends and the inability of working men to break out of thoughts about work. In this atmosphere the elderly people felt they would be out of place. In addition, they said the suburbs were badly provided with entertainment and social facilities suitable for elderly people, while transport costs were high. For a few people, the need was to get away from excessive commitments to local government and voluntary bodies. They found the committees increasing in their retirement rather than the reverse and decided that a move was the only way to ease out tactfully.

It was hoped that some additional light would be shed on motives for moving by the replies to a further question on the ideas people had in advance about the way they would spend their retirement (TABLE 5.2).

Over a third of people said they had had no ideas at all. People who had had to retire suddenly through ill-health and people who were very old at the time of the survey were strongly represented in this group, but most had no particular reason for not having considered their retirement. They had just not though about it until it happened.

From the point of view of motives for moving, the most interesting feature of the ideas which were described was the stress laid on wanting to live by the sea in retirement; a quarter of those in Bexhill and 17 per cent in Clacton gave this as their idea of retirement. These replies were much more numerous than those which referred more vaguely to getting away from towns. The move to resorts is a positive one to the sea, not just a flight away from the towns. The phrase 'to have a bungalow by the sea' was used, giving a more precise image to the ideal.

TABLE 5.2 Ideas about retirement

	Bexhill	Clacton
Sample number	503	487
PROPORTION WHO GAVE THE FOLLOWING REPLIES:	%	%
No ideas about it	38	37
To live by the sea	25	17
To get away from towns	12	4
To have a perpetual holiday	3	5
To be with relations, especially spouse	3	3
To rest and relax	16	19
To have a bungalow	2	6
To develop a garden	12	11
To pursue hobbies	13	6
To work full- or part-time	2	3
Other	12	9

Other ideas about retirement did not necessarily involve a move, though some did by implication, particularly 'to have a complete break', 'to have a perpetual holiday' and 'to rest and relax'. Many people in their replies to the questions about their previous home made it clear that the pace of city life was such that they felt unable to relax as they wished to. In addition it is frequently said of those who move to the seaside that they identify the 'holiday' of retirement with the previous holidays of their working life. And in this context it is interesting to note that the proportion of main holidays spent in Britain, which are spent at the seaside, remains fairly constant at about 70 per cent. (2) In spite of the congestion at resorts, high prices and attempts to popularize inland holidays, British people, if they go on holiday in Britain, tend to go to the seaside. Therefore the identification of retirement with a seaside holiday seems very likely. In addition the reasons that holiday-makers give for choosing seaside resorts are very similar to those given by the retired people. According to the British Tourist Authority, British seaside holiday-makers are looking for 'rest, relaxation, seeing the sea, sea-air, good weather and living in comfort'. (3)

The other main ideas about retirement were to do with hobbies, particularly gardening. Here again there is no need to move to go in for more gardening, but property in the retirement resorts is particularly geared to providing the sort of bungalow and garden which fulfil the image of the average mover.

Wanting to spend more time with a husband or wife was specifically mentioned by relatively few people but the implication of a shared retirement underlay the whole discussion of ideas about retirement. Retirement to resorts such as Bexhill and Clacton is, as we have seen, very much a feature of the elderly couple. The idea of moving has been developed mutually. The vast majority, more than 70 per cent, said that each had been as enthusiastic as the other about moving. Of the rest, about 3 per cent said they had had no choice but to move and the rest were equally divided between those who said the husband was most keen and those who said the wife was.

This approach to retirement does suggest a particular atmosphere of companionship in the marriage relationship. Ethel Shanas relates it to social class characteristics: 'It is ... white collar, middle class couples who occupy the retirement communities of the United States and Britain, and it is among these couples that one is likely to find a companionate, sharing, close relationship between husband and wife.' (4) Most writers who have described relationships within marriage have commented upon the greater emphasis on companionship by the middle classes, amongst older people at least. Amongst younger people they have found that class differences are breaking down in this respect, and working-class couples also increasingly stress companionship.

However, in the rush of a working life this companionship may be difficult to achieve. Willmott and Young describe the new type of 'absentee husband':

the executive who spends nearly all his time out of the home not so much spending money as making it. There are many workers in Woodford who snatch at every chance of overtime and stay in their factories night after night to earn money for a washing machine, a refrigerator or a small car.... But they do not ordinarily work anything like as long as some of their employers. (5)

These characteristics of the 'absentee' husband may

give some clues as to why so many of them should choose to move on retirement. For instance, it is highly likely that the couple may feel that if they are to achieve more companionship in retirement than during their working life, then, on retirement, a fresh start is needed. More important, for the husband who had devoted his life to his work, a new enterprise is also probably needed to help fill the gap. He may also want to leave the reminders that he is no longer needed in his firm.

However, Willmott and Young emphasise that absentee husbands are the exceptions. Most middle-class, working-age, suburban men spend their evenings at home and are particularly active in decorating, repairing and improving the house. Willmott and Young attribute this preoccupation with the house to three main reasons: first, pride of ownership, second, the opportunity to develop skills as a craftsman and, third, the attitude that the house is a sort of business, an investment which will appreciate. (6)

For these home-centred men, retirement from work probably presents the prospect of a mere extention of their evening and weekend activities to the whole week. It is not surprising that they may want a change - a 'complete break' as they so often put it. They would probably relish being able to devote their do-it-yourself skills and new leisure time to a different set of walls and windows, creating a new home in their retirement. Particularly, they may be more ambitious about the scale and skill of the gardening they would like to undertake. There is also the desire to realize the proceeds of the 'business investment' in the house. If the appreciation in local house prices has been watched with the pleasure which Willmott and Young describe, there is a built-in incentive, at the time when income is reduced by retirement, to obtain the proceeds of appreciation by selling the house and buying a cheaper one elsewhere. This will be particularly true if the house is too large or they feel that the area is deteriorating or likely to deteriorate.

For many couples, the retirement move may well be the first major decision that the two people have been able to make purely for themselves, without considering the children, since they first started a family. It may be no coincidence that some people said they chose Clacton because 'it's where we did all our courting' or Bexhill 'because we had our honeymoon here'. Retirement from work and the marriage or independence of children give the couple a chance to concentrate on their relationship with each other. What is more companionable than setting out on a new enterprise together, especially if it is one that has always been discussed as an ideal, namely the opportunity to get away from the city and live by the sea?

But then comes the choice of retirement home. For some people the decision to move at all is inextricably bound up with the choice of a particular place to move to, for instance the 'honeymooners' and those who are moving to be with a friend or relative. However, for at least half the movers, the choice of place is not a foregone conclusion.

Half the people who retired to Bexhill had considered alternative places, mainly along the Sussex coast, but also other parts of the South Coast, especially towards the west. (7) Fifty-eight per cent of those who moved to Clacton had considered other places. Once again Sussex predominated. Of those who had considered other places, three-quarters in Bexhill and half in Clacton had considered places in Sussex. In both Clacton and Bexhill, Eastbourne was the most frequently named alternative town but it was rejected on grounds of expense and the fact that it is very difficult to find bungalows, particularly new ones, within several miles of the sea front. A quarter of the people who had considered places other than Clacton had considered other parts of the Essex coast, whereas only 2 per cent of Bexhill people had done so. The coasts of Norfolk, Suffolk and Yorkshire were also mentioned more frequently in Clacton.

Most important, only about a tenth of the people who considered another place and therefore about 5 per cent of all the people interviewed had considered moving to places other than retirement resort areas and most of these others were country districts. It was extremely unusual for a person to say they had considered moving to a city or inland town, for instance to be near relatives or friends. The second important point was the overwhelming attraction of the Sussex Coast even for people who eventually moved to Clacton. It should be remembered that most of the Clacton movers came from North London.

What were retired people looking for in considering a number of places? Cost was an important feature; 77 per cent of those who chose Clacton on grounds of its low prices had looked at other places first. The same feature appeared in Bexhill, where 88 per cent of those who chose Bexhill on grounds of price had looked at other places. In Bexhill also 71 per cent of those who chose Bexhill because of the suitability of the property there had looked at other places. This category covers more than price; it really means that there were properties of the right size and cost within striking distance of the coast.

(In 1969 bungalows were still under construction within half a mile of the coast in Bexhill, which is unusual on the South Coast.)

The reasons given for selecting Bexhill or Clacton as a retirement home had a rather different emphasis from the reasons for moving at all on retirement. For instance though only 15 per cent of movers in Clacton and 10 per cent in Bexhill said their reason for moving at all was to be with friends or relatives, 32 per cent said they chose Clacton and 27 per cent Bexhill because they had friends or relatives living there or nearby. (8) Similarly though only 9 per cent in Clacton and 5 per cent in Bexhill said they moved because of the expense of their previous place of residence, 23 per cent in Clacton and 10 per cent in Bexhill said they chose that particular place because house prices were low enough. In other words, once the decision to move has been taken, usually on grounds of an improvement in environment and climate, other factors come in to play concerning the choice of place to move to. This is bound to be the case since a warm climate, for instance, is not something which strongly distinguishes one seaside resort from its neighbours, hard though the guide books may try to convince one to the contrary. There are not many people who can, like one respondent, confidently select Bexhill 'because the guide book said you would live ten years longer if you moved there'. (To be fair to Bexhill, it did not say so.)

In both Bexhill and Clacton the presence of friends and relatives was the most important reason for choosing the town but otherwise there were some significant differences between the two towns. Bexhill was more likely to have been chosen for the quality of the surroundings and town itself and, almost equally important, the availability of suitable houses. In Clacton it was the low price of property which particularly attracted retired people.

Before examining these reasons in more depth, it will be helpful to give the results of three other related questions: first, 'Did you have any friends, relations or children living here before you moved here?'; second, 'Had you ever been to Clacton/Bexhill during the winter time?'; and third, 'Had you ever been on holiday or for a day-trip around here?'.

People who retired to Bexhill were more likely than Clacton movers to have had friends in the town before they went there; 31 per cent had friends in Bexhill compared with 21 per cent in Clacton. However, only 2 per cent in Bexhill had children already living in the town compared with 7 per cent in Clacton. This difference also held true when widowed and married people were considered separately. However, the groups most likely to have had contacts already living in either town were single people and in Bexhill those who had been widowed before their move. These groups differed in that single people were more likely to be joining friends than relations whereas the widowed were more likely to be joining relations, particularly their children, than friends.

The reasons given by single people for choosing Bexhill and Clacton reflect this situation. They were particularly likely to say their reason was to join relations and friends; in Bexhill 43 per cent and in Clacton 44 per cent of them mentioned this.

Even when people had friends or relations in Bexhill and Clacton before they moved, they did not necessarily say they moved to be near them. Those with relations or children there were, however, much more likely to say they moved to join them than were those with friends. Of those in Bexhill who said they had friends in the town, 32 per cent said they came to join them, compared with 61 per cent of those who had relations and 58 per cent of those with children there. The equivalent proportions in Clacton were 28 per cent of those with friends, 70 per cent of those with relations and 80 per cent of those with children living there. As a result of this difference, though more people had friends in either town than had relations, the number who gave joining relations as a reason for their choice of the town was considerably larger than the number who said they were joining friends.

The old were also more likely than younger retired people to be joining people in the town. Of those who moved when they were 70 and over, 41 per cent in Clacton moved to be with friends and relations, compared with 32 per cent of all movers. In Bexhill the feature appeared only for those who moved after the age of 74, but of this age group 43 per cent moved to be with friends or relations, compared with 27 per cent of all movers. However, those aged under 60 were also likely to have moved to be with relations and friends. Some of these were single women or younger married couples who moved to take care of an old relative.

One of the problems sometimes mentioned in relation to retired people moving to the coast is that though they may be familiar with a resort in the summer months, they may never have seen it in the winter when the wind is cold. The retired people were therefore asked whether they had ever visited Bexhill or Clacton in the winter before they moved there. In Bexhill, 48 per cent and in Clacton 42 per cent said they had. We cannot tell of course, how many people who came in the winter were put off and decided not to retire there. However, many certainly were not; of those who chose Clacton and Bexhill for their climate and healthy air as many had been there in the winter as had not.

The identification of 'retirement' with 'holiday' and 'holiday' with 'seaside' holiday was mentioned earlier. But is there a more direct link in that elderly people choose for their retirement a place at which they have frequently spent their holidays. A British Travel Association survey of Bexhill certainly showed that visitors to Bexhill are very likely to be considering moving there on retirement:

> Contacts gave information on where they were spending or would spend their retirement; 36% would stay or were staying in their present town or village; 15% of the '35 and over' sample said they would move to Bexhill. Excluding from the sample those who had already retired, this would mean that 19% of the '35 and over' group sampled who had not yet retired claimed that they would retire to Bexhill when the time came, a figure which increased to 26% among repeat visitors. Whilst these figures may well be optimistic, they do testify to Bexhill's potential as a place for retirement. (9)

In Bexhill 78 per cent of the retired people said they had already been there on holiday or a day-trip; in Clacton the proportion was 92 per cent.

It is interesting that people who chose Clacton and Bexhill because of the price of houses, or Bexhill because it was the place in which they could find suitable accommodation, were the least likely to have visited the towns in winter or to have been there for a holiday or day-trip. This suggests that these towns may have been their second choice, not the place that had been visited most frequently in the past.

For some people there were strong emotional or nostalgic ties which brought them to Clacton or Bexhill. One man came back to Clacton because he had always liked it since he danced in the pier concert party there as a young man. Several had had their honeymoon in the town they chose.

The size of the towns was a point which a number of people mentioned. They felt that the towns were small enough for there to be a community, for people to identify with the town and to feel at home in it. This of course reflects the reason which some people gave for moving at all, namely their dissatisfaction with the quality of city and suburban life.

Just as relatives and friends played a role in the decision to move and in the choice of resort so they also helped with the process of moving itself. The majority of respondents found their houses through an estate agent or through newspapers and special property papers, notably 'Dalton's Weekly', but for a substantial minority (18 per cent in Bexhill and 23 per cent in Clacton) relatives and friends found the house, or in a few cases provided it. The rest either found it casually, when walking round the town, or obtained it in some other way, such as inheritance. A few, especially in Clacton, already owned their house before retirement and used it as a weekend cottage. When they moved in permanently they sold their London house.

Of the respondents in Clacton who said they had relatives or friends in the town when they moved 40 per cent had found their house through them. In Bexhill the proportion was only 26 per cent. In Clacton relatives were more likely to have helped than friends, and children were more likely to have helped than other relatives. In Bexhill it was the reverse; friends and relatives were most likely to have helped, children least. In a few cases a son or son-in-law bought a flat and let it, sometimes rent-free, to the elderly person.

For a minority there was no question of finding accommodation, because the place chosen had been determined by the availability of accommodation. Some of these have been mentioned, for instance those who had property provided by a relative or who inherited it, but there was also the retirement accommodation provided by particular firms and professional or other organisations. Several people were interviewed in one such flat block in Bexhill owned by a professional organisation. One woman, who had moved from London simply to get the flat, had always loathed Bexhill, mainly because of the large number of old people in the town, and came there only because the flat had been provided for her.

To summarise the actual moving process, it may be said first, that the people who retired to Bexhill and Clacton had given little consideration to moving to any place other than coastal resorts. Second, amongst the resort areas considered the Sussex coast stood out clearly as the most preferred retirement area, though many people had to reject moving there on grounds of cost. Third, the presence of friends and relatives played a large role in influencing decisions about the choice of a retirement resort, but it was also clear that the majority of movers were fairly familiar with the towns from previous excursions and holidays there. Last, for the actual process of selecting a house, their sources of information were largely the usual ones, namely newspapers and estate agents, but help was also frequently given by friends and relations, particularly in Clacton.

Part two

Life in the seaside resorts

6 The retired population of Bexhill and Clacton

> All the household were but two; and both of them obeyed, and both commanded.
> Ovid: 'The Metamorphoses' (Boucis and Philemon)

In previous chapters the retired people who moved to Bexhill and Clacton were considered in relation to the characteristics of their previous home and occupation, the timing and motives for their move and their reasons for choosing Bexhill and Clacton in particular for their retirement home. We now go on to look at the characteristics of these retirement movers at the time of the survey, that is the overall character, in 1968-9, of that section of the Bexhill and Clacton communities who had moved to the resorts to retire.

Though the majority of people had, as we have seen, moved to Bexhill and Clacton at about the age of 65, they had, of course, lived in the two towns for very varying periods since. In that time some of them had been widowed. The retired population of the two resorts had, therefore different age and marital status characteristics from those presented earlier as being typical of people at the time of their move. The majority (70 per cent in Bexhill and 80 per cent in Clacton) had moved to the town within the last ten years. This was partly a reflection of death rates but also of the very rapid growth of retirement resorts, particularly Clacton, in the previous ten years. However, women (other than married women) were more likely to have moved to the town earlier; nearly a quarter of widows and single women in Bexhill and 15 per cent in Clacton had moved there before 1954. This, of course, ties up with the greater age of widows but it also draws attention to another crucial point, namely the very great length of the retirement of many elderly women; their stay in the resort is not a short phase of their lives. (1)

THE AGE OF THE RETIRED POPULATION

As Clacton had grown more rapidly in the previous ten years and elderly people had moved there more recently than to Bexhill, it was to be expected that the retired people there would be rather younger than in Bexhill. However, against this, it must be remembered that Clacton men were older than those in Bexhill at the time when they moved to the town. (2) In fact, the two factors balance, and it was only widowed and single women in Bexhill who were older than their counterparts in Clacton. In Bexhill 42 per cent of them were 75 and over compared with 27 per cent in Clacton. The men's ages were remarkably alike in the two towns; about a quarter were 75 or over (Table 6.1).

TABLE 6.1 Age and sex of head of retired household

	Bexhill		Clacton	
	Men	Women	Men	Women
Sample number	335	143	391	88
Age	%	%	%	%
Under 55	-	-	1	-
55-9	1	3	2	1
60-4	8	10	10	11
65-9	34	16	33	31
70-4	30	28	30	30
75-9	18	22	17	11
80 and over	9	20	7	16

In England and Wales as a whole, in 1971, women aged 65 and over, were slightly more likely than those in the same age group in Bexhill to be aged 75 and over, and were much more likely than those in Clacton to be of that age. There was no significant difference in the ages of the men. However, these overall comparisons mean little. It is necessary to look at age in relation to marital status to understand the differences. Though in both towns the ages of married women were near the national average for elderly married women, widowed women were considerably older in Bexhill than they were nationally; 37 per cent in Bexhill were 80 and over compared with 29 per cent in England and Wales. (3) The explanation of this may be that if women are widowed relatively young they are more likely to return to their place of origin. In Clacton, however, both single and widowed women were considerably younger than the national average, though they were older

than married women in the town. The explanation of this
probably lies in the recent expansion of Clacton's retired
community so that the proportion of very old widows is
still small.

Married men were slightly older in Bexhill and Clacton
than were elderly married men nationally, but only in that
they were more frequently in their early 70s than late 60s.
In Bexhill there were also very slightly more married men
of 75 and over. There are a number of possible reasons
for this. Ethel Shanas lists them when commenting on
similar problems of interpretation of age and marital
status data in Britain and the USA:

> In both Britain and the United States middle class men
> with white collar backgrounds are more likely than
> other men to be married. From our data we cannot
> determine whether this difference between middle class
> men and other men (a) is the result of differential
> longevity - that is, of men in the white collar occupa-
> tions being more likely than other men to survive into
> old age - or (b) whether it is the result of these men
> marrying women considerably younger than they are, or
> (c) whether it results from a greater incidence of
> remarriage among these old men. All three of these
> causal factors may be operating to create the differ-
> ences in the two countries between the proportions of
> middle class men and of other men who are married. (4)

From rather inadequate data there was an indication
that the men in Bexhill were more likely than Clacton men
to have wives considerably younger than themselves. Of
those aged 75 and over 8 per cent had wives under 65,
compared with 1 per cent in Clacton.

MARITAL STATUS

The marital status characteristics of the elderly people
who had moved to Bexhill and Clacton were very different
from those of elderly people in England and Wales as a
whole. The proportion of people of 65 and over in England
and Wales in 1971 who were married was 50 per cent and
the proportion who were widowed was 38 per cent. (5) This
compares with 73 per cent and 14 per cent of retired people
and their household members aged 65 and over in Bexhill
and 80 per cent and 15 per cent in Clacton.

The presence of this unusually small proportion of
widowed people needs further examination. The fact that
widows and widowers less often moved to the resorts in the
first place (6) is not sufficient to explain the very
small numbers, because deaths amongst married couples would,

amongst the older retired people, offset the initial bias. The most likely explanation of the unusually small proportion of widowed people is that widows and widowers tend to leave the resorts after the death of their spouse. One lady of 91 living alone in Bexhill said rather wistfully that she would have returned to Folkestone had she known she would live so long after her husband's death. She had been widowed sixteen years. Unlike her, many of the others must have made up their minds to go. A comparison of the proportion of widowed women in each age group, in the resorts and nationally, shows that in the lowest age group, there were 5 percentage points less widows amongst the migrants to Bexhill than the national average for that age group. In the next group there were 8 percentage points less and, from that age on, the proportion of widows fell further and further behind the national average until, in the 75-9 age group, widows nationally represented 59 per cent of all women, whereas in Bexhill they represented only 26 per cent (Table 6.2). (7)

TABLE 6.2 Proportion of widows, by age group (%)

AGE GROUPS: WOMEN		Britain (cross-national)	England and Wales 1971 Census	Bexhill movers and their households	Clacton movers and their households
			Proportion of widows in each age group		
55-9		NA	14	9	-
60-4		NA	22	14	12
65-9	65-6	33	33	10	13
	67-9	42			
70-4		53	47	17	19
75 9		56	59	26	20
80 and over		68	72	50	54

The very recent expansion of retirement resorts helps to explain the large proportion of younger married people but it does not explain the small percentage of widows amongst the very old. It could be an explanation if there were a constant movement of very old married couples to the town. However, this is not the case; 90 per cent of the elderly people had arrived in Clacton and Bexhill under the age of 70 and the majority at about 65 years old.

Chapter 6

In addition the older people who arrived tended more often to be widowed.

Another alternative explanation might seem to be that Clacton and Bexhill have death rates for men much lower than the national average. However, this could be supported only if married men were shown to be very much older than the national average, but, in both Clacton and Bexhill, married men were only very slightly older than the national average for men of 65 and over; the difference was not sufficient to be an explanation of the lack of widows. In addition, for the explanation to be adequate, their wives would have had to be older than the average. This was not a feature of either town. Thus, though death rates are low, particularly in Bexhill, this does not explain the lack of widows. (8)

An explanation which is much more plausible is that whereas the national figure included people living in institutions this sample did not. There are many people living in homes and hotels in Bexhill and Clacton, and these people would include a large number of widowed people. The only way to check on this was to look at the age structure of the 1966 and 1971 Census populations for Bexhill and Clacton, including those living in non-private households. In fact this revealed that the whole population of 65 and over in Bexhill and Clacton in 1966 and 1971 exhibited the same characteristics of a shortage of widowed women in each age group over 65, compared with the national average. (9) The feature is not as striking as it is for movers alone because local old people would be less likely to move away in old age or widowhood. Nevertheless, the difference from the national average remains large, and the conclusion must be that women who moved there whilst their husbands were alive moved away when they were widowed.

Other resort towns exhibit the same feature of a smaller than average proportion of widows. It should be remembered again that these figures include local people as well as elderly people who have retired to the town. However, the same shortage of widows is found in the over-70s in, for instance, Sidmouth, Eastbourne, Hastings and Worthing and in the over-75s in Bournemouth, Torbay and Hove. Southend and Blackpool had proportions close to the national average. The feature is particularly striking if a comparison is made with large industrial towns where the proportion of widows amongst women aged 75 and over tends to be well above the national average and about 20 per cent higher than in Bexhill and Sidmouth. (10)

The situation in relation to single people also requires some discussion. Nationally 12 per cent of people of 65 and over were single, in 1971, compared with 13 per cent in Bexhill and 5 per cent in Clacton. The proportion of single people in Bexhill, though close to the national average, was grossly overweighted towards women. The proportion of single people in Clacton was well below the national average, but again women were more numerous than men. It seems that single men are particularly unlikely to move to retirement resorts. They were under-represented both amongst movers and in the Census population of Bexhill and Clacton; nine-tenths of all the single movers were women.

The difference between Clacton and Bexhill is probably explained largely by social class; in Britain women from the white-collar workers are more likely to remain single than working-class women are. According to the cross-national survey, 18 per cent of elderly females of the white-collar classes are single compared with 8 per cent of those in the blue-collar classes. (11) As Bexhill is much more middle-class than Clacton is, this is bound to be a factor in the difference between the two.

The conclusion in relation to single people is, therefore, that single women are much more likely than single men to move to retirement resorts, especially the more middle-class resorts.

THE RETIRED HOUSEHOLD AND THEIR FAMILY

We have seen that married couples, living alone, were the most usual type of household to move to Bexhill and Clacton. Though, over the period of time between this move and the date at which they were interviewed, a proportion of these people had been widowed, the typical household in both towns was still the married couple; 63 per cent of all the households interviewed in Bexhill and 68 per cent of those in Clacton were of this type, married couples without any other person living with them. In Bexhill 94 per cent and in Clacton 83 per cent of retired married couples lived by themselves, compared with only 68 per cent of married couples aged 65 and over in Britain as a whole. (12)

When a married couple did live with someone else this other person was rather unlikely to be a son or daughter. Only 3 per cent of married people and 3 per cent of widowed or single people in Bexhill were living with their children. In Clacton the proportions were a little larger, 7 per cent and 10 per cent but even these were very small compared with 27 per cent of married people of 65 and over in Britain and 38 per cent of other people of that age. (13)

Earlier, it emerged that people moving to Bexhill and Clacton were less likely to have any surviving children than people nationally and that those in Bexhill were less likely to have them than those in Clacton. (14) In Bexhill, 37 per cent of the retired people had no children, compared with 30 per cent in Clacton. There was an additional difference; in Clacton the widowed were less likely than the married to have any surviving children; 36 per cent had no children compared with only 24 per cent of married people. In Bexhill, however, the married were as unlikely as the widowed to have children; 37 per cent had none compared with 40 per cent of the widowed.

Retired people under 65 were particularly unlikely to have any children, possibly because of the greater number of single people in this age group. Or do childless people move when they are younger? People aged 65-9 were the most likely to have children, but after that the older a man or woman was the less likely they were to have surviving children. Half the people of 80 and over in Bexhill and a third in Clacton had no children at all. This is bound to have implications for the health and social services because these old people will need to depend more on outside help.

There were difficulties in comparing these data about numbers of children with the results of the cross-national survey which were processed differently. (15) However, it is possible to compare the male heads of retired households in this survey with the male respondents in the cross-national survey. The proportion of childless married and widowed men in Bexhill was 36 per cent, in Clacton 25 per cent and in Britain 16 per cent, (16) less than half the Bexhill figure.

But even those with children are not always able to call on them for help because of distance. As the elderly people in Bexhill and Clacton had moved away from their original home and from large centres of employment, it was to be expected that they would be further away from their children than old people usually are. Compared with elderly people nationally, those in Bexhill and Clacton were extremely cut-off by distance from their children. Nationally 42 per cent of elderly people with children live with their nearest child compared with only 7 per cent in Bexhill and 10 per cent in Clacton. In addition, nationally, a further 40 per cent live within half-an-hour of their nearest child, compared with 11 per cent in Bexhill and 15 per cent in Clacton (Table 6.3)

TABLE 6.3 Distance from nearest child

	Bexhill	Clacton	Britain* All respondents	Britain* White-Collar
Sample no.: heads of retirement units with surviving children	264	340	1911	464
DISTANCE FROM NEAREST CHILD	%	%	%	%
Living in same household	7	10	42	36
Living up to ½hr away	11	15	40	37
(of which living in same town)	(6)	(14)	-	-
Living up to 10min. away	-	-	24	21
Living ½hr but less than 1hr away	7	6		10
Living 1hr but less than 3hrs away	48	48		
Living 3hrs but less than 1 day away	19	19	18	17
Living 1 day or more away	8	3		

* E. Shanas et al., 'Old People in Three Industrial Societies', London, Routledge & Kegan Paul, 1968, p.193, Table VII-7, and p.240, Table VIII-6.

The majority of the retired people's children lived in London and this shows up in the concentration of children, about half, living 1-3 hours away from their parents. In this respect the two towns were remarkably alike. Equal proportions of people in the two towns also had children living from 3 hours to 1 day away. However, Bexhill people were more likely to have no child within a day's journey. Many of these children lived abroad. (One old lady admitted that she did not know where her son was.)

The fact seems inescapable that there is, in relation to proximity of children, an important difference between the group of people who moved on retirement and old people as a whole. Ethel Shanas sums up the national situation as follows:

> for every social class, old people who live apart from their children tend to have at least one child in the immediate vicinity. Half of all old people, irrespective of class, either share a household with a child or live within ten minutes distance from a child. Further ... it is unusual for an old person to have his nearest child one hour or more distant from him.... There are some class differences, however, among those old people who live this far from their nearest child ... persons of white collar backgrounds are the most likely of all old persons to report that they live an hour or more from their nearest child.

But

> The evidence is diametrically opposite to the common belief that aged parents within any social class are physically separated from their children. The immediate household of the old person differs by whether he is of white or blue collar background.... However, in most instances, if an old person has children and there is no child in his immediate household, then there is a child living within ten minutes distance from him. The responsibility or attachment of adult children to aged parents appears to override class.... (18)

What then are the possible explanations for the failure of Bexhill and Clacton to conform to this pattern? There are a number of probable contributory factors.

First, married couples nationally are less likely to live with their children than are widowed people and in both resort towns married couples constituted the bulk of households. In the cross-national survey, 32 per cent of married people of 65 and over lived with their children, compared with 54 per cent of widowed, separated and divorced people. In Bexhill 5 per cent of married people lived with their children, compared with 15 per cent of widowed, divorced or separated people. In Clacton the figures were 8 per cent and 17 per cent. In our survey also widowed people were more likely to live near their children even if not actually with them, than were married people. About a fifth of widowed people with children had them living in Bexhill or Clacton compared with 4 per cent of married people in Bexhill and 12 per cent in Clacton.

Second, the retired people in Bexhill and Clacton who had children had fewer than the national average. This is important because 'the chances of living further than thirty minutes journey from the nearest child are greater the smaller is the number of children'. (19) In Clacton 35 per cent and in Bexhill 40 per cent of those with surviving children had only one child compared with 25 per cent in Britain as a whole. (20) In Bexhill and Clacton those with more children were also likely to be nearer to them than those with only one child; only 6 per cent of people in Bexhill with one child had them living within 30 minutes' journey compared with 32 per cent of people with three or more children. In Clacton the proportions were 22 per cent for people with one child and 38 per cent for those with three or more. But nationally nearly three-quarters of married people and 60 per cent of widowed people with one child live within half an hour of them. (21)

Third and probably most important, there is a relationship between social class and proximity of children. White-collar workers were over-represented in Bexhill and Clacton compared with the national picture, and retired white-collar workers are less likely to live with their children and are more likely to live at a considerable distance from them. Their children also tend to be white-collar workers. Of these, many, by the nature of their employment, have to be geographically mobile. (22) Though many of the Clacton respondents were not white-collar workers themselves they came from that social group of foremen, supervisors, etc., whose children are most likely to be socially mobile upwards. (23) A proportion of these children are therefore likely to exhibit the same features of geographical mobility as the children of the more middle-class Bexhill people. Certainly, in our results there was no difference between skilled manual workers and the white-collar workers as far as distance from their children was concerned. (The sample of people in the other social classes who had children was too small for further differences to be sought.) It is therefore by no means certain that the retired people would have lived near their children even if they had stayed in their home town and not moved to the sea.

In the USA a survey of elderly people who had retired to Arizona and Florida went into this point more closely. It was found for instance that 'one half (49 per cent) of the children of the Florida respondents and two thirds (68 per cent) of those of the Arizona migrants were located outside their parents' home states'. In comparison only a quarter (28 per cent) of the children of people who remained in Wisconsin after their retirement had moved away from Wisconsin. Or to put it another way 'whereas two thirds (65%) of the Wisconsin respondents with families had one or more adult children living in their home communities, only one fourth (28%) of the migrants would have enjoyed a similar family situation had they retired instead in their home towns'. (24)

But the fact remains that those people who moved to Bexhill and Clacton had usually moved further away from their children rather than nearer them. The nature of the relationship and contacts between parents and children before the move is clearly important in a discussion of motivation for the move. If they were living near their children, why move away? If they were living a long way from their children, why not move closer? We have seen that only a minority of people, particularly in Bexhill, moved to be near relations or their children. Were their emotional links with their children looser than usual, or were they having a period of independence in early retirement which would give way to greater dependence in old age or widowhood? The experience of Willmott and Young suggests that the latter may well be the case and may be fairly typical of middle-class retired couples. These writers say that the contrast between working-class Bethnal Green and predominantly middle-class Woodford in the nature of family support for the elderly is that: 'in one, the generations are together throughout life; in the other, they separate when the children marry but rejoin each other when the parents grow old'. (25) They found in Woodford that 'the older the parents the more often they live in the same dwelling as a married child. There is a similar tendency for older parents (at any rate up to the age of 70) to live near their children if they do not actually live with them. This variation with age is largely, though not wholly, explained by widowhood'. (26) They conclude that:

> the reason why so many old people live with children in Woodford is, paradoxically, because they used to live so far away. The old people of Bethnal Green were down the street; their children had only to walk over the road to look after them or keep them company. But Woodford children lived so far off that even with cars they could not keep an eye on parents all the time, nor give them that assurance which old people need, of someone close by to call on in an emergency.... Where can they come to, except right into their children's homes? Most Woodford people own their own homes and do not want to sell them to move away to their parents, even if their jobs allowed. The parents had to leave their homes instead. (27)

The character of employment opportunities or lack of them in seaside resorts probably makes it even less likely that children will move to their parents. There is little employment for the professional and managerial classes and though within commuting distance of London, neither Clacton nor Bexhill are well situated for commuting. Bexhill, in particular, has a poor rail service to London.

Though children are the first relations to be considered in terms of family support, retired people in Bexhill and Clacton were in fact more likely to have surviving brothers and sisters than they were to have children. Whereas 37 per cent of all respondents in Bexhill had no children, only 16 per cent had no brothers or sisters. (28) In Clacton, 30 per cent had no children, 11 per cent no brothers or sisters. The older people were the less likely they were to have surviving brothers and sisters. But, though more people had brothers and sisters than children, in Clacton proportionately fewer brothers and sisters lived close by. In Bexhill, however, people who had brothers and sisters were more likely to have them living in the town than people with children were to have any of their children living there. The proportion of people who actually had brothers or sisters living with them was 5 per cent in Bexhill and 2 per cent in Clacton. Those who had them living in the town were 22 per cent in Bexhill and 19 per cent in Clacton.

Willmott and Young have written about the close relationship between single people and their siblings, both in East London and suburbia:'single people generally make up for the absence of other relationships by seeing more of their brothers and sisters ... Single people see their brothers and sisters much more often than do those who are, or have been, married.' (29) The cross-national survey found, in addition, that widowed people without children were also likely to live with siblings. (30) Bexhill and Clacton households showed the same features. Single and widowed heads of retirement units were much more likely to live with brothers or sisters or to have them living in the same town. A fifth of widowed and single men and women in Bexhill were living with brothers and sisters or other relations, compared with 3 per cent of married couples. In Clacton the proportions were 11 per cent and 4 per cent. Only 17 per cent of married couples in Bexhill and 18 per cent in Clacton had brothers or sisters in the town compared with 33 per cent of single and widowed women in Bexhill and 22 per cent in Clacton.

People living alone were also more likely than others to have brothers and sisters living in the town. Of all the people living alone, 25 per cent in Bexhill and 21 per cent in Clacton had brothers and sisters living in the town.

In both towns households consisting of several related people or friends were very likely to consist entirely of people of pensionable age. Of all three-person households interviewed, 50 per cent in Bexhill and 32 per cent in Clacton had all three people of pensionable age. In England and Wales, only 7 per cent of three-person households, containing an elderly person, had all three elderly. (31) In Bexhill, it was particularly common for several single or widowed women to be living together.

There was a notable difference between the two towns in this respect: in Bexhill respondents were much more likely to live with other elderly people. There were nearly twice as many people aged 60 and over living with respondents in Bexhill as there were in Clacton (67 compared with 37) and over twice as many people aged under 60 living with respondents in Clacton as there were in Bexhill (61 compared with 27). There were only 20 people in the Bexhill sample who were living with their children, compared with 36 in Clacton; most of these were unmarried children. One person in Bexhill, but 6 in Clacton lived with a married daughter and son-in-law; the Bexhill family had no grandchildren but all 6 Clacton families had grandchildren present. This also highlights a point frequently noticed, that married daughters are much more likely to live with their parents than are married sons. The same feature was also typical of those retired people who had very old parents living with them. In Clacton 5 out of 7 retired people who lived with old parents were daughters and so were 8 out of the 11 in Bexhill. Incidentally, the average age of these old parents in Bexhill was 88.

Because of the predominance of married couples the proportion of people living alone in the resorts was smaller than the national average. In Bexhill 22 per cent and in Clacton 19 per cent of elderly households had only one person, compared with 41 per cent in England and Wales as a whole in 1971. (32) However, it is important to notice that while the proportion of people who lived alone was smaller in the resorts than elsewhere, the proportion of widowed and single people who lived alone was larger. In Britain as a whole 43 per cent of the widowed and single lived alone compared with 64 per cent in Bexhill and 70 per cent in Clacton. (33)

CONCLUSIONS

The household characteristics of elderly people who retire to the resort towns are very important in that they have a direct bearing on the welfare of elderly people and possible demands on the social services. It is useful therefore to summarize briefly the main conclusions of this chapter.

The average retired household in the two resorts consisted of a married couple living by themselves.

2 Married couples in Bexhill and Clacton were less likely to have others living with them than were married couples nationally. They, and widowed people, were particularly unlikely to live with their children.

3 Though the proportion of people who lived alone was lower in Bexhill and Clacton than nationally, the proportion of the widowed and single who lived alone was much larger than the average.

4 Widowed and married people in Clacton and particularly Bexhill were far less likely than elderly people nationally to have any surviving children. Those that did have children had less than the national average.

5 The very old were less likely than younger people to have children. Half those of 80 and over in Bexhill and a third in Clacton had no children.

6 Those people in Bexhill and Clacton who did have children lived much farther from them than did elderly people nationally.

7 The elderly people in Bexhill and Clacton were more likely to have surviving siblings than children and were more likely to have them living in the town and with them than they were to have children there.

8 In Bexhill elderly people were much more likely than those in Clacton to be living with other elderly people. Women particularly lived with other elderly women.

9 There were fewer widows in the population in Bexhill and Clacton in all age groups of 55 and over than would be expected according to the national average. This held true for a number of other resorts and can be explained partly by the predominance of married couples amongst those moving to resorts and partly by the departure of widows from the resorts.

10 Bexhill had a particularly large proportion of single elderly women. Clacton did not have as many. Single men were rare in both resorts.

11 Compared with the national age range of those aged 65 and over, Clacton's elderly population was relatively young. Bexhill's was not, because the widows in Bexhill were much older than the national average. It must be remembered that the growth of the resorts has been very rapid in the last few years creating a 'bulge' of younger retired people who arrived in this period. In the course of time as movement to the towns slackens with decline in the availability of building land, this 'bulge' will move

Chapter 6

up into the older age groups and will produce large numbers of older widows. This feature is already present in Bexhill, where the rate of growth had slackened off by 1971. The departure of widows from the resorts will probably reduce the number and proportion of older widows to some extent but the numbers will still be large.

7 Family life and friends

> Forsake not an old friend; for the new is not
> comparable to him; a new friend is as new wine;
> when it is old, thou shalt drink it with pleasure.
>
> Ecclus. 9 : 10

One question with which this study needed to be concerned was whether the migration of elderly people has any particular effect on their social contacts and family life.

Kleemeier states the broad question in relation to American retirement communities, but he does not yet appear to have received a satisfactory answer:

> Such aggregation of dwelling units serving as they do a uniformly middle-aged or elderly segment of the population must have some significant bearing on the activities of their residents. What this influence may be is imperfectly known, but certainly it is reasonable to expect to find here different patterns of activity than those found among the elderly scattered throughout the community, living by themselves or with their families. (1)

It would require a more specialised survey comparing the social activities of elderly people in resorts with those of similar people in other types of town to give a full answer to such questions in Britain. This study has, however, been able to examine certain points and to indicate some further issues upon which research would be rewarding.

One of the most obvious points of concern was that moving in retirement might have an isolating effect on the movers. Most retired people in Bexhill and Clacton lived a long way from their children and had moved away from the town in which they had spent most of their working life, so it seemed possible that they might be more lonely or isolated than other elderly people.

The cross-national survey identifies four types of isolation amongst old people:
1. By comparison with their contemporaries; this might be termed peer - contrasted isolation:
2. By comparison with younger people; this might be termed generation - contrasted isolation:
3. By comparison with the social relationships and activities enjoyed by the same people at an earlier stage of the life-cycle, in youth or middle age; this might be termed age-related isolation or desolation.
4. By comparison with the preceding generation of old people; this might be termed preceding cohort isolation. (2)

This chapter will be concerned mainly with the first, comparing elderly people in resorts with elderly people elsewhere, as well as comparing different groups of elderly people in the resort. However, the third will also be considered, particularly in relation to differences between people before and after their retirement move.

As elderly people in Bexhill and Clacton lived much further from their children than most elderly people did nationally, their contacts with them were bound to be less than average; most elderly people in Britain meet at least one of their children on a day-to-day basis. (3) However, had this always been the situation or had the retirement move made it worse? Those who had moved to Bexhill or Clacton within the last ten years and who had surviving children, were asked whether they were seeing their children more, less or about the same as before their move. The largest proportion of people in Bexhill (43 per cent), and in Clacton an absolute majority (59 per cent), said that they were seeing their children less often (Table 7.1). Few people (16 per cent) were seeing more of their children, but in Bexhill 40 per cent saw them just as much as before, compared with 24 per cent in Clacton.

Married couples were more likely than widowed women to say that they now had less contact with their children. In Bexhill 44 per cent and in Clacton 61 per cent of married couples were seeing their children less, compared with 31 per cent and 50 per cent of widowed women.

The difference between Clacton and Bexhill is related to the class difference between the towns. In the previous chapter evidence was given that in middle age the white-collar groups are less likely to live near their children than are manual workers (4) and that similarities between classes in later life are caused by the movement of middle-

TABLE 7.1 Contact with children, brothers and sisters and close friends after the move

	Bexhill		
Recent movers*	Children	Brothers and sisters	Close friends
Sample no.	194**	299***	338
PROPORTION WHO WERE:	%	%	%
Seeing them more	16	29	24
Seeing them less	43	31	27
Seeing them the same	40	40	49
	Clacton		
Sample no.	285**	351***	393
PROPORTION WHO WERE:	%	%	%
Seeing them more	16	21	30
Seeing them less	59	50	33
Seeing them the same	24	29	36

* 'Recent movers' only, are defined as those who moved to Bexhill or Clacton after 1958.
** Those who had surviving children.
*** Those who had surviving brothers and sisters, including brothers- and sisters-in-law.

class old people to live near their children. In the case of Bexhill and Clacton they had not (yet) moved to be near their children, but many, particularly in Bexhill, were not more cut off from them than during their working life, because they had seen them relatively little even before their move.

Of course, the reasons why people were seeing less of their children were not entirely to do with their having moved. In some cases they would have been seeing less of their children wherever they had lived. For instance, a number of movers brought their teenage children with them when they moved but by the time of the survey nearly all these children had moved away to work, study or marry. It may be that in another, larger, town with more employment, some of these children might have stayed on with their parents but, even had they stayed in the area, there is an increasing trend for young single people to move away from their parents to have their own rooms or flat, not just out of necessity but out of a desire to do so. It is inevitable in these circumstances but the parents see less of them than before. Similarly, young people who had married or had their own children would find less time to visit their parents. These are only qualifications, however; the evidence was that it was the increased distance of parents from their children which had weakened contact so considerably.

The people who saw their children more often than before were of several types. First, there were those, often widowed women, who had moved to be nearer their children. Second, there were those who had not moved specifically to be nearer their children but that is how it had turned out. Third, there were those who said that since they moved to the seaside their children had visited them more often because they liked to come for holidays there.

The evidence then was that for the majority the move to the seaside did weaken contact with children; but what of contacts with other relations and friends? Apparently contact with siblings was not weakened as much as it was with children. Though in Clacton half the elderly people with brothers and sisters were seeing less of them than before the move, 21 per cent were seeing them more and in Bexhill the proportions were almost equal at 31 per cent and 29 per cent (Table 7.1). It has already been mentioned that widowed and single elderly people often develop or maintain close contacts with siblings. Certainly the single and widowed people were more likely than married couples to say they were seeing more of their brothers and sisters since the move. In Bexhill, 32 per cent of single and widowed people, compared with 27 per cent of married couples, were seeing their brothers and sisters more; 24 per cent compared with 34 per cent were seeing them less. In Clacton the feature was more marked; 29 per cent of the widowed and single were seeing their brothers and sisters more, compared with 19 per cent of married couples; 42 per cent were seeing them less, compared with 52 per cent of married couples.

A number of people had moved specifically to be near their brothers and sisters or had at least chosen Clacton or Bexhill in particular because they had relations there. In fact, it was because 25 per cent in Bexhill and 20 per cent in Clacton of people with brothers and sisters alive had them living in the town that contacts with siblings were less adversely affected by the move. In Clacton, only 10 per cent and in Bexhill 16 per cent of those with no brothers or sisters in the town said they were seeing them more than before.

It was contacts with close friends which were apparently least adversely affected by the move. Those who saw their close friends less than before their move were 27 per cent of all recent movers in Bexhill and 33 per cent in Clacton. This compared with 31 per cent and 50 per cent for brothers and sisters and 43 per cent and 59 per cent for children in the two towns respectively (Table 7.1).

There were, of course, some people who had friends or relations in the town when they arrived there, but there was not a significant difference between these and the rest in their impressions of how much they were seeing close friends. This suggests that the friends living in the town were not often close friends, which seems likely in that few people who had friends in the town chose to move there specifically to be with them. (5)

It was clear from the replies about 'close friends' that, for most elderly people, close friends were those whom they had known a long time. It was, therefore, to be expected that many might find that they had lost contact when they moved. In one estate of seaside bungalows owned by the Greater London Council, a study reported that the old people:

> still depended on visits from relatives and such old friends as they remained in contact with for much of their companionship. But, after an initial visit to see the new bungalow, these visits were often very sparing and tended to die away as friendship ties weakened. (6)

In the case of our respondents, the situation may, for a number of reasons, be less extreme. For one thing, a number had encouraged or persuaded friends to join them in the resorts. (7) These people were much less likely to have reduced contact with their close friends. Further, most of at least the Bexhill retired people came from a social class in which it was most likely that their friends, too, would move to the coast. Some even remarked that most of their friends had already gone and that they had felt left behind before they also moved. In such circumstances the friendship ties would already have been weakened by the time they moved. Also, some of the professional and managerial classes, having been more geographically mobile during their working life, may have been less likely to live very near their longest-standing friends even before retirement. Last, being more affluent, they could probably afford more frequent trips to see friends and were more likely to have a car to facilitate this.

A distinction must be drawn between contact with old and close friends and the possibilities of making new friends in the resorts. The retired people were much more likely to say their contact with close friends had deteriorated than that it was difficult to make new friends. Of the people who had moved to Bexhill or Clacton within the last ten years, the largest proportion (43 per cent in Bexhill and 46 per cent in Clacton) said that they found it easier to make friends than before they moved. A further 40 per cent in Bexhill and 27 per cent in Clacton said they found the situation the same as before. The rest, 17 per cent in Bexhill and 26 per cent in Clacton, found making friends more difficult (Table 7.2).

TABLE 7.2 Opinions about making friends, by marital status

	Bexhill			
	All	Married couples	Single	Widowed
Sample no.	332	242	46	44
PROPORTION WHO FOUND IT:	%	%	%	%
Easier to make friends	43	43	(52)	(41)
More difficult to make friends	17	16	(15)	(20)
The same	40	42	(33)	(39)
	Clacton			
Sample no.	389	302	20	67
PROPORTION WHO FOUND IT:	%	%	%	%
Easier to make friends	46	49	(35)	38
More difficult to make friends	26	25	(30)	32
The same	27	26	(35)	29

In giving their reasons for finding it easier to make friends, most people stressed the increased leisure of retirement and the greater possibilities it gave for making friends (Appendix 1, Table A1.19). Not only had they themselves more time for their social life but, as most people in the town were retired, there were always others to be found who had time to spare for an outing or a game of bowls. At the same time, it was stressed that retired people shared the same kinds of interests and

attitudes. This made them congenial company for each
other. This, of course, is the corollary of the argument
that suburbs and cities are unsuitable for retirement
because most of the residents there are working and have
no time for the retired.

There was also the 'We're all in the same boat' attitude. Sometimes this was a positive feeling about launching out on retirement together, best typified by the
people who revelled in pioneering new bungalow estates.
One couple, for instance, said proudly that when they had
married they had been the first to move into a house on a
new estate and on retirement they had repeated this feat.
They felt they had made a lot of friends that way. Another
couple said they had had 'a new lease of life' moving into
a new estate in this way. Such comments were common. The
more negative side of this attitude, however, appeared in
the replies that stressed the difficulties of old age,
particularly loneliness, and the value of the mutual help
and friendliness available in a retirement community. The
following comments were typical of this attitude:

'We go out more here and people are lonely and welcome
a chat. When you're on the sea front, people you sit
next to will talk to you.'

'People are so lonely here that they are all anxious to
make friends.'

'So many people live on their own and are lonely in
Clacton and one meets them when out and often goes
and has a cup of tea with them.'

Another point often commented on was the size of the
two towns. It was felt that being relatively small they
were more friendly than the cities and their suburbs.
People frequently used the word 'community': 'In a town
this size you feel part of a community.' 'Surely Bexhill
is the friendliest town in England', said one man who had
left Surrey because it was 'snobbish'. 'In a smaller
community people are more drawn together than they are in
a big town.' 'You can identify yourself with a smaller
town.' In addition, in Bexhill there were frequent
comments on the style of the town. It was felt to be
genteel; not too many of the shops had self-service.
There were an extraordinary number of comments on the
politeness and friendliness of people in the shops. 'It's
such a wonderfully friendly and courteous place', said an
88 year old, golf-playing ex-brigadier. 'I find people
so decent and polite, shopkeepers and even bus conductors',
said an elderly lady who had moved from London.

In summary it can be said that people who found it
easier to make friends tended to stress the value of
having a town which was mainly for retired people.

Chapter 7

The reasons given for finding it more difficult to make friends were varied. Some put the blame on Bexhill or Clacton, some on themselves and others on their personal circumstances. (8)

About a third of the people who found it more difficult to make friends said it was because the town was unfriendly or snobbish. Those in Bexhill were more likely to mention snobbishness, but those in Clacton also did sometimes:

'There is so much snobbery. Nobody speaks to you here.'

'The retired people living here are snobbish and unfriendly.'

'It's a question of social standing. If you don't play golf, bridge or bowls you're not wanted.'

There was also the question of money mentioned by a very few:

'It's difficult to make friends because people in Bexhill are very comfortably retired and it's very difficult to reciprocate hospitality.'

There were several versions of this. One elderly man from Clacton put a different twist to it:

'People here are very hard up and want to borrow money all the time so we don't encourage them.'

A number of people felt that people from different parts of the country did not make friends with each other easily, and that this made the town an unfriendly place for those who were in a minority, or generally made social contacts difficult:

'The people round here don't have much in common as we all come from different places. The funny thing is we retired here from the North which we didn't like because we're Southerners.'

In fact, if the remarks about making friends are analysed according to the area of origin of the respondent, a relationship appears between the two. People from the Midlands, North and abroad seemed to find it more difficult to make friends in Bexhill and Clacton than did people from the South, London and the Home Counties. The North showed up particularly clearly.

Many elderly people put their difficulties down to their age. They felt that they were neither able nor inclined to make friends any more:

'I could make friends if I wanted to, as people are very sociable but I'm too old to bother with making friends now. I used to go to clubs before we moved but I have no interest in them now.'

Some said they had always been used to meeting people at work or had relied on the friends with whom they had grown up, and now did not know how to set about making new friends:

'We grew up in Morden and never really had to make the effort to make friends.'

For the same reasons, a number of people drew a distinction between the type of friends they had in Clacton and Bexhill and those they had left behind:

'We have more friends here but they're not close.'

'We have acquaintances but not friends.'

An important point made by single women and widows was that they felt that they did not fit into the society there. They felt the social life was geared to married couples.

'It's difficult to make friends when you live alone. People don't seem to be interested in a single person.'

'People go out together in pairs.'

Widows and widowers felt this particularly because they had previously seemed to fit in. In addition, their distress in widowhood affected their desire to make or even keep friends. One widower said he was 'too lazy to do things on my own'. An elderly widow confessed she was 'afraid to make friends, especially living on my own; I'm a bit suspicious of people'. Another widow of 71 had retreated completely since her husband died three years earlier:

'I don't want to mix with too many people. I'm still grieving for my husband. I miss him dreadfully. I do needlework and mending. I can't watch TV; I've got rid of my set. I think I'll go into a home to get more company. I don't know what to do really. I sometimes think I'll have to move away from my memories of my husband.'

These comments made by widows and widowers about finding it hard to make friends are borne out by an analysis of opinions about making friends according to the marital status of the respondent (Table 7.2). Widowed people in both Clacton and Bexhill were more likely to find it hard to make friends than were married couples. This difference was particularly striking in Clacton where 32 per cent of widowed people found it harder to make friends. In addition, single people in Clacton reacted very much as the widowed did (30 per cent found it harder to make friends), whereas in Bexhill they were the least likely of any group (only 15 per cent) to have this difficulty. This feature may be associated with the fact that Bexhill has many single women but Clacton very few.

But some of the married couples themselves sometimes felt that their style of life was not suited to making friends because they were always together. The wives noticed this particularly as their husbands no longer went out to work, leaving them alone to go out for coffee and a chat. Some clearly found the change limiting and claustrophobic. Others did not mind: 'We don't need other friends because we have each other'. This exclusiveness of married couples helps to explain why so many widows feel cut off.

For a number of people in each town, health problems were an obstacle to making friends. The wife or husband of the sick person was also affected. For instance, one wife was virtually housebound because her husband had become too forgetful to leave alone.

Though many people spoke of age as affecting their ability to make friends, there was, in fact, no relationship between their replies and their age. What seemed more relevant was the age at which they made their retirement move. Those people who moved in their 60s were, in Clacton particularly, the least likely to say they had difficulty in making friends. In Bexhill 14 per cent who moved at this age said they found it more difficult to make friends, compared with 16 per cent of those who moved when they were younger and 32 per cent who were older. In Clacton, 21 per cent of those who moved in their 60s found it more difficult to make friends, compared with 46 per cent of those who moved when they were younger and 38 per cent of those who moved after they were 70. It will be remembered that 60-9 was the age at which the majority of people moved to the resorts and that people who moved when they were older or younger than this were more likely to be single or widowed. It is, therefore, impossible to tell whether these people found it more difficult to fit because of their age in relation to other new arrivals or because of their peculiar social position. However, there does seem to be more to the age effect than just marital status differences, because there were greater differences between the age groups than there were between marital status groups. It seems likely that people find it easier to make friends in the resorts if they move at roughly the same age as other people, namely in their 60s. One couple in Bexhill said, 'We should have moved earlier to become part of the community'. This is only a tentative conclusion, however, as there are other special features of the late and early movers which may be the cause of the apparent relationship. We know, for instance, that early movers frequently retired for health reasons, and poor health was felt to be an obstacle to making friends. The later movers may also have arrived at a time when their health had already deteriorated and they were unable to make new contacts by getting out.

It is possible, of course, to keep in touch with friends

and relations fairly adequately by telephone rather than by frequent visits; if you have a telephone, that is. The retired people in Bexhill were twice as likely as those in Clacton to have a telephone. In Bexhill 77 per cent had one, compared with 28 per cent in Clacton. The difference was maintained even within income groups. In Bexhill, 28 per cent of people with incomes of up to £7.50 had telephones compared with 5 per cent in Clacton. However, in each town it was the most affluent who were the most likely to have telephones. Currently, telephones are being stressed as an important means of contact for elderly people living on their own but it was the single and widowed, the people most likely to be living alone, who were least likely to have one. In Bexhill 64 per cent of those living alone had telephones compared with 77 per cent of all respondents. In Clacton only 20 per cent of people living alone had them, compared with 28 per cent of all respondents.

It is one thing to have relatively few family or other social contacts; it may be quite another to be lonely in these circumstances: 'Many isolated people do not feel lonely and some "integrated" people do feel lonely. Isolation and loneliness are not coincident. This is perhaps one of the most important findings of the cross-national survey.' (9)

The proportions of people in Bexhill and Clacton who said they were often, sometimes or never lonely were very close to those found in Britain as a whole by the cross-national survey (Table 7.3). But this result has to be scrutinized carefully because of the differences between household types nationally and in the resorts. For instance, the cross-national survey found that the widowed and single were more likely to say they were lonely than were married people. Recently-widowed people tended to be more lonely than those widowed some time ago. Of those in Bexhill and Clacton who were widowed, particularly within the last five years, very many more were lonely even than the national average. Only 13.4 per cent of widowed people in Bexhill and Clacton said they were never lonely, compared with 57 per cent of widows in Britain. It will be remembered that those in the resorts were much more likely to live alone than were widowed people nationally and were less likely to have any children. There was a big difference also between those who had been widowed before and after their move. People widowed recently or after their move were much more lonely. A third of those widowed within the last five years said they were often lonely.

Chapter 7

TABLE 7.3 Loneliness, by marital status

	Bexhill	Clacton	Britain*
	All	All	All
Sample number	498	485	2,483
ALL RESPONDENTS			
Proportion who said they were:	%	%	%
Often lonely	4	8	7
Sometimes lonely	17	17	21
(Rarely or) never lonely	78	75	72
MARRIED			
Sample number	335	363	1,204
Proportion who said they were:	%	%	%
Often lonely	2	3	3
Sometimes lonely	11	12	14
(Rarely or) never lonely	87	84	83
SINGLE			
Sample number	75	23	257
Proportion who said they were:	%	%	%
Often lonely	–	(4)	5
Sometimes lonely	23	(30)	23
(Rarely or) never lonely	77	(65)	72
WIDOWED			
Sample number	86	98	740**
Proportion who said they were:	%	%	%
Often lonely	19	24	13
Sometimes lonely	38	32	30
(Rarely or) never lonely	43	44	57

* E. Shanas et al., 'Old People in Three Industrial Societies', London, Routledge & Kegan Paul, 1968, p.271, Table IX-9, and p.272, Table IX-10.
** Women only.

On the other hand, married people in Bexhill and Clacton gave replies similar to those given by married couples nationally (Table 7.3). Single people were less lonely than the national average in Bexhill and, perhaps, a little more lonely in Clacton. (10) This is what one might have expected from previous findings. Clacton appears to be very much a retired married couples' town; Bexhill on the other hand has quite a number of single people.

The replies of widowed people about loneliness fit in with the remarks they made about having difficulty in making friends and with the evidence that many may move away from the resorts. However, in view of the fact that the resorts attract a disproportionate number of those without children, it is also perfectly possible that these people when widowed, would have been lonely anywhere. The existence of lonely widows living by themselves in resorts does not necessarily mean that the resorts made them lonely. They may even be happier than elsewhere. We know too little about the psychological make-up of the minority of elderly people who choose to move in retirement to be able to blame the character of retirement resorts for the unhappiness of the widowed there.

As the cross-national survey found, it is not necessarily those who appear most isolated who are most lonely. Many even of those who live alone say they are never lonely. However, elderly people who lived alone in Bexhill and Clacton were much more likely than others to say that they were often lonely; 14 per cent in Bexhill said they were often lonely, compared with 4 per cent of all respondents; in Clacton 27 per cent were often lonely, compared with 8 per cent of all respondents. Only 44 per cent in Bexhill and 35 per cent in Clacton of those living alone said they were never lonely, compared with 78 per cent and 75 per cent of all elderly people.

The proportions of those living alone who said they were often lonely were roughly the same in Bexhill as in Britain as a whole. In Clacton, however, people living alone were much more likely to be lonely. In Clacton these people were more frequently widows than they were in Bexhill or in Britain generally. In Clacton 84 per cent of people living alone were widowed compared with 65 per cent in Bexhill and 77 per cent in Britain. (11)

The findings of this survey tend to support the view that 'loneliness is related much more to "loss" than to enduring "isolation"'. (12) Thus, widows were more lonely than single people. However, isolation frequently coincides with loss. 'Isolation' and 'desolation' are often found together. This may be a particularly important feature of retirement resorts where the blow of the loss of a marriage partner cannot be softened by close contact with children living nearby or by the support of long-standing friends. Many widows apparently react to this situation by leaving the resorts.

PREFERENCE FOR YOUNGER OR OLDER PEOPLE

It is frequently said that the old prefer to be with younger people, who keep them lively and in contact with life. There seems, however, to be a clash between such statements and the popularity of resorts such as Bexhill, where over 40 per cent of the population is of retirement age and where the chances of meeting younger people are substantially reduced. In addition, those retired people who said they found it easy to make friends in the resorts, particularly stressed the advantages of having other retired people of similar interests and enough leisure.

The replies to a question about whether they preferred their own age group or younger people were remarkably similar in the two towns. The largest proportion (47 per cent in Bexhill and 45 per cent in Clacton) said they had no preference. The next largest group (31 per cent in Bexhill and 33 per cent in Clacton) said they preferred their own age group, and the smallest group (18 per cent in Bexhill and 21 per cent in Clacton) preferred younger people. (13) The different answers did not seem to be related to particular ages or social characteristics except that those who had surviving children were slightly more likely to prefer younger people.

Three-quarters of the people in Bexhill who preferred their own age group said it was because they had more in common with them. They shared interests and experiences. In Clacton two-thirds gave this reply.
    'Younger people can't converse.'
    'You can't talk about the war with young people, can you?'
    'You can't talk to young people - they argue with you.'
    'The young and old are in different worlds.'
Quite a number put this in rather stronger terms, expressing resentment or criticism of younger people:
    'Younger people are boring for older people.'
    'The enthusiasms of the young are so tedious.'
    'Young people are selfish.'
    'You can't talk to these young people, long-haired, good-for-nothing bastards.'

'Young people are such a job to get on with. They tell
you you're old fashioned. They smoke too much and they
make up too much and they wear tight trousers.'
'Young people today are very cheeky and insubordinate.'
'I don't think much of what little I see of younger
people.'
'I've no time for younger people. A long-haired lot of
noisy brutes.'

For others the trouble was not that they disliked young people but that, no longer having the physical strength and energy, they found them tiring (10 per cent in Bexhill and 11 per cent in Clacton) and noisy (11 per cent and 12 per cent):

'Well, when you get to our age you like to see young
people come but you like to see them go.'
'I like young people but I'm not sure that I would
like to live next door to them.'

A few people (2 per cent) felt that they particularly did not want to live near children:

'I don't want a lot of bawling brats around.'
'Children these days are very noisy and badly behaved.'
'I've not enough patience to cope with children now.'

It is worth noting that two of the most antagonistic of the remarks quoted were made by old people who were severely disabled. There was one remark which was extremely honest in this respect; an elderly man said, 'I have no preference about living with younger or older people. I am jealous of young people but I hate old people, who depress me.'

Two-thirds of those who preferred to live near young people, gave as their reason that young people were more lively and kept them more alert and aware of current trends. A number found old people depressing (12 per cent in Bexhill and 5 per cent in Clacton), too obsessed with themselves, their health and other problems. In addition some, particularly women, liked children and wanted to see more of them (6 per cent in Bexhill and 11 per cent in Clacton). A small number felt that they could contribute their experience to help young people.

'I would love to help look after babies. I could
babysit for people and contribute something by way of
experience.'
'It's necessary to have mixed age groups in order to
get discussion and new ideas.'
'They make you feel younger and more lively.'
'Old people have a very narrow outlook, they live in
the past and condemn everything modern.'
'Younger people are nice. They have nice helpful ways
about them. They are more lively than old folk.'

'I'm interested in young people because I was a teacher, but it's difficult to meet them because there are so many retired people here.'

In addition, some people were worried by the problems arising from there being such a large proportion of old people in the resorts:

'I like old people but I do find in Bexhill that there are so many who are in very bad health that they really need looking after and when everyone is old there is no one to help.'

'Old people are too fond of reminiscing. There are too many old people in Bexhill.'

'Old people are so set in their ways. There are too few young people in Bexhill.'

As the resorts have such large proportions of old people, it was rather interesting to look at those who said they preferred younger people, to see if they found making friends more difficult or were, in general, less satisfied with their choice of retirement area. This was to be expected because of the very large proportion of elderly people in the retirement resorts.

The evidence was that those who preferred younger people were more likely to be lonely. In Bexhill 67 per cent and in Clacton 70 per cent of those who preferred younger people said they were never lonely. This was less than those who preferred their own age group and those who had no preference (81 per cent, 79 per cent). In addition, people who preferred younger people were much more likely to find it more difficult to make friends: 31 per cent in Bexhill and 40 per cent in Clacton found it more difficult, compared with 16 per cent to 20 per cent of people who preferred their own age group. They were also more likely to say they saw close friends less frequently than before their move; 41 per cent in Bexhill and 47 per cent in Clacton gave this reply, compared with 25 per cent of people who preferred their own age group.

In conclusion then it does seem that the social contacts of elderly people in the resorts are affected both by their having moved and, though by no means always adversely, by the particular character of the towns themselves.

The move itself meant that, in Clacton particularly, those old people who had children were seeing them less than they had been. In addition there was less contact with old friends.

Because of the character of the resorts, elderly people who preferred the company of younger people seemed to be less satisfied with their move and more often lonely. Also, the widowed, and, in Clacton, the single, were likely to feel lonely and excluded. Widowed women in particular were very lonely, compared with the national average but then they were also less likely to have any children and were more likely to be living alone. It is not clear that the resorts made these widows lonely but rather that resorts attracted childless couples, the survivor of whom would probably feel lonely wherever they lived in widowhood. However, there was one feature, which while not confined to resorts was particularly marked there and which affected widows: that was the exclusion of widowed and single people from a society dominated by married couples. This was exacerbated by the fact that widows usually had no children living nearby into whose families they could be drawn.

In addition, for other relationships, retired people in the resorts were much more dependent on friends than on relatives and upon acquaintances rather than long-standing friends. This feature was likely to turn married couples in on themselves even further and to make it particularly difficult for a single or widowed person who needed help rather than casual company.

On the other hand, nearly half the retired people in the two towns said that it was easier to make friends there than in their home town. This they generally ascribed to the fact that the resorts were mainly for retired people like themselves. This throws considerable doubt on the widely held view that 'balanced communities' provide the best setting for social contacts. This view has, in fact, now been severely criticized, particularly in the American planning literature. Attempts to define 'balance' have shown that the concept is extremely vague and variable, and some writers, for instance Gans, have come to the view that far from heterogeneity being socially the most desirable character for a community, a certain degree of homogeneity is required.

The virtues ascribed to heterogeneity are more often associated with the degree and type of population homogeneity found in the typical new suburb. Much has been written about the alleged dangers of homogeneity, but frequently these allegations are based on the false assumption that, because the suburbs as a whole are statistically more homogeneous than cities as a whole, suburbanites are all alike.

In actual fact, many suburban sub-divisions are more heterogeneous than the urban neighbourhoods from which some of their residents came. For example in Levittown, New Jersey, many people felt that they were encountering a greater mixture of backgrounds than where they had lived before. The fact that most people were similar enough in age and, to a lesser extent, income, enabled them to become friendly with people of different occupations, religions, ethnic backgrounds or regional origins for the first time in their lives. Many felt that they had been enriched by experiencing this diversity. This would not have been possible if marked differences in age and income had also been present. It would seem, therefore, that in the large 'brand name' suburbs, at least, the relatively greater homogeneity of age and income provides the cultural and social prerequisites which allow people to enjoy their neighbour's heterogeneity with respect to other, less basic characteristics. (14)

Elsewhere Gans describes the role which similarity of backgrounds, values and interests plays in the selection of friends and acquaintances. As a result he concludes that 'although propinquity brings neighbours into social contact, a certain degree of homogeneity is required to maintain this contact on a positive basis. If neighbours are too diverse, differences of behaviour or attitude may develop which can lead to coolness or even conflict'. (15)

Rosow goes even further when he says, in relation to old people, that normal neighbourhoods 'have produced the bulk of the problematic group - the alienated group' and 'offer no assurance of effective social contact with others'. (16) He says that the basic reason for this is that for anyone, old or young, the people with whom they would choose to mix are predominantly of the same age. Added to this, he says, it has been found that young people have adverse views of the elderly, even when they come into contact with them frequently, and this rejection by younger people prevents integration of the elderly into the younger community. In an ordinary neighbourhood, old people are dispersed amongst the younger families and gradually movement and death reduce their contacts with their family and friends of their own age. For old people the physical proximity of friends may be particularly important for the maintenance of contacts, especially when physical mobility deteriorates in later old age. This may be the reason why segregated retirement communities attract people, namely because they concentrate rather than disperse potential friends.

As a result of this reasoning, Rosow goes on to 'hypothesise that the segregated neighbourhood will integrate them socially more effectively than the integrated neighbourhood'. (17) The concentration of people with common situations and problems and similar experiences and views may, he says, maximize opportunities for new friendships. This view does seem to coincide with the types of reasons given by our respondents for being happy with their retirement move. They emphasized the specialization of the resorts in catering for the elderly and the pleasure which they found in living in a place with a predominantly retired population.

In Rosow's view an ordinary neighbourhood is most likely to provide successful social relationships for old people if the old people concerned are long-term residents, if the area is a relatively stable, unchanging neighbourhood, if the area is socially homogeneous especially for social class and racial and religious groups, and if the group of family, relations and friends remain locally fairly intact. (18) From our survey it emerged that though our respondents had lived some time in their home district, many of them were very disappointed by the changes which were overtaking it. They particularly complained of the area 'going down' or changing its racial character, being built up or overwhelmed with traffic. In addition though they had lived there some time, they did not necessarily live near their children and even their friends had often moved away already, frequently to retire to the coast themselves. In Rosow's view, then, these neighbourhoods are far from ideal for the social integration of the elderly.

However, it is possible to have relatively homogeneous local areas which fulfil a role in assisting social contacts without having a whole settlement with large proportions of elderly people. In fact Rosow is talking about segregated neighbourhoods or apartment blocks, as well as whole communities. So these arguments in favour of concentrations of elderly people, though they may help explain the popularity of retirement resorts, may not be sufficient to justify whole towns rather than parts of them being predominantly occupied by old people, if there are other reasons which make such concentrations undesirable. On the other hand, in the absence of other substantial reasons concentrations of elderly people should not be condemned out of hand as socially undesirable.

8   In case of emergency

> Woe to him that is alone when he falleth,
> for he hath not another to help him up.
>
> Ecclus. 2 : 1

In the resorts, the style of social life emphasizes the married couple; other social contacts too are less often with relatives than with friends and frequently are with comparatively new friends and acquaintances rather than with life-long friends. The impression is that, though this way of life may be satisfactory for relatively young retired couples, the widowed may find that it gives them inadequate social support and that it is a 'fair weather' system that could well break down in cases of sickness or other types of emergency.

To pursue this point, all retired people in Bexhill and Clacton were asked whom they would call in case of an emergency. The replies showed, as in any area, an emphasis on unofficial sources of help, but with the particular feature that dependence was on neighbours and friends as much as on children and other relatives.

The most important group of people whom the elderly would call for help were neighbours. In Bexhill 29 per cent and in Clacton 31 per cent mentioned them. In addition 14 per cent in Bexhill and 7 per cent in Clacton mentioned friends, which gives a total for the two of 43 per cent for Bexhill and 38 per cent for Clacton.

This heavy reliance on neighbours and friends poses a peculiar problem in the resorts in that the neighbours and friends themselves are very likely to be old. There are large areas of Bexhill and Clacton, particularly the bungalow estates, where well over 80 per cent of the population are elderly. Doctors in the resorts frequently describe the situation in which they call on a neighbour to help them lift a collapsed patient only to find that the neighbour too has a severe heart condition. These situations which are a common occurrence in the resorts show what limited help even the most willing neighbour may be able to give.

The next most common source of emergency help mentioned in Clacton was children (22 per cent), though they were much less frequently mentioned in Bexhill (10 per cent). Of course only 53 per cent of retired people in Bexhill, compared with 70 per cent in Clacton, had any children at all. But there was still a difference. Only 19 per cent of those in Bexhill who had children would have asked them for help, compared with 31 per cent in Clacton. However, when the distance that children would have to come to see their parents is taken into consideration, the difference between the two towns virtually disappears. (1)

In Bexhill, elderly people were more likely to mention other relatives (20 per cent) than they were to mention children, but this was not the case in Clacton where only 10 per cent mentioned them. Probably, in Bexhill the absence of children in the locality led to greater dependence on other relatives. The 'other relatives' who would have been asked for help were frequently brothers or sisters, particularly in Bexhill. It will be remembered that women in Bexhill were much more likely than those in Clacton to have brothers or sisters living in the town; 33 per cent had them there compared with only 25 per cent in Clacton. (2)

There were some further differences between the two towns. For instance, those in Clacton were more likely to call some sort of welfare agency (8 per cent) than they were to call the doctor (5 per cent). In Bexhill it was the reverse; 9 per cent would have called the doctor, compared with 2 per cent a welfare agency. In each town, however, only 1 per cent would have turned to a priest or church organisation. This is a very small proportion considering that 37 per cent of all retired people in Bexhill and 23 per cent in Clacton went to church. (3) More people in Bexhill mentioned outsiders such as shopkeepers, telephone operators, milkmen, postmen, etc., than mentioned welfare agencies or the church. The response on welfare agencies, doctors and the church is particularly poor considering that 12 per cent of respondents in Bexhill and 14 per cent in Clacton said they would not know whom to call on for help. Of those living alone 8 per cent in Bexhill and 10 per cent in Clacton said they would not know whom to ask for help or had no one to ask. These slightly lower proportions may suggest that people living alone are more aware of their predicament and have thought ahead. But it also shows

that it is not just those living alone who may be in
difficulty. Elderly married couples may become extraordinarily cut off from other people, without perhaps
exciting the notice or sympathy that one isolated old
person may arous; 14 per cent of elderly couples would
not know whom to call on. In the course of interviewing,
one old man was discovered trying to nurse a desperately
sick wife all alone, though he was himself completely
distraught about her illness. Couples of elderly women
living together can also become extremely isolated. On
several occasions, interviewers making enquiries about
people in the sample, found that neighbours knew nothing
at all about couples of elderly women, even if they lived
in one of a number of flats in a converted boarding house.
Of all the people who lived with brothers or sisters or
other relatives (and these were almost entirely single
and widowed women living together), 12 per cent in Bexhill
and 21 per cent in Clacton said they would not know whom
to ask for help. In Clacton the situation of single
women appears to be particularly unsatisfactory, as the
previous chapter also showed in relation to loneliness.

So the statutory health and social services were not
seen as a major source of help in emergency. But how much
help were the elderly people who had moved to Bexhill and
Clacton already receiving from these services? This study
was not primarily designed to enquire into social services
for old people in the resorts. Because of the very limited
coverage of most of the social services, only very small
numbers of users of each service come up in a general
random sample of retired people. However, some comparison
could be attempted between the use of services by people
who had moved to retire in the two resorts and the use of
services nationally.

THE USE OF HEALTH AND SOCIAL SERVICES BY RETIRED PEOPLE

The service which has the widest coverage is that provided
by general practitioners. The people of Bexhill were
seeing their doctors slightly less than the national
average for old people. (4) Under a quarter of those aged
65 and over had seen their doctor within the last month,
compared with over a third in England and Wales. In
Clacton there was no significant difference from the
national average (Table 8.1).

There was a difference between the two towns in the
ratio of home visits to surgery consultations. The elderly
people were asked whether they usually visited the doctor
themselves or were visited by him. Seventy-four per cent

of those in Clacton said it was they who visited their doctor, compared with only 59 per cent in Bexhill. There was no difference between the towns in the proportions who said that they were visited by their doctor; in Bexhill 9 per cent said the doctor visited them compared with 8 per cent in Clacton. However, those in Bexhill were much more likely to say that it depended on the circumstances or the character of their illness whether or not they were visited; 33 per cent gave this reply compared with 18 per cent in Clacton.

TABLE 8.1 The use of health and social services

	Bexhill (people of 65 and over)	Clacton (people of 65 and over)	Great Britain* (1962) People of 65 and over living in private households
Sample number	409	387	
Proportions of people of 65 and over seeing following services	%	%	%
Doctor:			
Within last month	24	29	33.7 (a)
Within last three months	42	47	48.9 (a)
Chiropody	32	14	18.6 (b)
Out-patients	12	11	10.4
Home help (private and LA)	17	4	12.4 (d)
Home help (LA)	1	1	4.4 (c)
Home nurse	3	1	0.8 (c)
Health visitor	2	1	1.6
Meals-on-wheels	*	1	1.1 (c)

* P. Townsend and D. Wedderburn, 'The Aged in the Welfare State', London, Bell, 1965: (a) p.61 (b) p.51 (c) p.24 (d) p.23.

To check on the impression given in reply to the last question, the retired people were also asked whether they had gone to the doctor's surgery on the last occasion they saw him or whether he had visited them. The replies showed up the same style of difference between the two towns; 81 per cent in Clacton had gone to the surgery, 17 per cent had called him to their house and 2 per cent had received a visit from him without being asked. In Bexhill the proportions were 74 per cent, 21 per cent and 5 per cent.

The likelihood of receiving a home visit in Bexhill and Clacton was strongly related to age. In Bexhill 43 per cent of retired people aged 75 and over had received a visit at home on the last occasion on which they had seen a doctor, and in Clacton 27 per cent had. The percentage for Clacton was very low for such a vulnerable group of old people, and was only about the same as the national average for all patients. (5) Why there should be such a difference between the towns in this respect, is not at all clear.

It is tempting to try to explain it in terms of social class differences between the two towns. However, there was no clear relationship between home visits from the doctor and social class or income. This also rules out the effect of the existence of more private patients in Bexhill than Clacton. In addition, other surveys which found wide variations in the ratio of home visits to surgery consultations have also found little relationship between these variations and the characteristics of patients. (6)

In fourteen studies in the United Kingdom in the 1950s and early 1960s, the average proportion of home visits to surgery consultations per patient per year varied from 19 per cent to 44 per cent, with the most usual proportion being between 25 per cent and 35 per cent. (7) There are hazards about comparing the last visit, as in the Bexhill and Clacton study, with all visits over a year, but if the comparison is made, Clacton appears to be very low in home visits and Bexhill just about average.

A further difference between Bexhill and Clacton was that the proportion of private patients in Bexhill (10 per cent) but not in Clacton (1 per cent) was very high compared with the national average for elderly people. Townsend and Wedderburn found that 98 per cent of people of 65 and over had a National Health Service doctor, 1.9 per cent had a private doctor and 0.2 per cent had no doctor at all. (8) Elderly people are more likely than younger ones to be private patients: 'Older patients, whose habits with respect to medical practice were estab-

lished before 1948, may prefer a paying relationship with
the doctor, and some older patients with greater need for
medical attention may feel more comfortable as private
patients because of their greater demands on the doctors'
time.'

Being a private patient was strongly related to income
and social class. In Bexhill, 16 per cent of Class I and
12 per cent of Class II were private patients compared
with only 3 per cent of the skilled manual and non-manual
classes and none of the semi-skilled and unskilled. In
Clacton, where there were only four private patients
interviewed altogether, three were in Class II and one
had been a skilled manual worker. However, as Samuel
Mencher writes:
> It should be noted that although the upper classes tend
> to make greater use of private hospital, consultant and
> general practitioner service there is no evidence that
> on the whole they are making less use of the public ser-
> vices. In fact, all indications appear to the contrary.(9)

Apart from general practice, the health or social
service most frequently used by old people is the chiropody
service. However, there are very big differences between
areas in the level of provision of the service and the
use made of it. Nationally there is great variety between
different areas but on average about a fifth of people of
65 and over go to the chiropodist, of whom more than half
pay for treatment privately. (10) (11) In Bexhill 32 per
cent of retired people who had moved there went to a
chiropodist; in Clacton, however, only 14 per cent did so.
The explanation of the difference between Bexhill and
Clacton may be the social class composition of the towns;
Classes I and II are more likely to go to the chiropodist,
particularly private practitioners.

The scope for expansion of the service appears to be
very large since it has been estimated that about 48 per
cent of people of 65 and over need chiropody. (12) There
is great variety in the generosity of local schemes. For
instance, in Bexhill all people of 60 and over qualified
for the cheap service and there was no charge for people
on Supplementary Benefits. Private chiropodists were used
for the scheme. In contrast, Clacton had a free scheme
but it applied only to one county council chiropodist who
had to cover the whole of the coastal strip including
Frinton, Walton and Jaywich. Because of this the coverage
was bound to be much more limited.

There was also a very big difference between Bexhill
and Clacton in the proportions of people who had the
services of a home help. In Bexhill 17 per cent had one,
compared with only 4 per cent in Clacton. However, the

difference is totally explained by the large number of home helps in Bexhill who were privately hired. In each town only 1 per cent of the retired people had local authority home helps. (All these were attending people aged 70 and over.) This is a low proportion compared with the national average of 4.5 per cent. Recruitment is very difficult. In Bexhill:

> it has been found that many residents particularly in Cooden and Little Common, are paying such high hourly rates and providing transport to and from Sidley, the main recruiting area, that it has been impossible for the service to attempt to compete. (13)

The only other service being used by a substantial proportion of retired people in Bexhill and Clacton was the out-patients clinic. In Bexhill 12.4 per cent and in Clacton 11.0 per cent were currently attending a clinic. This is just above the national average of 10.4 per cent. It is possible that in some respects the out-patients service may be used to relieve pressure on general practitioners. Later we will consider whether doctors in the resorts are indeed over-extended.

In descending order of frequency of use, the other services asked about were: home nursing (3 per cent in Bexhill and 1 per cent in Clacton), health visitors (2 per cent in Bexhill, 1 per cent in Clacton) and meals-on-wheels (less than 0.5 per cent in Bexhill, 1 per cent in Clacton). In Clacton, all these services but in Bexhill only the meals-on-wheels service, were covering less than the national average proportion of elderly people. Bexhill's meals service as a whole was better than Clacton's because apart from the meals-on-wheels service, the Senior Citizen's Club provided 60 meals a day compared with only 25-30 at the Derby and Joan Club in Clacton. In both resorts, however, the meals-on-wheels services covered less than half the national average of people of 65 and over, 8 or 9 per 1,000 compared with 20 per 1,000 for all county districts in 1970.

Because of the difficulties of small numbers it was not worth reproducing the analysis of these individual service users according to income, social class, marital status and so on. Instead the users of all services were all considered together, according to the number of services they were seeing. It emerged that in Bexhill, elderly people were both more likely than those in Clacton to be receiving any services at all and to be receiving several. In Bexhill 37 per cent received no service, compared with 43 per cent in Clacton. Also, of those receiving services, 54 per cent in Bexhill compared with 68 per cent in Clacton received only one.

The number of services people were receiving was closely related to their age, but only in Clacton were those living alone significantly more likely to receive services than were other people. (14) In addition, though the very old were more likely to receive services, there were still many of them who received none. For instance, in each town a quarter of all people aged 75 and over received no services.

In spite of the serious limitations of this brief review of the services, a number of conclusions or at least further questions do emerge.

First, the provision of help in emergencies is largely seen by old people as a function of friends and neighbours, and yet, in the resorts, these friends and neighbours are very likely to be old themselves. The fact that old people often have no children or live a long way from them makes the family less effective in emergencies, though siblings, again usually elderly too, are seen as a source of help. Though few people actually mentioned statutory services as a potential source of help, the fragility of community support in the resorts may well imply a greater need than usual for help through official agencies.

Second, in only two instances were a larger percentage than the national average of elderly people receiving a particular service. Both were private services, chiropody and home help, and both were in Bexhill. In Bexhill, too, a relatively large proportion (10 per cent) of patients of general practitioners were private patients.

Third, in Clacton most services were being received by rather less than the national proportion of elderly people and in Bexhill by not significantly more.

These results suggest that though there may be a very great potential need for help, there is currently a poor level either of take-up or of provision of services. Bexhill differs from Clacton in that certain privately provided services are widely used there, whereas in Clacton incomes are too low to allow this. In a later chapter we will see that old people in Bexhill are also much more likely than those in Clacton to go to live in private nursing and residential homes or in hotels. Does this supplementation of the services provided by the state or local authority imply that the latter are inadequate, or do relatively wealthy people prefer private services? In Chapters 14-17 the provision of health and social services in retirement resorts is considered more generally to see what are current levels of provision, and what are the financial implications for local authorities of providing services for such large proportions of elderly people.

9   Leisure

> Absence of occupation is not rest,
> A mind quite vacant is a mind distress'd.
>   Cowper: Retirement, 1.623

> You could knit a sweater by the fire-side
> Sunday morning go for a ride.
> Doing the garden, digging the weeds,
> Who could ask for more?
> Will you still need me,
> Will you still feed me,
> When I'm sixty-four.
>   Lennon and McCartney

The old people led quiet lives centred on their homes and gardens. The men spent their time gardening, going for walks or sitting on the sea front and carrying out odd jobs or decorating around the house. The women spent their time in running the home, gardening and sitting on the front. A number did knitting and sewing or crochet work for their children and grandchildren. Most watched T.V. in the evenings. (1)

This picture of life in the Greater London Council's bungalows at Littlehampton very much fits that of the retired married couples interviewed in Bexhill and, in particular, Clacton. In Bexhill there was a tendency for people to have more activities outside their own homes, than the retired people in Littlehampton and Clacton had.

    The retired people in Bexhill and Clacton were asked to describe how they spent most of their time 'at this time of year', that is in the late autumn and winter. (2)

    The bulk of the activities mentioned were home-based. They were such things as housework and house maintenance, gardening, watching television, reading, listening to the radio, doing handicrafts and receiving visitors. Next came activities outside such as walking, motoring or sitting on the sea front, plus visiting friends. Last, there were small proportions who mentioned clubs or welfare work.

Elderly people in Bexhill were rather more likely than those in Clacton to spend their time motoring, reading, listening to the radio and in particular visiting friends or receiving visits from them. People in Clacton mentioned less activities altogether, but laid more emphasis on one or two, notably gardening and walking.

Women tended to mention more activities than men did. This difference was particularly noticeable in Clacton. The greater number of activities is largely explained by women's greater variety of home-based activities, such as playing cards or doing handicrafts, particularly knitting and sewing. However, they also mentioned visiting friends more frequently than men did and attending clubs and bingo and other organizations. In Bexhill, women also more often mentioned various sorts of social work or 'helping people'.

Married, single and widowed women also varied in the number of their activities. In Bexhill, single women mentioned the most activities; married women were next and widowed women mentioned least. In Clacton there were too few single women for analysis but again married women were more active than widows. There were also differences in the type of activities of married and widowed women. In Clacton, married women went motoring and visiting more, but widowed women did more reading and listened to the radio more. In Bexhill, married women motored and walked more than widowed women did but did not do more visiting. Widowed women listened to the radio more but mentioned reading about the same amount. It was the single women in Bexhill who read most and spent time at clubs and organizations and in welfare work.

The possession (3) of a television was near the national average for all households; 87 per cent had one in Bexhill, 92 per cent in Clacton and 91 per cent in the United Kingdom. (4) In Bexhill and Clacton, single and widowed people were much less likely than married couples to own or rent a television set. Single people (who were mainly women) in Bexhill were the least likely; only 69 per cent had one compared with 80 per cent of the widowed and 93 per cent of married couples. In Clacton there was not such a big distinction between the single and the widowed. There, 77 per cent of single people had a television, compared with 81 per cent of widows and 96 per cent of married couples. The ownership of a radio was much more evenly spread: over 90 per cent of all groups had one. Not to have a radio or television set appears to have been more often a matter of choice than necessity; there was little relationship with income.

The popularity of motoring as a leisure pursuit of retired people in Bexhill was related to much more widespread car ownership there than in Clacton; in Bexhill, 45 per cent of the retired people had a car, compared with 27 per cent in Clacton. In the past, too, those living in Bexhill had also been more likely to have a car; only 30 per cent had never had one, compared with 54 per cent in Clacton.

There was a closer relationship between car ownership and income than might have been expected, considering that a third of those who had once owned a car said they had given it up for health rather than financial reasons. However, another main reason for having given up a car was that a widow did not drive and so had to sell the car when her husband died. As widows tend to have lower incomes, this would reinforce the relationship between income and car ownership. Apart from financial problems, health and bereavement, people give a wide range of reasons for having given up their cars. One which was common but unexpected was petrol rationing during the war. Many of the retired people had not bothered to get another car after the war. Many also said they had become tired of heavy traffic or that on moving to the seaside they felt that a car was no longer needed.

However, 79 per cent of all the people with incomes of £20 and over in Bexhill had cars. Also 89 per cent of all those with over £20, who had ever owned a car, still did so, compared with 65 per cent of all respondents, and 75 per cent of married couples. This suggests that income is an important factor in determining whether or not an elderly couple retain their car. The doctors are in rather a quandary over this as some of their patients are at risk from heart attacks whilst driving, but if they were prevented from driving they would either become very cut off or would have an attack earlier because of the effort of walking. This becomes particularly crucial when old people live in one of the more remote bungalow estates, with poor shopping facilities.

A question about how one spends 'most of one's time' is not designed to bring out references to those leisure activities, such as going to the sea front or clubs, which may play an important role in putting variety into life but may be relatively infrequent. Some specific questions were therefore asked about these sorts of activities. The first of these was 'Do you go to any of the following more than once a fortnight on average throughout the year? (a) the cinema, (b) the sea front and promenade, (c) a public house, (d) sporting events, (e) a park.' (5)

Retired people in Clacton were slightly less likely than those in Bexhill to visit any of the listed places; 32 per cent visited none, compared with 25 per cent in Bexhill. This is compatible with the earlier finding that they had less outside leisure activities. There was an extraordinary difference in the park attendance (25 per cent in Bexhill compared with 5 per cent in Clacton). Both towns have parks but Bexhill's Egerton Park is a much more ambitious one, situated near the sea front and is considered one of the town's major attractions. Even so, park visiting is apparently very localised; half the people who went to the park regularly in Bexhill lived in two electoral districts near Egerton Park. In Clacton, park visiting was also very localised.

However, it is probably of more interest to look at the differences between the sexes and between married, single and widowed people than to look at the differences between the two towns. In both, women were less likely to visit any of the listed places. In Clacton, in fact, over a third of the women but only a quarter of the men visited none of them with any frequency. In Bexhill the figure was not far short of one-third of the women compared with one-fifth of the men. The biggest differences for individual items were in the proportions visiting the sea front, public houses and sporting events. More light is thrown on this by looking at marital status. For instance, it appears that married women were much more likely to visit public houses than were single or widowed women. There is still hesitation from most women about visiting public houses by themselves, even if they would like to. The only place that widows visited more often than married women did, and that only marginally in Bexhill, was the cinema. The difference between widowed and other women must partly be explained by their greater age, but they probably also suffer from the change in their social position on the death of their husband.

In Bexhill, women were much more likely than those in Clacton to go regularly to sporting events. This is largely attributable to the extreme popularity of bowls in Bexhill. There are a large number of high-quality greens there and bowls can be played all the year round on the indoor bowling green. One man said he had seen the indoor bowling green advertised in South Africa and had chosen to retire to Bexhill for that reason. The publicity brochure for Bexhill lays great stress on bowls.

There were too few widowed men in the samples for reliable conclusions to be drawn about any differences in the leisure pursuits of married and widowed men. The very thin evidence suggests that widowed men in Bexhill went to most of the listed places rather less than married men did, but this did not apply to Clacton and the results were not statistically significant.

In both towns the place visited by far the most often was the sea front; 69 per cent of retired people in Bexhill went there more than once a fortnight and so did 63 per cent in Clacton. What is the attraction? First, there is always something to watch there. The sea itself in winter is for most people endlessly attractive and in summer there are people, particularly children, walking and playing on the beach. (The children's trampoline on Bexhill beach is a notable magnet for elderly spectators, although there was considerable initial opposition to its purchase.) Then there are other people to talk to. In summer the benches along the front are always full of elderly people, and according to many respondents it is generally accepted that strangers talk to each other there. The lay-out of a seaside resort is also important; it is like a town cut in half along the line of the sea front. So a visit to the centre for shopping brings one nearer to, not farther from, the most open part of the town - the sea front with its uninterrupted sea view. It is natural for someone who has come into the centre to shop to walk down to the front to rest on a bench or to have a cup of coffee in one of the cafes. The shape of the town is semicircular instead of circular and has the sea front as its focal point. For this reason no matter how urbanised a resort becomes, it is still, as one resident called it, 'a compromise between town and country'.

In winter of course the pattern of life in resorts is rather different from that in the summer. Nevertheless it is notable that 63 per cent of the respondents in Bexhill said there were no major differences between their life in the autumn and winter and that in the summer. In Clacton only 45 per cent said there was no major difference. The people who said there were major differences mentioned particularly spending more time in their gardens, on the sea front or beach, or walking. Rather less mentioned that they received more visitors and visited more friends in the summer. Clubs provided outings by coach in the summer and the bowls clubs were much more active. Certainly, the summer sees more social life and a less home-centred way of living. This is in striking contrast to the working residents of holiday resorts whose social activities tend to end abruptly with the start of the summer season and the need to concentrate on catering for tourists.

Attending clubs of some sort was much more popular in Bexhill than in Clacton; 56 per cent of elderly people in Bexhill went to a club, compared with 40 per cent in Clacton. (6) Those in Bexhill were also more likely to go to church and to evening classes. In both towns more people went to clubs than to church and only a few went to evening classes.

According to the cross-national survey (7) 32 per cent of men and 46 per cent of women in Britain aged 65 and over go to church. In Clacton, only 19 per cent of men and 26 per cent of women went to church. Bexhill, with 32 per cent for men and 40 per cent for women, appears to be near the national average but it should be remembered that church attendance is most common amongst the higher social classes, (8) so Bexhill in fact has a below-average attendance for the social class composition of the town.

The reason for this below-average attendance in both towns is not entirely clear. One likely explanation is the break with the home area. The Greater London Council, in their survey of five of their seaside bungalow estates, found a big drop in church membership after the move out of London; whereas 17 per cent of men had attended a church before the move only 1 per cent were still attending. Similarly whereas 28 per cent of women had attended a church in London only 11 per cent still did. The report concluded that only the most regular churchgoers kept up their contact with a church after moving to the seaside. The question of distance from a church must be one factor in this: the bungalow estates tend to be remote from the old town core with its churches. (9) However, there are probably other reasons. First, there is probably hesitation about joining an unfamiliar congregation, just as there is about joining a new club. Second, there must be those who are glad to drop going to church and only continued going because of long-standing obligations. They will take the opportunity of a move to stop attending. Third, the process is probably cumulative. It has been shown that church attendance falls, even amongst people who previously attended regularly, if they move to an area in which few people attend. (10)

Another reason for the low church attendance may be the predominance of married couples in the population. Single and widowed women are, nationally, more likely to go to church than are married women or men. (11)

Retired people in Bexhill were also more frequently attenders of clubs and there was also a very remarkable contrast in the types of clubs that old people were attending in the two towns. In Bexhill, clubs specifically for old people played a relatively small part. Only 10 per cent of all the people who went to clubs in Bexhill attended old people's clubs, compared with 42 per cent of those who went to clubs in Clacton. The Bexhill people were much more likely to be going to clubs which catered for specific interests rather than old people's or social clubs; 39 per cent of the clubs attended in Bexhill were associated with specific hobbies or other interests, apart from politics, sports and church or charitable associations. In Clacton, only 18 per cent of the clubs attended were of this type. However, community centres played a bigger role in Bexhill than in Clacton and it should be remembered that such social clubs, though not called 'old people's clubs', are in retirement resorts attended largely by old people.

Bexhill prides itself on having 157 local societies and organisations, of which the variety is enormous. In this survey 118 different clubs and societies, other than old people's clubs, were mentioned by respondents in Bexhill, compared with only 45 in Clacton.

The types of clubs, other than old people's clubs, mentioned by the elderly people interviewed can be roughly categorized as in Table 9.1.

TABLE 9.1 Number of clubs, by type

	Bexhill	Clacton
Social clubs	22	4
Church and charities	33	2
Art, music and drama	24	10
Other hobbies	20	12
Sports	7	1
Professional associations	10	12
Clubs for the disabled	2	4
Total	118	45

The hobbies clubs covered a wide range, in Bexhill particularly, from the usual Photographic and Horticultural Societies to the Cat Club (300 members), the Cactus Club, the French Circle, the Philosophical Society, the Vegetarian Society and the Home Economics Society. Religious clubs and charities were represented by a vast selection including the Quaker Club, the Order of the Cross, the Teilhard de Chardin Society, the Commoners, the Missionary Working Party, and the Fellowship of Reconciliation.

Professional organizations were represented by, amongst others, the RAF Association, the Police Club, the National Provincial Bank Pensioners Association, the Civil Service Pensioners Alliance, the Old Southeronians, and the Federation of Post Office Veterans. Some of these organizations held few local functions. Others, like the Banker's Coffee Morning were a regular feature of Bexhill social life.

There was no difference between men and women in Bexhill in the proportion who attended clubs, but in Clacton more women than men went to clubs. This is rather curious because nationally more elderly men attend clubs than do elderly women. Nationally, the proportion of elderly retired men who go to clubs is 45 per cent (12) which is lower than in Bexhill (55 per cent) but higher than in Clacton (36 per cent). However, the proportion of elderly women who went to clubs, 56 per cent in Bexhill and 43 per cent in Clacton, was substantially higher than the national average (just under 30 per cent). In addition, widowed women in Bexhill and Clacton were more likely than married women to go to clubs, whereas nationally there was little difference between the two.

There was, in both Bexhill and Clacton, a relationship between club membership and social class. Broadly, between a half and two-thirds of the non-manual classes were likely to belong to clubs, compared with about 40 per cent of the manual classes. (13) Sillitoe remarks that there is a 'general tendency for club membership to rise with social class'. In particular, women in the top socio-economic groups are 'outstandingly active in adult social clubs and political organisations'. (14) This clearly helps to explain the difference between Bexhill and Clacton in their rates of club membership. It also helps explain the greater activity of women in Bexhill compared with the national average. It does not, however, explain the greater activity of women in Clacton, where the social class distribution is not skewed upwards. Nor does it explain the relatively greater activity of widowed, compared with married, women.

One explanation of the club-going of widows is that old people's clubs predominated in Clacton and women tend to form the majority of the members of old people's clubs. This is inevitable in that women tend to live longer than men. Associated with the predominance of women in old people's clubs is also the fact that there are many more widowed and single people in them than in the general population. In the Bexhill Senior Citizens Club, (15) 30 per cent of the members were married compared with 67 per cent of the general sample; 40 per cent were single, compared with 15 per cent, and 31 per cent were widowed compared with 18 per cent. In addition 52 per cent of the members lived alone, compared with 21 per cent of the sample. Of course, not all the members of the club were people who had moved to the town to retire, but most were. Only 17 per cent said they had always lived in Bexhill or had moved there other than to retire; this would compare with at least 50 per cent of the retired population of Bexhill. The characteristics of club members are probably to some extent affected by its location in the middle of the town where there are many bed-sitting rooms and converted flats occupied by single or widowed women. In previous surveys the club has found that most of its members live within half a mile of the club. However, other old people's clubs in the town also show the same feature, a predominance of women living alone, so location is only one factor.

Those who said they belonged to old people's clubs in Bexhill had almost exactly the same social class characteristics as all respondents, but in Clacton there was a slight downward skew in class amongst members of old people's clubs. (16) There were more than average semi-skilled and unskilled people and less than average professional and managerial.

In some cases, membership of a club or church can be a purely nominal membership, with little attendance and no effect on the social life of the person concerned. To check on this, those who went to clubs, evening classes, church or some other organized activity, were asked how often on average they went to any of these. Again there were some interesting differences between the two towns. In Clacton, though there were fewer members of clubs, those who were members attended more often; 18 per cent went more than three times a week compared with only 9 per cent in Bexhill. The reason for this is presumably the predominance of old people's clubs in Clacton. However, in both towns about two-thirds (64 per cent in Bexhill and 69 per cent in Clacton) of those who attended some sort of organization went at least once a week. The clubs were clearly very much part of the weekly routine rather than a rare occurrence.

Giving their reasons for not going to clubs, those who were not members most often said that they were too busy (20 per cent in Bexhill and 17 per cent in Clacton) or preferred home life (36 per cent in Bexhill and 23 per cent in Clacton). 'I don't enjoy women in the mass. I'm not a clubite.' More people in Clacton than in Bexhill (20 per cent compared with 4 per cent) made derogatory remarks about clubs. It seems logical to connect this with the different character of the clubs in the two towns, especially as the adverse comments in Clacton were often clearly directed at old people's clubs rather than clubs for hobbies. For instance, less that 1 per cent in Bexhill compared with 4 per cent in Clacton said that clubs had too many old people in them or made remarks which showed that they equated 'club' with 'old people's club':

'I'm not old enough to be interested in clubs yet.'
'I once went to a Darby and Joan Club but didn't like singing "Little Bo Peep, etc.".'

Of course some of the adverse comments were not particularly related to old people's clubs but just to any club:

'They're far too gossipy.'
'I don't believe in getting in with people like that - you pick up colds.'
'I don't like the struggle for power in clubs.'

The largest group of people who did not go to clubs were those (18 per cent in Bexhill and 14 per cent in Clacton) who said they could not because they were housebound, ill or infirm. The most frequently mentioned problem was in fact deafness. This distressing situation is one which clubs would do well to take into consideration. It is noteworthy that some people who could not even walk were being ferried to and from clubs and were thus able to enjoy company, while deaf people were denied this company or denied it to themselves through nervousness or self-consciousness.

Only a small number of people (30 per cent in Bexhill and 2 per cent in Clacton) said that they had difficulty in getting to clubs because the meetings were held in the evening. The difficulties that elderly people experience in going out on winter evenings are to some extent overcome by having afternoon meetings. As the membership even of hobby clubs is largely retired people, this is possible in the resorts. This is an important point; in most towns the proportion of retired people is not such that special interest groups can usually be held in the daytime - though old people's clubs are. Of course, premises have to be available for afternoon meetings. If schools have to be used, the possibilities of afternoon meetings are severely reduced.

Distance and poor transport facilities are mentioned as problems for some people (3 per cent in Bexhill and 5 per cent in Clacton). Of course expense comes into the question of distance from clubs. One old lady said that she felt 'Very isolated by the need to pay bus fares to go anywhere'. It should be remembered that some of these people had moved from towns which have reduced fares or free bus passes for people of pensionable age. In a place with a third or more of its population eligible for such a rebate such concessions are not usually viable propositions, though the Southdown Bus Company has now introduced such a scheme.

Some old people were in such straitened circumstances that, quite apart from bus fares, they found even the modest demands of club membership too much for them financially:

> 'I tried clubs but it was no good because it costs quite a bit to go - with raffle tickets, entry and tea to pay for.'

Clearly, not all these expenses were compulsory but pride leads people to feel that they have to contribute, not to be the odd one out. This can deter them from going at all.

Then there are those who would like to go but are too shy to take the leap:

> 'I'm not a mixer. I go red in the face at meetings.'
> 'I've no friends to go to clubs with. I never see anyone. I could be dead.'

It is a mistake to equate such social activities as club-going with a happy social life. Nevertheless for those who have few relations and no other means of making friends, a club can provide valuable contacts. Indeed, more than one person commented that 'everybody goes to clubs here because they are so lonely'.

Most surveys have suggested that the bulk of those who go to clubs are people who have adequate contacts through family, friends and neighbours. They are just varying their lives. According to the cross-national survey people who went to clubs,

> did not differ strikingly from non-members in the degree to which they were integrated into an extended family. Some individuals certainly seemed to find compensation in club and church activities for their lack of close relatives, but others seemed to have added club and church activities as well as friendships to a family life that was itself rich already. Three-quarters of those who had no relatives or who saw them infrequently did not belong to any club at all ... there is no sign of an inverse correlation between familial and extra-familial participation. A number of previous studies in the United States and Europe have pointed to the same conclusion. (17)

However, in the resorts there are many people with no day-to-day contact with relatives or long-standing friends and they may need other structured forms of social contact to take the place of those made through work and long residence in one area. This need may become particularly felt by widows who until that time may have found their home and husband sufficient company. Without children nearby, clubs may form an important point of contact. This may explain the relatively large proportions of women, particularly widows, who go to clubs in Bexhill and Clacton. It is worth repeating that only 30 per cent of the members of the Senior Citizens Club in Bexhill were married compared with 40 per cent single and 31 per cent widows, and that 52 per cent of the members lived alone. In this, as in many other ways, perhaps the resorts differ from the usual national picture.

SOME FURTHER QUESTIONS ABOUT LEISURE PURSUITS IN THE RETIREMENT RESORTS

This study has been able to give only limited attention to the complex subject of leisure in retirement resorts. For this reason one emerges with questions for further study rather than with firm conclusions. The following are some of the questions which may be particularly relevant.

1 In communities with large proportions of elderly people, are retired people less likely to feel excluded, more 'the heart of the community', and therefore more willing to take initiative to run the community life of the town and to take part in its organised social life?

2 Does the concentration of elderly people in resorts make more viable the organization of a variety of types of clubs and societies to cater for the many different interests of retired people? What are the factors involved? E.g. (a) a workable size of membership, (b) the possibility of holding meetings at suitable times of the day?

3 Is a town which has a large proportion of the professional and managerial classes likely to produce managerial skills to run such clubs, as well as a larger membership? Is there any relationship between club-going and satisfaction with the social life of the town?

4 Are people who live a long way from their relatives and long-standing friends likely to take more part in organised social life, such as clubs?

5 How important to retired residents are the facilities provided essentially for holiday-makers, e.g. the pier, the bandstand, sea-front cafes, etc.?

6 Why is the sea front such a magnet? In what ways does it act as a social centre? Do parks of the 'Prince's Street, Edinburgh type' operate in a similar fashion by bringing open spaces into the main shopping area of the town? Or is there something special about the sea as a means of breaking down social barriers?

7 To what extent is there a social split between long-standing local residents in the resorts and the people who move there to retire? Are the movers, for instance, mostly friendly with each other rather than 'locals'? Is such a split reflected in, for instance, old people's welfare committees being more concerned about 'local' old people than others, no matter how long they have lived there? Is a split also apparent in the membership of clubs? For instance, is the Darby and Joan mostly 'local' and the Senior Citizens Club mostly for those who moved on retirement? Is there less split in towns in which there is less difference in social class between 'locals' and 'movers'?

These are just some of the issues related to leisure activities which need further research in order to contribute even partial answers to Kleemeier's question about the distinctive character of life in retirement towns.

10 The financial position of retired people

> Not even a good man could easily endure old age and poverty conjoined
>
>   Plato: 'The Republic', Book 1

> 'She is poor; she has sunk from the comforts she was born to; and, if she live to old age, must probably sink more. Her situation should secure your compassion.'
>
>   Jane Austen: 'Emma'

Because Bexhill had such a predominantly middle-class retired population, it seemed likely that, there at least, average incomes might be well above the national average for the elderly. Nevertheless, there is quite severe poverty even in places like Bexhill. One has only to visit the ladies' waiting room of a South Coast railway station on a winter afternoon or evening to find old ladies who have come there for the warmth and the company. 'We're packed out in the evening, because they can't afford to keep the electric fires on in their rooms', said one attendant.

This chapter is largely about the incomes and savings of retired people in the resorts. (1) A discussion of housing expenditure is reserved until the following chapter.

Incomes (2) in Clacton proved to be substantially lower than in Bexhill; only 3 per cent of the respondents in Clacton had incomes of over £20 a week, compared with 27 per cent in Bexhill. Similarly, half the Clacton people but only 28 per cent in Bexhill had incomes of £10 or less a week (Table 10.1). The contrast between married couples in the two towns was even more marked. Only 4 per cent had incomes over £20 a week in Clacton compared with 34 per cent in Bexhill, while 41 per cent in Clacton had £10 a week or less compared with 13 per cent in Bexhill.

TABLE 10.1 Weekly net incomes, by marital status and sex

	Bexhill			
	All	Married couples	Single or widowed men	Single or widowed women
Sample number	377	249	19	109
WEEKLY NET INCOME	%	%	%	%
Up to £5.00	4	-	(-)	15
£5.01 up to £7.50	7	3	(8)	16
£7.51 up to £10.00	17	10	(15)	32
£10.01 up to £12.50	11	11	(15)	8
£12.51 up to £15.00	12	14	(15)	7
£15.01 up to £20.00	21	26	(23)	9
£20.01 up to £25.00	9	10	(15)	5
£25.01 up to £30.00	8	11	(-)	4
£30.01 and over	10	13	(8)	4
	Clacton			
Sample number	414	303	28	83
WEEKLY NET INCOME	%	%	%	%
Up to £5.00	5	-	(11)	22
£5.01 up to £7.50	17	11	(14)	40
£7.51 up to £10.00	29	30	(25)	28
£10.01 up to £12.50	21	36	(21)	5
£12.51 up to £15.00	12	15	(7)	2
£15.01 up to £20.00	11	13	(14)	4
£20.01 up to £25.00	2	3	(-)	-
£25.01 up to £30.00	1	1	(4)	-
£30.01 and over	*	-	(4)	-

The relationship which was expected to exist between social class and income did emerge from the data, as long as female heads of retirement units were considered separately. (3) The professional and managerial classes had substantially higher incomes than the other classes. However, these two classes in Clacton were not as affluent as those in Bexhill. (4) Only 5 per cent of men and married couples who were in the professional and managerial classes in Clacton had over £25 a week, compared with 31 per cent in Bexhill. In fact skilled non-manual workers in Bexhill were better off than the professional and managerial classes in Clacton. There was a similar contrast for women heads of retirement units; so the income contrast between Bexhill and Clacton was not just a result of class differences between the towns but of the fact that within any one class, Bexhill's retired people were likely to be more affluent than those in Clacton.

Single and widowed women had much lower incomes than men or married couples. In Clacton particularly, women's incomes were very low indeed; 90 per cent were £10 a week or less and 22 per cent, £5 or less. In Bexhill, two-thirds were £10 a week or less and 15 per cent, £5 or less. Even of the women in Social Classes I and II, 47 per cent in Bexhill and 78 per cent in Clacton had £10 a week or less. None of the Clacton women but 13 per cent of those in Bexhill had more than £20 a week. The incomes of single and widowed men (bearing in mind the small numbers on which the data are based) were roughly comparable with those of married couples; there were in Clacton just slightly more men in the lowest income groups. As most of these men were widowers, presumably the difference between them and married men is mainly accounted for by a smaller state pension.

In Clacton most of the women other than married women were widows. In Bexhill, however, nearly half were single women and their incomes were noticeably higher than those of widows; 51 per cent were over £10 a week compared with 18 per cent of widows. They were, however, lower than those of widowed or single men. This sex differential in incomes is, of course, a national feature which has been widely documented. (5) The causes of the difference are basically that women have less often worked than men have and, even if they have worked, their incomes and occupational pensions are lower. Widows have particularly low incomes because their husbands' pensions frequently end on death. (6) In addition, widows are older than married and single people, and nationally the incomes of elderly people have a downward gradient with increasing age. This downward gradient with age appeared quite clearly in Bexhill and Clacton for both married couples and for individuals. For instance, in Bexhill 21 per cent of men heads of retirement units aged 75 and over had incomes up to £10 a week, compared with only 11 per cent of those aged 65-9 and none aged under 65. In Clacton 60 per cent aged 75 and over had this low income, compared with 40 per cent aged 65-9 and 27 per cent of those under 65. Similarly for women, 44 per cent of women of 75 and over in Bexhill had incomes up to £7.50, compared with 15 per cent of those under 70. In Clacton, 74 per cent aged 75 and over had £7.50 or less, compared with 50 per cent under 70. In the cross-national survey the large income differential with age was mainly attributed to the employment of younger people (7) but the numbers of respondents in Bexhill and Clacton who were working were so small (6 per cent of men in Bexhill and 12 per cent in Clacton) that another explanation is necessary. The reasons which were regarded as secondary in the case of the cross-national survey are the primary ones in this case.

In societies that have been exposed to inflation and where at the same time the real income levels of the active population have also been rising, it is not surprising to find that the very old have benefited least. They will have had less opportunity to accumulate savings, and the real value of savings they have will have been reduced. (8)

Because of the difference in the proportion of earners in the cross-national survey sample (28 per cent of men aged 65 and over) it is not so necessary here to heed the warning: 'We must beware, however, of drawing any conclusions from this cross-sectional data about what happens to the financial resources of individuals as they age.' (9) Unless a retired person's income is initially large enough for them to have a surplus from which to increase their income from existing savings by wise investment, it is inevitable that over the years inflation will cause the relative value of their income from investments to fall. Unless increases in existing pensions compensate for these losses then the relative value of their total income will fall. If it then becomes necessary for them to cash some of their investments to supplement their income, the money income as well as its relative value will fall. This sequence is by no means unlikely.

There were difficulties in comparing incomes from this survey with national figures. The cross-national survey (1962) data were too out of date so the best source was the Family Expenditure Survey, but that used gross income whereas this was net of tax and other deductions. (10) There was another problem in that the Family Expenditure Survey's data were for household income. However, in most cases the Bexhill and Clacton data amounted to that too because the income asked for was that of the individual or married couple; 84 per cent of the households in Bexhill and 86 per cent in Clacton were either individuals or couples living alone. (11)

In spite of the difficulties of comparison, it is possible to see that Bexhill's incomes were well above the national average for people of 65 and over. In spite of the fact that Bexhill's were net incomes, there were far fewer in the £10 or less group than there were in the national figures. In addition, there were as many people with net incomes in Bexhill of over £30 a week as there were people with gross incomes at that level nationally.

The comparison of Clacton incomes with the national figures was less easy but it seemed that, in Clacton, elderly people were much less frequently than the national average in the top income brackets, even when allowance was made for the difference between net and gross income. It also seemed likely that the proportion with incomes of £7.50 or less was slightly lower than the national average and that the chief feature of Clacton incomes was that they were more bunched in the £7.50-15.00 (net) income group than were incomes nationally.

To sum up, then, Clacton's incomes were lower than the national average for the elderly in that they had a very low ceiling but the proportion of the very poorest was also probably below average. In Bexhill, incomes were above the national average but they were spread out over £10 rather than bunched in the very high ranges.

To anticipate a later discussion, one can suggest that the explanation of this income structure lies in the difficulty which lower income people experience in moving to retirement resorts and in the type and price of housing available there. With its high house prices, only the better off can afford to move to Bexhill. Clacton with hardly any houses to let is still too expensive for the very poorest, who would have difficulty in buying a house anywhere. On the other hand the types of houses built in Clacton are aimed at medium income retired people, so the more wealthy are not attracted there. Thus, there is a 'bunching' in the middle income group just as there is a 'bunching' in the skilled manual class.

Though Bexhill's incomes were well above the national average for elderly people, it should be remembered that nationally elderly people's incomes are low, so it does not follow that Bexhill's population is wealthy in comparison with the country's working age population; in fact compared with Bexhill's 10 per cent, (12) 42 per cent of all households in Britain in 1968 had gross incomes of over £30 a week. (13) It is important to make this point because, in discussions of the need for social services in the resorts, it is frequently said that people in places like Bexhill are too well-off to require publicly provided services. However, it can be argued further that elderly people usually have less financial obligations than younger people, especially with a family to support, so that it is inappropriate to compare retired

Chapter 10

couples' incomes with those of families. But Bexhill married couples had substantially lower incomes than all households consisting of one man and one woman; 13 per cent had over £30 compared with 33 per cent nationally. (14) But it may again be argued that younger couples are often paying heavy mortgages and saving for a future family. This is true but Bexhill married couples also had less income than outright owners of property nationally, of whom 35 per cent had over £30 a week and who in turn had less income than owners with mortgages. (15) It is clear, then, that in terms of income there is very little case for saying that the average retired person in one of the more 'exclusive' resorts is too affluent to require the sorts of services expected by the community generally.

However, it is often argued that, though they may have relatively low incomes, the capital assets of old people in resorts are so large that they should be used before any call is made on social services. In this survey, two questions were asked specifically about savings. These were, 'Do you have any savings or capital?' and 'Do you find that you are having to use your savings or capital to supplement your income?'

In Clacton, 84 per cent of the respondents said they had some capital, and in Bexhill, the proportion was even higher at 94 per cent. There was, however, an even larger difference between the towns in the amount of savings people had. (16) In Clacton the average amount was £1,067 and nearly half the people had less than £500. Only 5 per cent had over £5,000. In Bexhill, only a fifth had less than £500 and 33 per cent had over £5,000, the average being £5,224.

Also people in Clacton were more likely to be dipping into their already meagre savings; two-thirds said they were doing so compared with 42 per cent in Bexhill. They were using their capital not just for occasional luxuries but for routine bills such as the rates. Some of the people using their savings were still in their early 60s. This bodes ill for their financial situation in later old age. (17) It was those with least savings who were most frequently having to reduce them further. In Bexhill 58 per cent and in Clacton 73 per cent of those with less than £1,000 capital were using it up. Because of the relationship between low income and small savings, in both towns the highest income groups were the most likely to have large savings, and the least likely to need to draw on their capital. The poor, who most needed additional income from interest on capital, were continually reducing both.

Turning now to sources of income, the differences between Bexhill and Clacton again come out clearly. (18) Elderly people in Clacton were almost twice as likely as those in Bexhill to receive Supplementary Benefits; 7 per cent in Bexhill received them, compared with 13 per cent in Clacton. In addition, those in Bexhill were more likely to have additional sources of income besides their pension; 55 per cent in Bexhill, compared with 48 per cent in Clacton had superannuation on an occupational pension, 55 per cent compared with 35 per cent in Clacton had interest on capital and 15 per cent compared with 7 per cent had additional government pensions, mainly related to war service or previous employment in the army.

However, even more striking than the difference between the towns, was the relationship between sex, marital status and source of income. Women were much more likely than men or married couples to get Supplementary Benefits. In Bexhill, five times the proportion of women as men received them; in Clacton, a little under three times as many, reflecting the lower incomes of married couples in that town. Women were also far less likely than men to be receiving superannuation, or, in Bexhill, forms of government pension other than the old age pension. They were, however, slightly more likely to have income from rent, though only a small proportion even of women (11 per cent in Bexhill; 6 per cent in Clacton) received rents. Women were also more likely to have help from relatives. The replies about help from relatives probably under-estimated the number of old people who were receiving any financial help at all, as some were helped in kind, such as telephone installation. Also, people may have omitted to mention help if it were not regular income, but rather in the form of infrequent or irregular gifts.

The most common sources of additional income were superannuation and interest on savings. In terms of a continuing income, savings are particularly crucial for women in that their husbands' occupational pensions usually stop on widowhood. In only a fifth of the cases in Clacton and 40 per cent of the cases in Bexhill were widows receiving superannuation although more than half of the married couples were. The unsatisfactory position concerning occupational pensions for widows has been stressed in the national context: 'In view of the relative poverty of women over retirement age the question of the transference of pension rights to widows in private occupational schemes is clearly an extremely important one.' (19) The difference between Bexhill and Clacton in the proportion of people receiving superannuation is explained by the greater frequency of occupational pensions amongst the professional and managerial classes.

It is worthwhile looking more closely at those with the lowest incomes, first, those receiving Supplementary Benefits (7 per cent of respondents in Bexhill and 13 per cent in Clacton). One feature which distinguished them from others in the same income bracket was that they were less likely to have any savings; in Bexhill only 73 per cent and in Clacton 65 per cent had any savings at all. Also the savings they did have were smaller than average for people in the two resorts in that income group; in Bexhill they averaged £806 and in Clacton £346. However, it should be remembered that in the cross-national survey it was found that 30 per cent of all couples, 35 per cent of men and 41 per cent of women heads of households had no assets at all. (20) This was, admittedly, in 1962, but it does show that the people interviewed in Clacton, and even more so in Bexhill, were better off in terms of savings than the national average.

Those receiving Supplementary Benefits were, however, a minority even of those in the lowest income brackets; only a quarter of those with incomes of £7.50 or less had Supplementary Benefits. The other people must either have failed to apply for help, or must have been ineligible for some reason, probably having too much capital or being just above the income limits. According to managers of Social Security offices in the resorts, it is still extraordinarily difficult to persuade older retired people to claim benefits to which they are entitled. (21) Frequently, they insist on using up all their small savings before applying for help, whereas had they received a supplementary pension earlier, they could have kept their savings for an emergency.

To conclude, the financial situations of the retired people in the two resorts were rather different. In Bexhill they were better off than the national average for retired people but in Clacton they were probably slightly poorer than average in terms of income but with fewer people in the very lowest income groups. In both resorts elderly people were more likely than the average to have some savings, however small.

However, the situation of old people even in Bexhill gives no cause for complacency. Women, even from the professional and managerial classes, had low incomes, and very old women had the lowest incomes of all.

The main point to make is that though a couple may start their retirement with adequate income, supplemented on occasion by dipping into their savings, as the years go by this situation deteriorates. The value of their money falls and their savings diminish. In particular, widows usually find themselves substantially worse off after the death of their husband as occupational pensions schemes are either not transferred to the widow or are substantially reduced. The position in Clacton is particularly worrying because the retired people there have very small savings and most have already started to use these up at the beginning of their retirement. Their incomes are also low. In a few years Clacton will find there is a major problem of poverty, particularly in relation to the upkeep of owner-occupied houses. At present the younger retired people who have come in the last few years still dominate the town numerically but in a few years a large number of these will have much reduced incomes whilst facing the difficulties of advancing old age. In Bexhill the proportion likely to meet real hardship is very much smaller, but many even there will be operating tight budgets. That seems to be an inescapable feature of old age in Britain.

11   The present retirement home

> Ah, yet, e'er I descent to th' grave
> May I a small house, and a large garden have!
>   Abraham Cowley: The Mistress

The stereotyped view of a retirement home as being a 'bungalow by the sea' was certainly fulfilled by the results of the survey, particularly in Clacton, where 70 per cent of the retired people interviewed lived in bungalows, compared with 44 per cent in Bexhill. (1) In England and Wales in 1963 only 6 per cent of households lived in bungalows. In Bexhill 30 per cent of the retired people lived in houses rather than bungalows or flats, compared with 19 per cent in Clacton.

In both towns there has been a growing trend towards bungalow building. Only 3 per cent of the dwellings in the sample which were built before 1919 were bungalows. Of the inter-war dwellings, 56 per cent in Clacton and 22 per cent in Bexhill were bungalows, but 84 per cent of post-war dwellings in Clacton and 61 per cent in Bexhill were bungalows. There has been a parallel but, in Clacton particularly, much smaller trend towards flats, most of which have been built since 1945.

In Bexhill, 25 per cent of retired households lived in flats, compared with only 8 per cent in Clacton. In both towns, 2 per cent were living in unconverted rooms. The big difference between the two towns in the proportion of flats was most striking in the case of converted flats (16 per cent in Bexhill compared with 4 per cent in Clacton), but there were also more people living in purpose-built flats in Bexhill (9 per cent compared with 4 per cent).

Contrary to expectation more of the elderly people living in flats in Bexhill owned them rather than rented them; 57 per cent owned, 40 per cent rented privately, and

3 per cent rented from the council. The proportion of owner-occupiers in converted flats was lower than in purpose-built flats but, at 49 per cent, was still surprisingly high. In Clacton, 18 of the 39 people living in flats were owner-occupiers (46 per cent), 19 rented privately (44 per cent) and the other 2 (10 per cent) rented from the council. Unlike those in Bexhill, people living in converted flats rarely owned their home; only 2 out of 19 did so. Nearly all the bungalows and houses were owner-occupied; 97 per cent in Bexhill and 96 per cent in Clacton.

The property occupied by the retired people in Bexhill was generally larger than that in Clacton; 27 per cent in Bexhill had five or more rooms, excluding bathroom and kitchen, compared with only 18 per cent in Clacton. It was the inter-war housing in Bexhill which was particularly large. It was in this period that the bulk of the houses, as opposed to bungalows, were built and in both towns houses were considerably larger than bungalows and flats. Two-thirds of the houses had five or more rooms whereas over 80 per cent of the bungalows had only three or four. But bungalows in Bexhill were larger than bungalows in Clacton, and houses in Bexhill were larger than houses in Clacton.

OPINIONS ABOUT THE SIZE OF HOUSES AND ABOUT MAINTENANCE PROBLEMS

One of the most widely recognised housing problems of elderly people, particularly owner-occupiers, is the maintenance of large accommodation, which they are neither strong enough to maintain themselves nor can afford to pay to have maintained. To follow up this point, the elderly people in the two resorts were asked about their satisfaction with the size of their house, their general satisfaction with it and whether or not they had maintenance problems. As expected, they were much more likely to say their house was too large (12 per cent in Bexhill and 9 per cent in Clacton) than that it was too small (3 per cent in both). However, it would be wrong to overstress the complaints about size, since the vast majority (85 per cent in Bexhill and 87 per cent in Clacton) said they were satisfied with the size of their house. These included very many people whose house might seem rather large, for instance two-thirds of those with five or more rooms.

If the replies of people living alone are analysed separately, the results in the two towns are still remarkably similar. Though 23 per cent of people living alone

in Bexhill compared with 17 per cent in Clacton found
their accommodation too large, the difference is partly
explained by the larger size of the accommodation in
which those in Bexhill lived. There was, however, some
suggestion that people who lived with others were more
likely in Clacton than Bexhill to find their house too
large if it had five or more rooms. This was in spite of
the fact that in Bexhill houses were larger (more had six
or more rooms) and married couples in Clacton were
younger. Perhaps these two factors were offset by the
higher incomes in Bexhill which allowed people to employ
domestic help: 16 per cent of Bexhill retired people had
private domestic help compared with only 3 per cent in
Clacton.

   Older people were more likely than younger ones to
find their houses too large. Of those aged 80 and over,
23 per cent in Bexhill and 18 per cent in Clacton found
their houses too large. This compares with 9 per cent in
Bexhill and 8 per cent in Clacton of those aged under 70
and 11 per cent and 10 per cent aged 70-9. Widowed
people were also particularly likely to find their houses
too large; 26 per cent in Bexhill and 18 per cent in
Clacton said this, compared with only 9 per cent and 8
per cent of married people. Single people were the least
likely to be worried by the size of their accommodation.
Only 8 per cent in Bexhill and 4 per cent in Clacton
found it too large. This means that in both towns the
bulk of the people living alone, who also found their
accommodation too large, were widowed.

   In Bexhill, 27 per cent of respondents, and in Clacton
36 per cent, said they had problems with the maintenance
of their homes. The main worry turned out to be the
garden, not the house. In Bexhill, 73 per cent and in
Clacton 77 per cent of those with problems mentioned their
gardens. This far outstripped any of the other complaints.
As one man aptly put it, 'The garden seems to get larger
and larger every year', or a woman, 'The garden is a
nightmare'. Sometimes the problem was put in financial
terms - the inability to pay a gardener or the cost of
having one. One married couple in Bexhill said, 'The
garden is getting too much for us. We have spent over
£200 on it since 1960.' Some people said that it was
impossible to get a reliable gardener even if you could
afford one. No wonder that there is now a flourishing
firm of gardening contractors who advertise as follows:
'Is your garden a burden or a delight? Do you realise
that ... can make your garden easier to run, yet in its
simplicity a place of greater beauty and enjoyment.'

   The problem of managing housework was the next most

common complaint, but this was mentioned by only 13 per cent of those with problems in Bexhill and 17 per cent in Clacton. It was closely followed by the more general categories, 'financial problems' (11 per cent in Bexhill and 14 per cent in Clacton) and 'health problems' (6 per cent in Bexhill and 9 per cent in Clacton), which of course overlap with the first two.

Though financial problems were sometimes related to the difficulty of maintaining the garden, they were more commonly associated with the cost of decorations and repairs. Poor health was also mentioned in this context because it was preventing many people from continuing with the 'do-it-yourself' efforts in which they had taken such pride and they could not afford to pay professionals to keep the house up to the same standard. Apart from the strain caused to the health of elderly people by attempts to keep up large gardens and to do their own repairs and decorations, and apart from the financial burden of paying for help, great distress is caused to elderly couples when they are forced to watch their long-dreamed-about retirement house and garden deteriorate. Frequently, it is the widow who can no longer keep the garden 'as my husband would have liked it'.

Naturally it was the very old and the least wealthy who were the most likely to be in difficulty. Of those aged 80 and over, 36 per cent in Bexhill and 53 per cent in Clacton said they had maintenance problems, compared with 31 per cent and 39 per cent of those aged 70-9, and 19 per cent and 29 per cent aged under 70. Similarly of those with incomes up to £7.50, half mentioned maintenance problems compared with a quarter of those with incomes of over £15.

Women heads of retired households were more likely than men to mention maintenance problems. This was not just a function of their greater age, because the difference between their replies was maintained within age groups. Older women are frequently unable to carry out or pay for jobs which men of their own age could do themselves or pay for. Widows' incomes are substantially lower than those of married couples of a similar age, which explains their inability to pay for outside help. Their difficulty in doing the jobs themselves is a matter of common observation; old men are much more likely to tackle heavy gardening and decorating than are their wives. Having always done these tasks they continue to do so even when it is a physical struggle. When they die, their widows are faced with starting to do tasks for which they have had little practice. In these circumstances, the gardening, particularly lawn-mowing, is liable to become a 'nightmare'. It is worth noting, too, that gardening, being something that needs constant attention, is the job with which relatives, living at a distance, are least likely to be able to help. Similarly, it is a greater imposition to ask neighbours to help in this way than to ask them for emergency help, such as mending a fuse or a one-off task such as hanging some curtains.

Though women in both towns were more likely than men to mention maintenance problems, women in Clacton were much more likely to do so than were women in Bexhill. The proportions were 30 per cent in Bexhill and 56 per cent in Clacton. The difference between the towns was maintained within age groups; in any age group Clacton women were more likely to mention maintenance problems. There are several possible explanations for this: first, in Bexhill many more of the women were single, and single women were much less likely to mention maintenance problems. Single women had long had to adjust their way of life to what they themselves could manage. They were not faced with sudden widowhood which left them stranded. Some of them experienced something similar when a parent or friend died, or when they left an institution in which they had lived and worked, but these situations were not as common as widowhood. Second, but linked with the first point, many more of the Bexhill women, particularly the single ones, lived in flats without gardens and were also less likely to complain of the dwelling itself being too large. Third, the incomes of women in Bexhill were much higher than in Clacton and they were therefore more often able to afford domestic help and a gardener.

Widowed men are more likely to find difficulty with housework than widowed women are. (In some places, the home help service has recognised this problem, and has taken on the job of teaching newly widowed men to cook). But men are less likely than women to find themselves widowed and having to tackle unaccustomed tasks.

While there is this element of lack of practice, the fact remains that the problems of gardening, housework and decorating are brought about largely by old age and ill-health, while low incomes prevent the retired person from hiring services. Thus, 19 per cent of even all married couples and widowed and single men in Bexhill and 22 per cent in Clacton complained of problems with their gardens. In total, 25 per cent of the men in Bexhill and 30 per cent in Clacton complained of some sort of maintenance problem.

These replies about maintenance worries did not, however, give any idea of the severity of the problems. Were the difficulties so great, for instance, that the person concerned had become dissatisfied with the house? When the existence of maintenance problems was analysed by general satisfaction or dissatisfaction with the dwelling, it emerged that only 5 per cent in Bexhill and 13 per cent in Clacton of those who said they had maintenance problems were generally dissatisfied with their house. This compared with 2 per cent and 4 per cent of those who said they had no problems. Similarly, of those who thought their house was too large, 12 per cent in Bexhill and 15 per cent in Clacton said they were generally dissatisfied with it. So, because a fairly large proportion were experiencing certain difficulties with their house, it does not necessarily mean that many of them would be anxious to move.

The problem of maintenance is a general one for old people and the solution for owner-occupiers not at all easy to envisage, especially as the features, such as a large garden, which attract them in early retirement become problems in later old age. The situation is rather different in relation to council housing. A report on retired people who had moved out of council houses in London to GLC bungalows in Littlehampton summed up the situation as follows:

> The only problems that seem likely to arise are the requests of one partner to move nearer to relations after the death of the other partner and the inability of widows to cope with gardening as well as keeping their bungalows tidy as they grow older. These problems should easily be overcome with a flexible housing management and lettings policy. (2)

One is struck by the much greater suitability of such provision for old people than the position of owner-occupiers who have to fend for themselves all the time. Yet, in spite of these drawbacks about owning a house in old age, the vast majority of people did so in the two resorts; 85 per cent of retired people interviewed in Bexhill and 90 per cent in Clacton owned their house, flat or bungalow. It can be argued that they did so because they had no other alternative, but, in fact, 94 per cent of owners in Bexhill and 88 per cent in Clacton said they still preferred owner-occupation to renting; 81 per cent of tenants in Bexhill and 60 per cent in Clacton agreed with them. Only 10 per cent of tenants in Bexhill and none in Clacton said they preferred renting. The rest were unsure. So of all the elderly people, 92 per cent in Bexhill and 86 per cent in Clacton preferred buying and only 5 per cent and 8 per cent respectively renting.

We will now examine in more detail the characteristics of owner-occupation in Bexhill and Clacton.

Chapter 11

OWNER-OCCUPATION IN THE RESORTS

Though in both Bexhill and Clacton, owner-occupation was the order of day, not all types of households were equally likely to be owner-occupiers (Table 11.1). Married couples were more likely than other people to own their houses and, if they did not, they had an unfurnished tenancy from a private landlord or infrequently a local authority. Single and widowed people rented more frequently than did married couples. They were also more likely to be living in furnished accommodation, or with relatives or friends, sometimes rent-free.

TABLE 11.1 Tenure of dwelling, by marital status

	Bexhill			
	All	Married	Single	Widowed
Sample number	503	337	75	91
TENURE	%	%	%	%
Owner-occupiers	85	91	72	79
Rented privately unfurnished	11	9	17	16
Rented privately furnished	1	-	3	1
Rented from council and other	3	1	8	3
	Clacton			
Sample number	487	365	23	99
TENURE	%	%	%	%
Owner-occupiers	90	94	(83)	78
Rented privately unfurnished	5	4	(13)	8
Rented privately furnished	1	-	(4)	5
Rented from council and other	3	2	(-)	8

It was to be expected that widowed and particularly single people would own less often than married people. What is remarkable is that so many single people did own their house or flat. About four-fifths of single people in each town were owner-occupiers. In fact they were more likely to own their own houses than were all elderly people nationally; in 1971 45 per cent of people aged 60 and over were owner-occupiers. (3)

Tenure in Bexhill and Clacton was similarly related to household type. Those living with their spouse or with unmarried children were most likely to own. Of the people in Clacton who lived with married children, just under half owned the house themselves; in the other cases their child owned or rented it. Those least likely to own were people living alone or with relations other than their children.

Nationally there is a clear relationship between tenure and social class; whereas 52 per cent of all households in England and Wales were owner-occupiers in 1971, 85 per cent of those in Social Class I and 74 per cent in Class II owned their houses. (4) In Bexhill and Clacton there was some relationship between social class and tenure though in Clacton it was only the semi-skilled who appeared to own less frequently than other classes. However, these differences were slight compared with those associated with marital status and household type and the important point remains that in each social class in Bexhill and Clacton at least 70 per cent owned their homes, so even retired unskilled and semi-skilled workers in Bexhill and Clacton were almost as likely to own as were Classes I and II nationally.

Tenure was, in fact, much more closely related to income than to social class but only in that there was a point below which there was a sudden drop in owner-occupation and increase in private tenancies. This point was different in the two towns. In Bexhill less than 60 per cent of those with incomes of up to £10 owned their houses, compared with 75 per cent of those with up to £12.50 and 91 per cent of those with up to £15. In Clacton it was only those with £7.50 or less who were less likely to own. The main reason for the difference between the two towns is probably that prices in Bexhill were higher than in Clacton. In Bexhill, 60 per cent of owner-occupiers had paid £4,000 or more for their house, compared with 18 per cent in Clacton. (5) Of those who had bought a house in Bexhill in 1966 or later, 82 per cent had paid more than £4,000 compared with only 38 per cent in Clacton. With such vast differences in prices, the possibilities for lower income groups owning must clearly be much slighter in Bexhill than Clacton.

Of the people who did manage to buy, even those within the same income group, tended to have spent more on their house in Bexhill than in Clacton. In Bexhill even the lowest income groups had had to pay about £3,000 for a house, whereas in Clacton there had been much more property available below £2,000. For lower income people there may be an element of extravagance in deciding to move to Bexhill at all. In all income groups, Bexhill owners had consistently paid more for their homes. Of course for the wealthier people, Bexhill has a much bigger range of expensive housing. In Clacton even the highest income groups relatively seldom paid more than £5,000.

Houses in Bexhill were more expensive on average than bungalows and both were more expensive than flats, but there was also a greater range of types and prices of house, from the small terraced house to the palatial detached house in large grounds. In Clacton, where houses were newer and the stock more uniform, there was no significant difference in the prices of houses and bungalows; the median for houses was £2,973 and for bungalows £3,114. The flats, of which there were only eighteen in the sample, had a median of £3,623. The median price of houses in Bexhill was £4,667, compared with £4,409 for bungalows and £3,870 for flats.

Amongst the reasons that people gave for choosing to move to Bexhill and Clacton, house prices emerged as an important factor. A large proportion of those who moved to Clacton said they did so because of the relatively low price of houses there. They frequently mentioned having found the South Coast prohibitive in price. People who moved to Bexhill mentioned house prices much less often, but if they did, it was most frequently in relation to having tried to buy in Eastbourne. They said that in Eastbourne it was excessively expensive to buy property anywhere near the sea. (6)

To see how the prices in Clacton and Bexhill compared with those in Eastbourne, the 'asking prices' of more than 150 properties listed for sale by estate agents in Eastbourne in November 1969 were analysed. It must be remembered that these were 'asking prices' and that they were probably higher than the actual selling prices. The first striking point was that out of 108 bungalows advertised, only 30 (28 per cent) were in Eastbourne proper. The rest were either well inland or were further along the coast at such places as Pevensey Bay. Flats were much more common in Eastbourne itself. The prices of bungalows in the outlying areas were roughly comparable with those of recently bought property in Bexhill, but those in Eastbourne itself were considerably higher, mainly over £6,000. The leasehold prices of flats (median £5,389) were closely comparable with the prices of all recently bought property in Bexhill (median £5,273) but cost more than flats in Bexhill. Clearly, then, there was a strong downward gradient in price between Eastbourne, Bexhill and Clacton, as the comments of respondents had suggested, and there was also a scarcity of bungalows and houses near to Eastbourne town centre and the sea.

Another issue which is of relevance to the movement of elderly people to the retirement resorts, is the relationship between prices of property in the resorts and prices in the conurbations, particularly London. For instance, in 1969 the average purchase price of a dwelling in Greater London was £6,195. (7) So though prices in Bexhill were high in comparison with Clacton they still compared favourably with London, without even considering the quality of environment and housing. This was not the case for the other major cities. Average prices in the West Midlands, the most expensive of the other major urban areas, were lower than those along the Sussex coast. The average price of a house in the West Midlands in 1969 was £4,348.

At that time, the rapid escalation of house prices between 1971 and 1973 was yet to come. The effect was to more than double prices. By the end of 1974 the average price of a house in Greater London had risen to £14,890 and in the West Midlands to £10,118. (8) But the relative position of the Sussex coast remained much the same, and it continued to be the case that the price advantage which Londoners received in moving to the Sussex coast did not exist for people from the other great cities. This, besides geographical proximity and familiarity, may be an important factor in their choice of different retirement areas.

Turning now to current costs, as opposed to capital costs for owner-occupation, the most striking feature was that only 4 per cent of the owner-occupiers in Bexhill and 8 per cent in Clacton had taken out a mortgage or loan when they bought their present house. Most people (83 per cent in Bexhill and 81 per cent in Clacton) had raised most of the necessary capital through the sale of a house. Some had supplemented this with savings, a loan or help from relatives. About 10 per cent in each town used savings alone, but 23 per cent in Bexhill and 19 per cent in Clacton mentioned savings either alone or in conjunction with other sources of capital, such as the sale of a house.

In addition the mortgage or loans given were usually small in comparison with the total cost of the house. Half in each town had already been paid off by the time of the survey. (9) The remaining loans were too few in number for much to be said about them, except that most entailed repayments of less than £15 a month, and the average was £10.

Those people who did not own their last house before their retirement move, were more likely to have had a loan of some sort, though savings were still their most important source of capital. However, more than a third of even these people in Bexhill had raised the money by selling a house they had owned at some time previously. Of course this may have been property that they owned and rented to other people rather than a house which they had lived in themselves. In Clacton, those who did not own just before their move were much less likely to say they had raised money by selling a house. The only exceptions were those who were living with relations. Clearly this had been either a temporary measure or a solution to retirement which had not worked.

One remark frequently made about the people retiring to resorts is that they rashly spend all their savings on a house and fittings and leave themselves none to rely upon later. The implication is that they should buy cheaper property and keep more savings in reserve. The evidence of this survey is not good enough to deal adequately with the point about injudicious buying. There is certainly no positive evidence that the people buying expensive houses were cutting more deeply into their savings than those buying cheaper ones. Those with the cheapest houses were the least likely to have savings and were the most likely to be using up what they had. However, this must be partly related to their age, in that those who bought longest ago will have bought most cheaply and also have used up their savings in a long retirement. It is, of course, possible that in all the income brackets there is a tendency to under-estimate recurring costs and hence the income and savings required for a comfortable retirement. They may therefore have a tendency to buy an over-ambitious house.

We have already seen that many were worried by the effort and expense of maintaining their house and garden adequately. Two other items of expenditure which may present problems are rates, and for leaseholders, ground rent.

There were only 7 leaseholders among the Clacton owner-occupiers, compared with 40 in Bexhill, reflecting the greater number of flats in Bexhill. Ground rents were usually between £10 and £20 a year but there were some of less than £10 and one or two much higher, even over £50.

Rates were much higher in Bexhill than in Clacton. A third of the Bexhill owner-occupiers paid £100 or more a

year, and only 6 per cent paid less than £50. In
Clacton, the figures were reversed; 32 per cent of owner-
occupiers paid less than £50 and only 2 per cent more
than £100. (10)

In both towns houses had higher rates than did bungalows, and purpose-built flats higher than either. (11)
In Bexhill 56 per cent of the purpose-built flats had
rates of over £100 a year and in Clacton 25 per cent did;
this compared with 37 per cent and 15 per cent of the
houses. This is important as there is a tendency to think
that smaller accommodation is cheaper and that as people
get older and need to cut down on maintenance problems and
on costs, a smaller flat or bungalow may be the solution.
In fact, higher rates for flats may be a deterrent to such
a move. Even considering all types of property, there was
little saving in rates by moving from larger to smaller
housing. For instance, in Bexhill the median rates paid
by owner-occupiers for three-roomed, four-roomed and five-
roomed dwellings were £79, £82, and £90. In Clacton they
were £55, £58 and £68. Such small savings would hardly
warrant the cost of moving.

There was a close relationship between high income and
high rates. For instance, 68 per cent of owner-occupiers
in Bexhill with incomes of £30 and more paid more than
£100 in rates. However, at the lower end of the income
scale there was clear evidence of people paying extraordinary proportions of their income on rates. In Bexhill,
of those with incomes of up to £15 a week, 16 per cent
were paying £100 a year or more in rates and 36 per cent
were paying £80 or more. In Clacton only 1 per cent of
those with incomes of up to £15 a week paid £100 or more,
though 5 per cent did pay £80 or more. However, because
incomes were so low in Clacton, rates represented just as
great a proportion of income as they did in Bexhill. In
many cases, particularly in the lower income groups, rates
represented as much as 20 per cent of incomes and were
usually at least 10 per cent. (12) (13)

These figures refer to the amount of rates actually
paid, after any rebate had been deducted. Additional
questions were asked about applications for rebates. In
our survey, 12 per cent of owner-occupiers in Bexhill and
37 per cent in Clacton said they received a rate rebate.
It should be remembered that, in addition, those who
receive Supplementary Benefits usually have their rates
paid by the Supplementary Benefits Commission. The
proportions receiving Supplementary Benefits were in
Bexhill 7 per cent and in Clacton 13 per cent.

At almost all levels of rates paid retired people in
Clacton were more likely to be receiving rate rebates than

were those in Bexhill. They were also more likely to have applied for one. Much more important, though, the same was true at comparable income levels; at a given income level, people in Bexhill were less likely to have a rebate although for a given level of income they were paying more rates. There seems to have been no significant difference between the two towns in the numbers within each income group who had applied for rebates, so the difference must be ascribed to the larger amounts of capital saved by the Bexhill retired people. A certain amount of savings is disregarded, but beyond this the applicant becomes ineligible.

TENANTS

Although the vast majority of retired people in Bexhill and Clacton were owner-occupiers, a minority of 12 per cent in Bexhill and 6 per cent in Clacton were renting privately, mostly unfurnished flats and rooms. Only 1 per cent of the retired people interviewed in Bexhill and Clacton lived in local authority housing. Residential qualifications handicap them in getting on to waiting lists but fundamentally the problem is that local authority housing is very scarce in the resorts and there are other demands upon it. In Bexhill and Clacton in 1966 less than 10 per cent of households of all ages lived in local authority housing, compared with a quarter nationally. In addition the retired people who move to the town are regarded, often rightly (but not always), as being more affluent and better housed than local elderly people and, in some cases, too snobbish to consider council housing anyway. Besides, in most towns owner-occupiers are not accepted on housing waiting lists or, at best, are put on reserve lists.

Although they were few in number the private renters deserve attention because of the conditions in which they were living, particularly those who rented rooms. As mentioned earlier, most renters are single and widowed people, particularly widowed women. To supplement the information obtained about the small number of renters in the sample, an analysis was made of the situation of the elderly applicants on the Bexhill Housing Register. This information, though obviously skewed towards bad accommodation, is relevant because a very large proportion of these applicants had moved to the town at or after retirement. It is often argued that people who retire to seaside resorts are not the sort of people who put their names on housing waiting lists. Although this may be true

of the majority, it is also the case that 46 per cent of
all the elderly applicants on the Bexhill housing register
in August 1969 had moved to Bexhill when they were 60 or
more and 55 per cent when 55 and more. This in spite of
the fact that owner-occupiers were not accepted on the
ordinary waiting list for old people's housing and 85 per
cent of the retired people interviewed in Bexhill were
owner-occupiers.

The vast majority (86 per cent) of those who were on
the waiting list and who had moved to the town when they
were 60 or over had been in the town less than ten years
before they put their name down on the housing register.
Probably the most interesting feature is that 32 per cent
had been in the town only one or two years before they
registered. These people had never had adequate accommodation in the town, whereas those who applied after five
years or more were more likely to have suffered a deterioration in their circumstances. In fact, reading some of
the case histories, it was alarming to find instances of
people in their late 70s and 80s moving down to Bexhill
to live in a bed-sitting room in a large rooming house.
Immediately they realised their mistake and put their
names down for better housing but they were competing
with very many people. In addition, by moving they had
usually disqualified themselves for local authority
housing in the area from which they had come.

Not all the elderly applicants were desperately in
need of better accommodation, but it was apparent from
reading through the cases that the bulk were living in
conditions which were extremely unsuitable for old
people. It is worth quoting some of these.

> Case 1 We are still anxious to find somewhere to live.
> I retired from London in July 1949. I am now nearly
> 85 years of age and going through a very rough period.
> We pay £6 weekly rent here and about £1.50 a week for
> heating, etc. I was compelled to book the place in
> April 1966 as my wife was coming out of hospital at
> that time. We have no chance to save anything and the
> prospect of spending another winter here is daunting.

This case was referred by the Department of Health and
Social Security when they discovered that the couple could
not manage their rent and there were also medical reasons
why they should not be living on a top floor. The
desperation underlying the restrained tone of the letters
comes through all too clearly.

> Case 2 A couple living on a top floor were referred
> by their doctor: 'I should be grateful if these
> patients of mine could be considered for ground floor
> accommodation they can afford, as the husband (aged 74)

has osteo-arthritis of the spine and now also gets very breathless from emphysema and pre-cordial pain climbing the 62 stairs to their present flat. The couple have lived in Bexhill for the past eight years at various addresses. They moved to Bexhill from London in order to retire. Their present rent is £4.25p per week and their income £860 gross.'

An examination on behalf of the housing department found that the wife (aged 71) also had arthritis of the leg. Tradesmen did not call at the flat but left everything on the ground floor. The dustbin was also on the ground floor. Neighbours helped but the couple had not been out of the flat for three months because of difficulty with the stairs.

Case 3 Another couple aged 72 and 70 had never really unpacked their belongings because of the conditions in which they found themselves when they arrived. They had come along the coast from Bournemouth, to which they had originally retired. 'We were promised a flat in Bexhill before coming here but ended up with two rooms, one on the ground floor and one on the first floor in the middle of a house. The room where we eat has still got packed cases in it and we are very unhappy. Our furniture is in a shed going mildew.'

Seven months later they had moved to a four-roomed flat with a kitchen, but one bedroom and one living room were unusable because of the damp. Their income, including Supplementary Benefits was just under £9 and the rent was £3.50. They described the flat as follows:

'The wall is crumbling with damp and there is no gas to cook. I had to buy a small electric stove which stands on the table. My Sunday lunch I cook in a neighbour's house. When my husband was ill in the winter, he had to go outside for the lavatory and the steps he has to climb to bring a bucket of coal up to the house are nobody's business. I have not unpacked some of our things in the hope that I shall see another flat. The last people here left the house in such a bad condition, I cannot find the money to make it habitable. We have made two rooms and a kitchen presentable just so we can call it home.'

This seems a world away from the retirement 'dream house'.

Of course, such conditions are common enough in every town in Britain, but it is necessary to make the point that they do also exist in the retirement resorts and that it is, contrary to local belief, often people who have moved to retire there who are experiencing them. It is clear that though in many respects housing in the resorts is more suitable for elderly people than that found elsewhere, there is a minority in great need of better housing, who cannot without help afford decent private provision.

In both Bexhill and Clacton, people who were renting privately had incomes well below the average for retired people in the two towns. For instance, in Bexhill 27 per cent and in Clacton 41 per cent of private renters had incomes up to £7.50 a week. This compares with 11 per cent of all retired households in Bexhill and 23 per cent in Clacton. In fact the overwhelming problem for private tenants was that of low incomes in relation to rents. Of the single and widowed people who applied for accommodation in Bexhill, 52 per cent had incomes of less than £7.50 a week. These were almost entirely women and may be compared with the interviewed single and widowed women of whom 31 per cent had incomes of less than £7.50. As the rent for even the worst unselfcontained accommodation was usually about £3 a week in Bexhill, rent levels were bound to play a large part in bringing applicants on to the housing register.

Rents were considerably higher in Bexhill than they were in Clacton. This held true for all types of flats and rooms, in so far as one can tell from the extremely small numbers. Bexhill tenants paid a median rent of £4.15 a week and 16 per cent paid £6 and more. (14) Clacton tenants paid a median rent of £3.42 but none paid £6 or more a week. The rents paid by elderly people who were on the Bexhill housing register were lower. The median was £3.15. This was only to be expected because they lived in worse conditions.

The rental market in the resorts responds to the demand from old people for ground-floor accommodation, by making ground-floor flats the most expensive. The cheapest are in the attics. (In fact most of the 'ground-floor' flats are also up a flight of at least five or six steps.) Because of poor health it is often impossible for an old person to move to a cheaper flat without becoming housebound. It is interesting in this connection to note that in Bexhill 18 per cent of people living in converted flats or rooms in Bexhill said they had trouble with going up stairs; in Clacton the proportion was 41 per cent. This compares with only 10 per cent of those living in houses and bungalows in Bexhill and 23 per cent in Clacton.

In all, the situation of retired people in privately rented housing in the two resorts left much to be desired. Those in expensive flats were, on fixed incomes, exceedingly vulnerable to inflation of rents and rates. Those in the older type of converted flat or rooms were usually living in conditions which were particularly unsuitable for old people, and the rents for even that accommodation were high in relation to the low incomes of the occupants.

The problem was exacerbated by the exceedingly small provision of local authority housing for the elderly in resort areas. The view that people who retire to the coast have no need or desire for council housing is not borne out by an analysis of the applicants for old people's housing and, were owner-occupiers also eligible, it is likely that the difficulties which many had with maintenance and rates would be given expression by applications for rehousing by the local authority.

Since this survey was carried out the position of people in private rented accommodation has potentially changed because of the introduction of rent allowances. One says 'potentially' because of the difficulty of ensuring that those who are eligible for help with their rent come forward for it. The elderly are a group who, in the past, have, notoriously, failed to obtain their rights in this respect, sometimes out of ignorance, other times out of pride. This situation appears to be changing but it is worth noting, for instance, that though their incomes were low only 8 per cent of tenants in Clacton and 14 per cent in Bexhill had claimed rate rebates. If the rent allowances are to make a favourable impact on the situation of elderly tenants in the resorts, a very deliberate and continuing drive will be required by the local authorities and by voluntary groups.

PERMANENT RESIDENTS IN HOTELS AND BOARDING HOUSES

Another group of elderly people whose situation deserves special attention is the group living in hotels and guest houses. Though small relative to the whole retired population, the total numbers in certain resorts are large.

According to the 1971 Census, there were 255 people of pensionable age living as resident guests in Bexhill on 25-6 April 1971. They outnumbered the elderly visitor guests at that time of year, who totalled only 80. (15) In relation to their size, Bexhill and Worthing (with 660) had the largest proportions of elderly people living in hotels of all the Sussex resorts. In Clacton, there were only 65 resident guests of pensionable age at the time of the 1971 Census, compared with 240 visitor guests of that age. The South Coast is apparently more popular for hotel-living amongst elderly people than is the East Coast. Devon too is popular, but there the number of non-resident guests is much larger than in Sussex, reflecting the more flourishing state of the tourist industry in Devon.

In the hotels women of pensionable age outnumber the men by more than two to one. In addition, resident guests of pensionable age, in most resorts, vastly outnumber younger resident guests. In Bexhill 255 out of 275 resident guests were of pensionable age, and in Clacton 65 out of 105. It is apparent that hotels are performing some of the functions of old people's residential homes.

To examine this point further, a short questionnaire was sent to hotel and boarding house proprietors in Bexhill and Clacton, asking them about their resident guests. In addition a limited number of interviews were carried out with resident guests in hotels in Bexhill, Clacton and Eastbourne. These were by no means a random sample but they gave some indications of the reasons why elderly people move into hotels.

Of the guests in hotels in Bexhill and Clacton, (16) 78 per cent were widowed or single women, 17 per cent were widowed men and the remaining 5 per cent only were married couples. The census also showed that in Bexhill and Clacton there was a particularly small proportion of men living in hotels, even compared with other resorts, but it is a general feature that very few married couples live in hotels, in the same way that few live in old people's homes.

From the interviews in Bexhill, Clacton and Eastbourne it appeared that reasons for moving into a hotel were very distinct as between single, widowed and married people. The single people said they had never been used to living alone. Some had lived with elderly parents. Others had been used to living in institutions, schools and hospitals for instance, were used to a communal style of life, and unused to doing housework.

The widowed and married people, on the other hand, moved in to rid themselves of the commitments of keeping up a house and because their health had broken down. One couple, of whom the wife had osteo-arthritis, had moved to the hotel because domestic help had proved difficult to find and unreliable when found. The widowed also came to avoid the loneliness of living alone. One woman said she neither wanted to live with her daughter nor alone.

The distinction between these two groups is interesting from a policy point of view. The widowed and married people would be the most likely to respond to a policy of support in the home. The single people on the other hand were frequently totally unused to living outside an institutional establishment and did not wish to start catering for themselves. Between the two were those, some

single and some widowed, who needed company and some
support but who would probably have found this adequately
in a form of grouped housing such as local authorities or
housing associations provide. However, though this might
have been a solution when they made their original
decision to move to a hotel, by the time of the survey
most were very old and long unused to catering for themselves. More than half had lived in that particular
hotel about five years and nearly all the rest about three,
and some had lived in a number of other hotels previously.

Of course living in a hotel is not a solution which is
open to many, because it is so expensive. The weekly
charges for permanent residents in the seventeen hotels
and boarding houses in Bexhill and Clacton which replied
to this enquiry in 1969 ranged from £6 to £25 in winter
and from £7.50 to £25 in the summer. The winter mean
charge was £12.75 and the summer £15.50. This was not
more expensive than paying for a similar range of services
in one's own home, but not many people would be in a
financial position to consider having even a few of these
services, such as domestic help and a cook, even if they
could find them. The people interviewed in hotels mostly
had relatively large incomes and were from the professional
and managerial classes, but this was not a random sample
and the incomes reflected the places in which they were
interviewed. The two women who lived in low-priced
boarding houses had low incomes, under £10 a week. In
spite of relatively high incomes most of the people in
hotels were apprehensive about their financial position
in face of rapidly rising hotel charges. Some said that
though they could manage when they arrived, the charges
had risen several times since then. Further increases
would mean that they would have to leave. They did not
know where they would go. The fact that rent allowances
for furnished accommodation are likely to apply to
permanent residents in hotels will be a help, as long as
the old people are not disqualified on grounds of having
too much capital. As they rely heavily for income on the
interest from their capital this aspect of means testing
falls hard on the elderly.

Several mentioned other difficulties they had experienced with hotels, particularly the difficulty of having
to leave if the hotel closed in winter or wanted to take
holiday-makers in the summer. (17) A very old woman
said that in a previous hotel it was 'such a bore being
moved out in summer time'; she had stayed there six
years up to the age of 84, each year having to find somewhere else in the summer. This problem of elderly people
being moved out in the summer is still a very real one in

all the places that have a substantial trade for holiday guests, conference visitors and foreign students. The Eastbourne Medical Officer of Health finds this problem every year, and occasionally has to take elderly people made homeless in this way into Part III homes. In Bexhill the problem is minimal because of the lack of tourist trade now.

Despite these worries, all the people interviewed in hotels said they were satisfied with living there. The reasons they gave for liking the hotel matched their reasons for going there, namely to find company, warmth and service. However, there were in no way a representative sample. In particular, cheap boarding houses were under-represented. Also, as interviews could take place only with the permission of the hotel proprietor, they were bound to be a biased sample, because proprietors did not let interviewers see those whom they said were very old, sick or senile.

The proprietors themselves were not at all convinced of the suitability of hotels and boarding houses as accommodation for elderly people. Their main worry was that most people came into hotels because of infirmity but hotels, without nursing staff, were not equipped to look after the sick. Also, the demands made on hotel staff by elderly people were very great and in most small establishments this burden fell on the proprietor and his wife year in and year out. They thought, too, a large proportion of permanent elderly residents discouraged other younger guests and that if there were very old and sick people in the hotel it was difficult to maintain standards of cleanliness and service which would satisfy holiday guests.

Because of these difficulties most hotels had rules about how long they would allow an elderly person to stay if they became ill and could not afford a private nurse.

'We care for them so long as they can get to the bathroom and back.'

'Residents move to nursing homes when they cannot look after themselves or otherwise stay in their rooms with a nurse.'

The rules may seem harsh, especially when one considers the anxiety that elderly people in hotels must feel about falling ill, but it is well to remember that any other policy may involve a hotel proprietor in a scale of nursing for which the establishment is unsuitable. The unsuitability of hotels for residents who need nursing care is especially great if the proprietors are themselves elderly, which is often the case. Unable to engage staff so that they themselves could have a holiday, some of the elderly proprietors who wrote in reply to this enquiry had not had a proper break for twenty years. The health of one woman nursing eight over-80 year olds, had completely collapsed.

Of course most hotels do not take in elderly people out of kindness. It is a thriving business. In Clacton, where the hotel trade is still alive, relatively few hotels take elderly residents but they do expand their season by providing off-peak pensioners' holidays. Along the South Coast, however, staying holiday-makers are in a minority now and caravans and chalets have increasingly replaced hotels and boarding houses. Most of the visitors are day visitors.

In these circumstances, it is natural that hotel owners should recognize elderly people as their new area of business. Given the fact that any form of private sheltered housing is virtually unobtainable, and that old people's homes are very variable in quality and often regarded with distaste, hotels are bound to appear an attractive solution to old people who can afford them. Whether they are suited to performing this role is quite another matter.

CONCLUSIONS - RETIREMENT HOUSING

In Bexhill there was more variety of property, and, in particular, there were more purpose-built flats than in Clacton, where 70 per cent of the retired people lived in bungalows. The property in Bexhill was also larger than that in Clacton, even for equivalent types of dwelling such as bungalows.

Twelve per cent of retired people in Bexhill and 9 per cent in Clacton said their houses were too large, compared with 85 per cent and 87 per cent who said they were satisfied with the size. However, there were certain groups who much more frequently found their housing too large; for instance those living alone (23 per cent in Bexhill and 17 per cent in Clacton), the over-80s (23 per cent in Bexhill and 18 per cent in Clacton) and widows (26 per cent in Bexhill and 18 per cent in Clacton).

In Bexhill, 27 per cent and in Clacton 36 per cent of all retired people said they had maintenance problems with their homes. The main worry was the garden. In Bexhill 73 per cent and in Clacton 77 per cent of those who said they had maintenance problems mentioned their gardens. Widowed women were particularly likely to be worried about their gardens and other housing maintenance jobs; however, a fifth of the men were worried about maintenance too.

In spite of the problems of being an owner-occupier in old age, 85 per cent of retired people in Bexhill and 90 per cent in Clacton were owner-occupiers. Of these 94 per cent in Bexhill and 88 per cent in Clacton said they still preferred owner-occupation to renting. A majority of tenants agreed with them. Nationally, less than 50 per cent of people aged 60 and over are owner-occupiers.

House prices in Bexhill were much higher than those in Clacton, but lower than those in Eastbourne where there was a scarcity of property near the sea. Though prices were high on the South Coast, they still compared favourably with those in London. However, all the other conurbations had lower prices than the South Coast did, so it was not as easy for retiring people to move from these areas to the South Coast, hence, one reason for their choice of other retirement resorts.

Very few owners still had outstanding mortgages or loans on their houses. Only 5 per cent in Bexhill and 10 per cent in Clacton had taken out one when they moved and half of these had paid it off.

Rates were much higher in Bexhill than in Clacton. In Bexhill a third of owner-occupiers were paying £100 or more a year. In Clacton only 2 per cent paid this amount. Rates for purpose-built flats were higher than for bungalows and houses. In Bexhill fewer people received rate rebates, even though the rates were so high. Some were paying as much as 20 per cent of their income on rates.

The conditions under which private tenants lived in the resorts were often exceedingly unsuitable for old people, and the Bexhill waiting list had many hard cases, about half of them people who had moved to the resort to retire. Poor health, low incomes in relation to rents and lack of any capital were the overwhelming problems. In Bexhill rents were much higher than those in Clacton. The demand for property with a minimum of stairs is reflected in price differentials between ground-floor and first-, second- and third-floor flats. It is, therefore, by no means the fittest, but often the oldest, sickest and poorest who have the top flats.

One solution adopted by some elderly people was to live permanently in a hotel or boarding house. Charges for good hotel accommodation were high and rising rapidly with wage increases for staff. In some resorts there was also the problem of being evicted in summer. Most hotels had rules about the need for a resident to move out if they fell sick. In spite of these problems, the hotels did provide company, warmth, service and freedom from the problems of housekeeping and maintenance, which were appreciated by the residents. Except in name many differed little from old people's homes.

Chapter 11

In the resorts there is naturally much more property suitable for retired people than there is in any other type of town. The availability of relatively small bungalows with gardens has been one of the attractions of the resorts. However, there is still a problem of lack of variety of accommodation, particularly lack of accommodation suitable for the very old and more frail.

The fact that nearly a quarter of widows, the very old and those living alone in Bexhill and Clacton found their houses too large and that between a third and a half of all very old people and widowed women had trouble with their gardens, shows the need for a more appropriate style of housing provision for later retirement.

But who should provide this? Traditionally only the local authorities and, to a less extent, the housing associations have provided 'sheltered' style housing for the elderly. In Britain we have always tended to equate 'housing for the elderly' with 'subsidized housing for the elderly', and until the 1972 Housing Finance Act to provide subsidy almost invariably via local authority housing. As a result, frail, elderly owner-occupiers, such as those interviewed in this survey, have been unable to obtain sheltered housing.

The fact that they are owner-occupiers is often enough to disbar them from waiting lists. Clearly it is necessary for local authorities to provide housing for these people. Since the repeal of the 1972 Act they have had discretion in fixing rent levels, provided housing accounts balance. If objections exist to subsidized housing for owner-occupiers, there is nothing to stop them charging rents they think appropriate, subject to tenants' abilities to pay.

The major alternative is at present housing associations. The Hanover, Anchor and Abbeyfield Housing associations working on a national scale, and a host of local associations, are building and converting dwellings for elderly people. Many schemes have been provided in seaside resorts. There is often a problem however, in persuading an elderly person to risk selling their property, in which after all they are protected against inflating rents, in order to go into rented property. The old people are often also reluctant to sell their property and have nothing left to will to their children.

One of the most interesting solutions to this problem is that provided by the Guardian Housing Association Limited, an association linked with Anchor Housing Association but designed with these particular problems in mind. The type of accommodation is much the same as in the Anchor, Hanover and other housing association schemes, typically a group of self-contained one- and two bedroomed flats, with common rooms and wardens' accommodation linked by intercom with the flats. However, whereas the normal housing association schemes receive loans from the local authority or housing corporation plus subsidy and sometimes an annual welfare or housing grant towards the cost of the wardens' services and other welfare facilities, the Guardian scheme relies on the capital provided by the occupants themselves, obtained from the sale of their previous home.

Each tenant will have life-occupation of a new flat, subject to a simple agreement which provides for the original loan to be repaid if he decides to leave, or, in the event of his death, to pass to his executors, subject to a small technical deduction. There will be a weekly maintenance charge to cover such items as upkeep of building, insurance, rates, maintenance of the communal area, warden's salary, etc., but there will be no rent, as there will be no mortgage to be serviced. (18)

Such a scheme seems to be ideal for resort areas where there are so many elderly owner-occupiers, particularly widows, who need smaller housing and more care. The problem, of course, is to find sites. It would not seem unreasonable for a resort local authority to offer sites on the condition that a proportion of owner-occupiers already living in the town should receive first option on a share in the scheme just as local people do in most housing association rental schemes. This would overcome the charge that the scheme was bringing more old people into the area and would help to set up a system whereby younger retired people moved into privately built bungalows and older ones moved on into more 'sheltered' accommodation. Old people wanting to take part in such a scheme might often be found amongst those registered for local authority housing but who, because they are owner-occupiers, are on a 'deferred' list.

Since there is such a demand it seems logical that private enterprise should start to provide more 'sheltered housing' schemes. Some of the open-plan estates are halfway there already with payments for communal servicing of the grounds. The resorts would be ideal as testing grounds for private demand for sheltered accommodation. Some private schemes have already been built, mainly in and around London, but the costs are apparently only within the range of the really affluent. How the rent allowance system will affect this situation is not clear, but it might make private schemes of this type more viable.

However, at the present time, until housing associations, local authorities and perhaps even private builders produce more suitable sheltered-style housing, there is little chance of an owner-occupier finding anything either cheaper or more suitable than their own bungalow. But many find even the maintenance and rates of these a financial strain. Typically the owner-occupier in a resort has a modest income from state pensions and other sources and a few thousand pounds of capital, but in a time of inflation the capital does not seem enough to bridge the gap between their income and the expenditure needed to live comfortably in retirement.

One solution to this problem is to transfer most of their savings into an annuity which would give a higher income than investments. But, as we have seen, many retired people have small savings and the improvement from buying an annuity would be small compared with the radical difference that could be made to their circumstances if only they could draw on the capital represented by their house. Certainly, in Bexhill and Clacton, for the majority of retired people their major asset was their house. Eighty-five per cent in Bexhill and 90 per cent in Clacton owned their house. Eighty-two per cent of those in Bexhill who had bought their house in 1966 or later had paid £4,000 or more, 59 per cent had paid £5,000 or more and 26 per cent £6,000 or more. In Clacton 38 per cent had paid £4,000 or more. These figures may be compared with the average amount of savings and investments which was about £1,000 for respondents in Clacton and £5,000 in Bexhill; the very old and those with the lowest incomes had the least savings. Plainly, for most retired people, their house is their largest capital asset and it is an appreciating asset. Since 1968-9 many of these properties have doubled in value.

Though building societies will not usually give a mortgage to people over 65 years, unless there is some other form of security, recently there has been an expansion of home-loan-annuity opportunities, (19) which means that prospects are brighter for elderly home-owners who wish to stay on in their house but have difficulty affording maintenance. Under these, loans are granted to elderly home-owners of up to say 75 per cent of the value of their house. On this the owner can get tax relief while the annuity paid out is regarded largely as a repayment of capital and is, therefore, free of tax. The house still belongs to the owner who can move or will it, though the loan is a charge against it.

So the situation is more flexible for the home-owner than it was previously. Nevertheless, there is still a danger of exploitation by swindlers if old people do not know of an annuity scheme or fail to qualify for one. (20)

The government could do a good deal to help pensioners

at relatively little cost by helping the building societies or some other body to start a national householder's annuity scheme. (21)

Having said this, it is still true that 'it is often possible to make more difference to one's financial circumstances by the careful choice of a place to live than by any amount of juggling between different investments or annuity quotations'. (22)

The survey showed how much more expensive it was to buy a house in Bexhill, not only in terms of capital outlay, but also in rate payments. The choice of a retirement resort may make a lot of difference to an elderly person's financial position, and they should be realistic about this when taking the decision to move. A move which increases their invested capital by providing a margin between the price of the house bought and the one sold is obviously to be preferred to one that involves supplementing the proceeds of the sale from savings in order to buy the new house.

For the resort authorities any discussion of more varied housing provision raises the question of land shortage. Private builders and housing associations both complain of the limitations placed on them by the difficulty in obtaining land. In some resorts there is scarcely any open land available on which more diversified types of housing could be built. Here the only solutions are demolition and conversion. Already these are widespread in the resorts. In particular, large hotels and boarding houses, which close because of the changes in the style of seaside holiday, are being converted or demolished to provide flats. They are usually very suitably located being near the front and the town centre. A further possibility, not yet much explored, is the provision of accommodation above town centre shops. Such schemes could be either for sale, rented by a local authority or housing association or could even be in some scheme such as the 'Guardian' one.

Whatever the solutions adopted, it is clear that the housing authorities in retirement areas need to take seriously the provision of more accommodation for the very frail and old. In an earlier chapter we saw the problems that exist in the resorts in relation to emergency help and community support. Grouped housing schemes, whatever their tenure and whether they are provided for the sick or the poor or both, are one way of using scarce resources of personnel in the health and social services to the maximum advantage. They also enable old people to help themselves much more effectively and to remain independent with least anxiety.

Chapter 11

Meanwhile, until more is done to help them, frail old people have to make shift as best they can. The solutions have been to stay on in their owner-occupied house and, if necessary, just not maintain it; to buy something cheaper, perhaps a converted flat up a flight of stairs; to rent furnished rooms; to go to live in a hotel, boarding house or old people's home; or to return to live with their children, if they have any.

12 Moving from one retirement home to another

> In the past ten years he has moved restlessly from one
> Connecticut town to another, hunting for the Great
> Good Place, which he conceived to be an old Colonial
> house, surrounded by elms and maples, equipped with
> all modern conveniences and overlooking a valley.
> There he plans to spend his days reading Huckleberry
> Finn, raising poodles, laying down a wine cellar,
> playing bowls and talking to the little group of
> friends which he has managed somehow to take with him
> into his crotchety middle age.
>
> James Thurber: 'The Thurber Carnival'

It is tempting to regard moves in retirement as once-for-all moves, but for many of the retired people in Bexhill and Clacton this was by no means the case. Twenty-three per cent of respondents in Bexhill and 16 per cent in Clacton had had moves in retirement other than their original move at retirement. In addition, some intended to move again; 4 per cent in Bexhill and 5 per cent in Clacton said they were expecting to move within the year and a further 17 per cent in Bexhill and 31 per cent in Clacton wanted to move. The majority of these moves, past, planned and hoped for, were from one house to another within Bexhill and Clacton, but many were from town to town, usually from one seaside resort to another.

The characteristics of people who had already moved again after retirement were rather different from those of people with only one move. They were more frequently widowed. In Bexhill 26 per cent and in Clacton 28 per cent of second movers were widowed compared with 15 per cent and 19 per cent of those with only one move. To put it another way, of married couples only 18 per cent in Bexhill and 15 per cent in Clacton had had second moves, compared with 36 per cent of widowed people in Bexhill

Chapter 12

and 22 per cent in Clacton. This clearly indicates that many moves are made after widowhood, perhaps to find accommodation more suited to the changed circumstances or to be nearer friends or relatives.

Second movers were also older than the average. In Bexhill 76 per cent and in Clacton 80 per cent of them were 70 or over, compared with 56 per cent and 50 per cent respectively of people with only one move. The majority of these were, however, widowed people rather than married couples.

One quite interesting feature of second moves is the high incidence of people who had moved to retire when they were under 60. Of those who moved when they were under 60, 43 per cent in Bexhill and 35 per cent in Clacton had had second moves. This may have been partly related to the length of time that they had been retired but these people were not necessarily very old now. Perhaps the explanation is that the younger people are when they retire the more ambitious they are about the type of house and garden they will be able to maintain and the more likely they are to need to find something more modest later on. Certainly the relationship between age at the retirement move and a tendency to have had a second move was stronger than that between second moves and the current age of the head of the retired household.

About 60 per cent of the people who had had more than one move since retirement had moved only from one house to another in Bexhill or Clacton; about a third had moved from one town to another and the rest had had both types of move. (1)

As well as being more likely than elderly people in Clacton to have had more than one retirement move, those in Bexhill were also more likely to have moved several times. Of those with previous retirement moves before arriving in Bexhill 10 per cent had lived in three or more other towns compared with 6 per cent in Clacton; 17 per cent had had two or more addresses in Bexhill other than their present one compared with 6 per cent with two or more in Clacton. However, the majority of second movers in both towns had had only one retirement home other than their present one. They represented 66 per cent of all second movers in Bexhill and 81 per cent in Clacton.

Fifty per cent of those who had come to Bexhill from a previous retirement home in another town had come from another seaside resort. In Clacton the proportion was 46 per cent. The rest had come either from the countryside to which they had first retired or from the homes of relatives. These results confirm census findings that there is considerable movement from resort to resort. (2) The people who came from other seaside resorts had, however, had less previous retirement moves than had the others. For instance, no people from seaside resorts had moved between four different places whilst 15 per cent of the rest had. The seaside resorts do not seem, then, to make people more footloose. Do they, though, attract a disproportionate number of the footloose from other places? Without better information on the rate of movement of retired people generally, this question cannot be answered. Certainly a number of people seemed to find the resorts a permanent haven after a series of moves.

The period that movers had spent in their last retirement house varied from less than one year to more than ten. About a third in each town had lived less than two years at their last address. A further third had lived there between two and five years and the remaining third over five years. Rather surprisingly there was no difference in the length of stay for all movers and those who had lived in more than one retirement town; the same proportions stayed less than a year in their last house.

The reasons given for moving varied to some extent according to whether or not the previous address was in Bexhill, Clacton or elsewhere. (3) In both towns the most common reasons for moving within the town were to do with the house. In Bexhill, the house being too large was most frequently mentioned but in Clacton it was the expense of running the house or the level of the rates. These two may be different ways of saying the same thing but not necessarily. There were less large houses in Clacton and the more wealthy people in Bexhill may have been worried by problems of upkeep without necessarily being concerned about the cost. Obtaining domestic help or gardeners can be a problem quite apart from the cost. Problems with gardens were also mentioned more often in Bexhill. Again there were more houses with large gardens in Bexhill than in Clacton. Another large body of reasons given for moving were to do with the area in which the previous house was situated, with a particularly large number of complaints about areas that were too far from the town centre, sea front or public transport. There were other types of complaint, especially in Bexhill, but these were very particular, such as the discovery, when the leaves fell off the trees, that a newly bought house looked straight on to a cemetery. There were a number of people, very notably in Clacton, who said they had 'just not been able to settle' in their previous accommodation, or who had been lonely or distressed by its association with the death of a husband, wife or friend. Why this should have been more apparent in Clacton than Bexhill is not at all clear. It might be suggested that the community may support such people less effectively in Clacton, but movers into Clacton from other towns also stressed the same thing, whereas those into Bexhill did not. Perhaps the working-class people of Clacton were more likely to suffer from the absence of close family or neighbourly contacts, having been more used to them than the middle classes. Certainly in reply to other questions they more frequently said they missed their children, but then they more often had children to miss.

Compulsory moves accounted for 5 per cent and 8 per cent of last moves within Bexhill and Clacton respectively. These were mainly caused by landlords selling their property or dying. Though a small proportion of total moves, such evictions accounted for a large percentage of moves from rented accommodation.

The typical move within the towns was one to find a smaller house or garden, less stairs or a home nearer to the sea front or town centre. The following example is reasonably representative of the sequence of events but widowers were far less likely to be involved than widows and also in this case Mr Wilkins's income was far above the average, so he could afford much better accommodation than most people.

Mr Wilkins, (4) a widower of 72 had had three different homes in Bexhill. He and his wife had originally bought a bungalow but after two and a half years they had decided that the garden was too big and had moved to a chalet-bungalow. However, after three and a half years there, Mrs Wilkins had died and so Mr Wilkins had bought a purpose-built flat which was more manageable for him on his own. He was very active in various clubs where he played bridge, bowls and chess and was an officer of one club. In all he thought that Bexhill was 'the ideal spot for retirement. It has the right amenities'. He had no intention of moving. During his working life he had been a senior civil servant and though he had little savings, his superannuation gave him a very decent income of about £32 a week in retirement.

Moves from one town to another after retirement were frequently connected with the desire to be with friends or relatives or with loneliness or, sometimes, an inability to settle. Again this was much more true of Clacton than Bexhill. Nearly a third of the people who had moved into Clacton from another retirement address came to be near relatives or friends, compared with less than a fifth of people in Bexhill. However, the most

common reason for a move from one place to another was
dissatisfaction with the last retirement area. The
predominant criticism was just that the previous place
had not been by the sea. This was mentioned by 23 per
cent of the movers in Clacton and by 16 per cent in
Bexhill. Another less common reason was that the
countryside had been too isolated for an elderly person.

Dissatisfaction with the house was also frequently
given as a reason for moving from one town to another;
21 per cent of movers into Clacton and 41 per cent into
Bexhill gave reasons of this type. The difference
between the two towns brings to mind the reasons which so
many retired people gave for choosing Bexhill, namely the
availability of suitable accommodation. Clearly Bexhill
attracts many previously dissatisfied retirement movers
partly because it has a larger range of suitable property
than most towns.

It was interesting to see if the rates of residential
mobility after retirement suggested restlessness. Three
per cent of respondents in Bexhill and 1 per cent in
Clacton had had four or more moves since retirement.
These represented 12 per cent of those in Bexhill who had
moved more than once since retiring and 6 per cent in
Clacton. Of course, from the point of view of disruption
and loss of friends, a move from one part of a town to
another is not as crucial as that between different towns.
In Bexhill and in Clacton 1 per cent of the people who
had had more than one move since retirement had had moves
between four or more different towns, but many more had
had a mixture of moves between different towns and between
houses in the same town. We will now consider this very
special group of rapid movers in more detail.

Some of those who had moved frequently had been
continually seeking cheaper and smaller accommodation as
their means became restricted. At the same time their
security of tenure in the accommodation they found became
less as they moved into privately rented furnished
accommodation. Every social service agency and housing
management department in the retirement resorts is
familiar with the old ladies who move rapidly from one
bed-sitter to another, often ending up on the top floor
of a former boarding house. But moves to save money are
not just made into rented accommodation. Owner-occupiers
move to reduce their rates and to realise capital on the
sale of a more expensive house, by buying a cheaper house
or flat.

Mrs Carter, a widow of 75, had had four different
houses in four different towns since moving from London
and gave as her reasons for each move the need to save

money. She and her husband had originally bought a retirement house in Ninfield but after four years decided to get something smaller and cheaper as they were eating into their small savings. They therefore bought a semi-detached house at Tunbridge Wells. There they stayed another four years until the rates became too high for them to manage. Then they moved to a bungalow at Uckfield. While they were there Mr Carter died and his widow was left with even less income than before so she bought a converted flat in Bexhill for £2,250. This was in 1961 and she had lived there since, eking out a meagre existence with virtually all her savings gone and relying now upon Supplementary Benefits. She was now finding the stairs too steep for her and would really have liked to move nearer her daughter who came down from London every other weekend, but who herself found this a financial strain with rising rail fares.

However, a minority of the people who moved from one retirement resort to another were just very unsettled. Logical (or sometimes illogical) reasons were given for each move, but there was plainly an unsatisfied and probably unsatisfiable questing from place to place for the ideal retirement home, 'the Great Good Place'. The first and last examples below are of people moving round Bexhill itself. The second shows continuous moves from resort to resort.

Mr and Mrs Chapman, aged 84 and 82, had had five different homes in Bexhill since they moved there in 1946. All had been owned by themselves. The first three had been houses and the last two bungalows. The periods they had stayed in these houses varied, six years in the first, four years in the second, two in the third, three in the fourth and five in their present one. The reasons they gave for moving were, for the first one, that they wanted a change, and for the second, which was to a house in the same street, the same, plus the fact that they felt it was too big. The third house in which they stayed such a short time was 'unsuitable'. They left the first bungalow because they 'took a fancy' to the bungalow they were presently living in; its garden backed on to that of the first bungalow.

Although this couple said that they were quite happy with their move to the seaside and in fact had persuaded friends to join them there, the husband clearly missed his previous busy life. He would have liked to continue as a JP as he missed public life. When working he had been the proprietor of a manufacturing business

and there were clearly no financial problems about the
rapid series of moves. They had grandchildren and
great-grandchildren who visited them and they were
active in the church, played music and were also doing
A levels at a college of further education. The couple
said they had no further plans for moving to a different house.

Mrs Rawlings, a widow of 71, had had seven different
retirement addresses, all owner-occupied bungalows, and
all the moves had involved moves from one town to
another. She had been widowed only since the last
move. Mr and Mrs Rawlings's first retirement move was
from Ipswich to buy a bungalow at Leigh-on-Sea but they
stayed there only a year because it was situated in a
valley and they found it too damp. They then moved to
Southend where they stayed three years but they found
this 'uncomfortably near their relations' so they
moved to Westcliffe, also in Essex. They stayed only
a year there, complaining of subsidence under the
kitchen, and they then went to Thundersley (Essex)
where again they stayed only a year because they found
it too damp again. Then they moved back to Southend.
At this point and after only a year there, they decided
to move to the South Coast. They chose Hastings but
after only six months they decided they did not like
the bungalow, which was in a windy situation on a hill
above the town. They then moved to Bexhill where they
had been only a matter of a few weeks when the husband
died. After a few months, his widow was already
thinking of moving again. She said that she did not
think the seaside had 'the atmosphere' of the inland
towns. 'There is more going on in bigger towns.' She
said she expected to move shortly and go nearer London
which would be better now she was on her own. It is
worth noting that since the age of 20 and before
retiring she and her husband had lived in only two
places, Carlisle and Ipswich, and they had lived in
Ipswich sixteen years.

Mrs Cochran, a 76 year old widow, had had four different homes in Bexhill since she moved there in 1956.
She had been widowed before she moved. The first
place she bought in Bexhill was a house but she left
it within a year because she found it damp, and moved
to a bungalow. She stayed there five years but she
said she left it because her sister, who lived nearby,
didn't like it! She didn't specify why this should
have been so crucial. She then bought another bungalow

and again stayed five years, but this time she left
'because the vicar said it was too far from the church'.
She had lived one year in her present bungalow.

She gave an impression of restlessness although she
said she had no further plans to move from that bungalow or from the town. She was active in going to
clubs, the Townswomen's Guild, the British Legion, and
various church organizations. She was, however, not
at all well off. Her husband, an architect, had died
twenty years before and she had little capital and no
private pension.

In preliminary discussions with people concerned with
health and welfare services in the retirement areas, one
theme, amongst others, came out strongly, namely that
over the course of their retirement, old people, particularly women, suffer a decline in their standard of living.
The trend is shown in their income which falls first on
retirement, further when they are widowed and then
continues to fall in real terms with the passage of time.
This decline in income, it was said, is, in the resorts,
paralleled by declining housing standards. The retirement bungalow is sold by the widow when she can no longer
afford to maintain it and is not strong enough to care
for it herself. She then seeks a smaller flat. The
nadir of this decline is a furnished room in an ex-boarding house in the town centre.

Was this pattern confirmed by the results of this
survey? The incomes of widows and very old people were
certainly lower than those of couples and younger retired
people. But was this financial decline in fact
accompanied by residential mobility to adjust to changing
financial circumstances? Or are moves more typical of
people who are trying to obtain accommodation of a size
and type more suited to their needs, rather than just
cheaper? We have seen earlier that the most common reason
was to get smaller accommodation with less maintenance
problems and with fewer stairs.

The characteristics of people who moved again after
retirement fitted in with either view of the situation.
The people with more than one retirement move were older
than the average and were more frequently widowed than the
population generally. (5) In Bexhill they were also more
frequently single, but as single people were more likely
to live in rented accommodation, in which turnover rates
are higher, their greater mobility is not surprising. One
piece of evidence against the relationship of high mobility
with a downward trend in housing standards is that the
moving rate was about the same for all social classes.
There was no particular emphasis on the poorer social
classes.

The theory of declining housing standards usually implies a change of tenure from owning to renting in the final stages. It is therefore interesting to see whether changes of tenure did happen during, for instance, the most recent moves. In fact, nearly half the people who were renting at the time of the survey and who had moved previously had changed tenure at their last move. Only 15 per cent of owner-occupiers in Bexhill and 11 per cent in Clacton had changed tenure. The contrast was even more striking when the owner-occupiers were examined in more detail because it emerged that many of those who had previously been renting had only been doing so temporarily until they found somewhere suitable to buy. Most of the renters had been owner-occupiers before, but some had changed from furnished renting and vice versa.

There was also a relationship between the tenure of house and the number of retirement moves. The more often people had moved the more likely they were to rent, and the more likely they were to live in flats or rooms. Of those who had moved only once, 90 per cent in Bexhill and 93 per cent in Clacton owned their houses, compared with 70 per cent in Bexhill and 78 per cent in Clacton of those who had moved twice or more. Similarly 18 per cent in Bexhill and 7 per cent in Clacton of one-time movers lived in flats or rooms, compared with 50 per cent and 25 per cent of those who had moved more than once.

Just as those with several retirement moves were less likely to live in larger than smaller accommodation so there was a parallel trend from newer to older property but this was a much smaller swing particularly in Clacton, where there was less older property available. There must in fact have been a substantial minority of moves from older to newer property. This fits in with the view that many people were moving from older houses into new purpose-built flats, or bungalows, getting more suitable rather than worse accommodation. There was no one-way trend suggesting that most people moving into flats or bungalows had come out of houses.

The conclusion can be drawn from these findings that there were three overlapping features of the residential mobility pattern in the resorts. First, there was the desire of ageing and widowed people for more manageable property in terms of housework, maintenance and gardening. This might involve moves from houses to bungalows or flats or from bungalows with large gardens to flats and small houses. The shortage of suitable flat accommodation sent the poorer old people into converted property. This led to the second feature, which was that a number of people, particularly women, were forced by financial circumstances and the lack of suitable cheap accommodation into old, often unselfcontained property. This did not always entail a change of tenure, as many converted flats were put up for sale rather than let. (6) Third, amongst old people who lived in furnished rooms and converted rented flats there was a high mobility rate, partly as a result of compulsory moves and partly out of a search for cheaper accommodation with less stairs. Some of these people had come down the scale from their own retirement bungalows. Others, as described in the previous chapter, had lived in rooms since they arrived in the resort.

It can be concluded then that mobility is not necessarily a measure of housing hardship amongst old people. For the second two groups it is, but for the first it shows an ability to take steps to improve one's housing situation. In fact the commonest source of hardship is probably the inability to move out of large or unsuitable accommodation, either for financial reasons or because of unwillingness to face the upheaval and loss of familiar surroundings. Numerically this is the largest housing problem in the resorts, though the plight of the minority living in rooms is more strikingly bad and fits in more easily with the orthodox view of what a 'housing problem' is. To weigh up worry about repairs, rates, etc., against lack of modern amenities is an impossible task.

To turn now to the people who said they were going to move in the future or hoped to do so, we find that retired people in Bexhill were less likely than those in Clacton to want or expect to move out of the town. They were more likely to envisage a move within Bexhill. Four per cent of the respondents in Bexhill and 5 per cent in Clacton said they were expecting to move within the next year. Of these 2 per cent in Bexhill and 3 per cent in Clacton were moving to a different town, the rest to a different house within the town. Many more wanted to move, though. In Bexhill a further 12 per cent wanted to move to a different house and 5 per cent to another town. In Clacton the proportions were 17 per cent and 14 per cent.

The reasons elderly people gave for wanting to move to another house were much the same in Clacton and Bexhill, except that Clacton residents were more likely to want to move to rent. (7) The reasons were also much the same as those given by people who had already moved. In both towns the majority were concerned with the unsuitability of their present accommodation for a person of their age. They said the stairs were too much for them, so they wanted a bungalow or flat or they wanted a smaller place in which there would be less housework. Others said they wanted a flat instead of a bungalow or house; and a large number referred to the difficulties of maintaining their gardens. The other important group of reasons concerned the location of the house, and here the most common complaints were the distance from the sea front, town centre, shops or public transport.

There was a clear relationship between dissatisfaction with the house and a desire to move. This was only to be expected but, as was found in relation to previous retirement moves, there was a relationship between the desire to move not only to a different house but also to a different town. There are a number of possible explanations for this. For instance, a number of elderly people had moved to Bexhill and Clacton specifically because of the availability of what they considered suitable accommodation. If their house proved less satisfactory than expected or became less suitable as they grew older the motive for selecting the town in the first place would be negated and they might consider other resorts for a further move. This explanation, however, rather assumes that they had not settled well in the town over those years. Dissatisfaction with their house might have been for some people just a symptom of a more deep-rooted dissatisfaction.

The reasons given for wanting to move to another town were rather different for elderly people in Clacton than those in Bexhill (Table 12.1). Those in Clacton were, for instance, more likely to complain of too little to do and the unfriendliness of other residents. Comparing the numbers of clubs and societies operating in the two towns and the larger proportion of people in Clacton who said they were lonely this seems a likely complaint. Clacton residents also complained of the climate, particularly the cold wind, which they said was harmful to their health. Just about the same proportion of all respondents in each town wanted to return to where they came from or to be nearer friends or relations, but because a smaller proportion of Bexhill residents wanted to move at all, this group represented a much larger proportion of the moving group there. It seems then that there was in each town a core of people, 5 or 6 per cent, who wanted to return to their 'home' town or who missed their family. In addition to this basic group, Clacton had a larger group than Bexhill who were dissatisfied with the particular resort. These people would be the most likely to be amongst those who moved to another resort rather than back to the area from which they came.

TABLE 12.1 Reasons for wanting to move to another town

	Percentage of potential movers from the town		Percentage of all respondents	
	Bexhill	Clacton	Bexhill	Clacton
Sample number:	34	76	500	484
	%	%	%	%
To be near family	(44)	24	3	4
To return to area they came from	(21)	12	2	2
Don't like the people: unfriendly	(3)	7	-	1
Not enough life in the town	(18)	22	1	4
Too many old people in the town	(3)	1	-	-
Too expensive	(6)	3	-	-
Prefer countryside to seaside	(3)	5	-	1
Climate or health reasons	(18)	17	1	3
Don't like the town for unspecified reasons or prefer some other place	(9)	9	1	1
Want a change	(-)	4	-	-
Other	(12)	8	1	1

Those who expected or wanted to move seemed not to be significantly different from others in household characteristics or age except that in Clacton they were more likely to have children and to be living with them. This ties up with a later finding that people who lived with their children in Clacton were particularly likely to regret their move. (8) In addition people who lived with their children might have been moving because the young people's employment had changed.

Lonely people were more likely than other people to want to move right away from Bexhill and Clacton. In Clacton 35 per cent and in Bexhill 23 per cent of the people who said they were often lonely said they expected or wanted to move from the town compared with 13 per cent in Clacton and 6 per cent in Bexhill of those who said they were never lonely. Loneliness was not, however, related to a desire to move from one house to another within the town. This is rather interesting in that stress is often laid on the undesirability of certain estate layouts from the point of view of social contacts. Though design may be an important factor in loneliness, the lonely people themselves did not see the solution to their problems in terms of a local move and wanted to move right away from the town.

This chapter has been concerned with people who have moved or want to move from one retirement home to another, whether it be in the same town, another seaside resort or back in the area from which they came. A lot of the movement can be explained in terms of the need of ageing people to have accommodation more suited to their lower income and reduced physical capacity. Sometimes income is the main factor, in which case the accommodation they find may be less suitable, a bed-sitter up many flights of stairs for instance. In other cases, their income is sufficient to enable them to purchase a flat or bungalow with a smaller garden, in order to avoid the worry and expense of upkeep of the larger property they bought when they first retired. In a small number of cases, however, it was clear, from a history of constant movement, that the retired couple had not settled in any of their retirement homes and had become restless and footloose. In addition, from questions about the desire to move, it emerged that a small core of people, 5 or 6 per cent, wanted to move back to their home district. The next chapter picks up this point and examines the more general question of whether the retired people were glad or sorry that they had moved.

13 Satisfaction with the retirement move

> 'Which of us has his desire? or, having it, is satisfied?'
> W.M. Thackeray: 'Vanity Fair'

In reply to the question, 'In the light of your knowledge now, and given your time again, would you move to the coast on retirement?', 84 per cent of the retired people in Bexhill and 79 per cent in Clacton said they would move, 9 per cent in Bexhill and 17 per cent in Clacton said they definitely would not and the rest (7 per cent and 4 per cent) said they did not know what they would do. On the face of it this seems in Bexhill at least, a high level of satisfaction.

However, there are several problems in asking people whether they are satisfied with having made a decision of this type. First, some people may not have had the heart to admit, even possibly to themselves, that they regretted moving. There is no way to tackle this problem, other than to recognize that it may exist, and, as far as possible, to cross-check with replies to other questions about loneliness, satisfaction with the town, wanting to move and so on.

Second, a number of those interviewed had moved too recently to be able to assess the success of their move. Some admitted this but others may have reacted either to the enjoyable novelty of the move or to initial disorientation. The scale of this particular problem was reduced by the fact that the electoral list from which the sample was selected was one year old at the time of the interviewing, and so the proportion who had arrived very recently, that is in 1968, was exceedingly small, less than 1 per cent in each town. However, 34 per cent of those interviewed in Bexhill and 43 per cent in Clacton had had less than five years' experience of the resort.

An analysis of satisfaction according to length of stay in the town, in fact, brought out only one clear feature, that those who had arrived before 1958 in Clacton and before 1954 in Bexhill were least likely to regret their move. In Bexhill of those who moved before 1954 only 5 per cent said they would not move if given the chance again, compared with 9 per cent of those who moved later. In Clacton, the most dissatisfied were those who moved between 1959 and 1965; as many as 20 per cent who regretted their move, compared with only 13 per cent who moved after 1965 and 9 per cent who moved before 1959.

These results cannot, however, be assumed to show that the longer people stay the better they like it. On the contrary, it probably highlights the third and most difficult problem in asking about satisfaction, namely, that is, the satisfied who stay on in the resort and the dissatisfied who move away and fail to appear in the sample. Therefore any sample of current residents is biased towards the satisfied.

Ideally one would like to be able to estimate the proportion of people who move away, but this is extremely difficult. The 1966 sample census gives the numbers of people of pensionable age who moved out of Bexhill and Clacton in the year 1965-6 and in the five years 1961-6, but these totals, of course, include local long-term residents as well as those who had retired to the resort and were moving away again. It may be, for instance, that people who have worked much of their lives in a resort town, decide to retire elsewhere, even if only to another resort.

However, it is worth looking at these census figures. (1) They do show, for instance, that there were greater proportions of women amongst the people of pensionable age moving out of Clacton than there were coming in. Of those who moved between 1961 and 1966, 64 per cent who came in were women, compared with 71 per cent who moved out. In Bexhill there was no significant difference between the two; 69 per cent coming in were women, compared with 68 per cent who left. It should be remembered, however, that, since many of the people who moved to resorts to retire were under 65 at the time, the sex ratio amongst those making their retirement move into the town is not the same as the sex ratio for people of pensionable age. There will be more widowed women in the latter group.

The second feature that emerges is that the ratio of pensionable age people coming in, to those going out, was slightly over 4 to 1 in Clacton and slightly under in Bexhill. In Bexhill the people who left in 1965-6 represented 2.3 per cent of the population of pensionable age in 1966 and in Clacton they represented 2.0 per cent. Over the five-year period the out-movers represented 7.5 per cent and 6.9 per cent respectively of the pensionable age population in Bexhill and Clacton. The movement out of Bexhill was therefore at a slightly higher rate than that out of Clacton.

From the findings of the last chapter, the reason for this slightly higher rate would seem to be the older age structure of Bexhill and the greater financial ability to move, rather than any greater dissatisfaction with the resort. On the contrary, one may in fact put down some of the greater dissatisfaction found in Clacton to the inability of the people to move. The inability to move may be, as was said before, a greater hardship than the need to do so.

Though we already know that many people of all ages move from one resort to another and from the resorts to the cities, (2) it is not possible to say how many elderly people move back to the cities. But even if it were possible to make a close estimate of the numbers who move away, it still does not mean that a move away necessarily implies that the person concerned regrets their retirement move. They might have had from ten to twenty happy retirement years on the coast but decided to move to live with their children or to go into a home when they were widowed or became very frail. That this is frequently the case emerged from remarks made by the retired people themselves.

To arrive at an estimate of the numbers who regret their move, it is not really even possible to take the highest level of discontent (that felt by those who moved between 1959 and 1963) as the general level, because some of these too would have already left. However, this is probably the nearest one can get to the general figure, bearing in mind that it may be conservative, because people may have left, or may be exaggerated by particularly difficult features of that period, such as widowhood, with which the retired person may come to terms later. If this figure is taken, about 10 per cent of people in Bexhill would not have moved to the coast again and a further 6 per cent were doubtful. In Clacton the record was very much worse, 21 per cent would not move again and a further 6 per cent were doubtful. The Bexhill figures seem very reasonable ones, considering that any move may have its difficulties. For over a quarter of the people who moved to Clacton to regret their move or be doubtful if they would move again seems, however, excessive.

What were the reasons for this dissatisfaction and why

were there differences between the two towns? Also, were particular types of people more likely to regret their move?

As one might expect, the widowed were more likely than married couples to regret their move. In Clacton, 24 per cent of widowed people said they would not move if given the decision again, compared with 15 per cent of married couples. In Bexhill 12 per cent of the widowed regretted their move, compared with 9 per cent of married couples. In addition a larger proportion of the widowed were unsure what decision they would make (Table 13.1). The difference in satisfaction between married couples in Bexhill and Clacton was not statistically significant and it was the discontent of widows in Clacton which accounted for the great difference in satisfaction between the two towns.

TABLE 13.1 Considered views about the retirement move, by marital status

	Bexhill			
	All	Married	Single	Widowed
Sample number	503	337	75	89
PROPORTION WHO:	%	%	%	%
Would take the same decision again	84	85	87	74
Would not move	9	9	4	12
Did not know what decision they would take	7	5	9	13
	Clacton			
Sample number	487	365	23	98
PROPORTION WHO:	%	%	%	%
Would take the same decision again	79	82	(78)	66
Would not move	17	15	(9)	24
Did not know what decision they would take	5	3	(13)	9

Rather unexpectedly, however, no difference showed up between people widowed before and after their move. It seems that the situation of being a widowed person in the resorts is a problem, whatever the time at which one is widowed. There may well be, however, a serious underestimate of the number of dissatisfied people who are widowed after their move because of their tendency to move away. But again one must repeat that a move away on widowhood is not necessarily the same as regretting the initial retirement move. Many people may have enjoyed the earlier period of their retirement at the seaside, but still decide to move nearer to their family in widowhood or extreme old age.

Rather curiously, in Clacton, those who were living with their children were the most likely to say that they would not move, given the decision again; 35 per cent gave this answer. In Bexhill, there was no such pattern but there were also very few people who were living with their children. This result from Clacton points to the dangers of assuming too glibly that moves with children or to be near them are necessarily more satisfactory than those away from them.

People who said they were lonely were far more likely than others to say that they would not move to the coast again. In both towns they were about three times as likely to give this reply as people who said they were never lonely. In Bexhill 23 per cent and in Clacton 46 per cent of those who were often lonely said they would not move again, compared with 14 per cent and 21 per cent of those who were sometimes lonely and 7 per cent and 13 per cent of those who were never lonely. Since there was a relationship between loneliness in the resorts and a preference for the company of younger people, (3) it was not surprising that those who preferred younger people were also less likely to say that they would move again to the seaside. In Bexhill 77 per cent of these people said they would, compared with 86 per cent of the others. In Clacton 73 per cent said they would, compared with 81 per cent of the others.

One of the questions that seemed relevant to this study was whether or not some familiarity with the resort before the move had been important in helping a retired person to settle down happily. The existence of a relationship between previous holidays or winter visits to the town and satisfaction with the decision to move would suggest that people who were familiar with the place would be more likely to settle down. In fact, there was a relationship between the lack of a previous holiday or day-trip to Bexhill or Clacton and regret about the decision to move.

The lack of a winter visit was also a significant factor in Clacton but not in Bexhill. However, there may be no causal relationship. Lack of a previous visit to the resort was also associated with negative reasons for selecting the town, such as low house prices, rather than a positive liking for the town. (4) Often the town was not a first choice for those who had not already had holidays there. It may be, then, that the retirement move got off to a bad start by the resort itself being a 'second best'.

The reasons people gave for feeling that they would move to the coast again were predominantly to do with liking the sea and the healthiness of the environment, the cleanliness and fresh air. This type of reply covered 46 per cent of satisfied respondents in Bexhill and 63 per cent in Clacton. (5)

'I like to know the sea is there if I want it.'
'We had both been ill before we moved here. We thought the coast would be good for us and it has been.'
'The air is so clean and fresh.'
'We both adore the sea.'

The Greater London Council Study (6) asked tenants in a number of resorts about their health since their move to the sea. Six per cent said it had deteriorated, 34 per cent said it was about the same and 60 per cent said it had improved. The reasons they gave for the improvement were the 'slower, more relaxed pace of life, pleasant surroundings and fresh air'. These replies fit in well with the emphasis placed on a healthy environment by elderly people in Bexhill and Clacton.

Sixteen per cent of retired people in Bexhill and 13 per cent in Clacton said they were just happy or that the place was ideal for retirement:

'It's a good place for elderly people.'
'It's made my husband happy.'
'It's suitable for retirement.'
'It's the ideal place to retire to.'

The next largest group (10 per cent in Bexhill and 7 per cent in Clacton) said they liked the peace and quiet of the seaside and the absence of the traffic, noise and crowds of the city:

'London's difficult for old people to live in.'

Eight per cent of respondents in Bexhill and 6 per cent in Clacton said they liked the social activities and liveliness of the town or the ease with which they could make friends:

'There's more movement in the seaside than country.'
'There's a definite atmosphere about a seaside town - the gaiety in the summer. People on holiday give out a happy atmosphere.'

'If my husband were alive I would live in the country but being a widow I must live with people and so must live at the coast.'
'It's a nice town - they care about older people.'
'Bexhill is a place for intelligent retired people. My friend who has a bird brain hates it.'
'I have liked it much more than I expected to. I had always been amongst the poor and didn't think I would fit in here - a sort of inverted snobbery about it (A social worker).'
'It's such a wonderfully friendly and courteous place.'

Some people put all these reasons together:

'The sea's more attractive than I thought. The life of a town of this sort is very friendly and there's no rush.'

Some people seemed to have very contradictory feelings. For instance, one couple in Clacton said that they would still take the same decision to move because they were both 'passionately fond of the sea', but in reply to an earlier question about moving they had said that they hoped to return to London: 'We miss our family very much and the retired people living here are snobbish and unfriendly.' This particular reply suggests that their answer about not regretting the move was not entirely realistic. This was the only completely contradictory reply but it does highlight the problem mentioned earlier of possible unwillingness to admit to having made a mistake. However, it is perfectly possible to have very mixed feelings about a past decision.

The reasons people gave for thinking they would not move to the coast if they had the choice again were rather different for the two towns. (7) In Clacton, people were, for instance, more likely to mention that they would prefer to be nearer their children (12 per cent in Clacton compared with 5 per cent in Bexhill). However, respondents in the two towns were equally likely (23 per cent in each) to say that they missed their old friends or surroundings or that they had really been too old to pull up their roots so drastically:

'I'm fed up. I moved away from my friends.'
'I didn't want to come to Clacton. It was my wife that did.'
'I think with a car it's so easy to get to the sea for the day. There's no need to pull up your roots unless you live in a slum.'

In Bexhill the most common reason (36 per cent) for not retiring to the coast again was that the seaside was less pleasant to live in than the country. So the feeling was not so much that they should not have moved in retirement, but that they should have moved to the country rather than the seaside. Only 14 per cent in Clacton gave this reply. It will be recalled that dissatisfaction with the countryside as compared with the seaside was the most common reason for a second move in retirement to Bexhill. There appears to be a two-way traffic, looking for the 'right' retirement area:

'I'd prefer an inland town; there's more community spirit.'
'People are more to one than places. The country is just as nice as the coast.'
'I don't like these artificial South Coast towns.'
'I've seen as much of the sea as I can stomach (Ex-naval officer).'

Retired people in Clacton were much more dissatisfied with leisure facilities and social activities, particularly in the winter; 21 per cent said this would be their reason for not going there again, compared with only 7 per cent in Bexhill. Those in Clacton also missed city facilities more, including shops and transport. But in both towns people made strong statements about the lack of life in the town:

'Too quiet. It's like an elephants' graveyard.'
'It's a dead end here - people come here to die.'
'Sundays are worst.'

The discontented in Bexhill more frequently complained of the climate and deterioration in their health. However, it should be remembered that as there were far fewer discontented people in Bexhill the proportion of all respondents who complained about their health was lower in Bexhill than Clacton.

Only one person in Bexhill and two in Clacton said they would not retire to the sea again on grounds of expense.

It is interesting to compare these results with replies to a series of slightly different questions asked of people living in the Greater London Council bungalows by the sea. (8) They were asked, first, how they liked living at the seaside compared with living in London. In all, 79 per cent said they preferred living at the seaside. Eleven per cent liked it less and 9 per cent said it was about the same. These results are remarkably close to the present ones. The GLC tenants were also asked how satisfied or dissatisfied they were with living at the seaside. The answers were as follows:

Very satisfied	71%
Satisfied	23%
Dissatisfied	6%
Very dissatisfied	−

Last, the tenants were asked where they would like to live if given a choice now. Seventy-nine per cent said they would stay in the same seaside resort. Two per cent said that they would like to go to a different Kent, Essex or Sussex seaside resort and 4 per cent said they would like to move to the West Country. Nine per cent said they would like to move to the Home Counties and 1 per cent to the Midlands. It was only 5 per cent who said that they would like to return to London.

The GLC study found considerable variation in satisfaction between towns. They attributed this tentatively to the distance of the particular bungalow estates from the sea front and town centre. The differences that we found in a much larger and completely random sample in Bexhill and Clacton suggest, however, that there may be other factors involved, to do with the towns themselves, rather than just the individual GLC estates.

To follow up the question about satisfaction with their own move, the retired people in Bexhill and Clacton were asked whether they would encourage retired friends or relatives to come to live in Bexhill or Clacton, and whether in fact any had done so through their encouragement.

Rather fewer were definite about encouraging friends or relatives to retire to the coast than were sure that they themselves would take the same decision again; however, 68 per cent in each town said that they would encourage them. In Bexhill 19 per cent said that they definitely would not, compared with 26 per cent in Clacton; 13 per cent in Bexhill and 6 per cent in Clacton were unsure whether they would encourage them or not. The main reason given for not encouraging them was that it was very much a matter for the individual and no one could decide for another whether or not they would like it.

'I would encourage them if they were prepared to make new friends. If not they should not come.'

Of the people who said that they would not take the decision to move again, 69 per cent in Clacton and 58 per cent in Bexhill said they would not encourage friends to come, but 22 per cent said they would. This apparent discrepancy arose because some of the people who would not move again had personal reasons for having disliked the move and they did not feel others would have these. However, those affected by bereavement had no reason to suppose that others would not have the same experience.

In Bexhill, 26 per cent of all respondents said that friends or relations had actually moved there through their encouragement compared with 18 per cent in Clacton.

Both these seem large proportions and show the importance that personal recommendation has in stimulating retirement to resorts.

In Bexhill, single women were particularly likely to say that they would encourage people to move; 81 per cent gave this reply. In fact 37 per cent had actually persuaded friends or relatives to join them, compared with 25 per cent of married couples and 20 per cent of widows. It will be remembered that in Bexhill many single women lived with women friends or relations and in addition they were particularly contented with the town and were socially active. (9) In Clacton, though the numbers were too small to be reliable, the evidence pointed to the reverse, with only 48 per cent of single people saying they would encourage friends to join them, compared with two-thirds of other people. Only 9 per cent had had friends or relations join them compared with 19 per cent of married people and 17 per cent of widows. In contrast to Bexhill, single people in Clacton were a particularly lonely and discontented group. (10)

Lonely people were less likely than others to say that they would encourage their friends to move to the coast. Only just over a third of those who were often lonely said they would encourage their friends to move, compared with 74 per cent in Bexhill and 69 per cent in Clacton of those who said they were never lonely and over 56 per cent of those who were sometimes lonely. It was clear that some of the people who had persuaded friends or relations to move now lived with them. For instance, in Bexhill 40 per cent of those living with siblings or other relatives and 38 per cent of those living with friends had successfully encouraged friends to move. In Clacton this feature showed up for people living with friends, but again the numbers were extremely small.

In conclusion, then, it seems that the experience of retirement to the coast had not been one that most retired people had regretted. In addition those people who had regretted their move had done so, not so much because they regretted moving at all, 'pulling up their roots', but because they did not like certain features of the place they had chosen. The dissatisfied in Bexhill often said they thought they would have liked the countryside better and those in Clacton missed the activity and variety of the city. These results fit in with the comments of people who intended to move from the resorts; an unexpectedly large number of them were seeking another retirement resort on the coast or in the country rather than returning to the place from which they came.

In addition, fitting in with earlier discussion of

social life and leisure activities in the resorts, it emerged that married couples were unlikely to regret their move but that widowed people, and in Clacton single people, frequently did regret it. This applied to people widowed before they moved as well as after. Again this corroborates the view that social life in the resorts is very much oriented towards retired married couples to the detriment of those who live alone. In Bexhill this did not, however, seem to apply to single women, who were relatively numerous and very active and self-reliant.

In spite, then, of an initial feeling that 21 per cent in Clacton is a rather large proportion of people to regret having moved, a more detailed examination of the situation suggests that the problems are not so much intrinsic problems of retirement migration or of resorts in general but of particular features of the social life of Clacton which would seem amenable to improvement. Though the situation of widows is worse in Clacton, it would seem that generally any widow contemplating retiring to a resort alone should consider the matter very carefully, as she is fairly likely to regret the move. Even so three-quarters of widows in Bexhill and two-thirds in Clacton said they would make the same decision again.

There has been a tendency for a rather alarmist view to become current, that 'they're all miserable in these retirement resorts'. This research does not support that view. Though there are certain problems which have been described here and which should not be overlooked, the expressions of concern about the trend for retirement to the seaside tend to come from the authorities concerned with providing health and social services for the elderly people in resorts, rather than from any strongly voiced discontent by the retired people themselves. Such a body of experienced opinion should not, however, be disregarded and the third part of this book will consider the fears expressed by the relevant authorities concerning continued provision for retired people in the resorts.

Part three

Some policy implications of retirement migration

Introduction to Part three

Though the previous chapters indicated some ways in which retirement to the coast has not been an unqualified success for the people concerned, the general impression from this study has been that for most retired people the move turned out a satisfactory one. In fact a substantial proportion of those who had moved had persuaded their friends to follow suit. The main doubt cast on the desirability of retirement migration has been in relation to the provision in the resorts of emergency help and care in ill-health or poverty, rather than in relation to the day-to-day social life of the towns. The qualification to this appeared to be that the widowed in both towns and the single in Clacton seemed rather lonely and isolated.

However, planning policies have to take into consideration more than the wishes of one group of the population. Wider issues have to be considered. To draw an analogy, the desirability of cutting up the 'greenbelt' for residential purposes cannot be measured solely by asking the new residents whether they enjoy living there. Similarly the interests of people other than the retired should not be overlooked in resort areas.

The report 'A Strategy for the South-East' lists a number of problems facing policy-makers in the retirement areas:

> the high level of old people, reaching over 30% in some places and associated with retirement migration to the south coast is already creating problems in some towns. As a result of labour shortages, the staffing of some essential services is becoming difficult; the pattern of amenities and entertainment suited to old people is less attractive to holiday-makers; and because of the high incidence of low or fixed incomes, rate income and consumer spending in these towns is not rising as elsewhere in the region. These problems will be aggra-

vated if too many schemes aimed at moving older
people to the coast are encouraged; but we recognize
that in view of this attractiveness, especially in
climate, retirement to the towns on the south coast
will continue and has to be catered for. But in the
light of the future age structure of the region's
population further study of these problems is badly
needed. (1)

This study to be at all manageable has had to limit
itself to considering retirement migration from the point
of the retired people themselves, and could not possibly
attempt to examine all these aspects of retirement
resorts. Further studies are needed to consider such
questions as the compatibility of tourism and retirement
or ways in which the economic base of resorts might be
improved without adversely affecting their tourist and
retirement attractions. There are, however, two policy
questions which have already arisen out of the interviews
with retired people, which are important for their welfare
and which might with advantage be considered by prospective movers. These two are, first, the level of provision
of health and social services in the resort areas and,
second, but linked with that, the rate burden currently
being borne by residents in the resorts to pay for these
and other services. In the next chapters we consider
these in some detail. Unlike the first two parts of the
book, which were based largely on the social surveys in
Bexhill and Clacton, this third part considers the
situation in a wide range of seaside resorts and is based
mainly on documentary material and interviews with
officials from a large number of resorts. (3)

THE SUPPLY AND FINANCING OF HEALTH AND SOCIAL SERVICES IN RETIREMENT AREAS

> The greatest hazard of a massive and rising retirement
> population is a two way stranglehold on the health and
> social services; first by over-loading with excessive
> numbers in an age group heavily at risk, and secondly
> by consequent decline and displacement of persons of
> pre-pensionable age to run the services. (4)

Over recent years there have been many such statements by
officers from the retirement areas that services are in a
crisis situation. The arguments against further retirement migration to the coast hinge very frequently upon
the position of the social services in the resort areas.
There is now a fairly extensive literature on the general

Introduction to Part three

subject of services for the elderly (5) and it would be inappropriate in this study to duplicate this. The issue here is whether there is evidence that provision of services is less adequate or more strained in resort areas than elsewhere and if so, what are the financial resources available to remedy the situation.

To obtain an impression of total health and social service provision in the resorts, some of the key services have been selected for assessment. These are hospital provision for old people, residential homes, housing, and some of the community health services, namely the services provided by general practitioners, home helps, meals-on-wheels, home nurses and health visitors.

14 Hospital facilities in the retirement areas

The problem of shortage of geriatric hospital facilities is considerably greater in resorts than in other areas. Recommended provision for geriatric beds is based on a norm of 10 beds per 1,000 of the population aged 65 and over. (1) This figure was derived from the national average of beds occupied by chronic sick patients in 1960. Fourteen years later the average provision of geriatric beds in England was only 8.6 per 1,000 of the elderly population, but the resorts were almost invariably well below even this figure. (2)

In some cases provision was less than half the national average, let alone the target. The Sussex coast was in a particularly bad situation. For instance, in 1974, provision in Chichester and Worthing Area Health Districts was 3.5 and 3.7 per 1,000 respectively. Perhaps even more depressing is the fact that the resort areas appear even to have been losing ground since 1970. (3) It is not possible to make comparisons between all the old Hospital Groups and the new area health authorities but the figures for each type in 1970 and 1974 suggest a deterioration. For instance, the Isle of Wight which had 8.2 beds per 1,000 elderly people in 1969 had only 6.8 in 1974.

The shortage of geriatric beds has its effects not only on the hospitals but on many of the other services. The comments of three geriatric consultants from different resorts illustrate some of the problems:

The problem is so great that we cannot do our job properly since we have to discharge patients before we are satisfied they are quite ready, in order to release their bed for someone on the waiting list. It has been suggested that it might be a good idea to stop medicated survival but in this region at least there is no such thing as medicated survival happening anyway. Pressure for geriatric beds is too great to keep people lingering on: if it is clear that a person can be kept alive for perhaps another few weeks only with extreme medication, then that person is allowed to die. (4)

The 120 General Practitioners whom we serve have gradually become aware of the fact that the Geriatric Service is being overwhelmed and have sadly been forced again into a situation similar to that of five years ago, where they are only referring cases of great social or medical urgency. Apart from the misery caused to patients and their relatives and the frustration felt by the General Practitioners, the effect on the morale of all who work in the geriatric service may readily be imagined. (5)

The bed situation reached a stage of complete crisis this year when the geriatric assessment officer of the town, going round to give priority to the cases on the waiting list, was forced, because of the seriousness of individual situations and complete lack of available beds, to advise these patients, if they could possibly afford it, to enter private nursing homes, with which the area is fairly well endowed. The situation could therefore hardly be more strained before the term breakdown is adequately applied. (6)

One serious result of the shortage of geriatric beds is that other wards of hospitals frequently find that they have a number of elderly patients for whom their type of intensive nursing is not required but for whom there is no room in geriatric wards. This is not to say that acute wards will not legitimately have large proportions of elderly patients for whom their type of treatment is required. This will be increasingly the case as the population ages. (7) However, studies have shown that there is certainly a problem of the 'blocking' of beds required for acute cases needing short-term intensive care by elderly long-term patients needing more routine care. One such study undertaken by the Chichester and Graylingwell Group Hospital Management Committee, showed that 27 per cent of acute general beds were occupied by elderly people who were waiting to be transferred to a geriatric ward, a local authority home or some other form of indefinite care. (8) A survey of the Bournemouth and East Dorset Hospital Management Group showed that, but for the 'blocking' of beds by geriatric cases, about 1,600 more patients could have been taken off the general waiting list over a period of two years. (9) (10)

A further problem is that of falling turnover rates in geriatric wards. These are partly attributable to lower death rates, but a study in Birmingham (11) has suggested that it is also the result of staff shortages and the over-burdening of geriatric wards so that patients cannot receive the attention they need to prepare them to leave hospital quickly. In every hospital group which provided figures for this study the average length of stay of a geriatric patient had gradually increased over the last 5-8 years. For instance, in the period 1963-6 the average length of stay of geriatric patients in the Worthing Hospital Group rose from 4.8 months to 7.3 months. So the scarcity of beds was made worse in that instead of each bed catering for about three patients a year, the number was reduced to less than two.

Worthing exhibits in the most extreme form the problem facing the hospital services in most of the retirement areas, namely that the planned provision of geriatric places has not kept pace at all with the rate of movement of elderly people in the area. For instance, the geriatric consultant for the Worthing area reported in 1968 'since 1962 there has been in the Group Area an increase of population of 16,580, the vast bulk of these being elderly, but hitherto no provision of extra geriatric beds to deal with this increase.' (12) As a result:

> at Worthing it must be recognised that a planned shortage of geriatric beds will exist until 1981. Present provision is half and will not exceed three-quarters of that recommended. The only prospect here would seem to be extension of contractual arrangement with nursing homes or transfer of patients to Chichester when beds are available. (13)

But the Chichester District with only 3.5 geriatric beds per 1,000 elderly people, compared with Worthing's 3.7, would be in no position to help.

The situation in relation to psychiatric provision for the elderly is rather different because there is the added dimension that it has been policy for some time now to reduce the scale of institutional care for the mentally ill and to concentrate on community care. The ratio of psychiatric beds per 1,000 of the total population is now set at 1.8.

Because of the policy of reducing psychiatric beds, the retirement resorts are currently faced with an actual reduction in the numbers of institutional beds available to elderly people. The shortage of geriatric beds and welfare homes has in the past prompted doctors to try to obtain admission for their patients in psychiatric hospitals. Undesirable though this may have been, there was at least care for these people in the psychiatric hospitals. If the numbers of beds are severely reduced before alternative accommodation is available, the situation will be still worse.

In addition there seems grave doubt as to whether the figure of 1.8 beds per 1,000 of the total population is at all adequate for the resorts, because of the much greater incidence of mental illness amongst the elderly. For instance Kay, Beamish and Roth (14) estimated that 5.6 per cent of the population aged 65 and over were 'severely demented' and really needed institutional care; that is they failed in the common activities of everyday life. They estimated that a further 5.7 per cent were 'mildly demented'. This group, unlike the first, could be 'contained with support in the community or in a welfare home'. In a population of which a third is aged 65 and over, compared with 12 per cent nationally, the proportion of 1.8 per cent beds per 1,000 of the population is clearly quite inadequate to cater for such an incidence of mental illness. By Kay, Beamish and Roth's assessment, the need of beds for severely demented elderly people in this type of town would be nearer 1.8 beds per 100 than per 1,000.

Some practitioners, however, cast doubt on the validity of Kay, Beamish and Roth's figures, because they actually sought out dementia, rather than waiting for it to present itself as a problem. (15)

Nevertheless, one study in the Chichester area suggested that old people who retire to a seaside resort have a particularly high risk of mental illness. This was derived from a comparison of referral rates in Bognor Regis with those in the rest of the Chichester area. It was found that Bognor had both a higher referral rate for psychiatric illness in old people and also a higher referral rate for depressive illness. It was suggested that:

> the high rate in Bognor Regis may be related to its ecology, which is typical of a seaside resort to which the elderly retire, and in so doing risk isolating themselves from all that was previously familiar in their social environment - a situation which is aggravated when the spouse dies. (16)

This fits in with the finding of this study that widowed people in the resorts were more likely to say they were lonely than were widowed people nationally. However, it would be unwise to conclude from these very preliminary results that, if there are two people with the same class and family characteristics, the one living in a seaside resort is more likely to need psychiatric help. The point is that it appears that people with the characteristics associated with high referral rates are particularly common in retirement resorts. Bognor for example has 30 per cent of its retired male population in Social Classes I and II, and these classes have a high referral rate. (17)

Elderly people in Bexhill and Clacton, and so probably in Bognor too, frequently have no children, and people with no children have high referral rates. On the other hand, widows tend to be under-represented in the resorts and they are a group with high referral rates. It would be interesting to know whether retired married people in the resorts are more subject to depression, or at least to consulting their doctor about it, than are retired married people elsewhere.

Whatever the reason, however, the possibility that resorts do have particular psycho-geriatric problems has to be faced. Though figures are as yet available for Bognor only, very many of the officials and doctors interviewed in a variety of seaside places thought that the situation was particularly bad in the resorts. One psychiatric consultant in Sussex described the situation as 'explosive; we're sitting on top of a volcano'. According to Sainsbury, Costain and Grad's findings in Bognor and Chichester the introduction of an improved community service is likely to bring to light even more old people with psychiatric problems, especially the single, the very old and women with depressive illness. (18) So an improved service will almost undoubtedly increase pressure on the psychiatric services in the resorts. In such a situation and considering the shortage of geriatric beds, the precipitate closing of psychiatric hospitals may be at best ill-advised and at worst disastrous.

THE POSSIBILITY OF UNUSUAL NEED FOR INSTITUTIONAL CARE IN RESORTS

It can well be argued that the particular circumstances of the resorts, in that they have such a predominantly elderly population, make it likely that national average quotas for the provision of hospital or other institutional care, even if achieved, may be unrealistically low even for average needs in the resorts, quite apart from the question raised above, as to whether psycho-geriatric problems in resorts are particularly acute. A geriatric consultant explains the situation:

The problem is particularly acute in retirement areas, not simply because there are more old people but because the yardsticks for provision which are used are too rigid and do not allow for any circumstances other than straight numerical ratios. Provision for geriatric beds is made on the basis of 10 beds per 1,000 population aged 65 and over, but what the administrators fail to realise is that, in areas with a large proportion of the elderly, there is not the opportunity for neighbourly help and, because of this greater incapacity of the community to cope with its elderly, provision for geriatric beds should be made at a more generous ratio. (19)

This view is certainly logical in view of the proportion of childless people interviewed in this survey and the sheer proportions of elderly people. Doctors find that they are unable to ask neighbours for help when someone is ill, because the neighbours are themselves too ill or frail. The hospitals have similar problems in that many people are admitted to geriatric wards or psychiatric hospitals because they live alone without outside help or because some other elderly person upon whom they have depended dies or is taken ill. It is quite common for elderly couples to be admitted together. Another relatively common situation is that an elderly landlady is taken ill and a tenant whom she had been nursing is left alone. In a community in which there were more younger people such situations would be less common.

The ability and willingness of family and friends to care for an elderly person will naturally have an effect on the rate of admission to hospital or at least on the number of requests for admission. As long ago as 1956 Abel-Smith and Titmuss (20) discovered that the widowed and single were much more likely to be admitted to hospital than were married people. Later surveys have confirmed this finding. (21) In other words it is the amount of community support available which determines admission at least as much as the character of the illness. Apparently relatives themselves are willing to suffer enormous inconvenience and hardship in order to keep a patient out of hospital. This is particularly the case when the relative concerned is a husband or wife of the patient. (22) (23) But despite this willingness strong doubts are being expressed about the ability of the retirement resort communities to carry the burden of physical and mental illness there. For instance, according to work by Grad and Sainsbury, (24) elderly psychiatric patients are much more likely to represent a severe burden on their relatives and neighbours than are younger psychiatric patients, and they say that: 'We are obliged to consider whether their continued presence in the homes is leading to the production of more mental illness in the community.' (25)

The following remarks about the situation in Eastbourne serve to confirm this view:

Inability of the relatives and neighbours to cope often

reflects the mental confusion of the elderly, and of all the difficulties met with, this is one for which I have the most sympathy. Wandering at night, restless, eccentric and very often aggressive behaviour by day, if it has to be endured for long, can ruin family life and cause much suffering to adults and children alike. In many instances it is not in the interest of the health of the family to persist with the modern doctrines of closing psychiatric beds, calling the resulting distressed situation 'community care'. (26)

In other words, though good 'community care' is probably the ideal solution for the patients, it seems highly dubious whether in retirement resorts, because of the old age and frailty of such a large proportion of the 'supporting' community, such a role can be adequately fulfilled without massive supporting services and some would say perhaps even with them. Particularly in the case of senile dementia the strain of constant care may be too much to be relieved by any range of daytime domiciliary help. Nevertheless, it should be remembered that, whether or not it is given the new name of 'community care', the situation remains, at present, as it always has been, that the majority of both psychiatric and geriatric cases are cared for at home throughout the greater part of their illness and will continue to be.

In a situation in which family and friends find difficulty in helping elderly people, and in which the proportion of elderly people is so large, it is essential of course that community services provided by statutory and voluntary bodies should be particularly well developed to act as a substitute. In addition elderly people who are looking after a sick relative need supporting services such as home helps. One reason why the well-to-do are admitted to hospital less often is that they can afford to pay for private domestic help and nursing. In this context it should be remembered that:

> The rate of ten geriatric beds per 1,000 population over the age of 65, assumes that the standard of services for the elderly outside hospital will be brought generally up to the level of the best current practice. Even this level is capable of being raised further, and some areas fall well below it. The services for the elderly include not only health visitors, social workers, home nurses and home helps, but also residential accommodation provided under Part III of the National Assistance Act for those in need of care and attention.
>
> In addition the increase in housing accommodation for old people, ranging from separate, specially

designed dwellings to group schemes with a warden and
communal services, has also made it possible for more
to be cared for outside hospital. (27)

In the following chapters we will see whether the short-
falls in hospital provision, and the handicaps under which
elderly people labour to help their sick friends and
relatives, are adequately relieved by provision of housing,
residential homes and good supportive community services.

15 Housing and residential homes: public versus private provision

In relation to the provision of residential accommodation for old people, both the social services and housing departments are faced with the same problem in that they have to decide not just how much special residential provision for old people is required but also how much the local authority should itself provide and how much can be left to voluntary bodies or to private enterprise. It is extremely difficult to assess the 'demand' from old people for publicly provided housing. In this brief review of the situation in retirement areas, all that is attempted is a comparison between the amount of accommodation provided in the resorts and average provision in England and Wales. However, it is necessary to qualify heavily statements based on these comparisons, because of the peculiar character of the resorts.

LOCAL AUTHORITY HOUSING

In the resorts very small proportions of the housing stock are publicly provided. Nationally in 1971, 28.2 per cent of households in England and Wales lived in local authority housing. Of the resort county boroughs only Brighton (with 19.8 per cent), Eastbourne (19.1 per cent) and Hastings (15.4 per cent) had more than half this figure. (1) Southport had the lowest proportion at 7.3 per cent. The position was the same in relation to the non-county boroughs and urban districts in resort areas; only a handful had more than 15 per cent of households living in local authority housing and many much less. For instance, in 1971, Bexhill had 10.4 per cent, Clacton 6.6 per cent, Worthing 9.4 per cent and Hove 10.3 per cent.

Looking at council housing suited to old people, in 1970-1 there were on average 84.7 one-bedroomed local

Chapter 15

authority flats and bungalows for 1,000 people of 65 and over in England and Wales. (2) Brighton came close to this figure with 79.7 but the other resorts fell far behind. In descending order the figures were Eastbourne 59.5, Blackpool 57.5, Hastings 43.3, Southend 41.8, Torbay 23.2, Bournemouth 20.7 and Southport 17.5. These figures compare even more strikingly with the national average for county boroughs which was 117.8.

It is of course, possible to argue that with so many privately built bungalows and with such large proportions of owner-occupiers, the resorts do not need large numbers of local authority old people's dwellings. But it is interesting to note that there is no relationship between the provision of local authority housing for old people and the social class of the population. Eastbourne provides much more than Hastings, Southend and Southport, where the retired people are less well off than those in Eastbourne.

From the analysis of the Bexhill waiting lists it emerged that many elderly people who retire to resorts fall into great financial or other difficulties and need help to find adequate housing. Often they are referred to the housing department by their general practitioner, the Supplementary Benefits Commission or other social service agencies, when they have not considered applying or been unwilling to come forward of their own accord. It seems fairly clear that the more liberal a resort authority is about relaxing residential qualifications and accepting owner-occupiers on its waiting list, the more it will be forced to recognize substantial hidden 'demand' for local authority housing. Stereotypes, about the 'well-off' retired people not requiring sheltered housing, will be rapidly eroded.

Social services departments also have a role to play in housing, by making contributions towards the costs of wardens and other facilities in sheltered housing schemes run by housing departments or voluntary bodies. In 1972-3 of the 83 county boroughs 47 made contributions to grouped housing schemes, the average amount being £194.9 per 1,000 population aged 65 and over. (3) Of the 8 resort county boroughs only Torbay, Blackpool and Eastbourne made such contributions, covering a total of 274 units. The sums given averaged £280.5 per 1,000 elderly people in Torbay, £104.0 in Blackpool and £20.0 in Eastbourne.

On the other hand, all the resort counties, like all other county councils, made contributions to sheltered housing schemes in 1972-3. However, only one resort county, Hampshire, exceeded the county average expenditure per 1,000 elderly people of £1,071.9. The lowest expenditures were recorded by the Isle of Wight, £205.8, Dorset, £330.8, Essex, £397.7 and East Suffolk £424.7 per 1,000 elderly people.

It is easy to point to the small proportions of local authority housing in resorts but less easy to say how much should be provided. Most resort housing authorities, whilst admitting the deficiencies, blame their position more upon the difficulties of getting central government loan sanction, of building within the Housing Cost Yardstick and of finding suitable sites, than upon their own unwillingness to build.

The earlier chapter about the housing situation in Bexhill and Clacton suggested that the basic problem in resorts was lack of variety of accommodation for old people and that there are alternative solutions other than the provision of local authority housing. Housing authorities need to consider these possibilities. In fact they, like all housing departments, need to work out a unified housing strategy for their area. The strategy would have to consider private, local authority and voluntary housing, hotels and homes as integral parts of the whole housing effort in the resorts.

RESIDENTIAL HOMES FOR OLD PEOPLE

At present no clear yardstick exists by which to measure the adequacy of provision of local authority residential accommodation or Part III accommodation as it is usually called. (4) However, there are broad guidelines. The Department of Health states that '... experience so far would suggest that most authorities may find a ratio of between 15 and 25 places per thousand population aged 65 and over appropriate to their areas', (5) and recommends provision within the range of 18-22 places per 1,000. (6)

In March 1974 the average number of elderly residents in Part III accommodation, provided by local authorities or in joint-user premises, was 14.5 per 1,000 elderly people in England. (7) There was, however, a big difference between the county boroughs with 17.5 and the county districts with 13.0.

The retirement resorts had rather poor levels of provision in 1974 compared with the national average. Of the 8 resort county boroughs all but Bournemouth had less than the average for all county boroughs. In addition 9 of the 12 retirement county areas had below the average for all English counties.

In addition to the Part III accommodation provided by the local authority and in joint-user premises, places are also taken for Part III accommodation in voluntary and private homes for the elderly. In March 1974, places taken up in this way averaged 2.4 per 1,000 of the elderly population in England; 2.2 were in voluntary homes and 0.2 in private homes. In most of the resort county boroughs and in the resort counties of East and West Sussex this type of provision was more common than the national average and was clearly being used to make up some of the severe shortfall in statutorily provided accommodation. In many cases an apparent improvement since 1970 in the provision of Part III accommodation can be explained largely by increased use of voluntary and private accommodation. (8)

Because of the unsatisfactory levels of provision of local authority homes, admission to places in them is reserved only for those in the most urgent need. Most admissions are not taken off the waiting list but are either emergency cases or exchanges with hospitals who need to discharge a patient. (9) Thus the waiting list is neither a measure of need nor of backlog nor, even, as in the case of a housing register, does it confer priority. (10)

In such a situation many people who seek residential accommodation will turn to voluntary and private institutions for help. The chances of finding this type of accommodation are not the same in all resorts, because of their patchy distribution.

The largest concentration of voluntarily run homes is in the ring of counties round London and in Sussex, Hampshire and the Isle of Wight. Certain resort county boroughs even outside this ring have very remarkable numbers of places in voluntary homes. The outstanding examples in the resorts are Southport (30.5 places per 1,000 in 1970), Hastings (16.7), Brighton (16.4) and Southend (11.9). (11) However, as mentioned earlier, in many places large proportions of beds are taken up by local authorities as Part III accommodation.

The national distribution of private homes (12) is very different from that of statutory or voluntary homes. In 1970, 46 per cent of all the residents in private homes in county boroughs in England and Wales were in 8 seaside resorts: Bournemouth, Hastings, Torbay, Southend, Blackpool, Eastbourne, Brighton and Southport. Hastings had eight times the national average of residents in private homes per 1,000 elderly people. (13) Similarly, of those 11 administrative counties with more than 300 residents in private homes, 8 were in retirement areas and a ninth, Lancashire, contained a number of retirement resorts. Devon and West Sussex both had more than twice the national average of residents in private homes.

Private nursing homes (14) are also very numerous in retirement areas. Though not as concentrated in resorts as are private homes, the numbers of nursing home places in Bournemouth, Eastbourne and Hastings in 1970 equalled or exceeded the numbers in major cities like Manchester, Liverpool, Birmingham and Bristol. Hastings had in fact six times the national ratio of beds per 1,000 people, Southport, Bournemouth, Eastbourne and West Sussex more than three times and Brighton and East Sussex more than twice.

Taking old people's homes alone there are 4 resorts, Hastings, Bournemouth, Torbay and Blackpool and 1 county, Devon, where private provision in 1970 constituted about 40 per cent or more of all residential accommodation. If nursing homes are included this figure is 12 resorts and counties. Nationally private provision constituted 13 per cent of total accommodation, and if private nursing homes are included 25 per cent. However, it should be remembered that the resorts specialize in provision for the elderly and that voluntary and private homes and nursing homes cater for a by no means exclusively local population. People come from London and other cities to enter a home on the South Coast and local elderly people have to compete with these newcomers to obtain a place. Thus, though the supply of private homes appears ample in, for instance, Hastings, it is not necessarily easy to find a place in a private or voluntary home there. Nevertheless, it will be substantially easier than in most cities in England and Wales; in 1968, for instance, out of 79 county boroughs in England and Wales which sent in returns, 28 had no private homes at all, 26 had no voluntary homes and 15 had neither.

Despite the existence of competition for places by people arriving from other parts of the country where private homes are scarce and the environment less pleasant, private homes and nursing homes in the resorts are certainly helping greatly in relieving the stresses caused by shortages of geriatric beds and local authority homes. For instance, the hospitals discharge patients into private homes, nursing homes and hotels when other accommodation is not available or is unsuitable. In the seven years 1961-7, 10 per cent of all those discharged from the Hastings Geriatric Unit went into local authority residential homes and 11 per cent went into private homes or hotels. Of the ones who went to private homes and hotels 46 per cent went to nursing homes, 48 per cent into old people's homes and 5 per cent into hotels. (15)

The practice of discharging patients into private homes and hotels is not confined to the resorts but the scale upon which they have to be used seems particularly great. One may compare, for instance, the Hastings figures with those for Sutton Coldfield, a similarly middle-class area but with only 10 per cent of people aged 65 and over in 1966. There in 1971 only 2.7 per cent of discharges from the geriatric unit of the North Birmingham District Hospital were to private homes, nursing homes and hotels. (16)

Before old people are discharged from hospital into private homes or hotels, at least some assessment is made of their financial position to see if they or their relations can pay for such accommodation. A much more worrying situation in the resorts is that general practitioners have been more and more forced to send patients to private homes when they are unable to get them into a hospital or residential home or to provide them with adequate domiciliary services. Not the least worrying feature of this situation is that many old people can ill afford these homes. The Worthing Geriatric Consultant writes as follows:

> The Medical Social Workers arranged 72 temporary admissions to nursing homes in 1966 compared with 47 in 1965. These figures, given as they are, only represent part of the true situation, however, taking no account of the nursing home admissions arranged by general practitioners themselves, because a hospital bed could not be found. At the date of writing, 40 patients (25%) on my A-list (in need of accommodation) are in nursing homes, many of them in considerable financial distress. In spite of my repeated requests over the years no financial help from statutory sources has been made available for those unfortunate old people, though it must be clear to one and all that it is the lack of hospital beds which has brought about this plight. (17)

Similarly the Medical Officer of Health for Eastbourne writes:

> Nursing home beds are at a premium, and it is no unusual event for departmental staff to appeal to voluntary funds to the tune of thirty guineas a week in order to admit a sick aged person who could not be left alone for another day. (18)

Private homes, private nursing homes and hotels are all much more expensive than welfare accommodation. In 1970 the maximum charge in a local authority home was about £10 a week. Compared with this 43 per cent of nursing homes in East Sussex charged a minimum of £20 a week and 50 per cent of old people's homes a minimum of £10. (19) Clearly the charges were very high in relation to the incomes of most elderly people, though not necessarily in relation to the service offered. The Supplementary Benefits Commission is willing to go part way to help with these charges but there is usually a large sum to be found by the old person, or by relatives, or if they are fortunate, by a charitable body. In 1970 the board and lodging charge allowed in resorts was between £6 and £7 plus from £1 to £1.50 pocket money. However, the average minimum basic charge for a private nursing home was £13 a week and £20-4 was not uncommon. There were usually extra charges above the minimum quoted. (20) Since then, prices have escalated rapidly.

Apart from the cost, there is the question of the control of standards in private homes and hotels. Many hotels operate virtually as homes but are not registered as such. (21) A social services department official writes:

> This is a delicate problem because if a strong line is taken with these establishments and they are required to comply with all the regulations necessary for registration, they may well decide not to have old people any more (or at least cut down their numbers) and this will put an added strain on the already tight accommodation situation of old people. Basically these establishments are doing a useful and worthwhile job: but technically they are doing it illegally. (22)

The difficulty is that unless an establishment is registered it cannot be inspected to see that its provision is adequate for old people. (23) On the other hand, proprietors find it difficult financially to comply with existing regulations, particularly the fire precautions. There is at present no system of grants to help them, nor is it possible for welfare authorities to subsidize the rents of residents in private homes unless they have themselves placed the old person in the home.

One suggested method of helping to raise standards in private homes is that welfare authorities should be allowed to contribute to the rent of all elderly people in private homes not just those whom they have placed in them. But which authority should or would contribute in the case of private homes in the coastal resorts? The logical conclusion would seem to be that, in the case of someone moving straight into a coastal private home from somewhere else in the country, the authority from which they came would make the contribution. This would be the same procedure as that currently adopted by welfare authorities when they place their elderly residents in some statutory or voluntary institution elsewhere in the country. However, many of the residents of homes have migrated in earlier old age. Who would pay for them? The coastal authorities would need financial assistance if the whole burden were to fall on them. Most welfare authorities finally conclude that, 'In the long run the only effective answer to unsatisfactory private accommodation is for there to be adequate alternatives provided by the public authorities in terms of residential homes and good housing.' (24)

However, the question of what level of residential provision the resorts should make is complicated by the fact that at present private homes in the resorts draw their customers from much wider areas than a welfare authority. If it were decided to make provision only for local elderly people, any but the loosest definition of 'local' would cause great hardship to people who had moved there to retire and had broken their links with their home area. On the other hand if the welfare authority provided residential accommodation for all elderly people wanting it, it would have implicitly accepted a national rather than a local role, and would have to receive official financial assistance from central government. It is doubtful even then whether private homes would close. Some of the more expensive provide a level of service and amenities which more wealthy people would not want to see disappear, and which can provide an example for improvements in the public sector.

In spite of the costs, then, it seems that private homes will continue to be a major feature of the resorts, attracting elderly people from all over the country. However, it is equally clear that only a minority of the retired residents of the resorts could pay for a private home indefinitely out of their income, and that even in the very 'middle-class' resorts such as Bexhill most of the old person's capital is tied up in a house. It is most important to stress that even in these wealthier resorts, there are at present many people who are forced through lack of adequate public provision of residential homes, hospital beds and day hospitals to live in private homes and nursing homes which they can afford only for a short period. The existence of this private provision should not be made an excuse for inadequate public provision, particularly when there is very little supervision of conditions in private homes. In resorts like Clacton, where the level of incomes and savings is very low, discussion of extensive reliance on private provision is in any case superfluous, and adequate public provision will have to be made unless a crisis situation is to be reached in a few years' time when the present relatively young retired population has aged. Moreover, for reasons given in the last chapter, the need for institutional care in the resorts may be such that more than average provision is desirable. In the next chapter we will see whether there are also problems in relation to community health and domiciliary services or whether these compensate for shortages in the other services.

16 Community health and domiciliary services

THE GENERAL PRACTITIONERS

Nationally it has been found that doctors have to visit elderly patients much more often than younger patients. The consultation rate per 1,000 men aged 65 and over is 586 consultations per year, compared with 294 for men younger than that. The rate for elderly women is 641 consultations compared with 369 for younger women. (1) Clearly, in the retirement resorts, where there are such large proportions of elderly people, it is to be expected that doctors will have a particularly heavy burden of work per patient.

However, assessment of the total burden of work on a doctor must take into consideration the numbers of patients on his list as well as the average amount of work per patient. The average list size in 1973 in England and Wales was 2,386. (2) Only two Executive Council areas covering resorts had average list sizes above this average, Essex with 2,498 and Southend on Sea with 2,420. (Essex, however, cannot really be treated as a resort county like the others, because it is too heterogeneous.)

The average is, however, rather misleading because it disguises the fact that within the same area there are doctors with very large and very small lists. Thus in Southport, though the list average was only 2,277 there were 30 per cent of doctors with lists of 3,000 or more and 25 per cent with less than 1,600. However, even so only 4 resort areas, Southport, Blackpool, Southend and Essex had more than 10 per cent of doctors with lists of 3,000 or more.

The favourable situation of the resorts as to list size is apparently the result of relatively easy recruitment. There is little difficulty in obtaining a replacement when a practice has a vacancy, mainly because, apparently, the pleasant surroundings which attract retired people also attract doctors. The Clerk to one Executive Council writes as follows:

> There are a number of popular retirement areas on the Dorset coast, for example, Lyme Regis, Swanage and the areas of Poole on the Bournemouth boundary. All of those districts, although presenting a geriatric problem, are extremely pleasant places in which to live and there is never any very great difficulty in obtaining medical manpower for these areas. In Essex the situation is somewhat similar, in areas such as Frinton and Clacton-on-Sea. (3)

The Executive Councils try to discourage doctors actually moving to the coast to work part-time after retirement from their full-time practice, but of course they cannot prevent local doctors gradually winding down their practice into retirement. For this reason, average list sizes can be very misleading as a reflection of the load on particular doctors.

The unequal distribution of patients between lists, particularly the very large proportion of doctors in resorts who have very small lists, may be putting a strain on the more active doctors. The consultation rate for a list of 2,200 people containing 33 per cent of elderly people is about the equivalent for a list of 2,480 people with an age distribution near the national average. Such a calculation brings the average lists in resort areas to around the national average; for doctors with larger lists, the work burden must indeed be severe: a list of 3,000 with 33 per cent of elderly people is the equivalent of 3,600 at an average age distribution. In addition the workload per consultation is not necessarily the same for old and young people.

As a consequence most doctors in the resorts show a marked preference for taking on younger rather than older patients. A doctor from Southport describes the position:

> No doctor likes to refuse acceptance to elderly people who have newly come to the town, but experience has shown only too clearly that the numbers of items of service required annually by the over-sixty-fives is greatly in excess of the national average; also that, for the elderly living alone, the problems of disposal during illness become so acute that doctors with lists top heavy with older people ... and knowing that they have insufficient time to deal adequately with the problems they present, are reluctant to take on more time consuming responsibilities. (4)

Elsewhere the strongest statement that the burden on

doctors in resorts was greater than in other areas came from the Executive Council in West Sussex:

> From my own discussions with doctors in the coastal belt of West Sussex, in some parts of which 20-30% of the patients are over 65, I am quite satisfied that doctors are in general in these areas more hard pressed than elsewhere and that the more considerate and helpful a doctor is, the greater is the pressure upon him from his patients. I express this opinion in full recognition of the fact that in some of the urban areas of this country, doctors are having to deal with very much larger lists of patients than are those in the areas of which I am talking and that I am not really qualified to compare the pressures on a doctor with 3,000 patients in Wolverhampton for instance, with the pressures on a doctor with shall we say 2,500 patients in Worthing or the neighbouring coastal areas. (5)

In general, though, the Clerks of Executive Councils in resort areas held the view that though elderly patients do put a heavy burden on doctors, the smaller number of patients on each list and the attractions of the resorts as residential areas are usually enough to counterbalance this. In addition, the Executive Councils felt doctors were financially compensated by the opportunities in many resorts for having private patients and by receiving the extra capitation fee for people of 65 and over. (6) Considering the difficulties that many industrial areas have to attract doctors and the consequential burden of work on the ones who do go there, it would seem wrong to increase incentives for them to go to the resorts.

So far, however, this discussion of the doctor's workload has not considered the effects of the scarcity of hospital beds and local authority homes. This cannot be ignored. The Southport doctor referred to the 'problems of disposal during illness'. The Medical Officer of Health for Eastbourne wrote about the way in which general practitioners rely on private homes to help their patients who are waiting for hospital beds. Another medical officer said that many of the old people leaving hospital are more sick than those going in. In these circumstances, it would be foolish to pretend that an analysis of list sizes can adequately reflect the doctors' situation. It should also be remembered that a burden of frustration or anxiety can be more taxing than one of hard but fulfilled work. When there is a shortage of hospital beds and of local authority homes, it is inevitable that the burden of making arrangements for alternative care should fall on general practitioners. If there is, in addition, a shortage of domiciliary services, then the greater the burden

of work and anxiety on the doctors. In this connection
the remark about sympathetic doctors getting a particularly
heavy workload is relevant. Beyond the needs of the
physically ill much work with elderly people has to do
with loneliness and the need for reassurance.

A further difficulty for doctors in the resorts is the
one already discussed that when someone is taken ill, the
neighbours, being old too, are unlikely to be capable of
giving much help. In addition relatively few old people
in resorts have young relatives living within a distance
that would be any help in such a sudden emergency. This
situation means that greater demands are likely to be
made on the doctors and domiciliary health services, as
well as on the hospitals, than in a community of more
mixed age and with more local roots. As people tend to
know more about doctors than about other services and to
turn to them in emergencies, (7) the doctors are bound to
feel the effect of this increased need. If in addition
shortage of other health services prevents them from
acting as an efficient clearing-house, they are bound to
suffer severe strain and worry. The solution, however,
is not in the provision of more doctors but in improvements in other services.

THE HOME HELP SERVICES

The home help service is usually regarded as amongst the
most crucial of the domiciliary services. With the
emphasis, in both geriatric and psycho-geriatric work,
on community rather than institutional care, the home help
service will become increasingly important. And yet in
most of the retirement resorts the service is in desperate
straits.

In her study of the home help service in England and
Wales in 1967, Audrey Hunt made an assessment of the
extent to which the service was currently meeting needs.
She concluded that: 'At the minimum the provision of home
help for the elderly needs to be at least doubled, while
that for the younger chronic sick needs to be at least
trebled.' (8)

A reanalysis of Audrey Hunt's data for the retirement
areas shows that the situation there was even worse than
the national average. (9) In particular the South Coast
(10) presented a very dismal picture. Whatever the
measure - ratio of home helps to the elderly population,
the proportion of elderly population seen, the number of
hours per case - the resorts showed up badly. During one
week in 1967 only 2.4 per cent of the elderly people on

the South Coast received a home help, compared with 3.31 per cent in other resort areas and 4.12 per cent in the rest of the country. There was only 1 home help on the South Coast for 142 elderly people, compared with 1 for 81 in other resorts and 1 for 89 elsewhere in the rest of the country. The number of hours per case averaged 4.0 on the South Coast, 4.8 in other resorts and 4.6 in the rest of the country. It was not only the elderly who received a poor level of home help service; the young suffered because of the strain of catering for the old. In the resort areas other than the South Coast, though the numbers of home helps were quite large they were still insufficient to provide for such a large proportion of elderly people. On the South Coast the numbers of home helps were below the national average even for a population of average age.

The annual home help figures for the year ending 31 March, 1973, show that the situation has remained as bad. Not one of the resort county boroughs came near to approaching the ratio of home helps to the elderly population in all county boroughs (1 in 169), let alone the national average (1 in 84). Southend had the best figure (1 in 218) and Bournemouth the worst (1 in 577). Essex and Norfolk which are only partially retirement areas were the only resort counties to reach the ratio for all counties (1 in 182). Many resort county councils fell very far short of the average, the worst being the Isle of Wight (1 in 472), West Sussex (1 in 458) and Kent (1 in 393). (11)

The problem is basically one of recruitment. The reasons for the scarcity of labour are various 'but perhaps the most obvious is the fact that there is a comparatively small population of women from whom home helps are usually recruited'. (12) The resorts have particularly small proportions of middle-aged, working-class women. Also in areas where there is a large proportion of fairly wealthy people, there is the additional problem of competition with the private sector. (13) That this is indeed a problem is confirmed by the results of our survey which showed that 18 per cent of our respondents in Bexhill had private home helps, while only 1.6 per cent had local authority home helps. Similarly it was found that in Worthing, in 1966, 11 per cent of elderly people had private home helps compared with 2.4 per cent who had local authority help. (14) The proportions having private help were well above the national average and the proportions receiving local authority help were well below. Competition for labour also comes from the hotels in the summer.

Because of this shortage of staff, the service has suffered in two ways. First, in order to cater for increasing demand from larger numbers of old people, the hours allocated to any one person have had to be reduced. Again the reduction in hours per case shows up in the home help figures for 1973. On average in England and Wales each case received 142.6 hours a year. This was slightly less in the county boroughs, 126.2 hours. In the resort county boroughs the greatest number of hours were achieved in Brighton, Blackpool and Southend, with 109.9, 106.0 and 105.4 hours respectively. Cases in Eastbourne and Hastings received 91.4 hours, in Southport 83.1 hours and in Torbay and Bournemouth 66.6 and 63.2 hours respectively, half the national average. These figures are in spite of the fact that elderly cases usually need more time.

The services in the resort county councils had not been as curtailed but again the Isle of Wight, Kent and West Sussex show up particularly badly with 107.3, 104.2, and 67.0 hours respectively.

An alternative to cutting hours had been to refuse home helps to more marginal cases, for instance those with higher incomes or where there is a less critical situation. (15) In addition many doctors, mental welfare, medical social workers and health visitors feel that it is not worth putting in a request for a home help, even for an urgent case. If this failure to report cases reaches a large scale, as it appears to have in many resorts, the organizers of the home help service may themselves be unaware of the inadequacy of their service, and it will be impossible to assess the real need. This is a genuine problem - to persuade referral agencies to continue to contact the home help service in spite of near certainty of failure, and to persuade the home help organizers that they are not catering for all the need.

Possible solutions to the shortage of home helps have been put forward by many writers. Up-grading the whole service, providing uniforms and cars and better equipment have been some suggestions. (16) Some of the resort authorities have made efforts with badges and overalls, prizes and lectures and training schemes, but as Eastbourne has found, 'even when recruits are found, there is a very substantial turnover of staff which can only be checked by the introduction of better conditions of service, including pay'. (17) The home help organizer for Hastings describes the pay as 'appalling':

> For a single person working full-time, when tax and insurance is deducted, there is not much more left than for an Old Age Pensioner who is in receipt of retirement pension and supplementary benefit.' (18)

In effect, to quote Audrey Hunt, 'almost all the major improvements would involve spending more money'. (19) But the resorts may well be facing a much more fundamental problem of an acute shortage of such local labour. The solution in this case would be to raise wage rates until people, including men, were actually attracted by the pay, or to attract men to the area to work in other employment hoping that some of their wives will take up work in the home help service. Even then there may remain a permanent problem of recruitment to what is currently relatively unattractive work.

MEALS SERVICES

The provision of meals for elderly people is still, in most parts of the country, predominantly a 'meals-on-wheels' service. However, lunch clubs are developing in importance, particularly in urban areas.

The provision of meals in this way has both a preventive role, in avoiding under-nourishment which so frequently causes a breakdown of health and hence admission to a hospital or home, and also a support role for people who come out of hospital or are infirm and unable to cater for themselves. The lunch club has the added bonus of providing company.

The size of the meals service provided in an area can be measured both by the proportion of elderly people receiving meals and by the numbers of meals served to them. Nationally in the year ending March 1973 an average of 4,546.9 meals were served per 1,000 people of 65 and over in county boroughs; 43.5 per 1,000 of these people received meals at home. (20) In the county council areas fewer people received meals at home 35.7 per 1,000 and fewer meals were served altogether, 3,116.7.

In the resort county boroughs the service provided compared very badly with the average, in terms of the number of meals served per 1,000 of the elderly population. Only Bournemouth (4,824.5 meals) exceeded the average. All the others fell short of the average by more than 1,000 meals. Blackpool and Southport served only 892.5 and 1,530.9 meals per 1,000 elderly people.

In the three resorts which served the most meals, Bournemouth, Brighton, and Southend, a relatively large proportion of the population was being reached at home with at least one meal in the course of the week. During a representative week they were serving meals at home to more than 50.0 per 1,000 of the elderly population compared with the average of 43.5 for all county boroughs. This means that they must have been serving meals relatively few days per week to relatively large numbers of people. At the other extreme Eastbourne was serving its meals to relatively few people at home; only 8.3 people per 1,000 were receiving meals at home in the course of that week, and 49 per cent of the meals were served outside the home. In the case of Blackpool and Southport so few meals were being served at all that in spite of the fact that more than 70 per cent of the meals were served at home only 11.0 per 10,000 people were receiving them.

In the county council resort areas, too, the picture was better but still not encouraging. Only 3 counties out of the 12 (Essex, East Suffolk and West Sussex) exceeded the very much lower average number of meals served in all county councils (3,116.7 per 1,000 of the elderly population). Cornwall, the Isle of Wight and Norfolk were the worst, with 1,204.7, 1,317.0 and 1,844.7 respectively.

The intervention of social services departments in meals services appears to reduce the likelihood of a very poor level of service. All resort authorities where the local authority provided more than 10 per cent of the meals had a service which was better than the average for resorts. While some of the best services, for instance in Brighton, East Suffolk and Devon, were run voluntarily, in all the resorts where there was a very poor level of meals service it was run entirely or almost entirely by voluntary agencies. Perhaps in some of those authorities which provide no meals service themselves, there is also a lack of interest in supporting the voluntary service.

In summary the situation in relation to meals services in the retirement areas is very poor in the county boroughs and in need of increased frequency of service in the county areas. The voluntary services need to be either improved or supplemented by local authority provision. This extra provision may well need to be in the form of lunch clubs which have proved, in Greater London particularly, to be a very good way of providing frequent meals to large proportions of elderly people. The retirement areas currently lag behind the national average in the provision of lunch clubs. This may partly be put down to the distances to be covered in rural areas. But most of the retirement areas of which we are talking have concentrated areas of retirement homes in which lunch clubs could be located.

Chapter 16

HOME NURSING

The home nursing service has become very much a service for old people. Nationally 56 per cent of home nursing cases are aged 65 and over. (21) In the resorts, the proportion is nearer two-thirds. The proportion of nursing time spent on the elderly is even larger because most elderly cases need more intensive and long-term help. The home nursing service is therefore one of the most crucial in the resorts especially given the shortages of hospital beds.

On 30 September 1973 the average number of home nurses in post was 0.23 per 1,000 of the total population in the English county boroughs. In the counties it was 0.22. In terms of staffing for the total population the establishments of home nurses in resorts were above the national average. Were there not large numbers of elderly people the service would be considered adequate. However, if one looks at the elderly population the situation is very different. In the county boroughs the number of home nurses per 1,000 of the population aged 65 and over was 1.61 and in the counties 1.63. None of the resort county boroughs or counties reached this figure. The best proportions were in Southport and Somerset (1.57) and Brighton (1.52). The worst were in Bournemouth (0.92) and Hastings (0.97).

It can be argued, in any case, that in the resorts there is, quite apart from the large proportion of elderly people, a need for a better than average service because the character of the work of home nurses is affected by the severe shortage of hospital beds. Another problem is, yet again, the lack of young relatives and neighbours to help the patient: 'The bulk of the nurses' work these days is heavy bedside nursing. Often the only person to care for the patient is an elderly and infirm relative. Therefore nurses may become the main support of the household.' (22)

The home nursing service is apparently making intensive efforts to compensate for shortages in other services. In many cases, big increases in the service have been achieved without increases in staff. Recruitment to the home nursing service is not easy but none of the resorts described a desperate situation in this respect. Amelia Harris has stated that small staff sizes are not usually a reflection on recruiting difficulties but of the establishment permitted by the local authority budget. (23) Because of their large proportions of elderly people, resorts have to provide very much bigger services per head of the population than do other towns just to achieve average cover for the elderly. This has to be paid for. In addition there is the problem of the age and frailty of the neighbours and spouses of sick people in resorts, which probably necessitates a higher level of home nursing service. Certainly until the shortage of hospital beds is remedied, only increased staffing of the home nursing service can reduce the risk of neglect of sick old people. Such remedies can be achieved more quickly than large building programmes by hospital boards, but again, as in the case of the home help service, local authority resources have to be available.

HEALTH VISITING

The work of health visitors has been much less concerned with elderly people than has that of home nurses, but, especially in the retirement areas, an increasing proportion of health visitors' time is spent on the elderly. However, it varies very much from place to place. For instance, though nationally in 1969 only 9 per cent (24) of the cases visited by health visitors were 65 and over, in Worthing the proportion was 29 per cent, in East Sussex 24 per cent, in Southport 22 per cent and in West Sussex 14 per cent. In some resorts this trend has been resisted. In Southend, for instance, only 2 per cent of the cases visited were 65 and over and in Devon only 8 per cent. It has been found that the trend towards the attachment of health visitors to doctors' practices increases the proportion of the visitors' time spent on the elderly. This is bound to be the case as 'hidden need' comes to light through routine visiting in resorts. Also, health visitors will be working with doctors and nurses whose resources are over-stretched in trying to cater for the needs of the elderly.

In 1973 there were 0.13 health visitors per 1,000 of the total population in county boroughs. (25) In the counties there were 0.14. Two of the resort county boroughs exceeded this, Brighton with 0.21 and Eastbourne with 0.17, but only Bournemouth fell far short with 0.09. In the resort counties the range was smaller, from Norfolk with 0.10 to Somerset and East Sussex with 0.17.

However, again, if the staffing is related to the elderly population the picture is very different. The average staffing in county boroughs was 0.94 per 1,000 of the population aged 65 and over and in the counties 1.01. Of all the resort areas only Brighton and Somerset (1.06) and Essex (1.05) exceeded these figures.

In Bournemouth, Hastings and Torbay the staffing was

less than half the average and in Blackpool, Eastbourne, Southend, Southport and Devon only just above.

THE COMMUNITY HEALTH AND DOMICILIARY SERVICES: CONCLUSIONS

Of the community health and domiciliary services in resort areas only the general practitioners have a well-staffed service and yet in spite of this they come under enormous pressure because of the greater needs of elderly people and because of shortages in institutional and domiciliary provision.

The home help service is sadly deficient and suffers from severe recruitment problems. Meals services are poor particularly in the county boroughs, and in the resort counties and county boroughs there are less home nurses and health visitors per 1,000 of the elderly population than there are nationally. This is in spite of the fact that hospital provision is short and home helps scarce.

The total situation is, then, that no service even reaches the national average, except the provision of general practitioners. Given all the problems of large concentrations of elderly people plus the shortage in institutional care, the total situation of the health and social services in the resorts is gloomy.

However, one point needs to be made. Though the overall position is bad, there is variety between the resorts in the quality of any particular service. Thus amongst the county boroughs the ratio of home helps to elderly people was largest in Southend and smallest in Bournemouth; the borough serving the most meals per 1,000 elderly people was Bournemouth, the least Blackpool; that with the best ratio of home nurses to the elderly population was Southport and the worst Bournemouth; health visitors were most numerous in Brighton and least in Bournemouth. Though Brighton, with its smaller proportion of elderly people, did frequently appear amongst the places with the best service, it was by no means always the case that the places with the most elderly people had the worst service.

One problem in improving standards, however, is that many of the resort county council areas are very rural, and, quite apart from their problems of provision for elderly people who move there to retire, they have all the difficulties of providing services for a thinly scattered population. Long distances have to be covered between cases by home helps, meals services, district nurses, health visitors and doctors alike. For this reason the nature of the services they provide may have to be different and the cost per person will be high. Any improvement in the service means heavy financial commitments.

But of course, for all areas, rural or seaside town, the task of bringing all the services up to the national average, or even more ambitiously, up to the national target where one exists, would put an enormous financial strain on the local authority and would require a more rapid increase in health and social services expenditure than government plans envisage. In Chapter 17 the financial situation of the resorts is considered in relation to proposed improvements in the health and social services.

17 Paying for services for the elderly

> As long as local taxation is the main support for community services, homogeneity at the community level encourages undesirable inequalities. The high-income suburb can build modern schools with all the latest features; the low-income suburb is forced to treat even more minimal educational progress as luxury. Such inequity is eliminated more efficiently by federal and state subsidy than by community heterogeneity, but the latter is essential as long as such subsidies are ... small.
>
> Herbert J. Gans: 'People and Plans'

If the health and social services are to be improved in the retirement areas, as they clearly need to be, this inevitably means a higher rate burden for the local authorities concerned, or else savings on other items of expenditure. Are those authorities in a good position to make such savings or, once the present restrictions on public expenditure have been lifted, to levy more rates?

This chapter discusses the financial sitation of the resorts, starting with some general points about their economic situation and then goes on, in more detail, to describe their current rate income and expenditure.

Incomes in the resorts are low. The main reason for this is of course the very large proportion of retired people living there, but there are the additional factors that unemployment rates, particularly in the winter, are very high and that the work available is very seasonal and mainly in the service trades, particularly catering and retail shops, in which wage rates are relatively low. In more rural retirement areas, agriculture is the main source of employment and here again wages are low and work opportunities continually reduced by increased mechanisation. For all these reasons, the domestic incomes available to pay rates are low compared with the national average.

On the other hand, though the incomes of retired residents tend to be low, the rateable values of their houses are high. In 1973-4, for instance, in the 8 resort county boroughs only 18 per cent of domestic properties had rateable values of £150 or less compared with an average of 46 per cent in all the county boroughs in England and Wales. (2) This is partly because houses in the resorts have been built relatively recently but also because they are situated in areas of high environmental quality and are therefore regarded as commanding a high rent. This is particularly the case on the Sussex coast where there is the added factor of proximity to London. Because rates are based on the rateable value of the property, not the income of its occupier, there is an inevitable problem in that the quality and value of the house purchased by a retired person tends to reflect their past income and savings rather than their present income and hence ability to pay high rates.

In addition, because of the lack of industrial development, and the de-rating of agricultural land, the proportion of local expenditure which falls on residential property has tended to be very high in resorts, compared with the national average. The domestic proportion of the rateable value in the 8 resort county boroughs in 1973-4 was 56.4 per cent compared with 46.3 per cent nationally for county boroughs. (3) But this represented a marked improvement on 1970-1 when the resorts averaged 59.2 per cent against a national average of 44.0 per cent. (4) The resorts have in fact been all to aware of this problem and have tried to remedy it, against a national tendency in the opposite direction. The same applies to the resort non-county boroughs where the proportion in 1973-4 was 61.3 per cent, compared with a national average of 51.4 per cent, whereas in 1970-1 it had been 65.6 per cent compared with 50.8 per cent. In the resort urban districts, however, the position had deteriorated with an average of 65.0 per cent in 1973-4 compared with 56.7 per cent nationally, whereas in 1970-1 it had been 62.0 per cent compared with 54.8 per cent.

These three features - the low incomes of residents, the relatively high rateable values of their homes and the small contribution of non-domestic rateable value - have been the most important factors in the rating situation of the resorts.

In the last few years a number of changes in the national context have influenced the financial situation of the resorts. The first has been a major review of the

Chapter 17

Rate Support Grant system which has brought a better match between central government subsidies and local needs. Second, in April 1974, a much more thoroughgoing rate rebate scheme was introduced, 90 per cent of which is funded by central government. Third, the reorganization of local government has meant that the seaside resorts have been amalgamated with their neighbouring resorts and with the surrounding rural areas and inland towns into the new district councils. This has produced rather more heterogeneous authorities, with a more average distribution of population, needs, costs and incomes.

A further development since 1972 has been the increased rate of inflation which has led to much higher absolute rates of expenditure by local authorities throughout the country. In turn, the government has reacted by imposing strict controls on local government expenditure. In particular, in the period after 1975, there are to be no increases in expenditure on local authority social services unless they can be financed through savings elsewhere.

All these factors have contributed to changes in the financial climate in the resorts in the last few years. (5)

We will turn now to the main question: Can and should the resorts take on a further burden of rates to cover improved health and social services? To attempt an answer, we need to ask a series of supplementary questions.

First, how heavy is the current burden on the individual domestic ratepayer compared with that in other areas?

Second, what is the current level of expenditure on health and social services in resorts compared with that in other areas?

Third, what is the general level of expenditure and upon which services is expenditure particularly high or low?

Fourth, how much of total expenditure is covered by government grants, not through local rates?

In dealing with the first question, the relevant measure of the burden on domestic ratepayers is the 'average rate per domestic property'. As we mentioned earlier the less the industrial and commercial property, the heavier the rate falls on domestic ratepayers. In 1973-4 the average rates per domestic property in the resort county boroughs were £72.03 compared with a national average of £58.92, in the non-county boroughs £67.42 compared with £59.64 and in the urban districts £71.43 compared with £63.01. After reorganisation, (6) the picture is obscured by the wider areas over which the averages are taken. Thus in 1974-5 the average rates per domestic property were £83.00 compared with a national average of £86.43 for non-metropolitan districts and £79.91 for metropolitan districts. However, this does not mean that rates per domestic property in the coastal resort areas of the new authorities have fallen. They have just been averaged out with lower rates in the rural areas and inland towns. Rateable values did not fall between 1973-4 and 1974-5 and rate poundages rose steeply, so the problem, though disguised, must still be there. If one looks at the new districts of Bournemouth, Brighton, Eastbourne, Hastings, Southend, and Blackpool where the boundaries have changed least under reorganization, one finds the following average levels of rates per domestic property in 1974-5:

Bournemouth	£109.33
Brighton	£ 99.90
Eastbourne	£109.81
Hastings	£ 83.69
Southend	£ 96.62
Blackpool	£ 68.30

But while the burden of rates is very high in the seaside resorts, it should be remembered that most of the people interviewed in Clacton and Bexhill came from London. In the London boroughs the average rate per domestic property was, in 1973-4, £101.30 in inner London and £95.58 in outer London, rising to an average of £101.99 for both in 1974-5. So though rates were very high in the resorts, compared with other towns of a similar size or even the major cities, those people who gave excessively high rates as one of their reasons for leaving London still had some justification.

Why are the rates so high in the resorts? Is this because of particularly high expenditure on health and social services for the large elderly population? This turns out not to be the case.

In spite of their large proportions of elderly people the resorts do not spend much more than the average on social services (Table 17.1). In 1974-5 the resort areas were spending £8.59 per head on social services (other than concessionary fares), compared with £8.35 in all the non-metropolitan districts, £10.93 in the metropolitan districts, £17.61 in Greater London and £10.42 in all authorities. In fact, between 1970-1 and 1973-4 there was an adverse change in the relationship between per capita expenditure on social services in the resorts and nationally. (Local government reorganization makes it impossible to look at trends after that point.) In 1970-1, social services expenditure was 16.7 per cent higher in the resort non-county boroughs than the average for all

TABLE 17.1 Estimated expenditure per head of population in retirement areas on local authority health, social and housing services

	Social services	Local health authority services	Housing	Social services	Local health authority services	Housing	Social services (other than concessionary fares)	Housing
	1970-1			1973-4			1974-5	
Resort county boroughs	3.62	3.59	1.93	8.39	3.43	5.20	–	–
All county boroughs in England and Wales	3.27	3.41	4.72	9.57	3.47	10.38	–	–
Resort non-county boroughs	3.07	4.19	1.84	7.17	3.88	3.78	–	–
All non-county boroughs in England and Wales	2.63	3.83	3.50	7.04	3.77	5.31	–	–
Resort urban districts	3.04	4.24	1.65	7.60	3.96	3.09	–	–
All urban districts	2.38	3.53	3.30	6.63	3.47	4.84	–	–

Table continued over

	Social services	Local health authority services	Housing	Social services	Local health authority services	Housing	Social services (other than concessionary fares)	Housing
	1970-1				1973-4		1974-5	
Greater London	–	–	–	14.11	4.43	23.42	17.61	35.41
All resort non-metropolitan districts	–	–	–	–	–	–	8.59	7.71
All non-metropolitan districts	–	–	–	–	–	–	8.35	9.11
All metropolitan districts	–	–	–	–	–	–	10.93	17.20
All authorities	–	–	–	8.49	3.61	9.09	10.42	15.13

county boroughs; in 1973-4 it was only 1.9 per cent higher. It appears, therefore, that deficiencies in the social services in the resorts, relative to national average provisions, will have had little chance of remedy up to the point at which further expansion of services was embargoed in 1975.

After reorganization, responsibility for expenditure on local health services was transferred from the rates to the Area Health Authorities. But in 1973-4 expenditure on these services was also not high compared with the national average. In that year, the resort county boroughs were spending an average of £3.43 per head compared with an average of £3.47 for all county boroughs. The resort non-county boroughs were spending £3.88, compared with a national average of £3.77, and the resort urban districts £3.96 compared with a national average of £3.47. Again there had been an adverse trend since 1970-1 in the relative position of the resorts in their spending on local health authority services. In 1970-1 expenditure in the resort non-county boroughs on local health authority services was 9.4 per cent higher than the average, in 1973-4 only 2.9 per cent higher.

One service on which the larger resorts have always tended to make substantial savings is education. In 1973-4, the resort county boroughs spent on average £45.50 on education, compared with an average of £58.02 in all county boroughs. Though they too had small proportions of school age children, the resort non-county boroughs and urban districts were not able to make such large savings, however. For instance in 1973-4, the average expenditure per head in the resort non-county boroughs was £62.57, compared with a national average of £63.68. The reason for this inability to save on education was that, for all county-level functions, the contribution of a non-county authority towards the total county costs was based on the rateable value of the authority, irrespective of its age structure and use of services. Thus the county precept required of a non-county borough for education would reflect not the needs of the town but those of the whole county. In fact, if it had many hotels and highly valued houses, a retirement resort might pay a disproportionately large part of the county education costs whilst using a disproportionately small part of the service.

With local government reorganization all but one resort area (7) have become lower-tier authorities. All these have therefore changed over to paying a county precept for education. As a result the areas which used to be county boroughs are now in a similar position to the other resorts and no longer make such large savings on education. In 1974-5 the resort new districts spent £55.86 per head compared with an average of £64.35 for all non-metropolitan districts. (8)

The other service upon which resorts have always made savings is housing. This has remained a lower-tier function, so it is still within the hands of the district council to control. The resorts have traditionally been areas in which there have been very small proportions of local authority housing. In 1973-4 the resort county boroughs spent on average £5.20 per head, compared with £10.38 for all county boroughs, and the resort non-county boroughs and urban districts each spent less than £4.00 per head. After reorganization, the pattern was somewhat changed because the areas with which the resorts were amalgamated tended to have slightly higher proportions of local authority housing. Thus in 1974-5 expenditure on housing in the resorts had risen to £7.71 per head compared with a national average of £9.11 for non-metropolitan districts.

It is one of the dilemmas of the rating system, where there are large numbers of people living on pensions or other types of relatively low fixed incomes, that, despite the community's need for better locally provided health and social services, the individual's most urgent concern is to keep down expenditure and in particular to bring pressure to bear to keep down the level of rates. Thus though the resorts already have permanent Conservative majorities which are usually opposed to heavy public expenditure, they also have very powerful and active ratepayers' associations operating either within the Conservative Party or as an opposition party in the council. In the last few years of inflation and rapidly increasing expenditure by local authorities, the effect of these pressures in the resorts appears to have been quite markedly to keep down the level of expenditure over a whole range of services, so that total expenditure increased about 10 per cent less in the resorts between 1970-1 and 1973 4 than it did in similar authorities nationally (Table 17.2). As a result, whereas expenditure in the resort non-county boroughs had been substantially higher than the average in 1970-1, it was very close to the average in 1973-4. Expenditure in the urban districts was still high but closer to the average than before and that in the county boroughs was even further below the average than in 1970-1. In 1974-5 the average expenditure per head in the new districts covering the resorts was £5.50 less than the average for all non-metropolitan districts.

TABLE 17.2 Total net rate and grant-borne expenditure per head in the retirement areas

	1970-1 £ p	1973-4 £ p	Change 1970-1 to 1973-4 (%)	1974-5* £ p
Resort county boroughs	64.77	101.02	+ 56	-
All county boroughs in England and Wales	72.29	121.58	+ 68	-
Resort non-county boroughs	86.32	124.61	+ 44	-
All non-county boroughs in England and Wales	81.71	123.93	+ 52	-
Resort urban districts	86.88	126.08	+ 45	-
All urban districts in England and Wales	73.99	114.59	+ 55	-
Greater London	-	164.56	-	-
All resort non-metropolitan districts	-	-	-	127.69*
All non-metropolitan districts in England and Wales	-	-	-	133.19*
All metropolitan districts in England and Wales	-	-	-	153.33*
All authorities	-	123.12	-	150.34*

* Expenditure in 1974-5 is not comparable with 1973-4 because Health Authority Services and certain items of education expenditure were no longer rate-borne in 1974-5.

The exception to this control of expenditure in the resorts was expenditure on 'other rate fund services', a category which consists very largely of administrative costs. These rose from £5.80 per head in the resort county boroughs in 1970-1 to £9.94 in 1973-4, an increase of 71 per cent compared with a national increase for county boroughs in that period of 28 per cent (from £4.36 to £5.59 per head). In the resorts, there is abnormally high expenditure under this heading because of their tourist function. Activities such as administration of car parks, publicity, information services, parades and other attractions, and care of the foreshore are all included in this category. It is ironical that these services, which might in a sense be regarded as frivolous expenditure compared with social services, should have received priority. But the seaside resorts have to invest in such things, plus illumination of the front and good maintenance of parks, in order to keep their tourists and day-trippers. The rates would fall even harder on residents if shops, cafés and further hotels closed as a result of decline in tourism.

But, of course, not all expenditure falls on the rates; a large part is covered by central government grants, either through direct subsidies to certain services such as housing, or through the Rate Support Grant system. Nationally, rates represent less than half the total net rate and grant-borne expenditure, but the proportion varies between types of authorities, being lowest for rural districts and highest for the London boroughs.

The position of the resorts in relation to rate-borne expenditure has improved since 1970-1. In that year the resort county boroughs were having to cover 52 per cent of their expenditure themselves, compared with a national average of 43 per cent for all county boroughs. Similarly the resort non-county boroughs and urban districts had to cover 40 per cent and 42 per cent respectively, compared with an average of 38 per cent for both types of authority nationally. In 1973-4, the resort county boroughs were still having to cover 47 per cent compared with 40 per cent nationally but the smaller resorts were in a much improved position. The non-county boroughs were covering 35 per cent compared with 34 per cent nationally and the resort urban districts 38 per cent compared with 35 per cent nationally.

The explanation of the below average amount of grant-borne expenditure in the past lies in two factors, first the small expenditure on council housing, and therefore small amount of housing subsidy, and second the character of the Rate Support Grant system.

The Rate Support Grant is intended to compensate local authorities for certain factors which may reduce their income or increase their expenditure above the average. It is designed to off-set the deficiencies in local taxation described in the quotation at the beginning of this chapter. The Grant consists of a number of elements, the Domestic Element, the Needs Element and the Resources Element.

The Domestic Element is a national limited de-rating of all domestic property and because so much of their property is residential the resorts benefit from this grant. For the resort county boroughs the average grant in 1973-4 was £5.64 per head compared with £3.39 for all county boroughs, in the resort non-county boroughs £4.54 compared with a national average of 3.68 and in the resort urban districts £4.64 compared with £3.75. After re-organization, the position has not substantially changed. The resort local authorities are still areas where a large percentage (58.8 per cent) of the rateable value is domestic and therefore the Domestic Element is, at £9.81 in 1974-5, still higher than the national average for all non-metropolitan districts (£8.35) and for metropolitan districts (£7.25).

The Needs Element, which constituted about 58 per cent of the total Rate Support Grant for 1975-6 is designed to compensate for certain factors which may lead to above average expenditure, whether or not the authority actually has increased expenditure as a result of them. It is based on over a dozen factors related to the need for local authority expenditure. These include population size, growth, and density, education requirements and a number of items relevant to the provision of social services. (9) One of these relates to the proportion of elderly people. There are two problems about the Needs Element; one is to achieve fair weightings. The 1971 Green Paper 'The Future Shape of Local Government Finance', (10) recognized that the weightings being given to the various factors were inadequate and went on to say that 'the right objective would seem to be the distribution of grants in such a way that the cost for each local authority of providing a standard level of service should be a standard amount per head'. 'If the principle of equalisation to a standard cost per head is accepted, it ought to be possible to derive a formula which would get a great deal nearer to this ideal than the present needs element formula.' (11)

Since that report was produced efforts have been made to adjust the weightings. However, there is a more fundamental problem. The indices which are used, particu-

larly those intended to measure the need for social
services, are mostly measures of existing provision and
therefore financial obligation (e.g. number of home helps)
rather than measures of the need for that provision.
Thus in areas such as the resorts, which fall particularly
short in the provision of meals, home helps, residential
accommodation and day care places, the level of the Needs
Element of the Rate Support Grant is cut reflecting
existing provision, rather than increased to encourage
improvement. This problem has now been realized and in
the White Paper, 'The Rate Support Grants for 1975-6 for
England and Wales', (12) it is stated that the regression
analysis used for the purposes of calculating the Needs
Element of the Rate Support Grant,

> has shown that authorities in areas with large numbers
> of low income households tend to spend less, other
> things being equal, than authorities elsewhere, though
> their true spending needs can be no less. In the
> course of the analysis, the expenditure estimates of
> these authorities have therefore, in effect, been
> adjusted upwards to compensate. Had this not been
> done, the formula would have under-presented the
> spending needs of the authorities concerned.

It is not made clear, however, how large this adjustment is and upon what basis it is made. It is to be
hoped that recognition of the problem will, however, lead
to more fundamental changes in the nature of the indices
used, in order to measure need rather than current
provision. This would certainly help the resorts, which
at present receive a relatively small sum per head from
the Needs Element, £2.50 lower than the average for all
non-metropolitan counties in 1974-5.

Currently the resort authorities suffer less from this
aspect of the Needs Element than they would otherwise
because it is based on expenditure per head, rather than
per adult or per household. As only the head of household
pays rates, equal expenditure per head means that each
household will tend to have to pay less in an area where
there are least children and the smallest households -
that is in a retirement resort. Should the system of
Rate Support Grant be changed to remove this anomaly, (13)
the resorts would find that they received even less from
the Needs Element calculation.

The Resources Element of the Rate Support Grant is
intended to compensate authorities for reduced rate
income. If the area's rateable value per head is below a
'national standard rateable value per head' (£154 in
1974-5) the authority receives financial help. In relation
to this grant, too, the resorts have come out very badly

because they have high domestic rateable values. Only Hastings and Southport out of all the resort county boroughs received any contribution from the Resources Element in 1973-4 whereas, on average, county boroughs received 11.9 per cent of their grant-borne expenditure in this way. In 1974-5, however, when the local authorities' boundaries had been changed, the new districts included more areas of older, cheaper residential property, and so received more from the Resources Element, an average of £15.47 per head compared with £17.79 for all non-metropolitan districts.

TABLE 17.3 Rate Support Grant per head of population 1974-5* (£ per head)

	All	Needs Element	Resources Element	Domestic Element
Greater London	58.35	43.45	2.25	12.65
Metropolitan counties and districts	72.70	41.13	24.32	7.25
Non-metropolitan counties and districts	62.26	36.12	17.79	8.35
Wales	92.85	40.36	38.32	14.17
All authorities	65.88	38.62	18.22	9.04
All resort non-metropolitan districts	58.87	33.59	15.47**	9.81

* Chartered Institute of Public Finance and Accountancy, 'Return of Rates', 1974-5.
** Calculated.

However, as discussed earlier, for the retirement resorts the rateable value of a house is not a good measure of the ability of the occupant to pay rates, because large proportions of the ratepayers are retired. Their house represents the bulk of their assets and their income is usually modest. The fact that they have a house worth £10,000 is not an adequate measure of their income, as it might be with a working couple. But even for working couples, there are problems in the system. The difference in valuations for identical houses in different parts of the country is substantially greater than the difference in wages for identical jobs. The occupants of the houses thus have higher rents and mortgage repayments, even before paying higher rates.

The latter difficulty about the Resources Element was again officially recognized in the Green Paper which suggests that:

> to take full account of these variations, a revised system might attempt to equalise not rate poundages but rate payments by comparable domestic rate-payers, by bringing into the distribution formula not only rate products per head of population but also variations in the rateable value of standard council houses and variations of average industrial earnings in each county or region. (14)

No steps have so far been taken to introduce such a system and even if they were they would still not deal with the problem of a predominantly retired population on low incomes. However, not all retired people are poor and it would not be satisfactory to have a new element of the Resources Element of the Rate Support Grant based solely on the proportion of elderly people in the population. This would, for instance, give the relatively well-to-do retired people in Bexhill an advantage over those in Clacton who are mostly poor. It may be argued that this type of anomaly is best dealt with through a rebate system.

A new rate rebate system has been introduced (in April 1974). Under this new scheme there is no minimum rate payment and therefore people with large rates but low incomes are much more effectively helped than by the old scheme, under which they had to pay just over two-thirds of the rate bill no matter how high it was. At the same time, local authorities receive 90 per cent of the cost of rebates compared with 75 per cent before, which helps to relieve them of the cost of running this much more generous scheme.

The introduction of this new rebate scheme is of the utmost importance to the resorts because of the factors already mentioned, namely the low incomes and high rates per domestic property. Even under the old rebate scheme large numbers of retired people in the resorts were receiving rebates. For instance in 1972-3, there were forty authorities in which more than 10 per cent of the households had rate rebates. All but seven of these were seaside resorts. (15) Clacton, Morecambe and Herne Bay were the areas with the largest proportions of people receiving rebates, (16) and they were spending roughly the equivalent of a penny rate in meeting the cost of the rebate scheme.

Chapter 17

CONCLUSIONS

The financial situation in the retirement areas can then be summarized as follows:

1 Incomes are low there because the majority of the population is retired and even the population of working age tends to have below average incomes because of seasonal employment and low rates of pay in catering and other service trades and in agriculture.

2 In spite of their relatively low current incomes, retired people in the resorts are usually living in highly rated properties, bought out of savings.

3 Because the retired people are on fixed incomes but live in highly rated properties, they fear and oppose fiercely any proposals for increased local government expenditure. Ratepayers' associations play an active part in resort politics and the authorities have been successful in keeping down expenditure on a wide range of services. But even so, because of dependence on domestic rates and because rateable values per dwelling are high, the actual rates paid per domestic property are higher than anywhere outside Greater London.

4 At present, in spite of very high rates and the retired population's greater need for health and social services, these services do not receive significantly more expenditure in resorts than elsewhere and in recent years their relative position has been deteriorating. Any substantial improvement in these services would have to increase the rate burden and politically this is unlikely to be an attractive proposition at local level.

5 It could be said that resources should be switched to social services from more apparently frivolous things such as the illumination of the front, but the seaside towns have to invest in such things to keep their tourists and day-trippers. The rates would fall even harder on residents if shops, cafés and further hotels closed. In addition, the retired population is very quick to complain about a decline in the standard of amenities in the town. They have, many of them, been attracted by these very features of the town, and the presence of retired people constitutes one of its industries and the main source of rate income.

6 In these circumstances, and because the standard of health and social services needs raising in retirement areas, there does seem to be some case for increased government help for expenditure on these services in the resorts, perhaps through a revision of the indices used for the Needs Element of the Rate Support Grant. Of more help probably would be a greatly increased weighting on

the Domestic Element of the Rate Support Grant to counteract the effects of a predominantly residential rateable value. It can be argued, though, that the improved rate rebate scheme has already greatly relieved the rate burden on the worst-hit individuals, and in any case, there are other areas of the county which would be hit by a diversion of resources to the resorts.

7 Ultimately it is for the local residents themselves to decide how much priority they intend their local authority to give to extra services and how much to keeping expenditure down. In the new more heterogeneous authorities, the retired will not have such an absolute hold on political control, a change which may lead to greater conflict in the future.

8 Fundamentally, however, the resorts epitomize the problems of a property rating system, in that in retirement areas property values are particularly ill-matched with current incomes. No amount of tinkering about with the present system will change this. Had the Layfield Committee on Local Government Finance recommended the substitution of a standard level local income tax, the resorts would have had reason to celebrate, but central government would have had to foot a very large bill.

Conclusions to Part three

Conclusions about the situation of the health and social services in the resorts can be divided into three parts: first, those about the need for services in the resorts; second, those concerning the supply of services; and third, conclusions about the financing of improvements.

THE NEED FOR SERVICES IN THE RESORTS

1 The age structure of the resorts means that they need much larger than average health and social services simply to deal with the normal demands made by elderly people. However, there is a qualification to this: in Bexhill and Clacton old people are not quite as old as the national average for elderly people; smaller proportions of people aged 65 and over in the two resorts are aged over 80. This is, though, likely to be a temporary phenomenon which has arisen because of the very recent migration of recently retired people into these towns. If migration rates decline, as they are bound to do as the land supply dries up, the age structure will become much more heavily weighted towards the very old.

However, there is some evidence to suggest that a number of the very old, particularly widows, leave the resorts and that therefore very old women may continue to be under-represented in the population. Old women tend to make more demands on the health and social services while elderly couples have been found to be able to support themselves much more adequately in the community.

2 Nevertheless this slight bonus for the services in the resorts, is much more than off-set by the old people's lack of relatives, or isolation from them. Even those who have children usually live far from them. For this reason

many old people are very isolated indeed. This means that they are more likely to need social services of all kinds and are more likely to need institutional care than are people whose relatives are near to look after them. Widowed people in Bexhill and Clacton were particularly likely to live alone.

3 The concentration of elderly people in estates where there are very few younger people makes it difficult for neighbours to help each other either in emergencies or with long-term help. 'Community care' is therefore less likely to be satisfactory in the resorts.

4 Isolated or lonely people are more likely than others to need psychiatric services. There is some evidence that the resorts make particular demands on the psychiatric services.

5 It is sometimes argued that people in resorts are so affluent that they do not need statutory health and social services. Average income levels of elderly people in Bexhill and similar resorts were higher than for elderly people in the country as a whole, so they are more likely to be able to afford private services. However, this point should not be overstressed. For one thing, the incomes of old people nationally are not a high standard against which to make a comparison. If one compared them instead, for instance, with households consisting of one man and one woman of any age, it would be clear that, relatively well-off though the retired people of Bexhill are compared with other pensioners, there are not many of them who could afford to pay for a range of medical and social services over an extended period of time. It is one thing to say that a retired couple are reasonably comfortable on an income of £15-20 a week. It is another to maintain that on this income they could afford to live in a private home, or to employ a gardener and a private home help or to have restaurant meals every day or a cook, a private nurse, private doctor, private hospital bed and consultant. Moreover it should be remembered that the people who are most likely to need all these things are widowed old ladies, and the majority of them, even in Bexhill, had in 1969 incomes below £10 a week. In addition Bexhill has, for a resort, an above average proportion of retired people in Social Classes I and II. Clacton has less than the average. In most resorts one would expect incomes to be somewhere between the two, though nearer to Bexhill's than Clacton's. As even in Bexhill there were relatively few people with high incomes (10 per cent over £30 a week) this suggests that the wealthiness of retired people in resorts can be exaggerated.

6 In addition money is not necessarily a guarantee of receiving a satisfactory service of the kind one wants. For instance, it cannot guarantee against unreliable service. Several people living in hotels said they could afford domestic help but could never rely on its being available so they had had to give up their home and move into a hotel. Similarly, high charges cannot entirely ensure that a private home or nursing home will be well run.

7 There is the further problem that old people with psychiatric disorders may require help in spite of themselves. They may not come forward for services which are vital to their support in the community, and if they have no relatives to care for them, the duty clearly falls on the health and social services.

8 With some social services, such as the home help service, one can see that the existence of private provision reduces demands on the publicly provided service. However, the relief is probably much more than off-set by the competition for recruits - a major problem in the resorts. And whereas the home help service is used for those in most need, the private service has little to do with need, just ability to pay. Thus the relief of pressing need continues to fall on the public service. In particular, emergencies have to be dealt with by the public service.

9 There is also the more general question whether the existance of people who can afford to buy health and social services should be any justification for a lower standard of public provision. If there is a National Health Service then it should provide for the health needs of the community. There is no reason why a sick old person should be required to pay for private nursing when it is to cover just such a period of sickness that they have been making their contributions for so many years.

CONCLUSIONS ABOUT THE QUALITY OF PROVISION OF SERVICES IN SEASIDE RESORTS

1 Overall, the situation of the retirement resorts is substantially worse than in other areas.

2 The hospital bed shortage appears to be a crucial problem, especially on the South Coast.

3 The provision of statutory residential accommodation is inadequate but only seriously so in a few places, particularly in the county districts.

4 The load of work on doctors is made worse by shortages in the other services which put a burden of worry and

organization on them. This partly explains their dissatisfaction. The solution is probably not more doctors but better hospital and domiciliary services.

5 The home help service is badly understaffed and the elderly are receiving far less help than elsewhere in the country, whilst needing more because of shortages of hospital beds and the lack of younger relatives and neighbours. The meals services in resorts are not up to national average standard.

6 Because of the shortages of hospital provision, home nurses are caring for many people who would normally be in hospital but even so fewer than the national average of elderly people. Doctors find difficulty in getting nursing help for chronically sick people. Further recruitment seems to be kept down by budgets rather than lack of applicants. Health visitors spend more time on the elderly in resorts than they tend to elsewhere but are able to cover smaller proportions of the total population than the national average.

7 There is extreme dependence on private provision of services, especially private homes and nursing homes. This dependence is not just by wealthy people but by those who are forced to go into private homes because they cannot get into a welfare home or hospital and cannot obtain adequate domiciliary help.

8 The provision of local authority housing is meagre, considering the numbers of elderly people living in multi-occupation and unsatisfactory flats. Provision of rent rebates in the private sectors (furnished and unfurnished) had helped to alleviate the situation of those whose problem is the high level of rent required for adequate accommodation. Housing associations providing for old people already living in the resorts should receive more encouragement.

9 There is heavy reliance on voluntary workers in the social services. Most of these in the retirement areas are elderly people themselves and the type of service that they can give is naturally affected. In some instances, self-help can be a great success. An example is the Bexhill Senior Citizens Club, run by its own members, providing all the expertise required, including its own accountant, and giving a variety of services from cheap meals to hobbies sessions and outings. Similarly the hospital car service and the delivery of meals-on-wheels are ones to which the elderly can effectively contribute but they cannot touch the core of the problem of heavy nursing and home help services. In addition, even in the services which can be voluntarily run, there are problems of scale in the resorts, where for instance

so many old people may require chiropody that voluntary secretaries have to give way to paid organizers, and where the scale of cooking and delivery of meals-on-wheels may get beyond the resources of the WRVS volunteers. Rather cruelly, but necessarily, it has to be said that the crucial health and social services in the resorts are not those which can be run by the well-intentioned volunteer especially the elderly person. The resorts will have to take some, probably locally unpopular, decisions about which services can continue to be left to voluntary agencies without risk of breakdown.

10 The recruitment of young women as home helps, hospital nursing auxiliaries, etc., is very difficult in the resorts. The attraction of industry and offices to the towns usually makes this situation worse in the first instance as they are attracted into office employment instead.

11 The planning of provision in the health and social services has not been adequately geared to information about the scale of migration to the resorts. It is difficult to apportion blame, but more effective collaboration between local and central government departments would probably have produced more realistic estimates. The ability of the Regional Hospital Boards to plan effectively has not been impressive but it is difficult to tell how much of this is due to lack of information about population trends, to concentration of resources in certain powerful sectors such as the London teaching hospitals, to lack of interest in the geriatric services by the medical profession or to financial difficulties which have restricted all major capital expenditure. In planning terms it is clearly much more difficult to put right miscalculations which involve large amounts of capital expenditure and a building programme than it is, for instance, to revise estimates about the need for home helps, health visitors or home nurses.

12 It does seem, from the plans now proposed, that the shortage of hospital facilities has been realized, but the backlog which has built up through lack of foresight in planning for the large-scale migration of elderly people cannot quickly be eliminated. In view of this unavoidable future shortage over a number of years, it seems desirable that a strategy be worked out to cope with this period. The question of the rate of closure of psychiatric wards may be one subject for discussion. Others might be the efficiency of voluntary domiciliary services and the role of private residential accommodation and possible financial help to patients in it.

It is to be hoped that the reorganization of the Health

Service and the dismemberment of the tripartite system into one more nearly approaching a total service to a community will help in this process of reform. In particular there is a need to end the situation in which patients are passed from one sphere of authority to another. To take an example, in the resorts it seems that hospitals, through pressure on their scarce beds, are sometimes sending patients back into the community when they are still very sick. Under the tripartite system, it was not the hospital doctors' responsibility that there was no home help to care for the old person, nor that the home nurse allocated was already overworked. The medical social worker experienced all the worry of trying to find a local authority or private home for someone leaving hospital, but it was the general practitioners and home nurses and health visitors who had to fight to provide some help for those who could not even get into hospital in the first place. Naturally, friction occurred between the members of the various authorities, each under immense pressure, each feeling that the others might be doing more. It is too much to hope that this will all go with administrative changes but the need in the resorts, as elsewhere, is to have health and social services planned for a whole community, with unified aims.

Whatever happens, the authorities concerned should not take refuge in the belief that old people can be deterred from moving, at least on a scale and within a period which would be useful to the services. The retired people are there and others will come to replace them and to occupy any new accommodation which the local authority allows to be built. Long-term policies of controlling building and encouraging industry may have effect eventually, but the issue of the quality of health and social services cannot be evaded meanwhile. In many respects the presence of large numbers of elderly people merely highlights existing fundamental deficiencies in the health and social services rather than causing those deficiencies.

FINANCING IMPROVEMENTS IN THE LOCAL AUTHORITY HEALTH AND SOCIAL SERVICES

1 The resorts are spending only slightly more than the average per head on local health services and on residential accommodation. Clearly with such a large elderly population they need to spend much more.

2 However, any substantial increases in expenditure which are not off-set by grants will put an intolerable rate burden on the residents of the resorts. Already

domestic rates paid are the highest in the country, outside London and a few major cities.

3 The resorts will continue to suffer from their lack of industrial and commercial rateable value. The more thoroughgoing rate rebate now introduced will help to alleviate the effect of this on domestic ratepayers, but other solutions are possible, such as a revised form of the Resources Element which might assess domestic and other rateable value separately, or a larger Domestic Element.

4 Though the retirement resorts have a problem in financing adequate services for the elderly, they do, unlike cities, have only the one major problem to solve. Therefore, while it seems right that remedies should be sought for the ways in which they are currently handicapped by the rate and grant system, it would be difficult to argue, over and above this, for redistribution of resources, towards what are, in many ways, relatively privileged areas.

18 Retirement to the seaside: success or failure?

INTRODUCTION

Retirement to the seaside has received much very bad publicity. Commentators have seemed only too anxious to seize on the idea that the majority of people who move regret doing so and become lonely and unhappy. (1) No actual surveys of retired people in the resorts have given support to this sweeping view. So why is it so popular? It is as if the writers dislike the idea that such a community could be a workable one.

One explanation is that attitudes towards the elderly, and even more the elderly en masse, are very negative. One survey of young people's attitudes to the elderly in the USA, came to the following conclusions:

> The old, uniquely amongst age groups, were perceived to possess a political power greater than their soundness of judgement might warrant. They were perceived as more emotionally ill, disagreeable, inactive, economically burdensome, dependent, dull, socially undesirable, dissatisfied, socially withdrawn, and disruptive of family harmony than youths or adults. (2)

If such views are widely held then it is clear that retirement resorts will have a bad 'image' irrespective of any objective criticisms which may be levelled at such communities. In particular, the view that retirement resorts are depressing seems to stem from the fear of the young and middle aged of confronting so inescapably the prospect of old age and death. Yet this study found that only a minority of the retired people themselves mentioned that they found the presence of many old people depressing.

But this negative attitude to the old is not the only explanation. Simone de Beauvoir who condemns bitterly such attitudes is also one of those who describes retirement migration in purely negative terms.

They go to the Mediterranean coast, and there they find
that the climate is bad for their rheumatism. They
also discover that rents are too high ... they know
nobody and they suffer from loneliness. Even if the
plans were sound in the first place, once they have
been carried out the old people find themselves with
nothing to do; they have merely postponed the time at
which they must adapt themselves. (3)

Her reaction is based on the belief that all elderly
people suffer very severely from giving up work and that
they try to overcome the trauma by doing something
different from the usual. She feels that this break with
long-accustomed surroundings, routines and friends is
bound to be unsuccessful.

However, she also admits that people's adjustment to
retirement is closely related to the spirit with which
they approach it. Those who look forward to it are much
more likely to be happy: "It is worth noting that the
state of mind in which retirement is faced has a direct
relationship to the manner in which it is experienced.'
(4)

The surveys in Clacton and Bexhill suggested, moreover,
that the people who had moved there were those who had
looked forward to retirement, had often retired early and
who said they had had little desire to work since.

Of course in having these views the retired offend
against the Protestant ethic, which is another potent
cause of condemnatory attitudes to retirement resorts.
Many, particularly of the American commentaries on retirement,
vehemently advocate work for old people. If they
cannot work for profit, they should do good works. This
attitude is partly a reaction against the idea that the
old are useless but it is often carried to such lengths
that, by implying that anyone who does not work is useless,
it becomes just as negative an attitude to the old. For
instance Clarke Tibbitts writes:

> No other culture has offered the length of life and the
> amount of free time now enjoyed by the industrialised
> countries of the Western World. What shall be done
> with it? An alternative is to encourage retired adults
> to live out their years in pursuit of time-filling
> hobbies, and such entertainment as circumstances afford,
> and in reflective vegetation - as a reward for past
> contributions. Or they may be regarded as a new and
> rich source of energy, experience and wisdom capable of
> attaining a self-realization and carrying important
> community responsibilities.

At any rate, the first alternative appears to
promise boredom, deterioration, dependency, conservatism,

depression and institutionalization. The second promises continued growth, preservation of the vital functions, purposeful living, continued social usefulness, and self-sufficiency. (5)

To a man of such views retirement resorts are clearly frivolous and likely to lead to 'deterioration'. They are devoted to the enjoyment of retirement in a relaxed fashion - long-term holiday resorts. The people who move there have ideals about rest and quiet and mutual enjoyment of leisure in retirement.

It is possible, in fact, that the pervasiveness of the bad image of the old, and of its 'be active at all costs' backlash, has something to do with the success of retirement resorts. In a community of the elderly, no elderly person need feel that he has to prove himself worthwhile by being active, politically or socially. He is one of the community, not an outsider in a community basically run by and for the young and working. He can be as socially inactive and politically irresponsible as he has been all his working life without it reflecting on him any more than it ever did. Nor, in relation to work, is there any need to feel the odd-man-out for being retired. No one is working. Most of the people who came to Bexhill and Clacton had the attitude towards work that they had done what could be reasonably expected of them, and perhaps more, and had earned a rest. Why, one asks, should the rich apparently find leisure enjoyable while the elderly are supposed to find it merely boring?

A further reason why the resorts have received a bad press is that unhappiness and problems are considered much more newsworthy by the media than are satisfaction and the solution to problems. This tendency has been accentuated by the fact that the local authorities have been quite rightly troubled by the situation of the health and social services in the resorts and many officers have written or spoken in public about these problems. Working as they do with those elderly people who are in trouble, it is natural that, from constantly seeing these people, they should come to the conclusion that a majority of the old who move to resorts are unhappy and regret their move. However, only a small minority of the elderly are likely to come within the scope of local authority or other health services at any one time. A random sample of the retired population presents, as we have seen in this survey, a very different picture of the incidence of unhappiness. A typical example of this impressionistic writing is that of a doctor from Essex. It is sensitive and true but he paints too bleak a picture of what the majority of retired people themselves feel.

Memories of childhood holidays and adult fantasies of peace and rejuvenation make the country and coast unrealistically attractive. Some find moving to a new home on retirement a pleasant experience and end their lives happily in a place where they have always wanted to live. Many, possibly the majority, realize that they have made a mistake when it is too late. They have moved from the familiar friend-populated place of their work to a new, strange world, new friendships are difficult to make, help is not available when needed and the winter, when it comes, appears a sad harbinger of death to come. (6)

For all these reasons - the distaste of the young for the elderly, the pervasiveness of the Protestant ethic in overvaluing work, and the very real worry about the health and social services - the retirement resorts have not been presented in a very flattering light. It is as well to remember these underlying factors when one reads about the 'Costa Geriatrica', 'old people's ghettoes', 'graveyards' and the 'wheel-chair society'.

SOME CONCLUSIONS OF THIS STUDY

This study was concerned to find out more about the process of retirement to the coast from the point of view of the retired people themselves.

It asked first of all whether there were features of the elderly people themselves which helped to explain why they were willing to move in retirement. It was not within the scope of the enquiry to look at the psychological make-up of these people. However, a number of features of their lives and opinions seemed to be different from the average.

First, they were less likely to have any children than were old people nationally. This probably allowed them to move more freely than most elderly people could contemplate.

Second, they had almost invariably owned the house they left to move to the resort. This had enabled them to take advantage of escalating house prices in the cities, especially London, to buy themselves a bungalow or house by the seaside.

These two factors clearly facilitated their move, but why did they have the desire to move? It was clear that their approach to retirement from work was inextricably bound up with their decision to move. Nearly all of them moved either in the year in which they retired or in the following year. The decision to move was one which had

been taken before retirement, not as a result of
experiences in their home town after retirement. Very
few said they would have liked to continue working and
even fewer had worked since moving. They felt they had
done their share.

So whatever the retired people said about the position
of the retired person in the cities or suburbs, they
themselves had had little experience of this. All they
were going on was the experience of others and their own
presentiments.

It is not surprising, therefore, that the emphasis in
the reasons given for moving to the seaside was on the
positive attractions of the resorts. Comparisons were
made with the physical defects of the cities, the dirt,
traffic and noise, but there were relatively few who
commented on the cities' social disadvantages for the
retired.

Thus while it is tempting and attractive to dwell on
the comments of the few who mentioned the exclusion of
the retired and elderly from the social life of the
cities, and to see the move to retirement resorts as a
conscious reaction to the attitude of society to the old,
the fact is that the retired people themselves rarely
mentioned this. They were concerned with the environmental advantages of the seaside compared with the cities.
Their reasons for moving were to do with the desire for a
better climate, clearer air, the sea and better health.

True, after they had been there some years, they had
become conscious of the social advantages of living in a
mainly retired community, and this figured prominently in
their reasons for liking the town and for finding it
easier to make friends. But, whatever the reasons for
the success of the move, improvement of environment and
health had been the initial motive.

The link with a previous holiday area is clear. It
was an area with a pleasant environment with which they
were familiar and which was, very often, not too far from
the area in which they had spent their working life. It
fitted in, too, with the image they had of retirement as
being a period of rest and quiet without the strain and
rush of town life.

So these were the ideas with which people retired to
the seaside. But how did it work out in practice?

The answer must be, I believe, 'Remarkably well',
according to the evidence of this survey. Social surveys
are certainly very fallible instruments but one cannot
select which parts of them to disbelieve just because they
contradict one's original expectations. It is a fact that
84 per cent of the people interviewed in Bexhill and 79

per cent in Clacton said they would, with hindsight, and given their time again, make the same decision to move. In addition 26 per cent of the retired people in Bexhill had actually persuaded friends or relations to join them in the town and so had 18 per cent in Clacton, a notable vote of confidence.

There were some, of course, for whom the move was not so successful. Widows were particularly likely to regret moving, 24 per cent of them in Clacton did so, and so did 12 per cent in Bexhill. In addition, there was considerable evidence that, whether or not they regretted their move, many men and women moved away when they were widowed. By no means all went back to the cities. They might go to other resorts, perhaps to join friends living there, or with some hope of finding a place which did not remind them of the time before they were widowed. There was a small minority of people who moved rapidly from one resort to another constantly searching for the perfect retirement home.

Such wanderings were unhappy but unusual. It was common, however, for retired people to have two or more homes after retirement. The first retirement home was frequently over-ambitious for later old age when the upkeep of the house and garden became too much. If this stage were reached, the fortunate moved into a more suitable flat, small bungalow or sheltered housing scheme. The less fortunate, or less affluent, were forced to stay on in their house or to move into even more unsuitable property, such as a converted flat up many stairs and with a high rent and little security of tenure. Others moved into hotels or private homes.

THE HEALTH AND SOCIAL SERVICES

It is the situation of such old people, in acute need of better health and social services, that worries the local authorities in the resort areas. Many feel that continued migration of old people to their towns will end in complete breakdown of the services. Certainly the review of the services in this study showed that most services were well below the national average in the proportion of elderly residents covered by them. In addition one can argue that, in areas where such a large proportion of old people have no children or relatives near and where even the neighbours are also predominantly elderly, the services need even greater coverage than the average.

There are three main problems in improving the services. One is national, namely to achieve adequate health planning and to give the necessary priority to geriatric serves which are so often neglected. The second is to overcome the financial handicaps which the resorts experience because of their lack of non-residential rateable value and the low incomes of the majority of their residents. The third problem is that of recruitment of staff for the health and social services in the resorts and constitutes possibly the biggest question-mark concerning the viability of the resorts. At present there are recruitment problems in the lower paid jobs, such as home helps and nursing auxiliaries, and it is difficult to obtain voluntary workers. However, in the highly paid jobs there is no such problem. Doctors are attracted to live in the retirement areas, and so are local government officers. The problem then seems to be that the very basic health and social services depend upon underpaid women workers and volunteers. This is possible in a community where there are many working-age women whose husbands are in employment. It does not work in the resorts. There is little employment for the husbands, and, if factories and offices do move to the resorts, as like as not the immediate effect is for nursing auxiliaries and home helps to become office cleaners and typists.

This situation threatens the viability of the resorts. It is not that the resorts are intrinsically incapable of attracting the necessary labour to provide a service for the new 'industry' of retirement. (It is not only doctors who would like to live there if jobs were available.) The mushrooming of private homes proves the contrary. Rather the special character of the resorts reveals the deplorably cut-price way in which the health and social services are expected to be run.

The plea from the local authorities is to discourage retirement migration. But this is to attack the wrong 'ill'. The problem lies in the health and social services not in the movement of elderly people to the coast. As far as the elderly people themselves are concerned, and they are the ones who matter in this case, retirement to seaside resorts is enjoyable, and not an 'ill' at all. The local authorities have to accept this and make such provision as they are allowed to, whilst lobbying for better pay and terms of employment for essential workers, both men and women, in the health and social services. They are, after all, the 'key' workers of the resorts.

THE EFFECT ON THE CITIES

Whilst there is an increased burden on the health and social services in resorts as a result of retirement migration, it is also the case that at the other end the major urban areas are losing a substantial proportion of their elderly population, largely as a result of the move to seaside resorts. (7) The cities benefit in two ways. First, the scale of provision of health and social services for the elderly will not need to be expanded as rapidly as would otherwise have been essential. Second, housing is made available to working-age people who are tied to the cities by the nature of their employment. In this way retirement migration is helping to relieve two problems out of the very many with which cities have to grapple. When one considers the immense problems of pollution, traffic, slum housing, violent crime, delinquency and racial discrimination which beset the cities, it does seem that the seaside resorts have little case against trying to tackle one service, namely provision for the elderly. In most other respects, particularly in terms of the quality of the environment, they are, after all, relatively privileged areas.

But it does seem clear that they will need greater financial help in order to provide this service. A changed Rate Support Grant formula which gave more help to counteracting the effects of a predominantly residential rateable value would be one suggestion.

HELPING MORE TO MOVE

If retirement migration is, on the whole, an enjoyable experience and has benefits for the cities in relieving their housing shortage, then a case can be made for helping more people to move. At present, for a number of reasons, movement out is almost entirely confined to owner-occupiers. They are by no means all affluent people. Many, particularly those who move to the cheaper resorts such as Clacton and Herne Bay, have been skilled manual workers or perhaps small shopkeepers, who managed early on in life to buy a house. Now this asset has appreciated and they are able to sell it and buy a bungalow in a seaside resort.

Because the movement out is confined to owner-occupiers, the houses freed for working-age people are also owner-occupied houses. There is, of course, a general effect of relieving shortage, but studies of the workings of the housing market suggest that this beneficial effect may not easily filter down to lower income people in the poorest houses. More crucially there is even less direct effect on the supply of vacancies in council housing.

For both these reasons, the desire to help tenants as well as owner-occupiers to move, and the need to relieve the shortage of cheaper rented property in the cities, an arrangement like the GLC's bungalows-by-the-sea scheme seems to be excellent. Under this, elderly council tenants in London move to seaside resorts. Compared with the movement of owner-occupiers the scheme is still tiny; 1,500 dwellings had been let in this way by January 1975. One of the reasons why it is small is that many seaside authorities have refused to allow the scheme to operate in their area. However, from the tenants' point of view it is very popular. There are about 4,000 tenants on the waiting list and publicity has been deliberately damped down to reduce a demand which cannot be met because of the difficulty of obtaining sites in resort areas.

The scheme has the advantage over individual moves that the GLC still keeps responsibility for the tenants and will help them move back to London if they want to. There is not then the problem of being unable to afford a further move if one regrets having left London. With this safeguard, the seaside resorts should be more, rather than less, willing to accept this type of development rather than owner-occupation, with all the risks that it entails for the very old and frail. In addition, the houses and, if necessary, gardens, are maintained by the GLC, or more usually by the resort's housing department under a financial arrangement with the GLC. This again reduces the problems in later old age.

The desirability of the expansion of the GLC's scheme and of the adoption of similar arrangements by other cities seems to be an obvious conclusion. It is not a new idea. As long ago as 1961, Hugh Mellor wrote that:

> What is needed is some administrative arrangement (similar to that operated under the Town Development Act 1952) whereby the cities could make arrangements with the coastal resorts to house some of their elderly residents in rented dwellings at the expense of the exporting authority, possibly aided by the Government. Alternatively a central housing authority building in these resorts might meet the need. If no more than an additional 20,000 people a year were provided for, in 10 years 100,000 dwellings in the big cities could have been freed - no mean contribution to solving the problem of our congested cities. (8)

Chapter 18

THE ROLE OF SEASIDE RESORTS

The opposition of the resort authorities to the GLC's bungalows scheme, whilst they are simultaneously granting planning permission for more bungalow building for owner-occupation, shows up their confusion about what policy they should adopt. Are they really opposed to retirement to their town and, if so, what measures should be taken? Or do they accept their role as a retirement resort? In which case, what are they doing to perform that role adequately?

As usual there are a number of competing interests and accessible coastline is a scarce commodity. There is the conservationist lobby, and the outdoor recreation lobby, by no means always seeing eye to eye with each other when it comes to the construction of marinas or the provision of water-skiing facilities. There are the traditional holiday hotels catering particularly for middle-aged and elderly holiday-makers and the caravan camps and holiday camps catering for younger families. There are those who wish to increase employment opportunities for local people and those who wish to keep the quiet atmosphere of the retirement town. There is even a conflict of interest between the retired people who have already arrived in the town and who want to preserve existing open space and those who wish to move there and want more land developed for residential building. All of these lobbies see the role of the coastal resort in a different way, and not all of them can be satisfied. All ignore (9) or devalue the claims of their rivals. But only of the retired is it said that it is in their own interests not to move to the seaside.

It is not part of this study to attempt to judge between these competing interests but something can be said about the compatibility of a retirement role with the others. After all, the resorts already have this role and it is not one that is easily going to be discontinued. Even if all new building of bungalows were stopped tomorrow, the existing stock would ensure a continuation of a large proportion of elderly people in the population.

Assuming then that the resorts will continue to have a retirement function, how compatible is this with the other interests just mentioned? Much more study is needed of this topic but the immediate impression is that it is no less compatible with each of the other functions than they are with each other. In fact, it is more compatible with the existing hotel trade than most of the others are. The holiday-makers in the South-East resorts in particular are very often middle-aged or elderly themselves and the same features of the town which appeal to them, appeal to the people who retire there. (10)

In relation to the compatibility of retirement with increased local employment, there has been a misconception that because of the presence of retired people the resorts have been losing young people at an accelerated rate. In fact retirement has nothing to do with the lack of employment in the area. Rather it has brought employment in the building trades and in shops and services. It is because of retirement that the resorts have reached their current size. Unless commuting had developed they would have remained very much smaller towns. Also, though like any small towns the resorts do lose young people, none of them except Brighton and Blackpool actually had a net loss by migration between 1961 and 1966 in the working age groups.

The presence of more employment in the resort towns would in fact help the retirement function, by providing more women's labour for the health and social services. But conversely, better pay and conditions of service in the health and social services would help the employment situation in the resorts. A high rate of unemployment in the resorts exists side by side with a shortage of labour in the services.

BALANCED COMMUNITIES

Something must also be said about the argument that resorts, because of their age structure, are 'unbalanced communities'. In what sense is an 'unbalanced' age structure a bad thing? The implications for the social life of the town were discussed in Chapter 7 and the conclusion was reached that there is no strong evidence that homogeneity of age is a problem in that respect. Indeed some commentators have said that it is of positive advantage in creating greater common ground between neighbours. This they considered of particular importance to the elderly who are less mobile and more dependent socially on close neighbours. The elderly people interviewed in Bexhill and Clacton confirmed this view by emphasizing the ease of making friends in a town where a large proportion of the people are retired like themselves. There is a problem of emergency help, but better services could alleviate this. Also we must not forget that even in the mixed-age communities in cities, the elderly are very often very isolated and fail to receive the help of younger neighbours even when they are there.

The economic arguments against unbalanced communities

have some basis. The disproportionate number of residents who are on low or at least fixed incomes in the resorts has its effect on the pattern of local authority expenditure. The absence of employment in industry and commerce means that the rates fall disproportionately on domestic ratepayers. However, these adverse features can be as easily changed by altering the structure of local taxation and government grants, as by aiming for greater heterogeneity of population.

The inevitable conclusion of this study is that elderly people are in general very satisfied with moving to the seaside and rarely regret it. Their move is motivated by a desire for a more congenial physical environment than the cities can offer and once they arrive in the resorts they find the added social advantage of being with other retired people with similar interests and time to spare. The blot on this picture is the situation of the health and social services which have failed to keep up with the demand. This is a soluble situation but the solutions do not lie solely in the hands of the local authorities concerned. More financial help is needed and so is a review of the way in which staff are recruited for the basic services.

The elderly people who leave the cities are passing a judgment on them as an environment in which to live. If there were more employment in the seaside resorts, would they have left during their working life? And would they have stayed in London if there had been less problems of traffic and dirt and noise? There was an Edwardian music hall song which went as follows:

Why can't we have the sea in London?
Why can't we have the seaside there?
If the pier was in the Strand,
You could go and hear the band,
Why can't we have the seaside there?
In the beautiful summer time,
London would be fine,
If we only had the seaside there.

Appendix 1: supplementary tables

Note: Parentheses around figures in Tables means that the percentages are based on a total sample number of less than 50; * = less than 0.5 per cent; - = nil.

TABLE A1.1 Larger local authorities in England and Wales with the highest proportions of elderly residents: proportions of people of pensionable age and of 65 and over, and net migration rates for people of pensionable age (urban areas with more than 15,000 inhabitants and 20 per cent or more of their population of pensionable age, in 1966).

Local authority	% population of pensionable age			% population 65 and over		Net migration rate 1965-6 people of pensionable age*	Net migration rate 1961-6 people of pensionable age*
	1961	1966	1971	1966	1971		
NORTH WEST COASTS							
LANCS.							
Blackpool CB	22.6	23.9	25.9	19.4	21.3	+ 1.6	+ 10.3
Morecombe & Heysham MB	26.0	30.7	31.4	24.7	26.6	+ 4.9	+ 41.8
Lytham St Annes MB	25.4	26.2	29.1	21.8	24.2	+ 9.4	+ 54.1
Southport CB	24.5	24.5	25.5	20.5	21.3	+ 2.6	+ 6.3
Thornton Cleveleys UD	25.1	25.7	27.9	20.9	23.4	+ 9.1	+ 50.2

Table continues

Appendix 1

Local authority	% population of pensionable age			% population 65 and over		Net migration rate 1965-6 people of pensionable age*	Net migration rate 1961-6 people of pensionable age*
	1961	1966	1971	1966	1971		
WELSH COASTS							
CAERN.							
Llandudno UD	28.3	28.8	32.1	23.6	26.9	+ 2.9	+ 17.4
DENB.							
Colwyn Bay MD	29.1	31.0	32.3	25.3	27.4	+ 3.2	+ 28.4
FLINT.							
Rhyl UD	22.1	22.7	25.7	17.8	21.5	+ 1.4	+ 22.5
SOUTH WEST COASTS							
CORN.							
St Austell UD	19.4	21.5	21.2	17.6	17.4	− 0.8	+ 9.4
DEVON							
Exmouth UD	27.3	28.9	29.8	24.9	25.3	+ 4.3	+ 40.0
Newton Abbot UD	21.8	21.7	23.8	17.8	20.2	+ 6.3	+ 21.6
Paignton UD	28.7	30.9	−	25.9	−	+ 7.3	+ 32.5
Torquay MB	26.1	26.5	−	21.7	−	+ 5.1	+ 22.8
Torbay CB	−	−	30.6	−	25.4	−	−
SOMERSET							
Weston-Super-Mare MB	24.9	24.4	27.7	20.3	23.3	+ 9.0	+ 34.4
SOUTH AND SOUTH-EAST COASTS							
HANTS							
Bournemouth CB	27.0	28.1	30.2	23.4	25.3	+ 1.8	+ 16.9
Lymington MB	27.1	30.4	32.2	25.8	27.0	+ 8.2	+ 50.2
Christchurch MB	21.0	23.9	28.6	19.8	23.5	+ 7.2	+ 39.7
DORSET							
Poole	19.6	21.1	21.5	17.1	17.7	+12.4	+ 19.8
IOW							
Ryde MB	22.8	24.5	26.6	20.1	21.8	+ 1.4	+ 19.4

Table continues over

Local authority	% population of pensionable age			% population 65 and over		Net migration rate 1965-6 people of pensionable age*	Net migration rate 1961-6 people of pensionable age*
	1961	1966	1971	1966	1971		
KENT							
Broadstairs & St Peters UD	29.4	30.8	32.7	26.1	27.9	+ 4.3	+ 46.3
Folkestone MB	22.9	23.6	26.5	20.1	22.3	+ 5.1	+ 17.2
Herne Bay UD	33.8	36.1	36.8	31.0	31.8	+ 9.5	+ 89.7
Margate MB	25.9	27.6	31.2	22.6	26.2	+ 6.1	+ 41.1
Ramsgate MB	21.5	23.0	24.8	18.6	20.8	+ 1.7	+ 23.6
Tunbridge Wells MB	22.8	22.6	22.1	18.6	18.4	+ 3.0	+ 12.0
Whitstable UD	28.5	27.5	27.5	22.9	23.3	+ 5.9	+ 47.7
E. SUSSEX							
Bexhill MB	37.0	41.2	44.2	34.7	38.4	+26.3	+ 92.4
Brighton CB	21.4	22.8	23.0	18.8	19.0	+ 2.1	+ 1.4
Eastbourne CB	29.8	33.7	33.4	28.1	28.4	+10.2	+ 49.0
Hastings CB	28.7	28.9	29.5	24.1	24.9	+ 2.2	+ 24.0
Hove MB	30.8	31.1	33.6	26.0	28.6	- 1.4	+ 18.7
W. SUSSEX							
Bognor Regis UD	28.4	31.4	31.0	26.6	26.3	+ 7.2	+ 48.5
Littlehampton UD	22.1	22.1	26.0	17.8	22.1	+ 5.5	+ 40.9
Shoreham by Sea UD	17.7	20.2	20.6	16.4	16.9	+ 6.5	+ 12.9
Worthing MB	36.3	38.0	38.8	32.4	33.9	+ 8.9	+ 50.6
EAST COASTS							
ESSEX							
Clacton UD	29.2	32.0	36.4	26.9	30.9	+20.6	+ 95.4
Southend CB	21.3	21.9	23.7	18.2	19.9	+ 1.9	+ 10.3
E. SUFFOLK							
Felixstowe UD	21.6	23.6	24.3	19.6	20.5	+ 9.3	+ 45.1
YORKS. ER							
Bridlington MB	26.6	28.8	31.2	23.9	26.3	+ 1.9	+ 26.8
YORKS. NR							
Scarborough MB	23.4	26.1	26.7	21.4	22.4	+ 5.7	+ 12.9

Table continues

Appendix 1

Local authority	% population of pensionable age			% population 65 and over		Net migration rate 1965-6 people of pensionable age*	Net migration rate 1961-6 people of pensionable age*
	1961	1966	1971	1966	1971		
INLAND YORKS.WR							
Harrogate MB	20.5	20.7	22.1	16.6	18.2	+ 3.4	+ 13.6
KENT							
Tunbridge Wells	22.8	22.6	22.1	18.6	18.4	+ 3.0	+ 12.0
ENGLAND AND WALES	14.9	15.5	16.1	12.4	13.3		

Sources: Census County Reports 1961, 1966, 1971 and Census Migration Reports 1966.

* Balance of immigration and emigration (population of pensionable age), expressed per 1,000 total resident population of all ages 1966.

TABLE A1.2 Smaller local authorities in England and Wales with the highest proportions of elderly residents: proportions of people of pensionable age in 1961, 1966 and 1971 (authorities with less than 15,000 inhabitants and 20 per cent or more of their population of pensionable age in 1966).

Local authority	% population of pensionable age		
	1961	1966	1971
NORTH-WEST LANCS.			
Grange UD	38.3	35.9	45.5
WALES & WELSH COASTS ANGLESEY			
Beaumaris MB	21.2	21.5	21.2
BRECON.			
Llanwrtyd Wells UD	28.0	34.1	26.5
Builth Wells UD	20.8	28.0	25.0
Hay UD	23.1	29.7	25.6
CAERN.			
Conway MB	24.2	26.6	28.0
Llanfairfechan UD	21.9	20.3	24.1
Penmaenmawr UD	25.7	31.8	27.4
Portmadoc UD	20.0	20.1	21.9
Pwhelli MB	20.9	22.5	22.2
CARD.			
Aberystwyth RD	19.8	22.7	19.6
Tregaran RD	20.6	27.0	23.1
New Quay UD	30.1	38.7	36.0
DENB.			
Abergele UD	24.1	27.3	31.1
Denbigh MB	19.8	20.1	19.9
FLINTS.			
Prestatyn UD	28.7	31.0	32.4
MERIONETH.			
Barmouth UD	21.9	22.3	26.1
Dolgellau RD	20.9	21.9	24.6
MONT.			
Llanidloes MB	21.2	21.4	25.1
RADNOR.			
Llandrindod Wells UD	21.6	20.9	25.9
SOUTH-WEST COASTS CORN.			
Bude Stratton UD	25.8	27.1	29.9
Fowey MB	22.8	23.1	-

Table continues

Local authority	% population of pensionable age		
	1961	1966	1971
CORN. (contd)			
Looe UD	25.1	20.5	28.0
Padstow UD	19.3	20.9	-
St Ives MB	22.5	25.2	26.5
Newquay UD	23.2	22.2	25.4
Bodmin MB	23.1	22.6	21.5
Launceston MB	20.8	24.4	23.8
Kerrier RD	21.5	21.4	21.1
Truro RD	20.1	22.0	23.1
Wadebridge & Padstow RD	-	-	21.3
DEVON			
Budleigh Salterton UD	36.4	38.8	43.0
Dawlish UD	25.3	29.6	28.7
Ilfracombe UD	26.0	26.5	31.7
Seaton UD	33.7	41.3	42.2
Sidmouth UD	36.0	42.8	44.3
Teignmouth UD	28.0	23.1	31.7
Lynton UD	24.6	26.4	23.4
Northam UD	24.0	26.8	29.4
Salcombe UD	24.5	21.7	28.5
Brixham UD	22.9	24.2	-
Barnstaple RD	19.8	21.5	22.1
Newton Abbot RD	22.6	25.3	26.8
Totnes RD	21.6	23.8	24.7
SOMERSET			
Clevedon UD	25.1	21.3	22.5
Minehead UD	29.3	32.3	35.4
Burnham on Sea UD	21.5	25.3	27.6
Williton RD	20.7	23.2	23.6
SOUTH & SOUTH-EAST COASTS			
DORSET			
Bridport MB	20.4	28.5	28.3
Lyme Regis MB	24.5	30.7	33.5
Swanage UD	25.0	28.3	30.1
Bridport RD	24.6	24.8	31.3
Blandford Forum MB	20.2	22.9	21.7
Shaftesbury MB	21.1	24.4	22.3
Sherborne UD	19.5	23.1	22.0
Wareham MB	20.6	21.0	20.1
Wimborne and Cranborne RD	20.7	20.9	22.9
HANTS			
Ringwood and Fordingbridge RD	21.7	24.4	24.5

Table continues over

Appendix 1

Local authority	% population of pensionable age		
	1961	1966	1971
IOW			
Ventnor UD	30.8	37.5	30.7
Sandown-Shanklin UD	23.3	26.9	30.7
Isle of Wight RD	22.3	23.5	26.9
KENT			
Hythe MB	26.5	30.6	30.0
Elham RD	22.1	22.1	24.9
Tenterden MB	22.9	30.0	27.4
Eastry RD	17.0	21.2	19.9
E. SUSSEX			
Seaford UD	28.7	32.5	33.4
Rye MB	19.0	21.2	24.4
Battle RD	24.0	26.9	27.4
Chailey RD	24.2	23.2	24.5
Hailsham RD	26.9	29.3	33.3
Uckfield RD	21.3	20.3	20.2
W. SUSSEX			
Southwick UD	19.4	22.1	23.0
Arundel MB	24.6	23.1	27.7
Chanctonbury RD	21.6	24.1	24.2
Chichester RD	20.9	21.0	23.6
Worthing RD	31.7	33.5	33.6
EAST COASTS			
ESSEX			
Brightlingsea UD	23.8	23.0	24.7
Frinton and Walton UD	30.9	34.2	40.8
West Mersea UD	25.0	30.5	26.9
Burnham on Crouch UD	20.8	23.0	21.7
LINDSEY (LINCS.)			
Woodall Spa UD	25.3	26.9	22.8
Mablethorpe UD	24.2	25.5	31.3
Skegness UD	21.7	23.7	26.8
Alford UD	23.5	20.4	23.3
NORFOLK			
Hunstanton UD	16.5	24.5	32.6
Cromer UD	25.0	29.9	31.2
Sheringham UD	25.6	34.9	32.6
Wells next the Sea UD	19.3	21.2	27.1
Downham Market UD	21.3	27.5	23.2
North Walsham UD	20.2	22.2	22.2

Table continues

Appendix 1

Local authority	% population of pensionable age		
	1961	1966	1971
E. SUFFOLK			
Aldeburgh MB	18.9	31.4	31.2
Southwold MB	34.7	40.8	43.5
W. SUFFOLK			
Sudbury MB	22.1	22.8	21.2
YORKS. ER			
Filey UD	22.3	26.4	33.6
Hornsea UD	24.4	22.7	24.5
YORKS. NR			
Scalby UD	22.6	22.0	25.2
ENGLAND AND WALES	14.9	15.5	16.1

Sources: 1961 Census County Reports; 1966 Census, unpublished data; 1971 Census County Reports.

TABLE A1.3 In-migrants of pensionable age in some retirement resorts and counties

	Percentage of population of pensionable age 1966**	In-migrants of pensionable age as a proportion of all in-migrants 1961-6*		
		Male	Female	All
ENGLAND AND WALES	15.5	-	-	-
CORN.	20.3	12.7	20.7	17.0
DEVON	20.9	13.5	23.3	18.8
Torquay	26.5	17.3	29.8	24.5
Paignton	30.9	18.7	32.8	26.4
Exmouth	28.9	22.6	35.4	29.1
DORSET	19.8	12.9	22.5	18.0
ESSEX	15.2	8.0	15.8	11.9
Southend on Sea	21.9	13.9	25.4	19.9
Clacton	32.0	31.4	44.6	38.8
HANTS	17.0	9.5	17.6	13.8
Bournemouth	28.1	17.7	31.0	25.1
ISLE OF WIGHT	23.2	15.5	28.4	22.4
KENT	17.5	10.5	19.1	15.0
Broadstairs and St Peters	30.8	22.1	34.2	28.9
Herne Bay	36.1	33.4	48.9	41.7
Margate	27.6	26.0	35.5	31.2
Ramsgate	23.0	17.4	28.7	23.4
Whitstable	27.5	19.9	34.3	27.6
NORFOLK	17.9	12.2	19.6	16.2
SOMERSET	18.3	11.0	19.6	15.6
Weston-Super-Mare	24.4	18.8	31.2	25.9
E. SUFFOLK	17.4	11.4	19.9	15.9
E. SUSSEX	25.8	19.3	33.3	27.1
Bexhill	41.2	39.7	57.1	50.3
Hove	31.1	18.0	34.6	27.5
Eastbourne	33.7	30.4	45.0	38.8
Hastings	28.9	21.8	33.9	28.9
Brighton	22.8	12.9	27.1	20.7

Table continues

Appendix 1

	Percentage of population of pensionable age 1966**	In-migrants of pensionable age as a proportion of all in-migrants 1961-6*		
		Male	Female	All
W. SUSSEX	23.8	17.9	33.2	26.3
Bognor	31.4	21.7	39.1	31.2
Worthing	38.0	29.3	49.2	41.3
CAERN.	22.2	15.2	25.9	20.8
Llandudno	28.8	13.2	29.5	22.1
DENB.	18.8	14.2	26.2	20.6
Colwyn Bay	31.0	18.3	33.3	26.9
FLINTS.	17.3	14.1	25.4	20.2
Rhyl	22.7	22.4	33.2	28.4
MERIONETH.	19.0	10.6	22.4	16.7
INDIVIDUAL RESORTS IN NON-RETIREMENT COUNTIES				
LANCS.	15.5	6.1	13.6	9.8
Blackpool	23.9	14.3	25.4	20.2
Morecombe & Heysham	30.7	22.4	39.6	31.6
Southport	24.5	10.5	23.5	17.6
Lytham St Annes	26.2	16.4	29.9	23.9
YORKS. NR	14.6	7.7	15.0	11.4
Scarborough	26.1	14.2	27.5	21.5
YORKS. ER	15.3	7.3	15.9	11.7
Bridlington	28.8	17.7	33.0	26.2

* General Register Office, Sample Census 1966, England and Wales, Migration Summary Tables, Part 1, London, HMSO, 1968, Table 5B.
** Sample Census 1966, County Reports.

TABLE A1.4 Main areas of origin of retirement movers: Movers of pensionable age into five regions or sub-regions, during the period 1961-6, analysed by region or sub-region of origin*

Former area of residence (origin)	Area of residence in 1966 (destination)				
	South-West Region	East Anglia Region	South-East Remainder Sub-Region	Wales Remainder Sub-Region	North-West Remainder Sub-Region
	%	%	%	%	%
Sample number	4,631	1,854	10,087	1,086	2,651
Northern Region	1	2	1	1	5
Yorks. and Humberside Region	3	4	2	3	14
North-West Region	6	3	3	45	48
East Midland Region	3	6	2	2	2
West Midland Region	13	5	4	19	6
East Anglia	1	–	2	1	1
Greater London	27	36	53	8	5
Outer Metropolitan Area	15	19	21	5	3
Remainder of S.E. Region	17	13	–	3	3
South-West	–	4	7	2	2
Wales	5	1	1	6	3

Appendix 1

Former area of residence (origin)	Area of residence in 1966 (destination)				
	South-West Region	East Anglia Region	South-East Remainder Sub-Region	Wales Remainder Sub-Region	North-West Remainder Sub-Region
	%	%	%	%	%
Elsewhere in the British Isles	3	3	2	1	4
Commonwealth and Foreign countries	5	3	3	2	2
All areas of origin	100	100	100	100	100

* General Register Office Sample Census 1966, England and Wales, Migration Summary Tables, Part 1, London, HMSO, 1968, Table 3B.

TABLE A1.5 Destinations of retirement movers: Movers of pensionable age from the main areas of origin of movers to the five main retirement areas, during the period 1961-6, analysed by origin and destination*

Area of residence at 1966 (destination)	Former area of residence (origin)						
	West Midland Region	East Midland Region	North-West Region	Yorks. & Humberside Region	Greater London	Outer Metropolitan Area	Remainder of South-East Region
Sample number	2,139	1,232	2,309	1,820	12,414	4,848	3,330
	%	%	%	%	%	%	%
Northern Region	3	4	8	22	1	2	2
Yorks. and Humberside Region	4	22	14	–	2	2	3
North-West Region	10	9	–	26	2	3	5
East Midland Region	9	–	5	17	2	3	4
West Midland Region	–	12	10	4	2	3	5
East Anglia	4	9	3	4	5	7	8
Greater London	4	5	6	4	–	19	19

Appendix 1

Area of residence at 1966 (destination)	Former area of residence (origin)						
	West Midland Region	East Midland Region	North-West Region	Yorks. & Humberside Region	Greater London	Outer Metropolitan Area	Remainder of South-East Region
	%	%	%	%	%	%	%
Outer Metropolitan Area	6	6	7	6	32	–	30
Remainder of South-East Region	18	18	13	9	43	44	–
South-West	29	13	11	9	10	15	22
Wales	13	4	23	2	2	2	2
All areas of destination in England and Wales	100	100	100	100	100	100	100

* General Register Office, Sample Census 1966, England and Wales, Migration Summary Tables, Part 1, London, HMSO, 1968, Table 3B.

TABLE A1.6 Areas of origin of people who had moved to Bexhill and Clacton to retire

	Bexhill	Clacton
Sample number	503	487
ORIGIN OF MOVERS	%	%
Greater London	45	63
Essex	4	16
Kent, Surrey, Sussex	24	4
Beds. and Herts.	3	6
Midlands	6	3
South-West	2	-
North	3	3
East Anglia	1	1
South	6	2
Wales, Scotland, N. Ireland	1	-
Abroad	5	-

TABLE A1.7 Migration by people of 65 and over, from the conurbations and to the retirement regions

	Gains and losses of people aged 65 and over					
	1960-1**			1965-6***		
	Loss	Gain	Net Gain/Loss	Loss	Gain	Net Gain/Loss
CONURBATIONS						
Greater London	19,240	6,030	-13,210	19,570	7,240	-12,330
West Midlands	2,550	1,060	- 1,490	2,690	1,200	- 1,490
West Yorkshire	1,690	1,240	- 450	2,200	1,250	- 950
Tyneside	1,230	520	- 710	2,050	500	- 1,550
South-East	2,890	1,820	- 1,070	2,950	1,850	- 1,100
Merseyside	1,470	1,000	- 470	1,730	1,010	- 720
All conurbations	29,070	11,670	-17,400	31,190	13,050	-18,140
Moves from one conurbation to another	2,080	2,080		1,250	1,250	
Gains/losses from conurbations	26,990	9,590	-17,400	29,940	11,800	-18,140
RETIREMENT REGIONS						
South-West Region	3,310	6,830	+ 3,520	3,730	8,800	+ 5,070
Wales II	1,220	1,690	+ 470	1,050	1,700	+ 650

Table continues over

Gains and losses of people aged 65 and over

	1960-1**			1965-6***		
	Loss	Gain	Net Gain/Loss	Loss	Gain	Net Gain/Loss
North-West Remainder	3,210	4,040	+ 830	3,060	4,920	+ 1,860
East*	4,460	7,530	+ 3,070	—	—	—
East Anglia*	—	—	—	1,560	3,320	+ 1,760
South-East						
Remainder*	5,150	11,880	+ 6,730	8,060	15,710	+ 7,650
South*	4,670	7,360	+ 2,690	—	—	—
All retirement regions	22,020	39,330	17,310	17,460	34,450	
Movement between regions	11,790	11,790		5,730		
Total gains	10,230	27,540	17,310	12,730	28,720	16,990

* Changes in definitions of regions prevent comparison of these regions in 1961 and 1966.
** General Register Office, Census 1961, England and Wales Migration Tables, London, HMSO, 1966, Table 5A.
*** General Register Office, Sample Census 1966, England and Wales, Migration Summary Tables, Part I, London, HMSO, 1968, Table 3A.

Appendix 1

TABLE A1.8 Movers of pensionable age, 1961-6*

	Men 65+	Women 60+	
Cornwall	2,180	4,250	
Devon	5,630	11,420	
Dorset	2,890	5,880	
Essex	7,200	15,220	
Hampshire	8,150	16,910	
Isle of Wight	1,030	2,150	
Kent	8,510	16,480	
Norfolk	3,070	5,730	
Somerset	4,010	8,370	
East Suffolk	1,970	3,780	
East Sussex	8,810	19,170	
West Sussex	6,500	14,510	
Caernarvonshire	890	1,660	
Denbighshire	1,070	2,280	
Flintshire	1,100	2,290	
Merionethshire	200	460	
IN LANCASHIRE			
Blackpool	1,500	3,010	
Southport	530	1,460	
Lytham St Annes	660	1,490	
Thornton Cleveleys	640	1,190	
IN YORKSHIRE			
Scarborough	470	1,090	
Harrogate	500	1,460	
	67,510	140,260	TOTAL
			217,770

Total pensionable population of England and Wales

	1966	7,301,890
	1961	5,496,497

* General Register Office, Sample Census 1966, England and Wales, Migration Summary Tables, Part 1, London, HMSO, 1968, Table 5B.

TABLE A1.9 Social class characteristics of some retirement resorts, 1966

	Proportion of population 65 and over in 1966*	Proportion of males in Social Classes I and II		Total population 1966*
		Retired**	Economically active**	
CORNWALL				
St Ives MB	21.7	30.4	23.6	9,110
Newquay UD	17.0	26.7	28.6	12,860
DEVON				
Budleigh Salterton UD	31.4	52.3	29.1	4,070
Dawlish UD	25.2	26.4	37.3	8,540
Seaton UD	32.6	51.3	18.8	3,440
Sidmouth	36.7	53.8	28.6	10,640
Teignmouth UD	19.5	29.4	26.7	12,590
SOMERSET				
Minehead UD	26.2	27.9	20.9	7,370
Burnham on Sea UD	21.2	25.0	19.7	11,010
DORSET				
Bridport MB	18.9	29.4	20.5	6,440
Swanage UD	24.6	44.9	28.5	7,860
ESSEX				
Clacton UD	26.9	19.8	21.8	33.040
Frinton and Walton UD	28.2	30.1	29.2	11,170
West Mercia UD	24.6	43.8	28.3	3,380
Burnham on Crouch UD	19.8	21.1	23.8	4,400
Southwold UD	36.2	53.9	37.7	2,180
Cromer UD	24.9	22.7	21.0	5,660
KENT				
Herne Bay UD	31.0	27.4	24.2	24,350

Table continues

TABLE A1.9 (contd)

	Proportion of population 65 and over in 1966*	Proportion of males in Social Classes I and II		Total population 1966*
		Retired**	Economically active**	
SUSSEX				
Bexhill MB	34.7	41.1	27.8	32,160
Eastbourne CB	28.1	37.8	25.3	65,060
Hastings CB	24.1	25.7	20.4	70,030
Worthing MB	32.4	40.2	27.5	83,900
Littlehampton UD	17.8	24.0	17.4	88,170
Bognor Regis UD	26.6	30.4	24.5	30,860
HANTS				
Bournemouth CB	23.4	29.9	22.7	155,620
ISLE OF WIGHT				
Ventnor UD	26.7	26.1	28.0	6,410
Sandown-Shanklin UD	21.9	30.9	30.5	13,890

* Sample Census, 1966, County Reports.
** Unpublished figures supplied by the Registrar General.

TABLE A1.10 Age at retirement move

	Bexhill			Clacton		
	Heads of retirement units at the time of the move					
	All	Male	Female	All	Male	Female
Sample number	495	400	95	476	421	55
	%	%	%	%	%	%
Under 55	5	5	8	4	4	5
55-9	14	12	18	9	10	4
60-4	39	40	36	31	29	45
65-9	32	33	26	43	46	22
70-4	8	8	7	9	8	15
75 and over	3	3	4	4	2	9

TABLE A1.11 Surviving children: proportions of men with no surviving children at the time of the survey; Bexhill, Clacton and Britain

	Male heads of retirement units, by marital status at the time of the move				Men of 65 and over	
	Bexhill		Clacton		Britain*	
	All	Married or Widowed	All	Married or Widowed	All	Married or Widowed
Sample number	403	399	427	419	1,004	964
	%	%	%	%	%	%
No surviving children	36	36	25	25	20	16
One or more	63	64	75	75	80	84

* E. Shanas et al., 'Old People in Three Industrial Societies', London, Routledge & Kegan Paul, 1968; calculated from Tables VI-1 and VI-2, pp.137, 139.

TABLE A1.12 Likes and dislikes about the pre-retirement house

	Bexhill	Clacton
Sample number	503*	487*
LIKES	%	%
Nothing liked	8	18
Size suitable	25	9
Nice garden	31	13
Well built	25	15
Liked design	9	14
Attractive	25	6
Warm	7	2
Location liked	9	7
Just liked it	20	32
Other and no reply	4	7
DISLIKES		
Nothing disliked	61	48
Too large	11	13
Too much housework	4	11
Garden problems	8	3
Out of date	5	8
Cold	6	5
Too small	2	1
Sad associations	2	3
Location	6	6
Just disliked it	-	*
Other and no reply	10	14

* The percentages add up to more than 100 as more than one reply could be given.

TABLE A1.13 Likes and dislikes about the pre-retirement area: analysed for all movers and those from Greater London

	Bexhill		Clacton	
	All	From Greater London	All	From Greater London
Sample number	503*	225*	487*	307*
LIKES	%	%	%	%
Nothing liked	9	13	16	15
Convenient for city	20	27	13	16
Near work or transport	15	17	18	21
Convenient for shopping, etc.	24	30	24	31
Good entertainments, etc.	4	5	4	5
Near countryside or open space	35	25	20	17
Good class area	24	26	14	15
Liked neighbours	23	24	15	16
Just liked it	9	9	17	10
Other and no reply	6	3	9	8
DISLIKES				
Nothing disliked	46	62	55	53
Area deteriorated	11	14	11	12
Coloured immigrants and Jews	3	5	8	12
Too much traffic	20	27	13	14
Too industrial	5	4	4	4
Being too built up	15	20	8	7
Suburbia characterless / No entertainments	7	8	1	*
Just disliked it	1	1	1	*
Other and no reply	15	8	3	8

* The percentages add up to more than 100 as more than one reply could be given.

TABLE A1.14 Consideration of other retirement areas

	Bexhill	Clacton
Sample number: Those who had considered other places	256*	202
PLACES CONSIDERED	%	%
Sussex Coast	74	51
Kent Coast	12	15
Essex Coast	2	25
Devon/Cornwall	12	9
Dorset, Somerset and Hants	23	18
Lancs and Yorks Coasts	*	2
Norfolk and Suffolk	2	7
Elsewhere	12	10

* The percentages do not add up to 100 because more than one place could be mentioned.

TABLE A1.15 Main reason for choosing Bexhill and Clacton

	Bexhill	Clacton
Sample number	500	487
PROPORTION WHO GAVE THE FOLLOWING REASONS:	%	%
Climate - air healthy	10	9
Flat land	5	5
Knew the town well	7	11
Had friends or relations there	27	32
Price of property	10	23
Liked the town, its surroundings and amenities	18	6
Liked the house	16	6
Convenient for London	2	4
Other	4	4

TABLE A1.16 Date of move to Bexhill and Clacton

	Bexhill		
	All	Married couples and widowed and single men	Widowed and single women
Sample number	503	357	146
DATE OF MOVE	%	%	%
In 1968*	1	–	1
1966-7	19	21	16
1964-5	15	18	7
1959-63	35	36	34
1954-8	19	18	20
Before 1954	12	7	23
	Clacton		
Sample number	487	396	91
DATE OF MOVE	%	%	%
In 1968*	–	1	–
1966-7	18	18	19
1964-5	25	27	20
1959-63	37	38	33
1954-8	11	10	13
Before 1954	8	6	15

* Because the Electoral list used for the sampling frame was a year old at the time of the survey only 1 per cent in either town said they had moved there in 1968.

Appendix 1

TABLE A1.17 Age by sex and marital status: people of 65 and over, Bexhill, Clacton and England and Wales

Age	Bexhill 1968 Movers and their households*				
	All	Married	Single	Widowed and divorced	Single, widowed and divorced
Sample no.	318	297	6	18	24
MEN	%	%	%	%	%
65-9	36	36			(35)
70-4	33	35			(13)
75-9	21	21			(22)
80 and over	10	9			(30)
Sample no.	303	233	87	84	171
WOMEN	%	%	%	%	%
65-9	36	48	25	18	21
70-4	29	30	31	24	27
75-9	19	15	28	21	25
80 and over	15	7	17	37	27
	Clacton 1968 Movers and their households*				
Sample no.	349	311	4	34	38
MEN	%	%	%	%	%
65-9	37	38			(26)
70-4	35	35			(37)
75-9	20	20			(24)
80 and over	8	7			(13)
Sample no.	352	254	28	74	102
WOMEN	%	%	%	%	%
65-9	45	49	(46)	36	39
70-4	32	31	(36)	32	33
75-9	14	14	(11)	15	14
80 and over	10	6	(7)	16	14

Table continues over

	England and Wales 1971**				
Age	All	Married	Single	Widowed and divorced	Single, widowed and divorced
Sample no.	–	–	–	–	–
MEN	%	%	%	%	%
65–9	43	48	46	23	29
70–4	28	29	27	24	25
75–9	16	15	15	22	20
80 and over	13	9	12	30	26
Sample no.	–	–	–	–	–
WOMEN	%	%	%	%	%
65–9	33	49	31	23	25
70–4	27	30	26	26	26
75–9	19	14	20	23	22
80 and over	20	7	22	29	27

* To compare the age structure of our sample with the Census age data, it was necessary to make some adjustments to the survey data. First, only people of 65 and over were included, to standardize the age group. Second, all other members of the household who were 65 and over (not just the respondent or their spouse) were included.

** Census 1971, Great Britain, Age, Marital Condition and General Tables, London, HMSO, 1974, Table 9.

TABLE A1.18 Proportions (%) of women in each age group who were widowed - some seaside resorts and inland cities, 1971*

Towns in ascending order of proportion of widows in 75 and over age group	Age groups				
	55-9	60-4	65-9	70-4	75 and over
			% widowed		
Bexhill	12	18	23	33	48
Sidmouth	12	15	24	33	50
Worthing	13	20	27	36	52
Eastbourne	13	20	28	38	54
Hastings	14	20	30	38	54
Clacton	12	20	25	37	56
Hove	15	23	31	42	57
Bournemouth	14	21	31	42	58
Torbay	14	21	29	41	58
Brighton	13	22	32	43	60
Southport	15	24	33	47	61
Southend	13	21	32	45	63
Blackpool	15	23	34	49	65
Greater London	13	22	33	47	66
Leeds	16	24	35	49	66
Manchester	17	26	37	51	68
Birmingham	14	23	35	50	68
Liverpool	18	27	39	53	69
Coventry	14	22	35	51	71
Sheffield	15	23	36	52	72
England and Wales	14	22	33	47	65

* Census 1971, Great Britain, County Reports, and Census 1971, Great Britain, Age, Marital Condition and General Tables, London, HMSO, 1974.

TABLE A1.19 Main reasons for finding it easier to make friends

	Bexhill	Clacton
Sample number	142	181
REASONS	%	%
Retired people have interests in common	18	22
When you are retired you have more time to make friends	40	27
There are plenty of social facilities	15	19
It is a friendly place: size of town	21	25
Other	6	7

TABLE A1.20 Main reasons for finding it more difficult to make friends

	Bexhill	Clacton
Sample number	53	102
REASONS	%	%
Unfriendly place	25	28
The town is rather snobbish	13	6
Not been in the town long	–	7
Bad health	11	11
Too shy to make friends	13	4
Difficult since widowed	2	3
Difficult when got older	34	24
Other	2	18

Appendix 1

TABLE A1.21 The number of services received

	Bexhill				
	All	All 65 & over	All 75 & over	Living Alone	With no reported health problems
Sample no.	498	409	134	106	
Proportion of people receiving following numbers of services*	%	%	%	%	
None	37	34	26	38	
One	34	34	31	30	
Two	21	22	28	18	
Three	7	8	11	9	
Four or more	2	2	4	5	
	Clacton				
Sample no.	481	387	98	86	271
Proportion of people receiving following numbers of services*	%	%	%	%	%
None	43	39	32	36	53
One	39	43	39	37	36
Two	13	13	21	20	9
Three	4	4	5	5	3
Four or more	1	1	3	2	*

* All services including those who had seen their doctor within the last three months (see Table 8.1)

TABLE A1.22 Ways of spending most of the time

	Bexhill	Clacton
Sample number	502	487
PERCENTAGE OF RESPONDENTS WHO MENTIONED: *	%	%
Household duties	52	56
Gardening	46	39
Watching TV	35	32
Reading	34	22
Listening to the radio	12	5
Handicrafts	12	19
Walking	21	26
Motoring	17	7
Sitting on the sea front	9	6
Cards, bingo, etc.	7	6
Attending organizations or clubs	12	13
Doing social work, helping people	7	3
Visiting friends or receiving visits	26	7
Other (including working)	27	18

* More than one activity might be mentioned so the percentages do not add up to 100.

TABLE A1.23 Use of leisure facilities

	Bexhill			Clacton		
	All	Men	Women	All	Men	Women
Sample no.	503	213	290	487	207	208
Proportion of people visiting the following more than once a fortnight on average throughout the year:	%	%	%	%	%	%
Cinema	3	2	3	5	4	5
Sea front	69	73	66	63	70	57
Public house	7	10	5	9	13	6
Sporty event	12	16	9	8	14	4
Park	25	26	24	5	4	5
None	25	20	29	32	26	37
Proportion of people attending:	%	%	%	%	%	%
Clubs	56	55	56	40	36	43
Evening classes	7	3	10	2	2	2
Church	37	32	40	23	19	26
Other organized activities	3	1	5	1	-	1
Attending none of these	57	65	51	74	80	70

TABLE A1.24 Social class and weekly net income of retirement units, by sex of head of retirement unit

		Bexhill				
		Men and married couples			Women	
Corrected* income range	All	Professional + intermediate	Skilled non-manual workers	Skilled manual, semi-skilled and unskilled workers	Professional + intermediate	Skilled, semi-skilled and unskilled
Sample no.	377	166	60	40	56	53
WEEKLY NET INCOME	%	%	%	%	%	%
Up to £5.00	4	–	–	–	11	21
£5.01 up to £7.50	7	2	–	(19)	14	21
£7.51 up to £10.00	15	8	12	(19)	22	38
£10.01 up to £12.50	11	10	19	(11)	8	9
£12.51 up to £15.00	12	11	20	(26)	8	3
£15.01 up to £20.00	22	26	37	(11)	11	9
£20.01 up to £25.00	10	13	12	(–)	11	–
£25.01 and over	18	31	2	(14)	15	–

Appendix 1

		Clacton					
		Men and married couples				Women	
Corrected* income range	All	Professional + intermediate	Skilled non-manual workers	Skilled manual workers	Semi-skilled and unskilled	Professional + intermediate	Skilled, semi-skilled and unskilled
Sample no.	414	74	52	149	54	26	55
WEEKLY NET INCOME	%	%	%	%	%	%	%
Up to £5.00	5	1	2	1	–	(12)	25
£5.01 up to £7.50	17	7	13	12	17	(31)	44
£7.51 up to £10.00	29	16	19	38	35	(35)	25
£10.01 up to £12.50	22	20	31	26	28	(12)	2
£12.51 up to £15.00	12	11	21	14	13	(4)	4
£15.01 up to £20.00	11	30	10	7	7	(8)	–
£20.01 up to £25.00	3	9	4	–	–	(–)	–
£25.00 and over	1	5	–	1	–	(–)	–

* Income range corrected to eliminate the effects of different response rates by various social classes.

284 Appendix 1

TABLE A1.25 Weekly gross income of elderly households in Great Britain and average tax paid, 1968*

	Head of household aged 60 and over** %	Head of household aged 65 and over** %	Retired and unoccu-pied*** %	Average weekly household expenditure on tax and National Insurance in new pence****	
				Single-person households (all ages)	Households with one man and one woman (all ages)
Sample no.	2,240	1,549	1,770	1,161	1,936
WEEKLY GROSS INCOME					
Under £6	7	9	10	−0.65	5.15
£6 but less than £8	15	19	19	5.30	
£8 but less than £10	10	13	13	30.30	
£10 but less than £15	20	24	23	125.25	32.90
£15 but less than £20	13	12	11	273.25	177.96
£20 but less than £25	9	7	7	⎫	
£25 but less than £30	7	4	5	⎬ 741.15	379.40
£30 but less than £40	9	6	6	⎭	583.75
£40 and over	10	6	6		1,168.25

* Department of Employment and Productivity, 'Family Expenditure Survey: Report for 1968', London, HMSO, 1969.
** Ibid., p.86, Table 28.
*** Ibid., p.86, Table 27.
**** Ibid., p.30, Table 4, and p.35, Table 5.

TABLE A1.26 Savings and their current use

	Bexhill	Clacton
Sample number	377	414
AMOUNT OF SAVINGS Proportion of those with savings who had:	%	%
Less than £500	19	49
£500-999	14	19
£1,000-2,999	26	23
£3,000-4,999	9	6
£5,000-6,999	6	3
£7,000-9,999	9 ⎫	
£10,000-14,999	9 ⎬	2
£15,000 or more	9 ⎭	
CURRENTLY USING SAVINGS (those with savings)		
Yes	42	66
No	58	34

TABLE A1.27 Sources of income

	Bexhill		
	All	Married couples and single men	Widowed and single women
Sample number	414	298	116
SOURCES OF INCOME* MENTIONED:	%	%	%
Old age pension	85	86	83
Superannuation/ occupational pension	55	61	40
Wages or fees	7	8	3
Interest	55	56	53
Supplementary Benefits	7	3	16
Other government pensions, etc.	15	17	9
Rents of property	5	2	11
Help from relatives	1	1	2
Other	1	1	–

	Clacton		
Sample number	475	386	89
SOURCES OF INCOME* MENTIONED:	%	%	%
Old age pension	89	87	97
Superannuation/ occupational pension	48	54	21
Wages or fees	12	14	2
Interest	35	35	35
Supplementary Benefits	13	9	33
Other government pensions, etc.	7	8	6
Rents of property	4	4	6
Help from relatives	1	*	4
Other	2	2	2

* All sources were asked for so the percentages do not add up to 100.

TABLE A1.28 Type of dwelling

	Bexhill movers	Clacton movers
Sample number	498	480
DWELLING TYPE	%	%
House	30	19
Bungalow	44	70
Purpose-built flat	9	4
Converted flat	16	4
Unconverted rooms	2	2
Other	-	1

TABLE A1.29 Price of house by weekly net income of retired household

	Weekly net income				
	Up to £10.00	£10.01 to £15.00	£15.01 to £20.00	£20.01 and over	All
Bexhill					
Sample number	63	76	90	112	357
COST OF HOUSE	%	%	%	%	%
Under £3,000	(42)	26	14	4	15
£3,000-3,999	(31)	39	29	15	25
£4,000-4,999	(25)	21	22	28	24
£5,000-5,999	(3)	9	29	28	21
£6,000 and over	(-)	5	4	25	15
Clacton					
Sample number	182	123	56		399
COST OF HOUSE	%	%	%		%
Under £2,000	21	12	(2)		13
£2,000-2,999	36	37	(32)		33
£3,000-3,999	33	36	(34)		36
£4,000-4,999	8	12	(16)		12
£5,000 and over	1	3	(16)		6

TABLE A1.30 Rates as a percentage of income of head of retired household

	Weekly income					
	£5.01–£7.50	£7.51–£10.00	£10.01–£12.50	£12.51–£15.00	£15.01–£20.00	£20.01–£30.00
BEXHILL						
Median rates paid	–	£75	£78	£77	£80	£88
Median rates as percentage of:						
Lowest income of range	–	19%	15%	12%	10%	8%
Middle income of range	–	16%	13%	11%	9%	7%
Highest income of range	–	14%	12%	10%	8%	6%
CLACTON						
Median rates paid	£61	£63	£64	£70		£76
Median rates as percentage of:						
Lowest income of range	23%	16%	12%	11%	10%	
Middle income of range	19%	14%	11%	10%	8%	
Highest income of range	16%	12%	10%	9%	7%	

TABLE A1.31 Gross rents in Bexhill and Clacton

	Bexhill	Clacton
Sample number	51	35
	%	%
Less than £2.00	2	(14)
£2.00 to £2.99	24	(23)
£3.00 to £3.99	22	(31)
£4.00 to £4.99	16	(26)
£5.00 to £5.99	22	(6)
£6.00 to £6.99	10	-
£7 and over	6	-
Average (mean) rent	£4.40	£3.25
Median rent	£4.13	£3.42

TABLE A1.32 Resident guests of pensionable age in hotels, 1971*

	Residents of pensionable age			All resident guests	Visitors of pensionable age		
	Male	Female	Total		Male	Female	Total
EAST SUSSEX	455	1,265	1,715	2,555	755	1,935	2,690
Brighton	65	130	195	525	90	240	325
Eastbourne	110	280	395	550	485	1,195	1,675
Hastings	65	215	280	380	90	265	355
Bexhill	45	210	255	275	20	60	80
Hove	95	260	355	460	25	85	115
WEST SUSSEX	260	665	920	1,265	130	320	450
Bognor Regis	30	65	95	130	15	50	65
Worthing	175	490	660	775	60	175	240
DORSET	65	145	215	555	250	630	880
ISLE OF WIGHT	20	55	75	205	245	830	1,075
ESSEX	120	275	395	950	110	270	380
Southend	70	140	210	350	25	40	65
Clacton	10	55	65	105	60	180	240
DEVON	410	705	1,115	2,145	1,200	2,800	4,000
Torbay	130	275	410	700	665	1,585	2,250
Exmouth	25	85	115	135	45	100	145
Sidmouth	30	75	105	125	100	230	330

* Office of Population Census and Survey, Census 1971, England and Wales County Reports, London, HMSO, 1972-3, Tables 12 and 17.

TABLE A1.33 Number of moves since retirement

	All movers		Movers with two or more moves	
	Bexhill	Clacton	Bexhill	Clacton
Sample number	500	487	118	80
Number of moves since retirement:	%	%	%	%
1 only	76	84	-	-
2	16	13	66	81
3	5	2	22	14
4	2	1	8	4
5 or more	1	*	4	1
Number of towns lived in:			%	%
Bexhill or Clacton only			59	60
2			31	34
3			7	5
4 or more			3	1
Number of addresses in Bexhill or Clacton:			%	%
None other than present			31	34
1 other			53	60
2 others			12	4
3 others			2	1
4 or more			3	1
Respondents with moves within town only			59%	60%
Respondents with moves elsewhere only			31%	35%
Respondents with both types of move			10%	7%

TABLE A1.34 Reasons for last retirement move: people with more than one retirement move

	Move into town		Move within town	
	Bexhill	Clacton	Bexhill	Clacton
Sample number	38	30	80	50
REASONS*	%	%	%	%
House too big	(8)	(7)	21	12
Too much garden	(11)	(1)	12	6
Rates: house too expensive to run; financial reasons	(3)	(7)	5	18
Wanted bungalow or ground-floor flat; stairs difficult	(3)	(-)	6	4
Other to do with house	(16)	(7)	20	16
Area too quiet; too far from town centre or front	(13)	(3)	6	8
To move to seaside from other area	(16)	(23)	-	-
Other to do with town or area	(26)	(13)	14	2
Temporary stay while found a house	(-)	(3)	11	10
Compulsory move	(-)	(-)	5	8
Couldn't settle, lonely, etc.	(5)	(17)	4	16
To be near children, relatives or friends	(18)	(30)	4	6

* More than one reason might be given, so the percentages add up to more than 100.

TABLE A1.35 Reasons for expecting or wanting to move to a different house in the same town

Number of respondents expecting or wanting to move to a different house in the same town	Percentage of potential movers		Percentage of all respondents	
	Bexhill	Clacton	Bexhill	Clacton
Sample number	68	89	499	485
REASONS	%	%	%	%
Prefer bungalow or ground-floor flat; stairs too much	16	20	2	4
Prefer flat or maisonette to bungalow or house	9	7	1	1
Want smaller accommodation; too much housework	16	13	2	2
Want smaller garden or no garden	21	18	3	3
Other reasons for dissatisfaction with house	18	15	2	3
Prefer to rent	-	11	-	2
Want to be nearer sea	12	13	2	2
Want to be nearer town centre, shops, bus route	13	13	2	2
For a change	-	4	-	1
Unavoidable move	1	3	*	1
Other	12	7	2	1

TABLE A1.36 Immigrants and emigrants of pensionable age, Bexhill and Clacton, 1965-6 and 1961-6*

	1965-6			1961-6		
	Male	Female	Total	Male	Female	Total
BEXHILL						
Immigrants	280	860	1,140	1,200	2,710	3,910
Emigrants	110	200	310	320	670	990
CLACTON						
Immigrants	310	570	880	1,370	2,460	3,830
Emigrants	50	160	210	210	520	730

* General Register Office, Sample Census 1966, England and Wales, Migration Tables, vol.I, Tables 3A and 3B.

TABLE A1.37 Reasons for moving to the coast again

	Bexhill	Clacton
Sample number: those who would move to the coast again	420	348
Proportion who mentioned:	%	%
Climate, healthy, clean, fresh air	19	32
Likes the sea	27	31
Just happy; loves it here	16	13
Peace and quiet; away from city or traffic	10	7
Likes the social activities; lively	7	3
Easy to make friends; likes the people	1	3
Not as quiet or isolated as the country	1	*
Other	4	3
No reply	15	7

TABLE A1.38 Reasons for NOT moving to the coast again

	Bexhill	Clacton
Sample number: those who would NOT move to the coast again	44	81
Proportion who mentioned:	%	%
Too far from children	(5)	12
Miss your old friends and surroundings: too old to pull up roots	(23)	23
Prefers country to seaside	(36)	14
Not enough to do, especially in winter	(7)	21
Prefers city; wants better transport, shops etc.	(2)	10
Climate disliked: bad for health	(16)	10
Expensive	(2)	2
Other	(7)	6
No reply	(7)	1

TABLE A1.39 Geriatric beds per 1,000 of the population aged 65 and over in retirement areas

Hospital group	Rate (1970)*		Area health authority	Rate (1974)**
St Helens Group Colchester***	8.8		Colchester***	7.3
Torquay	7.7	(1968)	Torbay	5.0
Isle of Wight	8.2	(1969)	Isle of Wight	6.8
Southport	12.3		North Sefton	14.5
Hastings****	7.2	(1968)	Hastings****	6.3
Chichester	5.7	(1969)	Chichester	3.5
Worthing	5.3	(1969)	Worthing	3.7
Eastbourne	7.2		Eastbourne	6.7
West Cornwall	10.5		Cornwall	5.9
Bournemouth and East Dorset	8.2	(1969)	East Dorset	7.5
North Devon	11.9		North Devon	9.5
			England	8.6

NB: The two types of area are not comparable.
*   Source: Hospital Management committees of the groups
**   Source: The Department of Health and Social Security.
*** Which includes the Clacton area.
****Which includes the Bexhill area.

TABLE A1.40 Local authority housing in resort county boroughs: stock at 1 April 1971*

	Proportion of local authority housing in the total housing stock 1971**	Numbers of					Number per 1,000 of the elderly population at June 1970		
		1 Bedroom			2 Bedroom		1 Bedroom flats and bungalows	2 bedroom flats and bungalows	1 and 2 bedroom flats and bungalows
		Flats	Bungalows	Flats		Bungalows			
Blackpool	11.0	1,636	70	274		–	57.5		66.7
Bournemouth	10.4	517	242	838		156	20.7		43.5
Brighton	19.8	2,439	174	2,545		17	79.7		157.8
Eastbourne	19.1	1,127	16	439		6	59.9		82.7
Hastings	15.4	546	203	913		19	43.3		97.1
Southend	12.1	1,189	182	1,199		46	41.8		79.8
Southport	7.3	168	130	103		100	17.5		29.5
Torbay	12.1	407	152	533		140	23.1		50.9
England and Wales	28.2	412,152	125,984	498,477		79,876	84.7		175.8
All County boroughs	–	187,482	37,651	201,359		11,274	117.9		229.3

* Institute of Municipal Treasurers and Accountants, 'Housing Statistics (England and Wales), Part I, Rents as at 1st April 1971', IMTA, December 1971.
** Registrar General, Census 1971, England and Wales, Housing Tables Part I, London, HMSO, 1974.

TABLE A1.41 Residents in residential homes in retirement areas at 31 March 1974

Retirement areas by old local authority	Population aged 65 and over June 1973	No. of residents aged 65 and over per 1,000 of population				Total Part III accommodation	
		In LA accommodation	In joint-user premises	Part III accommodation provided			
				In registered voluntary homes	In registered private homes	March 1974	December 1970
RESORT COUNTY BOROUGHS							
Blackpool	33,500	9.2	–	1.7	–	10.9	10.3
Bournemouth	38,500	17.7	–	1.9	–	19.6	19.5
Brighton	32,200	16.8	–	3.9	–	20.7	17.7
Eastbourne	20,800	17.0	–	1.8	1.0	19.8	18.1
Hastings	18,200	10.2	–	4.2	–	14.4	15.8
Southend on Sea	34,100	16.4	–	6.0	–	22.4	25.2
Southport	18,200	15.3	–	3.1	–	18.4	18.3
Torbay	28,200	7.2	–	3.5	0.3	11.0	10.3
All English CBs	1,879,700	17.2	0.3	1.6	0.1	19.2	18.9

Table continues over

Retirement areas by old local authority	Population aged 65 and over June 1973	No. of residents aged 65 and over per 1,000 of population				Total Part III accommodation	
		In LA accommodation	In joint-user premises	Part III accommodation provided		March 1974	December 1970
				In registered voluntary homes	In registered private homes		
RESORT COUNTY COUNCILS							
Cornwall and Isles of Scilly	69,500	13.8	–	1.4	–	15.2	14.9
Devon	98,600	10.2	–	1.9	–	12.1	12.4
Dorset	68,100	11.6	–	0.7	0.1	12.4	14.3
Essex	149,900	15.2	–	1.4	–	16.6	15.7
Hants	132,200	8.9	0.9	2.2	–	12.0	11.1
Isle of Wight	23,700	11.9	–	1.0	0.6	13.5	13.4
Kent	211,900	8.7	1.4	1.7	–	11.8	12.4
Norfolk	76,000	15.4	–	1.0	–	16.4	17.6
Somerset	99,700	12.6	–	1.6	1.0	15.2	13.0
East Suffolk	43,800	10.9	0.2	1.1	0.3	12.5	11.4
East Sussex	104,200	11.7	0.5	4.3	0.3	16.8	15.7
West Sussex	109,200	9.6	–	3.3	–	12.9	13.8
All English CCs	3,483,400	12.6	0.4	1.7	0.1	14.8	14.6
GLC	998,400	14.1	–	5.0	0.3	19.4	19.4
All England	6,361,500	14.2	0.3	2.2	0.2	16.9	16.7

Source: Department of Health and Social Security.

TABLE A1.42 Residents in residential homes in retirement areas at 31 December 1970

	Population aged 65 and over June 1970	All residents			
		In LA and joint-user premises	In registered voluntary homes	In registered private homes	In registered nursing homes*
		Residents per 1,000 of the total population aged 65 and over June 1970			
RESORT COUNTY BOROUGHS					
Blackpool	29,700	8.6	5.4	11.0	6.9
Bournemouth	36,700	18.4	7.8	18.6	13.5
Brighton	32,800	15.1	8.5	4.4	10.4
Eastbourne	19,200	17.1	6.0	6.6	15.8
Hastings	17,300	11.6	13.4	25.0	21.4
Southend on Sea	32,800	19.8	10.3	7.7	3.4
Southport	17,000	17.0	21.7	4.2	14.4
Torbay	24,200	5.4	7.4	17.1	5.2
All English CBs	1,827,700	18.8	3.8	2.9	2.6

Table continues over

	Population aged 65 and over June 1970	All residents			
		In LA and joint-user premises	In registered voluntary homes	In registered private homes	In registered nursing homes*
RESORT COUNTY COUNCILS					
Cornwall	61,500	13.1	4.1	5.5	2.5
Devon	83,300	10.0	4.4	11.0	4.5
Dorset	56,800	13.4	3.2	4.4	2.3
Essex	139,500	15.5	3.7	2.5	4.9
Hants	125,000	8.3	6.0	5.0	3.0
Isle of Wight	20,000	14.1	6.3	6.9	2.2
Kent	202,600	11.4	4.0	6.1	4.7
Norfolk	67,000	17.6	2.1	2.7	4.6
Somerset	88,200	12.5	4.7	6.5	2.4
East Suffolk	41,700	10.8	3.0	5.9	11.1
East Sussex	92,000	13.3	11.8	4.1	12.6
West Sussex	96,200	9.9	8.8	8.5	
All English CCs	3,186,100	13.8	4.6	3.6	3.5
GLC	366,400	15.1	6.5	2.1	4.9
All England	5,380,200	15.5	4.7	3.1	3.9

Source: Department of Health and Social Security, Social Services Statistics 1970, Tables 1 and 2, H48 (1970) Extract.

* The statistics for nursing homes were kindly provided by the Community Health Division of the DHSS. N.B. These are for beds not residents so strictly speaking are not comparable with the others which allow for vacancies.

TABLE A1.43 Principal medical practitioners: analysis by list size, 1 October 1973

Executive Council area	Total number of patients on list of principals for whom council is responsible	Total number of principals	No. and % of principals by list size											Average list size
			Under 1600		1600–1899		1900–2499		2500–2999		3000 or more		
			No.	%	No.	%	No.	%	No.	%	No.	%	
England and Wales	50,751,266	21,266	2,289	10.8	2,261	10.6	7,405	34.8	5,873	27.6	3,438	16.2	2,386
Bournemouth	161,757	79	11	13.9	14	17.7	40	50.6	14	17.7	–	–	2,048
Isle of Wight	111,936	53	15	28.3	–	–	34	64.2	2	3.8	2	3.8	2,112
E. Sussex, Eastbourne & Hastings	599,363	268	37	13.8	42	15.7	102	38.1	61	22.8	26	9.7	2,236
Brighton	184,842	86	16	18.6	16	18.6	33	38.4	14	16.3	7	8.1	2,149
W. Sussex	508,519	224	21	9.4	25	11.2	106	47.3	59	26.3	13	5.8	2,270
Norfolk	443,920	201	20	10.0	38	18.9	87	43.3	43	21.4	13	6.5	2,209
E. Suffolk	246,029	114	10	8.8	16	14.0	64	56.1	24	21.1	–	–	2,158
Cornwall	404,382	195	32	16.4	30	15.4	93	47.7	33	16.9	7	3.6	2,074
Devon, Exeter & Torbay	678,921	329	48	14.6	72	21.9	141	42.9	63	19.2	5	1.5	2,064
Somerset	615,838	276	40	14.5	43	15.6	111	40.2	58	21.0	24	8.7	2,231
Essex	1,206,871	487	30	6.2	36	7.4	183	37.6	147	30.2	91	18.7	2,478
Southend	174,260	72	6	8.3	8	11.1	15	20.8	34	47.2	9	12.5	2,420
Blackpool	161,497	73	12	16.4	8	11.0	26	35.6	17	23.3	10	13.7	2,212
Southport	91,098	40	10	25.0	6	15.0	6	15.0	6	15.0	12	30.0	2,277

Table continues over

Appendix 1

Executive Council area	Total number of patients on list of principals for whom council is responsible	Total number of principals	No. and % of principals by list size									Average list size
			Under 1600		1600-1899		1900-2499		2500-2999		3000 or more		
			No.	%	No.	%	No.	%	No.	%	No.	%	
NE London	1,182,107	482	49	10.2	48	10.0	149	30.9	124	25.7	112	23.2	2,453
SE London & Kent	2,010,338	814	60	7.4	74	9.1	262	32.2	283	34.8	135	16.6	2,470
SW London & Surrey	2,063,732	891	91	10.2	108	12.1	359	40.3	213	23.9	120	13.5	2,316
E. Midland Region	3,597,089	1,433	98	6.8	133	9.3	444	31.0	469	32.7	289	20.2	2,510
W. Midland Region	5,301,321	2,144	230	10.7	159	7.4	692	32.3	628	29.3	435	20.3	2,473
Yorkshire & Humberside	4,920,130	1,958	134	6.8	191	9.8	666	34.0	532	27.2	435	22.2	2,513
North Region	3,345,465	1,357	120	8.8	108	8.0	482	33.3	425	31.3	252	18.6	2,465
NW Region	6,823,526	2,750	268	9.8	243	8.8	833	30.3	800	29.1	606	22.0	2,481

TABLE A1.44 The home help service in retirement areas
(data for year ending 31 March 1973)

Retirement areas by old local authority	Total no. of home helps as at 30 Sept. 1972	Ratio of home helps to total population	Ratio of home helps to population aged 65+	Average hours per case
COUNTY BOROUGHS				
Blackpool	131	1:1145	1:252	106.0
Bournemouth	66	1:2255	1:577	63.2
Brighton	128	1:1279	1:249	109.9
Eastbourne	45	1:1560	1:445	91.4
Hastings	57	1:1299	1:318	91.4
Southend	154	1:1061	1:218	105.4
Southport	32	1:2664	1:570	83.1
Torbay	90	1:1182	1:301	66.6
COUNTY COUNCILS				
Cornwall and Isles of Scilly	217	1:1767	1:309	152.5
Devon	332	1:1383	1:289	140.2
Dorset	230	1:1622	1:289	135.9
Essex	815	1:1501	1:180	133.7
Hampshire	465	1:2226	1:278	135.4
Isle of Wight	49	1:2218	1:472	107.3
Kent	530	1:2623	1:393	104.2
Norfolk	398	1:1140	1:184	189.4
Somerset	468	1:1300	1:208	116.3
East Suffolk	220	1:1212	1:195	170.1
East Sussex	380	1:1190	1:270	115.8
West Sussex	234	1:2141	1:458	67.0
All CBs (in England and Wales)	11,478	1:1215	1:169	126.2
All CCs (in England and Wales)	20,420	1:1358	1:182	145.1
London Boroughs	6,082	1:1209	1:162	114.3

Source: The Chartered Institute of Public Finance and Accountancy, The Society of County Treasurers, 'Local Health and Social Services Statistics 1972-73', cols 179-84.

TABLE A1.45 Meals services in retirement areas during the year ending 31 March 1973*

	Main meals served per 1000 population 65+	No.persons served at home (during representative week) per 1000 population 65+	% meals served at home	% meals** provided by the LA 31.3.72
RESORT COUNTY BOROUGHS				
Blackpool	892.5	11.2	72	-
Bournemouth	4,824.5	50.6	52	100.0
Brighton	3,216.8	50.3	79	3.0
Eastbourne	3,073.8	8.3	51	9.4
Hastings	2,533.9	28.2	66	-
Southend	3,482.6	64.2	86	-
Southport	1,530.9	11.9	71	76.7
Torbay	2,053.5	25.9	63	-
RESORT COUNTY COUNCILS				
Cornwall	1,204.7	13.4	98	-
Devon	2,006.9	23.5***	92	0.6
Dorset	2,514.9	15.5	70	6.0
Essex	3,529.3	55.7	70	7.7
Hampshire	3,073.4	16.1	63	-
Isle of Wight	1,317.0	21.7	80	-
Kent	2,074.6	44.9	81	2.1
Norfolk	1,844.7	20.4	94	-
Somerset	2,675.2	20.0	92	12.4
East Suffolk	3,187.2	56.1	88	-
East Sussex	2,904.3	49.8	85	12.6
West Sussex	3,451.7	57.1	79	7.1
CBs in England and Wales	4,546.9	43.5	63	47.5
CCs in England and Wales	3,116.7	35.7	75	8.4
London Boroughs	9,491.6	59.5	52	74.4
England	3,067.8	34.2	74	41.7

* The Chartered Institute of Public Finance Accountancy, 'Local Health and Social Services Statistics 1972-73'.
** Department of Health and Social Security.
*** Estimated.

TABLE A1.46 Home nurses in retirement areas, 1973

Retirement areas by old local authority	Home nurses in post as at 30.9.73	
	per 1,000 total population	per 1,000 population aged 65 and over
COUNTY BOROUGHS		
Blackpool	0.30	1.34
Bournemouth	0.24	0.92
Brighton	0.31	1.52
Eastbourne	0.34	1.16
Hastings	0.24	0.97
Southend on Sea	0.23	1.12
Southport	0.33	1.57
Torbay	0.30	1.15
All English CBs	0.23	1.61
COUNTY COUNCILS		
Cornwall and Isles of Scilly	0.24	1.36
Devon	0.23	1.09
Dorset	0.21	1.15
Essex	0.18	1.50
Hampshire	0.19	1.47
Isle of Wight	0.25	1.15
Kent	0.21	1.38
Norfolk	0.21	1.28
Somerset	0.25	1.57
East Suffolk	0.23	1.42
East Sussex	0.25	1.10
West Sussex	0.26	1.21
All English CCs	0.22	1.63

Source: Department of Health and Social Security, Statistics and Research Division 2(a).

TABLE A1.47 Health visitors in retirement areas, 1973

Retirement areas by old local authority	Health visitors in post as at 30.9.73	
	per 1,000 local population	per 1,000 population aged 65 and over
COUNTY BOROUGHS		
Blackpool	0.12	0.54
Bournemouth	0.09	0.35
Brighton	0.21	1.06
Eastbourne	0.17	0.58
Hastings	0.12	0.47
Southend on Sea	0.11	0.52
Southport	0.11	0.52
Torbay	0.13	0.48
All English CBs	0.14	0.94
COUNTY COUNCILS		
Cornwall and Isles of Scilly	0.15	0.84
Devon	0.12	0.58
Dorset	0.11	0.64
Essex	0.13	1.05
Hampshire	0.12	0.96
Isle of Wight	0.15	0.70
Kent	0.12	0.78
Norfolk	0.10	0.64
Somerset	0.17	1.06
East Suffolk	0.10	0.63
East Sussex	0.17	0.75
West Sussex	0.15	0.68
All English CCs	0.14	1.01

Source: Department of Health and Social Security, Statistics and Research Division 2(a).

Appendix 2: definitions

1 According to the Census definition a HOUSEHOLD is 'one person living alone or a group of persons living together, partaking of meals prepared together and benefiting from a common housekeeping'. Any individuals or groups living in the same dwelling but having separate catering arrangements form separate households.

2 The HEAD OF HOUSEHOLD (HOH) is the person who is responsible for paying the rent/mortgage and in whose name the house or tenancy stands. With a married couple this will usually be the husband; in the odd case where it is the wife, the husband should be regarded as the head. Where the house or tenancy is in the name of more than one of the occupants and these are not a married couple, the head of the household is the male, or where there are several people of the same sex with equal claims to be the HOH, the HOH is the oldest. (This may arise with single people sharing a house.)

3 A RETIREMENT UNIT was defined as an individual aged 55 and over or a married couple of whom the man was 55 and over, who had moved to Bexhill or Clacton after retirement from work or with a view to retirement. When a single or widowed person lived with another single or widowed person, the person interviewed was regarded as an individual 'retirement unit'. This was done to avoid the complications arising from the fact that single or widowed individuals had often joined forces in a common household at a late stage in the retirement.

4 HEAD OF RETIREMENT UNIT was used to refer to the husband, in the case of a married couple and to the individual interviewed in all other cases. The use of the term 'head of retirement unit' rather than 'head of household' prevented complications when an elderly person or couple lived with their children or with friends, to whom the questionnaire was irrelevant. In the vast

majority of cases, the 'head of the retirement unit' was the head of household but it was to deal with the other cases that the concept was introduced. As far as possible, the phrase is not used in the text, but it is used in the tables, for the sake of precision.

5 The SUBJECT or the RESPONDENT was the person who actually answered the questionnaire.

6 A RETIREMENT MOVE was one made after retirement from work or with a view to retirement, after the age of 55. Some elderly people made several of these moves.

7 A RECENT MOVER was someone who had moved to Bexhill or Clacton since 1958 (i.e. 1959-68). This need not have been their first move since retirement from work.

8 'OF PENSIONABLE AGE' or 'OF RETIREMENT AGE' means 65 and over for men and 60 and over for women.

9 NET INCOME means income after the deduction of tax and National Insurance.

Appendix 3:
the sampling method and response

The grant for the study of elderly people who move to retirement areas provided for a social survey of about 1,000 people. There were no other initial constraints on the type of sample. In practice the problems of obtaining a random sample of people who had retired to coastal resorts were considerable.

There were two basic decisions to be made, that about the nature of the sampling frame and that about the geographical areas to be studied. In practice one was very much a function of the other.

Several possibilities of obtaining lists of elderly people in retirement areas were explored. These were as follows:

1 THE EXECUTIVE COUNCIL REGISTER

This was not usable because it was not possible to have access to individual addresses. The only arrangement possible was that the Executive Council should send a letter to a sample of their patients asking if they would be willing to answer a questionnaire. If they were willing, their address would be released. If, however, they refused or, more probably, did not reply at all, no access would be given. This drawback effectively ruled out the use of Executive Council Registers as it would produce both a very low and an extremely biased response rate. The less active and more withdrawn people would be least likely to reply.

2 DEPARTMENT OF HEALTH AND SOCIAL SECURITY

An obvious possibility for providing a sample of retired

people was the Department of Health and Social Security. However, the Department is not allowed to release names and addresses and was therefore unable to help. Also, lists of retired people drawing pensions are centralized, not held by the area offices of the Ministry. The lists would not, of course, include people who had moved to resorts who were too old to qualify for a pension, or those who were too young.

3 RUNNING NATIONAL SAMPLES

Another possibility was to add some questions to one of the running national sample surveys undertaken by the market research organizations. A block of questions could be asked of people living in coastal areas to find out their age, length of residence in the present town, whether they were retired and where they lived previously. From these an appropriate sample could be obtained for a subsequent full interview by the same market research organization or the sample could be purchased to be given to another.

The attraction of this method was that it would provide us with a scattering of people in many different places and this would concentrate our emphasis on the people who retire rather than the places they retire to. It would off-set the problems of one area attracting wealthier people than another and minimize the risk of local factors becoming unjustifiably emphasized. On the other hand, local background would be missing and opinions could not be put into a local context.

However, there was no possibility of using this method because no national 'omnibus' survey was anywhere near large enough to yield 1,000 interviews in coastal retirement resorts, let alone 1,000 such interviews with old people. In any case the market research firms felt that the sort of questions would be unsuitable to be added on to an ongoing survey.

4 'AT RISK' REGISTERS

The possibility of using lists of elderly people compiled by voluntary welfare organizations was explored (e.g. Bexhill Caring Community). These were too incomplete and out of date.

5 SIFT AND SAMPLE FROM THE ELECTORAL LIST

Eventually it was decided that the most satisfactory method for carrying out our survey was to select an over-large sample from the electoral list and discover by an initial visit which of the sampled people had moved to the town to retire or after retirement. The size of the initial sift would depend on the proportion of people of 60 and over in the voting-age population (those over 21 at that time) and the proportion of migrants in the elderly population. The only information we had about the proportion of migrants was from a survey of Worthing (1) in which it was found that 40 per cent of the people of 60 and over had moved to the area after reaching the age of 55. The proportion of people of 60 and over in the voting-age population was obtained from the census.

The basic problem about this method was one of cost. To obtain a sample of about 1,000, the interviewers would have to contact at least 6,000 households to establish which of them would be relevant. The lower the proportion of elderly people in the town, the larger the number of households that would have to be contacted to produce a sample of 1,000 and the greater the cost.

One way in which the size of the sift might have been reduced was to have taken particular wards with particularly high densities of elderly people. However, there was evidence that the characteristics of elderly people in different parts of the resorts varied, and we feared that such selection might bias our sample in ways that we could not tell. (2) We therefore decided to take a simple random sample.

THE SELECTION OF STUDY AREAS

The cost of doing a 'sift' to obtain a sample restricted our choice of area to those with large proportions of elderly people. This was in fact compatible with the aims of the study which was directed towards the situation in those areas having the largest proportions of elderly people.

The number of areas to be studied was largely a function of the need to have a satisfactory size of sample for each place. The alternative, to take a large number of places so that local features would be cancelled out, was ruled out because of the administrative costs and problems of selecting samples and organizing interviewers in a large number of resorts. On the basis of sample size, it was decided that the largest number of resorts for which reliable results could be obtained for basic questions was three and for sub-samples of widows, single people and so on it seemed desirable to have only one area or two.

As a basis for selection of survey areas, a list of 'retirement areas' was drawn up. For these purposes a 'retirement area' was (arbitrarily) designated as one with 20 per cent or more of its population of pensionable age ($1\frac{1}{2}$ times the national average) and with a net annual immigration level of 1 per cent or more of the total population. The (then) Ministry of Housing and Local Government provided a list of local authority areas with 20 per cent or more of their population of pensionable age in 1966 and with net annual immigration rates between 1951 and 1961 and for 1960-1 of 1 per cent or more of the total population. This information had been derived from the 1951, 1961 and 1966 Census returns. Thirty-three of the 35 areas listed were coastal areas and 18 were on the South Coast. This list laid the basis for the selection of study areas, but it was incomplete in that certain published data for 1966 related only to areas with more than 20,000 population. This cut out in particular the string of small resorts along the south Devon coast. Details of these resorts had to be derived from unpublished census material.

From other census data it emerged that resorts varied considerably in the social class structure of the retired population. If contrasting areas were to be chosen, class seemed one criterion which might be relevant. Another seemed to be location. Although the South Coast of England is the retirement area 'par excellence', there are a number of others which are of interest, for instance, Somerset, Devon and Cornwall and the coasts of North Wales, Lancashire, Yorkshire, Norfolk and Essex.

Eventually it was decided to select Bexhill, which, of all towns in the country with more than 20,000 inhabitants, had the largest proportion of elderly people in 1966, and Clacton, which besides not being on the South Coast, had a lower social status but also a very large proportion of elderly people.

The decision to omit Devon was taken very reluctantly because it is possible that its relative remoteness may give it particular features. However, this disadvantage in the choice of study areas had to be weighed against the fact that the samples in Clacton and Bexhill were large enough to enable a number of conclusions to be drawn about groups such as widows, and even about smaller groups such as widows whose husbands had died before the move, and this was probably more valuable than variety of geographical area. Pilot surveys to test the questionnaire were carried out in Clacton and Eastbourne.

THE SAMPLE

According to the 1966 Census, the proportion of people aged 60 and over in Bexhill was 44.1 per cent and in Clacton 35.7 per cent. As the electoral lists contained, at that time, only the people aged 21 and over in the year it was in force, the first figure needed to decide the size of the sift was the number of people of 60 and over as a proportion of people of 20 and over, of whom there were 25,330 in Bexhill in 1966 and 25,800 in Clacton. The proportions of people aged 60 and over amongst this 'adult' population were 56 per cent in Bexhill and 45.8 per cent in Clacton. This calculation is based on the assumption that Bexhill resembled Worthing in that 40 per cent of its over-60s were people who had moved there to retire. For Clacton a slightly lower figure was taken because it had a smaller total proportion of elderly people.

Using these very rough assumptions, it was calculated that in Bexhill a 1 in 10 sample of the 24,070 on the electoral list should produce an effective sample of 500 or so. In Clacton a 1 in 9 sample of the 28,204 was expected to produce this.

The following were the instructions given to interviewers about how to find the appropriate interviewees:

WHOM TO INTERVIEW

The sample has been drawn from the Electoral List and each interviewer will receive sheets on which names have been ringed at regular intervals. These actual people are the sample. It will be necessary to call on each of the people whose name is ringed (except where marked Y (people under 21) or S (Service Voters)) but many of them will not be relevant to the survey. We wish to interview only those who are 55 or over and who have moved to Clacton or Bexhill after retirement or with a view to retirement. Thus if a man of 59 is still working in London but has moved in preparation for retirement in a few years time, he will be relevant to the survey, just as a man would be who had already retired. Retired local people are not relevant to the survey, nor are people living in local authority old people's homes.

The number of names has been calculated on the assumption that substitutes will not be made for people who have moved or died. There is one exception to this rule: if a married person has died, or is for some other reason unable to answer the questionnaire, e.g. they are out, deaf, infirm etc. their husband or wife should be interviewed instead.

The arbitrary lower age limit of 55 was taken in order to include people who were still working but had moved with their retirement in view. Preferably the interviewers asked the respondents themselves the necessary questions to find out if they were eligible for the survey but, failing that, they were allowed to ask other members of the family or neighbours. People who lived in old people's homes and hospitals were not interviewed. People who lived in hotels and boarding houses were interviewed but the completed interviews were not included with the others when the analysis was made.

In the event the effective sample in Bexhill fell short of 500 and a supplementary 1 in 25 sample was drawn from the remainder of the Electoral List in order to produce a large enough sample. The reasons for this appear to have been that the figure of 40 per cent was an over-estimate for the proportion of eligible elderly people and that response rates from those who were eligible were lower in Bexhill.

THE RESPONSE

The results of the sifting operation are summarized in Table A3.1.

Though it is possible to give the response rate to the total sift, it is not possible to say what the response rate was amongst those who were eligible for interview. This is because of the existence of a proportion of people who could not be contacted and whose neighbours could not say whether or not they would be eligible. There were 182 such people in Bexhill and 141 in Clacton. In addition it is not known how many of the people who lived in Old People's Homes or had died or who had moved would have been eligible for interview. There were 71 dead in Bexhill and 72 in Clacton; 297 who had moved in Bexhill and 438 in Clacton. The numbers were large because the Electoral List was one year old when it was used. This was unavoidable because of the timing of the survey. For these reasons it is not possible to use the results of the sample to say exactly what proportions of Bexhill or Clacton's population were people who had moved there to retire.

Appendix 3

TABLE A3.1 Response to Bexhill and Clacton survey

	Bexhill		Clacton	
Ineligible because local or too young	1,897	57%	1,578	51%
Moved away or empty house	297	9%	438	14%
Dead	71	2%	72	2%
Weekend bungalow, not permanently resident	8	*	122	4%
Lived in old people's home: not known if eligible	28	1%	17	1%
No contact: not known if eligible	182	6%	141	5%
Unable or unwilling to answer for health reasons including some who must have been ineligible but were too sick to say or were away in hospital	99	3%	53	2%
Eligible but refused	187	6%	204	7%
Gave interview but lived in hotel or boarding house	4	*	1	*
Gave interview included in analysis	503	15%	487	16%
	3,276		3,113	

However, it is necessary to check whether the sample can be taken as representative of people who moved to these towns. The only means of checking the responding sample for bias is by comparing the respondents with people who were eligible but who refused or could not reply because of poor health. A little information is available about these people in that the Electoral List shows the sex of the non-respondents and the names of other people living at the same address. This is an inadequate source of information but the best available. From it Table A3.2 has been constructed to compare respondents and eligible non-respondents.

This shows that women were over-represented amongst both the refusals and health cases. The latter would be expected because of the greater age of the women but it is not known why they should refuse more often than men.

Whatever the reason the effect of this lower response rate is to make women slightly under-represented in the sample.

TABLE A3.2 Non-respondents compared with respondents, by sex and household type

	Refusals	Health cases	Refusals and health cases	Respondents including those in hotels and guest houses	Respondents refusals and non-response
BEXHILL					
All	187	99	285	507	792
	%	%	%	%	%
Males	31	27	29	42	37
Females	69	73	71	58	63
Living alone	15	15	15	21	19
Living with spouse only	61	35	52	63	59
Living with five or more 'unrelated' people	4	21	10	1	4
Others	20	29	23	15	18
CLACTON					
All	204	53	252	488	740
	%	%	%	%	%
Males	35	21	32	42	39
Females	65	79	68	48	61
Living alone	15	29	17	18	17
Living with spouse only	65	23	56	68	64
Living with five or more 'unrelated' people	3	8	4	*	1
Others	17	40	23	15	17

Clearly also the proportion of people who lived alone was much greater amongst the people who could not be interviewed for health reasons than it was amongst the responding sample. This means that any estimate of those in difficulty or isolation which is based on the respondents only will necessarily under-count those in difficulties.

The health cases were also more likely than respondents and people who refused an interview to live with people other than a spouse. Many women for instance lived with other women, either related or unrelated to them. Women non-respondents were much more likely than men to be living alone.

What effect does this have on the reliability of the whole sample? In Bexhill females were under-counted by 5 per cent and men over-counted by 5 per cent. In Clacton the proportion was 3 per cent. People living with their spouses only were also slightly over-represented, by 4 per cent in both Bexhill and Clacton. People living alone were under-counted by 2 per cent in Bexhill and 3 per cent in Clacton and people living with relatives or friends by 6 per cent in Bexhill and 3 per cent in Clacton. These errors are not very large, but they have had to be allowed for in drawing conclusions about the retired population of the two resorts.

However, it should be borne in mind that these calculations only take into consideration known eligibles who refused and people who were sick. There were a further 182 people in Bexhill and 141 in Clacton who could not be contacted. If many of those were eligible, and particularly if they could not be contacted because they were eccentric or sick, there could be further errors in the sample. On the other hand all sick people have been included in the estimate of bias and some of them would not have been eligible for the survey.

STATISTICAL SIGNIFICANCE

In a study with so many statements based on survey material, it would have been unnecessarily cumbersome to quote significance tests every time. As a solution, significance has only been mentioned when a conclusion was not statistically significant but, because the problem was small sample numbers and there was other corroborative evidence, it was felt worth quoting. Thus where a conclusion was below the 95 per cent level of significance on a Chi-square test a reference has been made to this fact, such as 'but this is not a significant difference' or 'but the numbers are rather small'. In all other cases this level can be assumed; in most the 99 per cent level was reached.

Appendix 4: questionnaire

University of Birmingham Centre for Urban and Regional Studies
retirement survey questionnaire

		Punch no.	Column no.
Name of interviewee ...			1
Address ...			
			2
Name of interviewer	Write list number in column 1		
Supervised/back checked	Write Elector's number vertically in columns 2-5		3
Edited			4
	BEXHILL ONLY		
Questions remaining to be coded	Put X in first section of column 2		5

INTRODUCTION

I am taking part in a university survey about retirement, especially retirement to seaside resorts, and have a questionnaire which is aimed at finding out whether people are satisfied with moving to the seaside. I wonder if you would mind telling me if you moved here either with a view to retirement or after retirement?

(IF YES)

      The information you give will be treated completely confidentially

A. INTERVIEW OBTAINED

B. RESPONDENT ELIGIBLE
    But (i) Refusal (either by subject or by someone on their behalf)
        (ii) No reply (after 5 calls)
        (iii) Not available for health reasons
        (iv) Not available for other reasons (SPECIFY)

C. RESPONDENT INELIGIBLE   (REASON)

319 Appendix 4

2.

			Punch no.	Column no.
1(a)	Dwelling type (FROM OBSERVATION)	No reply	Y	6
		Whole house	X	
		Whole bungalow	O	
		S/C purpose built flat/ maisonette	1	
		S/C converted flat/ maisonette	2	
		Rooms (no conversion)	3	
		Guest house/hotel	4	
		Other (STATE)	5	
(b)	Date of construction (FROM OBSERVATION OR IF NOT POSSIBLE ASK AT THE END OF THE INTERVIEW)	No reply	6	
		Post-1945	7	
		Inter-war	8	
		Pre-1919	9	

2(a) May we start by asking who there is in your household? (SEE DEFINITION)

Relationship to subject (RING H.O.H.) (SEE DEFINITION)	Sex	Age	Marital status			Paid job (Hours per week)		
	M F		M S Wid. Div. Sep.			Full (over 30)	Part (11- 30) Up to 10	Not (0)
A. Subject								
B.								
C.								
D.								
E.								
F.								
G.								
H.								

(b) IF SUBJECT WIDOWED
How long have you been widowed?   Number of
(WRITE IN NUMBER OF YEARS)   ... years

3(a)	Do you have any children now living?	No reply	Y	7
		Yes	X	
		No	O	
(b)	IF YES	How many do you have?		
		1	1	
		2	2	
		3	3	
		4	4	
		5	5	
		6	6	
		7+	7	

GO TO PAGE 4

3.

FOR OFFICE USE ONLY (CODES FOR Q.2(a) and (b))

	Punch no.	Column no.		Punch no.	Column no.
A. AGE OF SUBJECT			F. TIME OF WIDOWHOOD		
No reply	Y	8	No reply	Y	(10)
Under 55	X		Before retirement move	X	
55-9	0				
60-4	1		After retirement move	0	
65-9	2				
70-4	3				
75-9	4		G. LENGTH OF WIDOWHOOD		
80+	5		No reply	1	
			0 - 1 year	2	
B. SEX OF SUBJECT			Over 1 but less than 5	3	
No reply	6				
Male	7		Over 5 but less than 10	4	
Female	8				
			Over 10 but less than 15	5	
C. MARITAL STATUS OF SUBJECT					
			Over 15 but less than 20	6	
No reply	Y	9			
Married	X		Over 20	7	
Single	0				
Widowed	1		H. NUMBER OF PERSONS IN HOUSEHOLD		
Divorced/separated	2				
			No reply	Y	11
D. HOUSEHOLD TYPE			1	X	
No reply	3		2	0	
Living alone	4		3	1	
Living with spouse only	5		4	2	
			5+	3	
Living with married children (with or without spouse)	6		I. NUMBER OF FEMALES AGED 60 AND OVER IN HOUSEHOLD		
			No reply	4	
Living with un- married children (with or without spouse)	7		0	5	
			1	6	
			2	7	
			3 or more	8	
Living with siblings or other relatives	8		J. NUMBER OF MALES AGED 65 AND OVER AND FEMALES AGED 60 AND OVER IN HOUSEHOLD		
Living with others	9				
E. AGE OF SPOUSE					
No reply	Y	10	No reply	Y	12
Under 55	X		0	X	
55-9	0		1	0	
60-4	1		2	1	
65-6	2		3 or more	2	
70-4	3				
75-9	4		K. NUMBER OF EARNERS IN HOUSEHOLD		
80+	5				
			No reply	3	
			0	4	
			1	5	
			2	6	
			3 or more	7	

Appendix 4

		4.	Punch no.	Column no.
ASK ALL				
4(a)	When did you move to this address? (WRITE YEAR AND RING CODE)	No reply In 1968 1966-7 1964-5 1959-63 1954-8 Before 1954	O 1 2 3 4 5 6	13
(b)	When did you move to this town? (WRITE YEAR AND RING CODE)	No reply In 1968 1966-7 1964-5 1959-63 1954-8 Before 1954	O 1 2 3 4 5 6	14

QUESTIONS 5-16 APPLY TO ALL EXCEPT THOSE IN GUEST HOUSES OR HOTELS (SEE Q.1). GUEST HOUSES AND HOTELS GO TO Q.17

5(a)	Do you (or your husband) own this house (bungalow, flat, etc.), rent it from the council, rent it privately, or have some other arrangement? IF RENTED PRIVATELY Is this rented unfurnished or furnished? (CODE ONE ONLY)	No reply Owner-occupied - whole house or flat Owner-occupied - letting out part of house to other household Rented council Rented privately, unfurnished Rented privately, furnished Other (SPECIFY)	Y X O 1 2 3 4	15
(b)	IF OWNER-OCCUPIED Is the house (bungalow, flat, etc.) - freehold or leasehold?	No reply/Don't know Freehold Leasehold	5 6 7	
6	How many rooms do you have? (Excluding bathroom and kitchen, unless you use the kitchen as a main living room?)	No reply/Don't know 1 2 3 4 5 6+	Y X O 1 2 3 4	16
7	Do you consider this accommodation the right size for your needs? (in terms of number of rooms)	No reply/Don't know Too small About right Larger than you really need	5 6 7 8	

		5.		Punch no.	Column no.
8	Regarding your house (bungalow, flat, etc.) would you say that on the whole you are satisfied with it or dissatisfied or have you no particular feelings about it?		No reply/Don't know Satisfied Dissatisfied No feelings either way	Y X O 1	17
9	Do you have any problems with the upkeep of your house or garden? IF YES, what are these? (RECORD ANSWERS IN FULL BELOW)		No reply Yes None	2 3 4	

OWNER-OCCUPIERS ONLY. IF RENTING, GO ON TO Q.15

10(a)	Could you tell me how much this house (bungalow, flat, etc.) cost, when you/your husband bought it? WRITE ACTUAL AMOUNT AND RING CODE £ ...		No reply/Don't know Under £2000 £2000 - 2999 £3000 - 3999 £4000 - 4999 £5000 - 5999 £6000 - 6999 £7000 - 7999 £8000+ Inherited other than from deceased husband	Y X O 1 2 3 4 5 6 7	18

IF INHERITED, GO TO Q.11. OTHERS CONTINUE

	(b) Did you/he obtain a loan of any kind in order to buy this house (bungalow, flat, etc.)?		No reply/Don't know Yes No	Y X O	19
	(c) Could you tell me what were your sources of capital to buy the house (bungalow, flat, etc.) CODE ALL SOURCES GIVEN		No reply/Don't know Bank loan, Private loan Building society Insurance company Local authority Sale of previous dwelling Savings Other (SPECIFY)	1 2 3 4 5 6 7 8	

Appendix 4

		6.	Punch no.	Column no.
	ASK ALL OWNER-OCCUPIERS			
11(a)	How much do you pay in rates each year for your house (bungalow, flat, etc.)?	No reply/Don't know	Y	20
		£50 - 9	X	
		£60 - 9	O	
		£70 - 9	1	
	WRITE AMOUNT AND RING CODE	£80 - 9	2	
		£90 - 9	3	
	£ ...	£100 or over	4	
(b)	Do you receive a rate rebate?	No reply	5	
		Yes	6	
		No	7	
(c)	IF NO, Have you ever applied for one?	No reply	Y	21
		Yes	X	
		No	O	
12	IF BOUGHT ON MORTGAGE OR LOAN - (SEE Q.10c) OTHERS GO TO Q.13			
	What are your mortgate/loan repayments per month?	No reply/Don't know	1	
		Less than £2	2	
		£2 but less than £4	3	
	WRITE AMOUNT AND RING CODE	£4 but less than £6	4	
		£6 but less than £8	5	
	£ ... PER MONTH	£8 but less than £10	6	
		£10 but less than £15	7	
		£15 but less than £20	8	
		£20 or more	9	
13	IF LEASEHOLDERS - (SEE Q.5b). OTHERS GO TO Q.14			
	How much is the ground rent for your house (bungalow, flat, etc.) per year?	No reply/Don't know	Y	22
		Less than £10 per annum	X	
		£10 - 19	O	
		£20 - 9	1	
	WRITE AMOUNT AND RING CODE	£30 - 9	2	
		£40 - 9	3	
	£ ... per annum	£50+	4	
14	ASK ALL OWNER-OCCUPIERS			
	When you made your last move, would you have preferred to rent?	No reply	5	
		Yes	6	
		No	7	
		No preference	8	
	ASK RENTERS ONLY: OTHERS GO TO Q.22			
15(a)	How much do you pay in rent each week for this house (flat, etc.) including rates?	No reply/Don't know	Y	23
		Less than £2	X	
		£2 but less than £3	O	
		£3 but less than £4	1	
	Rates if paid separately	£4 but less than £5	2	
	£ ... per annum	£5 but less than £6	3	
		£6 but less than £7	4	
		£7 but less than £8	5	
	Rent including rates	£8 but less than £9	6	
		£9 but less than £10	7	
	£ ... per week	£10 or more	8	

Appendix 4

		7.		Punch no.	Column no.
15(b)	Do you receive a rate rebate?	No reply		Y	24
		Yes		X	
		No		O	
(c)	IF NO, have you ever applied for one?	No reply		1	
		Yes		2	
		No		3	
16	When you made your last move would you have preferred to buy?	No reply/Don't know		4	
		Yes		5	
		No		6	
		No preference		7	

QUESTIONS 17-21 ARE FOR THOSE IN GUEST HOUSES OR HOTELS ONLY. OTHERS GO TO Q.22

Punching

Return to Col. 15 for hotel section

17	What made you decide to live in a guest house/hotel? RECORD ALL REPLIES IN FULL AND CODE ALL	No reply/Don't know	Y	15
		Spouse deceased	X	
		Poor health or infirmity	O	
		Unable to manage house or flat	1	
		Always been used to living in hotel/guest house or club or being catered for	2	
		Social life	3	
		Has nursing facilities	4	
		No worries or responsibilities	5	
		Other	6	
18(a)	What do they charge here at present per week, including meals? WRITE AMOUNT AND RING CODE £ ... IF COUPLE GIVE TOTAL CHARGE; NOT PER PERSON	No reply/Don't know	Y	16
		£0 - 4	X	
		£5 - 9	O	
		£10 - 14	1	
		£15 - 19	2	
		£20+	3	
(b)	Do they charge any more in summer?	No reply/Don't know	4	
		Yes	5	
		No	6	
(c)	How much more do they charge then? WRITE AMOUNT £ ... per week			

Appendix 4

		8.	Punch no.	Column no.
19(a)	Do you remain here all the year round or do you move out during the summer months, other than for your own holidays? IF 'ALL YEAR' GO ON TO Q.20 IF 'MOVE OUT'	No reply/Don't know All year Move out in summer	Y X O	17
(b)	Did you move out during the summer just gone for more than a month? IF 'NO' GO ON TO Q.20 IF 'YES'	No reply/Don't know/ Was not in hotel Yes No	1 2 3	
(c)	For how long did you move out? WRITE PERIOD AND RING CODE ...	No reply/Don't know Less than 2 months 2 - 4 months More than 4 months	4 5 6 7	
(d)	Why did you move out? RECORD BELOW	No reply/Don't know	Y	18
(e)	Where did you move to? PROMPT - TYPE OF ACCOMMODATION; PLACE WRITE ANSWER IN FULL AND CODE	No reply/Don't know Friends/relatives Another G.H./H. in town Another G.H./H elsewhere Other (SPECIFY)	Y X O 1 2	19
20	Do you find it difficult to keep up with the amount that is charged for accommodation here, or do you manage easily, or just manage?	No reply/Don't know Manage easily Just manage Difficult to manage	Y X O 1	20
21(a)	Regarding this guest house/hotel would you say that on the whole you are satisfied with it or dissatisfied or have you no particular feelings about it?	No reply/Don't know Satisfied Dissatisfied No feelings either way	2 3 4 5	
(b)	What do you like or dislike about it?			

END OF GUEST HOUSE/HOTEL SECTION

8A.

THIS PAGE IS FOR OFFICE USE ONLY

	Punch no.	Column no.
Age at retirement move (H.R.U. at that time)		23
N.R.	Y	
Under 55	X	
55 - 9	0	
60 - 4	1	
65 - 9	2	
70 - 4	3	
75 - 9	4	
80 - 4	5	
85 - 9	6	
90+	7	
Time of retirement move in relation to date of retirement of H.R.U. at that time		24
N.R.	Y	
Never worked	X	
Before retirement	0	
Same year as retirement	1	
Up to 1 year after	2	
1 but less than 2	3	
2 but less than 3	4	
3 but less than 4	5	
4 but less than 5	6	
5 but less than 10	7	
10 but less than 15	8	
15 or more	9	

Appendix 4

		9.		Punch no.	Column no.
	ASK ALL, INCLUDING THOSE IN GUEST HOUSES/HOTELS				
	Q.22 SHOULD BE ASKED ABOUT ALL SUBJECTS WHO ARE SINGLE WOMEN, SINGLE OR MARRIED MEN OR WIDOWS WHOSE HUSBANDS DIED BEFORE THE RETIREMENT MOVE. FOR WIDOWS WHOSE HUSBANDS DIED AFTER THE RETIREMENT MOVE, WHETHER OR NOT THE WIDOW HAS WORKED, THE QUESTION SHOULD REFER TO HER DECEASED HUSBAND. FOR WOMEN LIVING WITH THEIR HUSBANDS THE QUESTION REFERS TO THE HUSBAND. THIS APPLIES TO THE REST OF QUESTIONNAIRE WHERE YOU/YOUR HUSBAND APPEARS.				
22	At what age did you/your husband retire from full-time work? WRITE AGE AND RING CODE ... years old	No reply/Don't know Never worked full-time Not retired yet Under 59 60 - 4 65 - 9 70 - 4 75+ Husband died before retirement		Y X O 1 2 3 4 5 6	25
	IF NOT YET RETIRED GO TO Q.25(b). IF DIED GO TO Q.26 IF RETIRED, CONTINUE				
23	What year was that? WRITE YEAR AND RING CODE ... year	No reply/Don't know In 1968 1966 - 7 1964 - 5 1958 - 63 1954 - 8 Before 1954		Y X O 1 2 3 4	26
24	What was your/his main reason for retiring? RECORD BELOW	No reply Ill-health Compulsory retirement age Redundant Voluntary retirement Other (SPECIFY)		Y X O 1 2 3	27
	IF RETIRED				
25(a)	Would you/he have preferred to continue working?	No reply/Don't know Yes		6 7	
OR	IF STILL WORKING	No		8	
(b)	Do you/does he prefer to continue working?	No preference		9	

328 Appendix 4

		10.	Punch no.	Column no.
26	How many different towns have you/your husband lived in for more than a year since you were/he was 20? WRITE NUMBER AND RING CODE ... Number	No reply/Don't know 1 2 3 4 5+	Y X O 1 2 3	28
27	Where did you/your husband live when you were/he was 40? NO CODE WRITE REPLY BELOW ...			
28(a)	Where did you/your husband move to when you/he left the place you/he lived in when you were/he was 40?	When was that?		
(b)	Where did you move to after that? ASK ALL TOWN MOVES UP TO AND INCLUDING PRESENT TOWN WRITE ALL ANSWERS IN TABLE BELOW	When was that?		

(a) Place Moved to   (b) Date of move to (a)

11.

			Punch no.	Column no.
29	CHECK FROM Q.23, 28(a) and (b) WHICH PLACE THEY LIVED IN JUST BEFORE RETIREMENT MOVE So, just before moving to retire, you lived in ... JUST A CHECK QUESTION	FOR OFFICE USE ONLY No reply/Don't know Greater London Surrey/Sussex outside Greater London Essex outside Greater London Other parts of S.E. Midlands S.W. Other (SPECIFY)	Y X O 1 2 3 4 5	29
30	And you retired to ... ? JUST A CHECK QUESTION THE ORIGINAL RETIREMENT MOVE MAY NOT HAVE BEEN TO BEXHILL/CLACTON CHECK THAT THIS DOES NOT ALTER THE RESULT OF THE INSTRUCTION AT Q.22 CONCERNING WIDOWS	FOR OFFICE USE ONLY Number of places lived in since retirement move, including Bexhill/Clacton No reply Bexhill/Clacton only Two Three Four or more	 4 5 6 7 8	28 (cont)
31	Just before you left ... (29) PLACE JUST BEFORE RETIREMENT MOVE			
(a)	Was your household the same as it is at present? PROMPT: OR HAS ANYONE LEFT THE HOUSEHOLD, OR JOINED IT? IF DIFFERENT CONTINUE; IF SAME GO ON TO Q.32	No reply/Don't know Same Different	Y X O	30
(b)	Who lived in the household then? RELATIONSHIP TO SUBJECT. RECORD BELOW AND CODE	No reply Spouse deceased No longer living with children No longer living with brothers or sisters Now living with children, not before Now living with brothers or sisters, not before Other changes (SPECIFY)	1 2 3 4 5 6 7	

Appendix 4

		12.	Punch no.	Column no.
32	Now, thinking about the house you lived in then (that is just before you moved to retire) did you own this house or rent it from the council, or rent it privately or did you live with relatives?	No reply/Don't know	Y	31
		Owner-occupier of whole house or flat	X	
		Owner-occupier, letting part of house to other household(s)	O	
		Renting from council	1	
	I.E. HOUSE IN PLACE NAMED IN 29 AND 31	Renting privately, unfurnished	2	
	IF RENTED PRIVATELY,	Renting privately, furnished	3	
		Living with relations	4	
	Was this rented unfurnished or furnished?	Other (including hospitals, schools & other institutions & tied housing and hotels) SPECIFY	5	
33	What sort of dwelling was this?	No reply/Don't know	Y	32
		House	X	
	PROMPT: A HOUSE OR BUNGALOW OR FLAT OR ROOMS?	Bungalow	O	
		Flat	1	
		Room/Rooms	2	
		Other (SPECIFY)	3	
34	How many bedrooms did the household have?	No reply/Don't know	4	
		1	5	
		2	6	
		3	7	
		4	8	
		5+	9	
35	Thinking about that house, what did you like or dislike about it at the time you left?	No reply/Don't know	Y	33
		Nothing liked	X	
		Size suitable	O	
		Nice garden	1	
	RECORD ALL REPLIES BELOW	Well built	2	
	LIKES	Modern design/labour-saving	3	
		Attractive	4	
		Warm	5	
		Other	6	
	DISLIKES	Nothing disliked	Y	34
		Too large	X	
		Too small	O	
		Too much garden	1	
		Too much maintenance and housework	2	
		Sad associations	3	
		Cold	4	
		Other	5	

Appendix 4

			13.	Punch no.	Column no.
36	Thinking about the area in which you lived then, what did you like or dislike about it at the time you left? RECORD ALL REPLIES BELOW LIKES		No reply/Don't know	Y	35
			Nothing liked	X	
			Convenient for City/London	O	
			Near countryside	1	
			Near to work, transport	2	
			Convenient for shopping	3	
			Entertainment available	4	
			Good class residential area	5	
			Liked neighbours and friends	6	
			Other	7	
	DISLIKES		Nothing disliked	Y	36
			Area deteriorated socially	X	
			Too much traffic; too noisy and busy	O	
			Dirty, smelly	1	
			Industrial surroundings	2	
			Too built up; lack of open space or country	3	
			Suburbia characterless	4	
			Not enough entertainments, amusements	5	
			Other	6	
	ASK ALL				
37	What was your <u>main</u> reason for wanting to <u>move</u> on retirement? WRITE ALL ANSWERS BUT <u>CODE ONE ONLY</u>		No reply/Don't know	Y	37
			For sea air/better climate/cleanliness	X	
			For flat countryside	O	
			Get away from town/London	1	
			Health reasons	2	
			To join friends/relatives	3	
			Wanted to live by seaside	4	
			Wanted quiet place	5	
			Always wanted to	6	
			Wanted a complete change	7	
			Wanted retirement to be like a holiday	8	
			Other	9	

332 Appendix 4

		14.		Punch no.	Column no.
	IF MARRIED COUPLE NOW OR AT MOVE OTHERS GO TO Q.39				
38	Who was most keen that you should move on retirement, you or your husband/wife?	No reply/Don't know Husband more keen Wife more keen Both same Other		Y X 0 1 2	38
	ASK ALL				
39	How many addresses have you lived at since you first moved to retire? (Including present address) WRITE NUMBER AND RING CODE ... Number IF ONLY ONE, GO TO Q.41	No reply/Don't know 1 2 3 4 5+		3 4 5 6 7 8	

40 Now, could we take each of these in turn?
    WRITE ALL REPLIES IN TABLE BELOW
    REPEAT QUESTIONS FOR EACH DWELLING

	What type of dwelling was the last one you lived in before this? SEE LIST BELOW	In which town was this?	Did you own it or rent it? If rented, from council or privately? Unfurnished or furnished? (Please state if Housing Association) SEE LIST BELOW	How long did you live in it?	And why did you leave it?
Last house					
The one before that					
Etc.					

CHECK LIST OF DWELLING TYPES	CHECK LIST OF TENURE TYPES
Whole house	Owner-occupied - whole house or flat
Self-contained, purpose-built flat/maisonette	Owner-occupied - letting part to other household(s)
Self-contained, converted flat/maisonette	Rented from council
Rooms (no conversion)	Rented privately, unfurnished
Guest house/hotel	Rented privately, furnished
Other (SPECIFY)	Other (SPECIFY)

16.

		Punch no.	Column no.
	ASK ALL		
41(a) Did you consider any other towns to which you might have moved when you chose to come to Bexhill/Clacton?	No reply/Don't know Yes No	Y X O	39
IF NO, GO TO Q.42	FOR OFFICE USE ONLY		
IF YES (b) What were these? RECORD NAMES	No reply/Don't know Sussex coast Kent coast Essex coast Devon/Cornwall coasts Dorset/Somerset/Hants coasts Lancashire/Yorkshire coasts Denbigh/Flint/Cheshire coast Elsewhere	1 2 3 4 5 6 7 8 9	
42 What was your main reason for moving to Bexhill/Clacton rather than another town? WRITE ALL REPLIES BUT CODE ONE ONLY	No reply/Don't know Climate, air, healthy Pleasant surroundings Been on holiday here Had friends here/near Had relatives here or near Recreational and other amenities Price of property Accommodation available Flat land Convenient for London Other (SPECIFY)	Y X O 1 2 3 4 5 6 7 8 9	40
43 Did you have any friends, relatives or children living here before you moved here?	No reply/Don't know Yes No Friends Relatives Children	Y X O 1 2 3	41
44 Had you ever been to Clacton/Bexhill during the wintertime?	No reply/Don't know Yes No	4 5 6	
45 Had you ever been on holiday or for a day trip around here before you moved here?	No reply/Don't know Yes No	7 8 9	

Appendix 4

		17.	Punch no.	Column no.
46	How did you come to hear about this particular dwelling/hotel? WRITE REPLY AND <u>CODE ONE ONLY</u>	No reply/Don't know Estate agents Newspapers Through friends Through relatives Saw a board on the house while going round town Other (SPECIFY)	Y X O 1 2 3 4	42

ASK ALL WITH CHILDREN (SEE Q.3(a)). OTHERS GO ON TO Q.50

47	Do any of your children now live in Bexhill/Clacton?	No reply/Don't know Yes, live with subject Live elsewhere in town No	5 6 7 8	
48(a)	Where do your children (the rest of your children) live? WRITE DOWN ALL PLACES MENTIONED; IF UNKNOWN PLACE MAKE SURE OF LOCATION	No reply/Don't know No other children except those in town	Y X	43
(b)	How long would it normally take to get to where the nearest one lives? APART FROM ANY THAT LIVE IN THE SAME TOWN	No reply Less than ½ hour 30 minutes - 1 hour 1 - 3 hours Over 3 hours but less than 1 day 1 day or more	O 1 2 3 4 5	

ASK OF 'RECENT MOVERS' ONLY - (THOSE WHO HAVE MOVED TO THE TOWN <u>SINCE</u> 1958 - SEE Q.4(b) CODES 1-4.)

OTHERS GO TO Q.50

49	Do you see your children more now than before you moved here, or less, or about the same?	No reply/Don't know More Less Same	6 7 8 9	
	ASK ALL			
50	Have you (both HOH and housewife) any brothers or sisters living now? INCLUDES BROTHERS & SISTERS OF DECEASED HUSBAND OR WIFE	No reply/Don't know Yes No	Y X O	44

Appendix 4

18.

			Punch no.	Column no.
	IF NO, GO TO Q.53; OTHERS CONTINUE			
51	Do any of them live in Bexhill/Clacton?	No reply/Don't know	1	44 (cont)
		Yes	2	
		No	3	
	ASK OF 'RECENT MOVERS' ONLY OTHERS GO TO Q.55			
52	Do you see your brothers and/or sisters more now than before you moved here, or less, or the same?	No reply/Don't know	4	
		More	5	
		Same	6	
		Less	7	
	ASK OF ALL 'RECENT MOVERS', OTHERS GO TO Q.55			
53	Would you say that you have more close friends now than before you moved here, or less, or the same?	No reply/Don't know	Y	45
		More	X	
		Same	0	
		Less	1	
	ASK OF 'RECENT MOVERS' ONLY			
54(a)	Do you think it is easier to make new friends here than where you lived before, or more difficult or about the same?	No reply/Don't know	2	
		Easier	3	
		More difficult	4	
		Same	5	
	FOR ALL EXCEPT 'SAME'			
(b)	What do you think is the main reason for that?			
	RECORD ALL ANSWERS BELOW AND CODE ONE MAIN REASON			
	EASIER	Many retired people with interests in common	Y	46
		When you're retired you have time to make friends	X	
		Not so pre-occupied with work, more interest in people	0	
		Social facilities available to help make contacts	1	
		Other	2	
	MORE DIFFICULT	The established community does not accept newcomers easily	Y	(46)
		Unused to making friends outside work contacts	X	

Appendix 4

	19.	Punch no.	Column no.
54(b) cont. MORE DIFFICULT	As you get older it is more difficult to make friends	O	
	The town is a bit snobbish	1	
	Have not been in town long	2	
	Health bad	3	
	Other	4	
55(a) How do you spend most of your time at this time of year? RECORD ALL REPLIES AND CODE ALL	No reply/Don't know	Y	47
	Walking	X	
	Gardening	O	
	Household duties	1	
	Motoring	2	
	Reading	3	
	Watching TV	4	
	Listening to radio	5	
	Sitting on sea front	6	
	Entertaining visitors	7	
	Other	8	
(b) Are there any important differences between the way you spend your time in the summer and winter? IF YES, What are these? RECORD BELOW	No reply/Don't know	Y	48
	No	X	
	Yes	O	

56	Do you go to any of the following more than once a fortnight on average throughout the year?	LEAVE BLANK FOR 'NO REPLY' RING YES WHERE APPLICABLE	
		No	1
	(a) the cinema?	Yes	2
	(b) the sea front and promenade?	Yes	3
	(c) a public house?	Yes	4
	(d) sporting events?	Yes	5
	(e) a park?	Yes	6
57(a) Do you have any pets?		No reply	7
		Yes	8
		No	9

(b) IF YES, what sort?

338 Appendix 4

			Punch no.	Column no.
	20.			
	ASK ALL			
58(a)	Do you go to any sort of club or society?	No reply/Don't know Yes No	Y X O	49
(b)	IF YES What sort(s) of club or society? WRITE NAME(S) AND TYPE(S) BELOW	FOR OFFICE USE ONLY No reply/Don't know Old people's club Ratepayers' or residents' association Townswomen's Guild or WI Specific interest club (not O.P.'s) Working Men's Club Sports Club Religious club or society Other	1 2 3 4 5 6 7 8 9	
59	IF 'NO' IN Q.58(a), OTHERS GO TO Q.60 Is there any special reason why you don't go to any? RECORD BELOW AND CODE ONE MAIN REASON.	No reply/Don't know No club in neighbourhood/too far away Housebound or ill No knowledge of clubs Too busy with other things Prefers quiet life without too many commitments or social contacts Has not been in town long Prefers house and garden Held in the evening Other	Y X O 1 2 3 4 5 6 7	50

60	Do you go to evening classes, church or any other community activities?	No reply
		No
		Yes Evening classes
		    Church
		    Other (SPECIFY)
			Y
			X
			O
			1
			2
				51

61	IF 'YES' IN Q.58(a) AND/OR 60 OTHERS GO TO Q.62 Taking all these and the clubs or societies together, how often do you go out to them? WRITE FREQUENCY BELOW AND RING CODE	No reply/Don't know More than 3 times a week 1-3 times a week Less than once a week but more than once a fortnight Once a fortnight or more than once a month Once a month Less than once a month	3 4 5 6 7 8 9	

Appendix 4

21.

			Punch no.	Column no.
62	If for some reason you (and your wife/husband) found yourself(selves) in sudden need of help of any kind, whom would you ask for help?	No reply/Don't know Children Other relatives Neighbours Friends Doctor Priest Welfare agency Other (SPECIFY)	Y X O 1 2 3 4 5 6	52
63	Would you say you are: (a) Often lonely (b) Sometimes lonely (c) Never lonely?	No reply/Don't know (a) Often lonely (b) Sometimes lonely (c) Never lonely	Y X O 1	53
64	With whom did you spend last Christmas Day or eat your main Christmas Day meal? CODE ALL APPLICABLE	No reply/Don't know Alone With spouse With children Other relatives Friends In hotel or boarding house, etc. Other (SPECIFY)	2 3 4 5 6 7 8 9	
65(a) (b)	Would you say that you prefer to live among people of your own age or would you rather have younger people - for example, young married couples - around you? IF (i) OR (ii) Why is this? WRITE OUT REPLY BELOW AND RING CODE	No reply/Don't know (i) Own age (ii) Younger people (iii) No preference CODES FOR (i) <u>OLDER PEOPLE</u> No reply/Don't know Older people have more in common with each other It's difficult to keep up with younger people You feel an encumbrance with younger people Older people quieter and more peaceful Other reasons	Y X O 1 2 3 4 5 6 7	54
		CODES FOR (ii) <u>YOUNGER PEOPLE</u> No reply/Don't know Younger people are more active and stimulating with more interests Old people think about themselves too much; their aches and pains Depressing with only older people around It's nice having children around Other reasons	 2 3 4 5 6 7	(54)

22.

			Punch no.	Column no.
66	Before you/your husband/wife retired, what ideas did you have about the way you were going to spend your retirement? RECORD BELOW AND CODE WHERE POSSIBLE	No reply/No ideas	Y	55
		To live by the sea	X	
		To develop a nice garden	O	
		To have a perpetual holiday	1	
		To travel	2	
		To make a complete break with the routine of working life	3	
		To get away from towns/suburbs	4	
		To rest and relax in peace	5	
		Other	6	
67(a)	In the light of your knowledge now and given your time again, would you move to the coast on retirement?	No reply/Don't know	Y	56
		Yes	X	
		No	O	
(b)	Why is that?			
68	Would you encourage retired friends or relatives to come to live in Bexhill/Clacton?	No reply/Don't know	Y	57
		Yes	X	
		No	O	
69	Through your encouragement, have any of your retired relatives or friends come to live in Bexhill/Clacton?	No reply/Don't know	1	
		Yes	2	
		No	3	
70(a)	Do you expect to move from this house within the next year? IF NO, GO TO Q.71. IF YES, CONTINUE	No reply/Don't know	4	
		Yes	5	
		No	6	
(b)	Would you be moving to a different town or another dwelling in this town?	No reply/Don't know	7	
		Another town	8	
		Another dwelling in same town	9	
(c)	Why do you expect to move? RECORD BELOW			

Appendix 4

		23.		Punch no.	Column no.
	IF YES IN 70(a), GO TO Q.73.				
	IF 'NO' CONTINUE				
71(a)	Would you like to move to a different dwelling in Bexhill/Clacton?		No reply/Don't know Yes No	Y X O	58
(b)	IF YES IN 71(a) Why would you like to move? RECORD BELOW				

72(a)	Would you like to move to a different town?		No reply/Don't know Yes No	1 2 3	
(b)	IF YES Why? RECORD BELOW				

	ASK ALL	LEAVE BLANK FOR 'NO REPLY'		
73	Here are some things which quite a few older people have difficulty in doing without help. Do you, or would you have difficulty in:	RING YES WHERE APPROPRIATE No		4
	(i) Walking up hills	Yes		5
	(ii) Going out of doors on your own	Yes		6
	(iii) Going up and down stairs on your own	Yes		7
	(iv) Getting about the house on your own	Yes		8
	(v) Getting in and out of bed on your own?	Yes		9

342 Appendix 4

24.

		Punch no.	Column no.
IF LIVING WITH SPOUSE			
OTHERS GO TO Q.75			
74(a) Does your husband/wife have difficulty with any of these?	No reply/Don't know Yes No	Y X O	59
(b) IF YES, which?	Walking up hill Going out of doors Going up/down stairs Getting about house Getting in and out of bed	1 2 3 4 5	
75(a) Do you own a car? IF YES, GO TO Q.76 IF NO	Yes No	6 7	
(b) Have you ever owned a car?	Yes No	8 9	
IF YES			
(c) Why did you give it up? CODE ALL REPLIES	No reply Financial reasons Health reasons Spouse deceased; cannot drive self Other	Y X O 1 2	60
THOSE LIVING WITH RELATIONS OR IN HOTELS GO TO Q.78			
OTHERS CONTINUE			
76(a) Do you have a home-help coming in to help you with the housework?	No reply/Don't know Yes No	3 4 5	
IF YES			
(b) Is she from the council?	No reply/Don't know Yes No	6 7 8	
IF YES IN (a)			
(c) How often does she come? WRITE FREQUENCY BELOW AND RING CODE ...	No reply/Don't know Daily Three times a week Once a week Less than once a week but more than once a fortnight Once a fortnight or less	Y X O 1 2 3	61

… Appendix 4

			Punch no.	Column no.
	ASK ALL BUT THOSE IN GUEST HOUSES AND HOTELS			
77(a)	Do you have any cooked meals brought by the meals-on-wheels service?	No reply/Don't know Yes No	4 5 6	61 (cont)
	IF YES			
(b)	How many times do they bring meals each week? WRITE NUMBER BELOW AND RING CODE ...	No reply/Don't know More than 4 a week 2-4 a week One a week or less	Y X O 1	62
	ASK ALL			
78(a)	Does the district nurse call on you?	No reply/Don't know Yes No	2 3 4	
	IF YES			
(b)	How often does she call? WRITE FREQUENCY BELOW AND RING CODE ...	No reply/Don't know Once a week or more Less than once a week	5 6 7	
	ASK ALL			
79(a)	Does the health visitor call on you at all?	No reply/Don't know Yes No	Y X O	63
	IF YES			
(b)	How often does she call? WRITE FREQUENCY BELOW AND RING CODE ...	No reply/Don't know Once a week or more Less than once a week	1 2 3	
	ASK ALL			
80(a)	Do you ever see the chiropodist?	No reply/Don't know Yes No	4 5 6	
	IF YES			
(b)	How often do you see him? WRITE FREQUENCY AND RING CODE ...	No reply/Don't know Once a month or more Less than once a month	7 8 9	
	ASK ALL			
81(a)	Are you attending a hospital out-patients department or clinic?	No reply/Don't know Yes No	Y X O	64
	IF YES			
(b)	How often do you go? WRITE FREQUENCY BELOW AND RING CODE ...	No reply/Don't know Once a week or more Once a month but less than once a week Less than once a month	1 2 3 4	

344 Appendix 4

	26.		Punch no.	Column no.
	ASK ALL			
82(a)	Apart from the services we have mentioned, do you have any other regular services, either privately or from a welfare organization? (e.g. regular private nursing)	No reply/Don't know Yes No	5 6 7	64 (cont)
	IF YES			
(b)	Which one(s)? WRITE ANSWERS BELOW			65
	ASK ALL			
83(a)	Do you usually visit your doctor when you need him or does he visit you?	No reply/Don't know Visits doctor Visited by doctor Depends on illness or circumstances	3 4 5 6	
(b)	Are you a private or National Health Service patient?	No reply Private N.H.S.	7 8 9	
(c)	When did you last see your doctor? RECORD BELOW AND RING CODE	No reply/Don't know Within last month Between 1 and 3 months ago Between 3 months and a year ago More than a year ago More than 10 years ago or never	Y X O 1 2 3	66
(d)	On that occasion, did you call him or visit him because you were ill or wanted help, or did he call without your asking him to? RING APPROPRIATE ANSWER	No reply/Don't know (a) Patient visited doctor (b) Patient or spouse called doctor (c) Doctor visited without being called	4 5 6 7	

27.

84	ASK ALL WHO HAVE EVER WORKED SEE Q.22 Did you/your husband continue working full-time after your retirement move? No reply ... Yes ... No ...	ASK ALL (e) Did you/did he have any formal qualifications of any kind? No reply ... Yes ... No ... IF YES	
	IF YES, Did you/he (a) continue commuting back to the place you left or back to London? (b) find employment locally? (c) Other (SPECIFY)	(f) What were these? WRITE OUT BELOW ... ... (g) If proprietor of a business or a manager - about how big an organization was this? Roughly how many people worked there? No reply ... 25 or more ... 10 - 24 ... Less than 10 ...	
85(a)	What was your/your husband's last occupation before you/he retired from full-time employment? What job did you/he actually do? WRITE OUT BELOW		

	FOR OFFICE USE ONLY	Punch no.	Column no.
(b) What type of firm or organisation did you/he work in? (Give type of firm, what it made, etc.) WRITE OUT BELOW	FROM Q.22 AND Q.2 Employment status of subject (if male or single) or husband No reply Working full-time Working part-time Retired completely from work Never worked	4 5 6 7 8	66 (cont)

(c) Were you/was he self-employed?
No reply ...
Yes ...
No ...
IF NOT SELF-EMPLOYED
	SOCIAL CLASS
	I A Professional
	II B Intermediate
	III C1 Skilled N.M.
	     C2 Skilled M.
	IV D1 Semiskilled N.M.
	    D2 Semiskilled M.
	V E Unskilled
	   F Armed Forces
	   G Indefinite, not stated
		Y
		X
		O
		1
		2
		3
		4
		5
		6
			67

(d) Did you/he have anyone working under you/him - for example, Were you/was he a supervisor or foreman? Or if in Police, Civil Service, Forces, etc. what rank or grade did you/he hold? No reply ... Yes ... No ... IF YES, Grade ...	Working full time after move (a) commuted (b) worked in retirement town	7 8 9	

Appendix 4

		28.	Punch no.	Column no.
86(a)	Could you tell me your (and your husband's/wife's combined total weekly net income from all sources? (i.e. after deductions) WRITE AMOUNT AND RING CODE £ ... p.w. IF REFUSAL IN (a), SHOW SCALE AND ASK: (b) Well, would you indicate into which of these groups your (and your husband's/wife's combined) total weekly net income would fall? RING APPROPRIATE CODE	No reply/Don't know	Y	68
		Up to £5 (£260 p.a.)	X	
		Over £5 to £7.10s (£261 - £390 p.a.)	O	
		Over £7.10 to £10 (£391 - £520 p.a.)	1	
		Over £10 to £12.10 (£521 - £650 p.a.)	2	
		Over £12.10 to £15 (£651 - £780 p.a.)	3	
		Over £15 to £20 (£781 - £1,040 p.a.)	4	
		Over £20 to £25 (£1,041 - £1,300 p.a.)	5	
		Over £25 to £30 (£1,301 - £1,560 p.a.)	6	
		Over £30 to £40 (£1,561 - £2,080 p.a.)	7	
		Over £40 (Over £2,081 p.a.)	8	
87(a)	ONLY TO OLD PEOPLE, MARRIED AND SINGLE, WHO ARE PART OF A NON-RETIRED HOUSEHOLD OTHERS GO TO Q.88 Could you tell me the total weekly net income from all sources, of your household - that is, the combined net income of all the members of this household? WRITE AMOUNT AND RING CODE £ ... IF REFUSAL IN (a) SHOW SCALE AND ASK: (b) Well, would you indicate into which of these groups the total weekly net household income would fall? RING APPROPRIATE CODE	No reply/Don't know	Y	69
		Up to £5 (£260 p.a.)	X	
		Over £5 to £7.10 (£261 - £390 p.a.)	O	
		Over £7.10 to £10 (£391 - £520 p.a.)	1	
		Over £10 to £12.10 (£521 - £650 p.a.)	2	
		Over £12.10 to £15 (£651 - £780 p.a.)	3	
		Over £15 to £20 (£781 - £1,040 p.a.)	4	
		Over £20 to £25 (£1,041 - £1,300 p.a.)	5	
		Over £25 to £30 (£1,301 - £1,560 p.a.)	6	
		Over £30 to £40 (£1,561 - £2,080 p.a.)	7	
		Over £40 (Over £2,081 p.a.)	8	

Appendix 4

			Punch no.	Column no.
	QUESTIONS 88 AND 89 APPLY TO OLD PEOPLE'S INCOME ONLY, NOT TO INCOME OF YOUNGER MEMBERS OF HOUSEHOLD, IF ANY			
88	From what sources do you get your income?	No reply/Don't know	Y	70
	PROMPT Old age pension	O.A.P.	X	
	Superannuation or private pension	Superannuation	O	
	Wages, salary, or fees	Wages, salary, fees	1	
	Interest from capital	Interest	2	
	NB. BOTH HOH AND SPOUSE			
	Supplementary benefit	Supplementary benefit	3	
	Other govt. grants and pensions	Other Govt. grants, pensions	4	
	From letting part of your house/rents	Rent	5	
	Help from relatives	Help from relatives	6	
	Other (SPECIFY)	Other (SPECIFY)	7	
	CODE ALL THAT ARE MENTIONED			
89(a)	Do you have any savings or capital?	No reply/Don't know	Y	71
		Yes	X	
	IF YES	No	O	
(b)	About how much do you have in savings or capital?	No reply/Don't know	1	
		Less than £500	2	
		£500 - £999	3	
	WRITE AMOUNT AND RING CODE	£1,000 - £2,999	4	
		£3,000 - £4,999	5	
		£5,000 - £6,999	6	
		£7,000 - £9,999	7	
		£10,000 - £14,999	8	
	IF YES IN (a)	£15,000+	9	
(c)	Do you find that you are having to use your savings or capital to supplement your income?	No reply/Don't know	Y	72
		Yes	X	
		No	O	
	TO ALL EXCEPT THOSE IN HOTELS AND BOARDING HOUSES			
90	Do you own or rent any of the following?:	No reply	1	
		A radio	2	
	CODE ALL OWNED OR RENTED	A T.V.	3	
		A washing machine	4	
		A refrigerator	5	
		A telephone	6	
		None	7	

END OF INTERVIEW

Check for Questions Omitted and Date of Construction (Q.1)

30.

	Punch no.	Column no.
EMPLOYMENT STATUS OF PRESENT HEAD OF RETIREMENT UNIT		73
N.R.	Y	
Full time	X	
Part-time or seasonal	0	
Not at all	1	
Employment Status immediately after retirement move (of Head of retirement unit at that time)		
N.R.	2	
Had never worked	3	
Continued work	4	
Stopped work	5	
If continued		
N.R.	6	
Commuted	7	
Employed locally	8	
Other (including bought business)	9	

USE OF SERVICES INDEX			74
Home Help	No reply	X	
Meals on Wheels	None	0	
District Nurse	One	1	
Health Visitor	Two	2	
Chiropodist	Three	3	
Outpatients	Four	4	
Other	Five	5	
Doctor within	Six	6	
last 3 months	Seven	7	
	Eight	8	

Appendix 4

31.

	Punch no.	Column no.		Punch no.	Column no.
CHARACTER OF LAST RETIREMENT MOVE		75	Length of stay at last address		77
PLACE					
N.R.	Y		N.R.	Y	
Within Bexhill or Clacton	X		0 - 1 year	X	
Into Bexhill or Clacton	O		Over 1 up to 2 years	O	
			Over 2 up to 5 years	1	
TENURE			Over 5 up to 10 years	2	
			Over 10 years	3	
N.R.	1				
Changed tenure	2		Number of addresses in Bexhill or Clacton		
Did not change tenure	3				
			N.R.	4	
TYPE OF DWELLING			None other than present	5	
N.R.	4				
Changed type	5		1 other than present	6	
Did not change type	6		2 other than present	7	
			3 other than present	8	
INTO BEXHILL OR CLACTON ONLY			4 or more	9	
ORIGIN					
N.R.	7				
Other seaside place	8				
Other	9				
PREVIOUS TENURE		76			
N.R.	Y				
Owner-occupied	X				
Privately rented (furnished)	O				
Privately rented (unfurnished)	1				
Lived with relations	2				
Other	3				
PREVIOUS TYPE					
N.R.	4				
House	5				
Bungalow	6				
Flat (either type)	7				
Rooms	8				
Other	9				

Appendix 5: list of resorts used for analysis of local authority finance

The eight county boroughs included in Tables 17.1 to 17.3 were: Blackpool, Bournemouth, Brighton, Eastbourne, Hastings, Southend, Southport and Torbay.

The non-county boroughs were: Bexhill, Bridlington, Christchurch, Colwyn Bay, Falmouth, Folkestone, Harrogate, Hove, Hythe, Lymington, Lytham St Annes, Margate, Morecombe and Heysham, Penzance, Ramsgate, St Austell, St Ives, Scarborough, Tunbridge Wells, Weston-Super-Mare, Weymouth, Worthing.

The urban districts were: Bognor, Littlehampton, Shoreham, Clacton, Felixstowe, Newquay, Teignmouth, Sandown-Shanklin, Seaford, Southwich, Frinton and Walton, Skegness, Thornton-Cleveleys, Llandudno, Exmouth, Newton Abbot, Broadstairs, Herne Bay, Whitstable, Cowes, Ventnor.

All non-county boroughs and urban districts were included which had 20 per cent or more of their population of pensionable age in 1966 and which sent in rate returns to the IMTA (now CIPFA). In the case of urban districts a minority of retirement resorts sent returns to the IMTA.

Since local government reorganization these authorities have now been included in the following new authorities:

County	Districts
Cornwall	Penrith, Carrick
Devon	South Hams, Teignbridge, Torbay, East Devon
Dorset	West Dorset, Weymouth and Portland, Bournemouth
Somerset	West Somerset
Avon	Woodspring
Hampshire	New Forest
Isle of Wight	South Wight, Medina
West Sussex	Chichester, Arun, Worthing, Adur
East Sussex	Hove, Brighton, Lewes, Hastings, Eastbourne, Rother

Appendix 5

Kent	Shepway, Dover, Thanet
Essex	Tendring, Maldon, Southend
Suffolk	Suffolk Coastal, Waveney
Norfolk	Great Yarmouth, North Norfolk
Lincolnshire	East Lindsey
Humberside	North Wolds, Holderness
North Yorkshire	Scarborough
Lancashire	Blackpool, Lancaster
Merseyside	Sefton (omitted as Metropolitan District)
Clwyd	Colwyn
Gwynedd	Aberconwy

Notes

INTRODUCTION

1 Michael B. Barker, 'California Retirement Communities', Special Report to Centre for Real Estate and Urban Economics, Institute for Urban and Regional Development, Berkeley, University of California, 1966, pp.ix-x.
2 Census 1971, Great Britain, Advance Analysis, London, HMSO, 1972, Table 1.
3 Maureen Messent, To Devon on the Retirement Special, 'Birmingham Evening Mail', Monday, 23 March 1970, p.10.
4 See Hugh W. Mellor, Retirement to the Coast, 'Town Planning Review', no. 33-4, April 1962-3; and John Barr, For Old People Only, 'New Society', 25 November 1965.
5 The National Corporation for the Care of Old People have always taken a keen interest in these developments. In 1967 they organised a conference, mainly of delegates from the local authorities concerned, to consider retirement migration and, in the same year, gave a generous grant to the Centre for Urban and Regional Studies for an exploratory study of the subject. This report is the result of that study.
6 Barker, op. cit., p.x.
7 Men of 65 and over and women of 60 and over. These figures were very kindly extracted for me from the 1968 Census of France by Mme Françoise Cribier, Laboratoire de Géographie Humaine de L'Université de Paris I.
8 Retire to the Fountain of Aphrodite, 'Guardian', 24 November 1972; and Places in the Sun are Pricey, 'Sunday Times', 14 November 1971.
9 'Kieler Nachrichten', no. 44, 21 February 1970, p.68.

Notes to Chapter 1

CHAPTER 1   FROM INLAND SPAS TO SEASIDE RESORTS

1. Quoted in E.W. Gilbert, 'Brighton, Old Ocean's Bauble', London, Methuen, 1954, p.10.
2. For a full account of the rise of seaside resorts in England see J.A.R. Pimlott, 'The Englishman's Holiday - A Social History', London: Faber & Faber, 1947; Gilbert, op. cit., Ch. 2; E.W. Gilbert, The Growth of Inland and Seaside Health Resorts in England, 'Scottish Geographical Magazine', vol. 55, 1939.
3. E.W. Gilbert, 'Old Ocean's Bauble', p.12.
4. Ibid., p.17.
5. E.W. Gilbert, Pioneer Maps of Health and Disease in England, 'Geographical Journal', 124 (1958), part 2, p.173.
6. See Pimlott, op.cit., for a full account of the 'holiday with pay' situation.
7. E.W. Gilbert, 'Brighton, Old Ocean's Bauble', pp.16-17.
8. Registrar General, Census 1961, England and Wales: Age, Marital Condition; and General Tables, London, HMSO 1964, Table 9.
9. Sample Census 1966, Regional Migration Reports, London, HMSO, 1974, Table 5B.
10. See Appendix 1, Table A1.3.
11. Cf. 'Air Ministry Meteorological Office, Climatological Atlas of the British Isles', London, HMSO, 1952.
12. E.g. M.J. Gardner, M.D. Crawford and J.N. Morris, Patterns of Mortality in Middle and Early Old Age in the County Boroughs of England and Wales, 'British Journal of Preventive Social Medicine' (1969), 23,0.135; and R.K. Macpherson, F. Ofner and J.A. Walsh, The Effect of Prevailing Air Temperature on Mortality, 'British Journal of Preventive Social Medicine' (1967), 21, pp.17-21.
13. E.g. G. Melvyn Howe (for the Royal Geographical Society), 'National Atlas of Disease Mortality in the United Kingdom', London, Nelson, 1963, pp.54-6; Gardner et al., op. cit., p.138; and Ministry of Health Reports on Public Health and Medical Subjects, no. 95, 'Mortality and Morbidity during the London Fog of December 1952: Report by a Committee of Departmental Officers and Expert Advisers appointed by the Ministry of Health, H.M.S.O.'.
14. George Cheyne, 'An Essay on Health and Long Life', London, 1724, p.11.
15. Ibid., p.206.
16. P.R. Gould and R.R. White, The Mental Maps of British School Leavers, 'Regional Studies', vol. 2, November 1968, pp.161-82.

17 P.R. Gould, 'On Mental Maps', Michigan Inter-University Community of Mathematical Geographers, Discussion Paper No.9, Ann Arbor, Department of Geography, University of Michigan, 1966.
18 Gould and White, op. cit., p.162.

CHAPTER 2   THE SCALE OF THE MOVEMENT TO THE COAST

1   And at January 1976 the Migration Reports of the 1971 Census had still not been published for the regions being considered here.
2   In the 1961 Census most data were given for those of 65 and over, not for people of pensionable age. The reverse was true in the 1966 Census.
3   The data in this paragraph are derived from the General Register Office, 1961 Census, England and Wales: Migration Tables, London, HMSO, 1966, Table 9.
4   D. Lowenthal and H.C. Prince, English Landscape Tastes, 'The Geographical Review', vol. 55, 1965, p.187.
5   See Appendix 1, Table A1.4.
6   These regions contain large areas which have very little retirement migration, such as Cheshire, in the North-West, Gloucestershire and Wiltshire in the South-West, Berkshire, Oxfordshire and Bedfordshire in the South-East and the inland areas in Wales and East Anglia. This makes their use as 'retirement regions' very unsatisfactory, but it is the only material available.
7   See Appendix 1, Table A1.5.
8   General Register Office, Sample Census 1966 England and Wales Migration Summary Tables Part II, London, HMSO, 1968.
9   Countryside Commission, 'The Planning of the Coastline', London, HMSO, 1970.
10 The question of links with holiday experiences is discussed further in Chapter 6.
11 A 'retirement move' was defined as one which was made after retirement from work or, if made before retirement from work, one which was specifically made with retirement in view.
12 This movement between resorts is considered in more detail in Chapter 12.
13 See Appendix 1, Table A1.6.
14 One has to remember the serious qualifications about the reliability of the sample census in relation to migration, especially for small areas.
15 Data for people aged 65 and over are used in comparing 1961 and 1966, because these are the only data available for 1961.

16 See Appendix 1, Table A1.7.
17 See Appendix 1, Table A1.8. The sixteen counties are: East Sussex, West Sussex, Isle of Wight, Caernarvonshire, Devon, Cornwall and the Isle of Scilly, Dorset, Denbighshire, Merionethshire, Somerset, Norfolk, Kent, East Suffolk, Flintshire, Hampshire and Essex. The resorts in Lancashire and Yorkshire are: Blackpool, Morecambe and Heysham, Southport, Lytham St Annes, Scarborough and Bridlington.

CHAPTER 3   WHO ARE THE MOVERS?

1 See Appendix 1, Table A1.9.
2 See Appendix 1, Table A1.9.
3 If one includes all the men interviewed who were retired, not just those of 65 and over, the proportion who retired before they were 60 is increased by about 4 percentage points but there are no comparable national figures available for all retired people.
4 The Civil Service, The Fulton Report, vol.4, 'Factual, Statistical and Explanatory Papers, Evidence Submitted to the Committee under the Chairmanship of Lord Fulton 1966-68', London, HMSO, 1968, p.379.
5 E. Shanas et al., 'Old People in Three Industrial Societies', London, Routledge & Kegan Paul, 1968, pp.315.
6 There is probably a slight undercount of those who retired for health reasons because the response rate of people in poor health was lower. This, however, is also likely to have been a feature of the cross-national survey (see Appendix 3).
7 The employment of retired people in the tourist trade during the summer months in Clacton is commented upon in National Parks Commission, 'The Coasts of East Anglia', London, HMSO, 1968, p.43.
8 Census 1971, Great Britain. Summary Tables (1% Sample), London, HMSO, 1973, Table 13.
9 A. Harris, Moving House by Elderly People, 'Labour Mobility in Great Britain 1953-1963', Government Social Survey, Appendix VIII.
10 Harris, op. cit., Tables 114 and 116.
11 It should be remembered that the only data available were for those people who stayed in the town; those who moved away, or died, were excluded. They were not, therefore, a true cross section of all the people who had moved to the town at one time.
12 See Appendix 1, Table A1.10.

13 This difference was not, however, statistically significant.
14 See Chapter 5 for reasons for moving.
15 Information is available on children only at the time of the survey. There will have been some people whose children had died but we can take the figures as sufficiently good for purposes of comparison with national figures for all men of 65 and over, some of whom would also have lost children since the age of 65 or so.
16 See Shanas et al., op.cit., p.230, for a discussion of this.
17 See Appendix 1, Table A1.11.
18 Shanas et al., op.cit., p.233.
19 A similar feature has been found in the USA amongst people who return to Florida and Arizona. According to one survey 'one fifth (22%) of the migrants had no children' and migrants with children had fewer on average than retired people who had not moved on retirement. See Gordon L. Bultena and Douglas G. Marshall, Family Patterns of Migrant and Non-migrant Retirees, 'Journal of Marriage and the Family', vol.32, no.1, February 1970, p.90.

CHAPTER 4 THE MOVERS' HOMES IN THE CITIES AND SUBURBS

1 Dr Johnson, 'Letter to Boswell', 20 September 1777.
2 There is a problem of data comparability in making any statement, however. According to a survey of labour mobility in Britain, the proportion of people aged 60-4 who had lived more than 20 years at the same address was 53.2 per cent and for people aged 65 and over 52.4 per cent. However, the labour mobility survey counted all changes of address not just moves between towns as was done in the retirement survey. See A. Harris, Moving House by Elderly People, in 'Labour Mobility in Great Britain 1953-1963', Government Social Survey, Appendix VIII.
3 Office of Population Censuses and Surveys, The General Household Survey Introductory Report, London, HMSO, 1973, p.92.
4 Ibid.
5 Ibid.
6 The numbers of semi-skilled and unskilled workers in Bexhill were too small for analysis.
7 See Appendix 1, Tables A1.12 and A1.13.
8 Compared with 8 per cent of dwellings nationally (see M. Woolf, The Housing Survey in England and Wales 1964, Government Social Survey, London, HMSO, 1969, p.143.)

Notes to Chapters 5 and 6

CHAPTER 5 THE MOVE ITSELF: MOTIVES AND CHOICES

1 Cf. also A. Harris, 'Labour Mobility in Great Britian 1953-1963', Government Social Survey, London, HMSO, Appendix VII, p.129, Table 116, in which elderly long-distance movers were shown to give improved surroundings as one of their main reasons for moving.
2 British Travel and Holidays Association, Visitors to Hastings 1962-63, unpublished document, 1964, p.6.
3 Ibid., p.32.
4 E. Shanas et al., 'Old People in Three Industrial Societies', London, Routledge & Kegan Paul, 1968, p.231.
5 P. Willmott and M. Young, 'Family and Class in a London Suburb', London, Routledge & Kegan Paul, 1960, pp.19-20.
6 Willmott and Young, op. cit., pp.24-6.
7 See Appendix 1, Table A1.14.
8 See Appendix 1, Table A1.15.
9 British Tourist Authority (Research Department), Survey of Staying and Day Visitors to Bexhill, Summer 1964, unpublished report, February 1965, p.11. Quoted by kind permission of Bexhill Corporation.

CHAPTER 6 THE RETIRED POPULATION OF BEXHILL AND CLACTON

1 See Appendix 1, Table A1.16.
2 See above, p.40.
3 See Appendix 1, Table A1.17.
4 E. Shanas et al., 'Old People in Three Industrial Societies', London, Routledge & Kegan Paul, 1968, p.229.
5 Census 1971, Great Britain: Age, Marital Condition and General Tables, London, HMSO, 1974, Table 9.
6 See above, p.40.
7 These percentages are far too large to be explained by sampling error. It was estimated that women heads of household were underrated by 5 per cent at the outside. See Appendix 4.
8 See the Registrar General's 'Statistical Review of England and Wales for the Year 1970. Part II Tables, Population', London, HMSO, 1972, Table E, Column 16, ratio of local adjusted death-rate to national rate.
9 See Appendix 1, Table A1.18.
10 See Appendix 1, Table A1.18.
11 Shanas et al., op. cit., p.230.
12 Ibid., p.186.
13 Ibid., Table VI-18a, pp.156 and 157.

14 See above, p.41.
15 Comparison of the family structure of the retired households with that of elderly people nationally is rather difficult because of the difference in the way the samples were selected. In this survey only the person selected was asked about his or her family and we analysed these findings according to the characteristics of the head of the retirement unit. The cross-national survey collected information about all the people of 65 and over in the households they selected. Thus a married couple with one child appears in our analysis as a married man with one child but in the cross-national survey as one married man and one married woman with one child if they were both of 65 and over, and as one married man with one child if only the husband was 65 or over. We did not analyse our material separately to cut out people under 65 or to identify men with wives under 65. However, the category of 'men' in the CNS is roughly comparable with the category 'Male Heads of Retirement Units' aged 65 and over in this survey. Although the latter excludes additional men in the households, there were very few indeed in either town. Their inclusion would have meant that a very slightly larger proportion of men would have had no children, because of the disproportionate number of single men amongst additional members of the household. There was no group in the CNS comparable with 'Female Heads of Retirement Units' all of whom were widowed, divorced or single.
16 Shanas et al., op. cit., calculated from Tables VI-2, pp.137 and 139.
17 There is a slight problem in making this comparison with elderly people nationally in that this sample included people under 65 while the CNS did not, but, in fact, the proportion of our respondents aged 65 and over who lived with their children was even lower than the proportion of those aged under 65. In Bexhill 5 per cent of those of 65 and over lived with their children, compared with 7 per cent of all respondents. In Clacton the proportions were 8 per cent and 10 per cent. The reason for this is that more of the younger respondents had single children in their teens or early 20s still living with them before moving away to marry or to work. The retired people in Clacton more often had unmarried children living with them.
There is another problem of comparison in that no information was collected in this survey about the children of members of the household other than the respondents. Their inclusion would alter the results

about children to the extent that a few of our respondents had very old parents living with them; in Bexhill there were eleven respondents who had parents living with them; and in Clacton seven. There were also widowed friends living with some of the widowed and single women interviewed; they may have had children, but not living with them. In fact inclusion of all· these additional people would probably have swung the results even further from the national ones, because of the relatively large numbers, especially in Bexhill, of spinsters and widows living without their relations.

18 Shanas et al., op. cit., p.239.
19 Ibid., p.161.
20 Those aged 65 and over.
21 Shanas et al., op. cit., Tables VI-20a and VI-20b, pp.159 and 160.
22 E.g., S.M. Lipset and R. Bendix, 'Social Mobility in Industrial Society', London, Heinemann, 1959, p.206: 'Therefore professionals and semi-professionals had the highest rate of geographical mobility of any occupational group.'
23 E.g. C.R. Bell, 'Middle Class Families, Social and Geographical Mobility', London, Routledge & Kegan Paul, 1968, p.49.
24 G.L. Bultena and D.G. Marshall, Family Patterns of Migrant and Non-Migrant Retirees, 'Journal of Marriage and the Family', vol.32, no.1, February 1970, p.90. This conclusion assumes, however, that the children would not have had a greater motive for staying if their parents had not moved. Even if this point were taken into consideration the scale of difference would probably still be great.
25 P. Willmott and M. Young, 'Family and Class in a London Suburb', London, Routledge & Kegan Paul, 1960, p.41.
26 Ibid., p.40.
27 Ibid., p.43.
28 Including brothers- and sisters-in-law.
29 Including brothers- and sisters-in-law.
30 Willmott and Young, op. cit., London, Routledge & Kegan Paul, 1960, pp.53-4.
31 Sample Census 1966 England and Wales: Household Composition, p.292, Table 38. These data were not available for 1971.
32 The figures quoted are for one- two- and three-person households only, in order to achieve comparability with those for the 1971 Census for England and Wales. Households larger than this were, however, very few (only 1 per cent of the total in Bexhill and 2 per

cent in Clacton) so that the figure is only a slight distortion. In fact 21 per cent of all households contacted in Bexhill and 18 per cent in Clacton were single-person households.
33 Shanas et al., op. cit., p.186, Table VII-1.

CHAPTER 7   FAMILY LIFE AND FRIENDS

1   Robert W. Kleemeier (ed.), 'Aging and Leisure', London, Oxford University Press, 1961, p.272.
2   E. Shanas et al., 'Old People in Three Industrial Societies', London, Routledge & Kegan Paul, 1968, p.260.
3   Ibid., p.212, Table VII-21.
4   See above, pp.73-4.
5   See above, p.58.
6   Greater London Housing Department, Seaside Bungalows Survey, unpublished report, part V, pp.3-4.
7   See below, pp.177-8.
8   See Appendix 1, Table A1.20.
9   Shanas et al., op. cit., p.273.
10 The numbers of single people in Clacton were too small, however, for statistical reliability on this point.
11 Calculated from Shanas et al., op. cit., pp.274, 279.
12 Ibid., p.276.
13 It is worth noting that the proportions of people in Bexhill and Clacton who said they preferred living with old people were substantially smaller than those found by the Building Research Station (see W.V. Hole and P.G. Allen, Dwellings for Old People, 'Architects Journal', vol.94, 9 May 1962, pp.1017-26; and W.V. Hole and P.G. Allen, Rehousing Old People, 'Architects Journal', vol. Aa 3, 8 January 1964, pp.75-82), the Department of the Environment (see survey in Stevenage, quoted in K.J. Haines and J. Raven, Old People: Study of Living Patterns, 'Architectural Journal', 26 October 1966, pp.1051-66), and in a survey of Hanover Housing Association (see D. Page and T. Muir, New Housing for the Elderly (an assessment study of the Hanover Housing Association's first sixteen housing schemes for elderly people), London, Bedford Square Press for the National Corporation for the Care of Old People, 1971, Table 6), but all these surveys were carried out in groups of dwellings exclusively for old people. In interpreting the results there is, as here, the problem of post facto rationalization of the present situation (see Haines and Raven, ibid.).

14 H. Gans, 'People and Plans: Essays on Urban Problems and Solutions', Abridged Edition, Harmondsworth, Penguin Books, 1972, pp.143-4.
15 Ibid., p.127.
16 I. Rosow, Retirement Housing and Social Integration, in C. Tibbitts and W. Donahue, 'Social and Psychological Aspects of Ageing', New York, Columbia University Press, 1962, p.333.
17 Ibid., p.337.
18 Ibid., p.338.

CHAPTER 8   IN CASE OF EMERGENCY

1 See above, pp.71-2.
2 See above, p.76.
3 See below, p.112.
4 The questions about the use of services were asked of the subjects themselves and do not refer to their spouses.
5 Office of Health Economics, 'General Practice Today', Paper No.28, London, Office of Health Economics, 1968, p.11.
6 As Ann Cartwright comments, 'Once again an attempt to explain wide variations in consultation rates by differences in the characteristics or attitudes of patients has been abortive.' See Ann Cartwright, 'Patients and Their Doctors', Institute of Community Studies, London, Routledge & Kegan Paul, 1967, p.37.
7 Office of Health Economics, op. cit., p.11.
8 P. Townsend and D. Wedderburn, 'The Aged in the Welfare State, London, Bell, 1965, p.61. See also Cartwright, op. cit., p.11.
9 Samuel Mencher, 'Private Practice in Britain', Occasional Papers on Social Administration, no.24, London, Bell, 1968, p.36.
10 18 per cent of all people aged 65 and over living in private households in England and Wales in 1966 (Office of Health Economics, 'Old Age', Office of Health Economics, 1968, p.23).
11 Amelia Harris, 'Social Welfare for the Elderly', Government Social Survey, vol.1, London, HMSO, 1968, pp.60, 101.
12 J. Williamson et al., 'Old People at Home: Their Unreported Needs', 'Lancet', May 1964, pp.1,117-20.
13 East Sussex County Council, 'The Health of the Community', 1968, p.58. The situation of the home help service in other resort areas is discussed further in Chapter 16.

14 See Appendix 1, Table A1.21.

CHAPTER 9 LEISURE

1   Greater London Council Housing Department, Seaside Bungalows Survey, unpublished report, part V, Littlehampton Bungalows, p.4.
2   See Appendix 1, Table A1.22.
3   Including hiring.
4   Department of Employment and Productivity, 'Family Expenditure Survey Report for 1969', HMSO, 1970, p.98, Table 51.
5   See Appendix 1, Table A1.23.
6   See Appendix 1, Table A1.23.
7   E. Shanas et al., 'Old People in Three Industrial Societies', London, Routledge & Kegan Paul, 1968, p.269.
8   Cf. Peter Dodd, Who Goes to Church? 'New Society', 29 April 1965, pp.22-3.
9   A survey in the USA showed a fall off in church attendance with increasing distance from the church (B.G. Zimmer and A.H. Hawley, Suburbanization and Church Participation, 'Social Forces', 37, May 1959, pp.348-54.
10 Cf. F. Boulard, 'An Introduction to Religious Sociology', trans. M.J. Jackson, London, Dacton, Longman & Todd, 1960, p.14.
11 Dodd, op. cit.
12 K.K. Sillitoe, 'Planning for Leisure', Government Social Survey, London, HMSO, 1969, pp.60-1.
13 Though, in Bexhill, professional people attended less than the skilled non-manual workers.
14 Sillitoe, op. cit., p.62.
15 A questionnaire was circulated with the kind help of the Secretary and members.
16 Cf. Emily White, 'The Over-Sixties Club and the Community', National Council of Social Service (no date), p.19, in which she points out that in Lancashire retirement resorts, the old people's clubs still tend to cater for lower income groups rather than the sort of people who tend to retire there. A number of people commented that there was in Bexhill a social class difference between the large and relatively middle-class Senior Citizens Club and the working-class Darby and Joan Club. They also said that migrants tended to go to the Senior Citizens Club and local people to the Darby and Joan. These points were not followed up but may be an interesting reflection on the social life of the town.

17 Shanas et al., op. cit., p.269.

CHAPTER 10 THE FINANCIAL POSITION OF RETIRED PEOPLE

1 Since this study was done inflation has led to a deterioration in the real income of retired people. The situation in resorts like Clacton is therefore likely to be even more precarious than described here.
2 In the survey, respondents were asked for the joint income of married couples and the individual income of all other people, that is the income of the 'retirement unit'. This was net of tax and other deductions (Winter 1968-9).
3 The analysis of income by social class revealed that there was a lower response rate from Classes I and II (about 75 per cent) than from the other classes (about 90 per cent). However, a calculation of the income range, corrected for the true social class proportions suggests that the effect is not great. Of course, most of the refusals may have been concentrated in the higher income groups within the social classes, so the effect may have been greater than the calculation suggests. However, it can probably be safely said that there is only a slight downward bias in the income figures given. (See Appendix 1, Table A1.8 and Appendix 3.)
4 See Appendix 1, Table A1.24.
5 E. Shanas et al., 'Old People in Three Industrial Societies', London, Routledge & Kegan Paul, 1968, p.364; D. Cole and J. Utting, 'The Economic Circumstances of Old People', Occasional Papers in Social Administration, no.4, Welwyn, Codicote Press, 1962, p.53; and A.B. Atkinson, 'Poverty in Britain and the Reform of Social Security', University of Cambridge, Department of Applied Economics, Occasional Papers 18, Cambridge University Press, 1969, p.49.
6 Cf. 'Occupational schemes have in the past granted relatively few pensions to the widows of deceased employees', and 'even by the end of the century only two thirds of pensioner households will be receiving occupational pensions'. 'Most existing schemes include only limited provisions for the payment of pensions to the widows of employees. In 1967 only 10% of schemes had unconditional widows' pensions (although more included an option which allowed the employee to "buy" a widows pension by foregoing part of his own pension)', Atkinson, op. cit., pp.47, 51. See also Ministry of Pensions and National Insurance,

'Financial and Other Circumstances of Retirement Pensioners', London, HMSO, 1966, Appendix V.
7 Shanas et al., op. cit., p.379.
8 Ibid.
9 Ibid., p.377.
10 See Appendix 1, Table A1.25.
11 Data were collected about the income of whole households even when it was a larger unit but the information was not good enough to be used. Most of the respondents knew little or nothing about the income of the people with whom they were living, whether children, relations or friends, and a follow-up to interview other members of the household was not considered worthwhile, considering the small numbers involved.
12 Net incomes.
13 Department of Employment and Productivity 'Family Expenditure Survey Report for 1968', London, HMSO, 1969, p.86, Table 26.
14 Ibid., (again gross income for the national figure).
15 Ibid., p.84, Table 22 (again gross income).
16 See Appendix 1, Table A1.26.
17 In particular these levels of savings would not last long if private nursing home accommodation were needed at £20-£150 a week.
18 See Appendix 1, Table A1.27.
19 Cole and Utting, op. cit., pp.73-4.
20 Shanas et al., op. cit., p.382, Table XII-15.
21 The failure of many eligible elderly people to apply for Supplementary Benefits or National Assistance is well documented in Ministry of Pensions and National Insurance, op. cit., Tables III 2 and III 4(2), and in Atkinson, op. cit., pp.55-9.

CHAPTER 11 THE PRESENT RETIREMENT HOME

1 See Appendix 1, Table A1.28.
2 Greater London Council Housing Department, Seaside Bungalows Survey, unpublished report, Part V, p.4.
3 Office of Population Censuses and Surveys, Social Survey Division, The General Household Survey, Introductory Report, London, HMSO, 1973, p. 96.
4 Ibid., p.109.
5 See Appendix 1, Table A1.29.
6 See above, p.56.
7 Department of the Environment, 'Housing and Construction Statistics', no.11, HMSO, 1974, Table 38.

Notes to Chapter 11

8   Department of the Environment, 'Housing and Construction Statistics', no.13, London, HMSO, 1975, Table 38.
9   In 1968, 10 per cent of retired or economically inactive owner-occupiers had outstanding mortgages (England and Wales). See Department of the Environment, 'Housing Statistics Great Britain', no.19, November 1970, p.73, Table IV.
10 In 1973-4 the average rates per domestic hereditament were £79.90 in Clacton and £94.21 in Bexhill (Institute of Municipal Treasurers and Accountants, Return of Rates Levied per Head of Population (England and Wales) 1973-74', July 1973). See below, Chapter 17, for a more detailed discussion of the rates situation of the resorts.
11 This difference has been documented nationally in 'Committee of Inquiry into the Impact of Rates on Households', The Allen Report, London, HMSO, 1965, p.65: 'in England and Wales other things being equal, the highest rates are paid by householders in flats'.
12 See Appendix 1, Table A1.30.
13 The proportions of income spent on rates were much higher in the two resorts than the figures quoted for retired people in the South in 1963-4 in the Allen Report. For households with retired heads the proportion of household income spent on rates was 5.3 per cent; for those with incomes of less than £6 a week 9.2 per cent and for those with incomes of £6-10 was 7.8 per cent (Committee of Inquiry into the Impact of Rates on Households, London, HMSO, 1965, p.366).
14 See Appendix 1, Table A1.31.
15 See Appendix 1, Table A1.32.
16 That is guests in the 17 hotels which reported having resident guests. Of the 47 hotels and boarding houses contacted in Clacton, 17 replied and of the 45 in Bexhill 23 replied of which 2 had closed. Only 2 of the Clacton establishments had elderly resident guests, compared with 15 in Bexhill. The total of elderly residents in these establishments was 12 in Clacton compared with 120 in Bexhill.
17 Julian Mounter, Enter Holiday-makers: Exit Old People, 'The Times', 10 April 1967.
18 The Guardian Housing Association, information booklet, 1971.
19 Cf. the Save and Prosper Scheme described in Round-Up, 'The Times' 23 December 1972.
20 Some of the schemes set minimum valuation on the houses they will consider. These will therefore exclude poorer owner-occupiers in greatest need of such a scheme. Also many widows hold their property

    in trust, under their husband's will, for their
    children. They, too, would be ineligible.
21 Timothy Johnson, How to Retire in Comfort; Old People's
    Finances, 'Sunday Times', 16 August 1970.
22 Ibid.

CHAPTER 12   MOVING FROM ONE RETIREMENT HOME TO ANOTHER

1 See Appendix 1, Table A1.33.
2 See above, p.28.
3 See Appendix 1, Table A1.34.
4 All the names used in examples are fictitious.
5 See above, p.67.
6 See above, pp.129-30.
7 See Appendix 1, Table A1.35.
8 See below, p.173.

CHAPTER 13   SATISFACTION WITH THE RETIREMENT MOVE

1   See Appendix 1, Table A1.36.
2   See above, pp. 28, 31.
3   See above, p.95.
4   See above, p.59.
5   See Appendix 1, Table A1.37.
6   Greater London Council Housing Department, Seaside
    Bungalows Study, unpublished report, part IV, p.19,
    Table 82.
7   See Appendix 1, Table A1.38.
8   Greater London Council Housing Department, op.cit.,
    part VI, pp.30-1, Tables 52, 53 and 54.
9   See above, pp.77, 108, 172.
10 See above, p.92.

INTRODUCTION TO PART THREE

1 South East Economic Planning Council, 'A Strategy for
   the South-East', London, HMSO, 1967, p.62, para.246.
2 There has now been some work done on the economic
   impact of retirement to the South West. This is by
   Ian Gordon of the University of Kent. See Ian Gordon,
   'The Retirement Industry in the South West: A Survey
   of its Size, Distribution and Economic Aspects',
   London, Department of the Environment, for the South
   West Planning Council, 1975. This appears also in a
   shortened version, South West Economic Planning
   Council, 'Retirement to the Southwest', London, HMSO,
   1975.

3   Neither Clacton nor Bexhill was a health or social services authority, so wider areas had to be considered in any case.
4   K.O.A. Vickery, Post Retirement and Later Days, 'Royal Society of Health Journal', vol.89, no.4, July-August 1969, p.84.
5   E.g. A. Harris, 'Social Welfare for the Elderly', Government Social Survey, London, HMSO, 1968; G. Sumner and R. Smith, 'Planning for Local Authority Services for the Elderly', University of Glasgow, Social and Economic Studies, no.17, London, Allen & Unwin, 1969; and Bleddyn Davies, 'Social Needs and Resources in Local Services', London, Michael Joseph, 1968.

CHAPTER 14   HOSPITAL FACILITIES IN THE RETIREMENT AREAS

1   Ministry of Health, 'The Hospital Plan for England and Wales', Cmnd. 1604, London, HMSO, 1964, p.5.
2   See Appendix 1, Table A1.39.
3   Ibid.
4   Communication.
5   Dr R.B. Franks, in Borough of Worthing, 'Annual Report on the Health of Worthing for the Year 1966', p.62.
6   L.P. Robinson, L.M. Mackenzie and A.A. Gregory, 'Problems of the Elderly in a Seaside Resort and Retirement Areas', unpublished paper to the Royal Society of Health Sessional Meeting, Southport, 1966, p.5.
7   It is, unfortunately, a fact which many surgeons and physicians are unwilling to recognize, persisting in regarding elderly patients in their wards as 'intruders'.
8   Chichester and Graylingwell Group Hospital Management Committee, Hospital Facilities for the Elderly, unpublished report, April 1970.
9   A Review of Waiting Lists by Bournemouth and East Dorset Hospital Management Committee, unpublished report.
10 Concern about the similar situation in Devon has led to the initiation of a very large-scale study of health and welfare services for the elderly in that county. This is being undertaken by the Institute of Biometry and Community Medicine of the University of Exeter.
11 M.B. Devas and R.E. Irvine, The Geriatric Orthopaedic Unit: A Method of Achieving Return to Independence in the Elderly Patient, 'British Journal of Geriatric Practice', vol.6, no.1, March 1966, p.23.

12 Borough of Worthing, 'Annual Report on the Health of Worthing for the Year 1968', p.52.
13 West Sussex County Health Department, The Frail, Sick and Demented Elderly in West Sussex, unpublished report, 1969, p.6.
14 D.W.K. Kay, P. Beamish and M. Roth, Old Age Mental Disorders in Newcastle Upon Tyne, 'British Journal of Psychiatry', 110, 1964, p.153.
15 West Sussex County Health Department, op.cit., Appendix I, p.13.
16 P. Sainsbury, W.R. Costain and Jacqueline Grad, The Effects of Community Service on the Referral and Admission Rates of Elderly Psychiatric Patients, in 'Psychiatric Disorders of the Aged', Report on the Symposium held by the World Psychiatric Association at the Royal College of Physicians, London, 28-30 September 1965, published by Geigy (UK) Ltd., Manchester (no date).
17 B. Abel-Smith and R. Titmuss, 'The Cost of the National Health Service', NIESR, Occasional Papers, XVIII, CUP, 1956.
18 Sainsbury, Costain and Grad, op. cit., p.29.
19 Communication.
20 B. Abel-Smith and R.M. Titmuss, The Cost of the National Health Service in England and Wales, National Institute of Economic and Social Research Occasional Papers, no.18, Cambridge, 1956, p.140.
21 Sainsbury, Costain and Grad, op. cit., p.31.
22 J. Grad and P. Sainsbury, An Evaluation of the Effects of Caring for the Aged at Home in Psychiatric Disorders in the Aged, 'Reports on the Symposium Held by World Psychiatric Association at the Royal College of Physicians, London, 28-30 September 1965, published by Geigy (UK) Ltd., Manchester, p.235.
23 J. Grad and P. Sainsbury, The Effects That Patients Have on their Families in a Community Care and Control Psychiatric Service - A Two Year Follow-up, 'British Journal of Psychiatry', 114, 1968, p.277.
24 Ibid., p.269, Table VII.
25 Ibid., p.277. Though Grad and Sainsbury say that their conclusions are not necessarily a condemnation of community care as long as adequate supportive services are available to the families. Whether or not such services are available in the resorts will be discussed in Chapter 16.
26 County Borough of Eastbourne, 'The Health of Eastbourne', 1969, pp.50-1.
27 Ministry of Health, op. cit., p.50.

CHAPTER 15 HOUSING AND RESIDENTIAL HOMES: PUBLIC VERSUS PRIVATE PROVISION

1 See Appendix 1, Table A1.40.
2 See ibid., Table A1.40.
3 Chartered Institute of Public Finance and Accountancy, 'Local Health and Social Services Statistics 1972-73', November 1974.
4 Under Part III of the National Assistance Act 1948, County, County Borough and London Borough Councils have a duty to provide residential accommodation for people who by reason of age, infirmity or any other circumstances are in need of care and attention which is not otherwise available to them. Local authorities may provide this accommodation in homes managed by themselves or in homes run by voluntary organizations by arrangement with them. This accommodation is frequently referred to as Part III accommodation.
5 Department of Health, 'Development of Community Care, Revision to 1975-6', Cmnd. 3022, London, HMSO, 1966, pp.22-3.
6 Department of Health, 'Health and Welfare: The Development of Community Care', London, HMSO, 1963, p.2.
7 See Appendix 1, Table A1.41.
8 See Appendix 1, Tables A1.41 and A1.42 and compare local authority and joint-user provision in 1970 and 1974, especially for Brighton, Eastbourne, Essex and Somerset.
9 In those counties where the exchange system is used.
10 There is therefore no point in trying to use the lengths of waiting lists in various resorts as a measure of the quality of the service being provided there; they are meaningless.
11 See Appendix 1, Table A1.42.
12 Private homes have to be registered under Section 37 of the National Assistance Act 1948. They may accommodate the aged and infirm who need looking after but may not provide actual nursing care.
13 See Appendix 1, Table A1.42.
14 Private nursing homes differ from private homes in that they provide nursing facilities and are registered under Section 187 of the Public Health Act 1936.
15 Information kindly supplied by R.E. Irvine, Physician Superintendent of St Helen's Hospital, Hastings. (The figures exclude deaths and discharges when the destination was unknown.)
16 Information kindly supplied by R.W. Parnell and D.M. Keating, North Birmingham District Hospital, Sutton Coldfield.

17 Dr R B Franks, in Borough of Worthing, 'Annual Report on the Health of Worthing for the Year 1966', p.62.
18 K.O.A. Vickery, Post Retirement and Later Days, 'Royal Society of Health Journal', vol.89, no.4, July-August 1969, p.85.
19 Rents, like house prices, vary from one resort to another. In East Sussex Eastbourne has the most expensive private homes, with Brighton, Hove and Bexhill next, while those in Hastings and St Leonards are rather noticeably cheaper.
20 Communication.
21 These are very numerous. See Appendix 1, Table A1.10.
22 Communication.
23 The subject of conditions in private homes has been discussed extensively by P. Townsend in 'The Last Refuge', London, Routledge & Kegan Paul, 1962; by C. Woodroffe and P. Townsend in 'Nursing Homes in England and Wales: a study of public responsibility', London, National Corporation for the Care of Old People, 1961; and in another NCCOP publication, 'Private Homes for Old People', London, NCCOP, 1967; there is no need to discuss it at length here. We may note, however, that all these found very variable conditions and a situation of very inadequate inspection and assistance by the Health and Welfare authorities. Similar comments were made by officers in the resorts.
24 Devon Council, 'The County Welfare Services in Devon', 1948-68, p.30.

CHAPTER 16 COMMUNITY HEALTH AND DOMICILIARY SERVICES

1 W.P.D. Logan and A.A. Cushion, 'Morbidity Statistics from General Practice Volume 1. Studies on Medical and Population Subjects, No.14, London, HMSO, 1958, p.56, Table 5A.
2 Information kindly supplied by the Department of Health and Social Security.
3 Communication.
4 L.P. Robinson, L.M. Mackenzie and A.A. Gregory, 'Problems of the Elderly in a Seaside Resort and Retirement Area, unpublished paper to the Royal Society of Health Sessional Meeting, Southport, 1966, p.5.
5 Communication.
6 This is the prevailing view. If the consultancy rate of elderly people is nearly twice that of younger people it is difficult to see how $42\frac{1}{2}$p added on the

Notes to Chapters 16 and 17

£1.10 basic capitation fee can adequately reflect the additional work involved for an elderly patient.
7 See above, p.100.
8 Audrey Hunt, 'The Home Help Service in England and Wales', Government Social Survey, London, HMSO, 1970, p.405.
9 The material was kindly provided by Audrey Hunt and the Office of Population Censuses and Surveys, Social Survey Division with the permission of the Department of Health and Social Security on whose behalf the survey of the home help service was carried out.
10 Including Cornwall, Devon, Somerset and Dorset.
11 See Appendix 1, Table A1.44.
12 East Sussex County Council, 'The Health of the Community', 1968, p.58.
13 Nationally, 80 per cent of home helps are aged 35-59, and 85 per cent of married or widowed home helps belong to the manual working classes and 93 per cent to Classes III, IV and V (Hunt, op. cit., p.33).
14 A. Harris, 'Social Welfare of the Elderly', Government Social Survey, HMSO, 1968, vol.1, p.73.
15 Cf. Borough of Worthing, 'Annual Report on the Health of Worthing for the Year 1966', p.68.
16 For a discussion of these attempts see A. Harris, 'Social Welfare of the Elderly', Government Social Survey, London, HMSO, 1968, vol.1, pp.14-16.
17 County Borough of Eastbourne, 'Annual Report of the Medical Officer of Health for 1966', p.48.
18 County Borough of Hastings, 'Annual Report of the M.O.H. and Chief Welfare Officer', 1967, p.42.
19 Hunt, op. cit., p.28.
20 See Appendix 1, Table A1.45.
21 Department of Health and Social Security, 'Annual Report 1969', Cmnd. 4462, London, HMSO, September 1970, p.189.
22 Cf. Borough of Worthing, 'Annual Report on the Health of Worthing for the Year 1965', p.54.
23 Harris, op. cit., vol.1, p.60.
24 Department of Health and Social Security, op. cit., p.189.
25 See Appendix 1, Table A1.47.

CHAPTER 17 PAYING FOR SERVICES FOR THE ELDERLY

1 Unless otherwise stated financial information in this chapter is drawn from the annual reports of CIPFA (IMTA) on 'The Return of Rates'.

2   Department of the Environment, 'Rates and Rateable Values in England and Wales 1973-74', London, HMSO, 1974.
3   Ibid. See Appendix 5 for a list of authorities included in this analysis.
4   Department of the Environment, 'Rates and Rateable Values in England and Wales 1970-71', London, HMSO, 1972.
5   Cf. V.A. Karn, Retiring to the Seaside - A Study of Retirement Migration in England and Wales, unpublished PhD Thesis, University of Birmingham, June 1974, Ch. 17.
6   See Appendix 5 for a list of the authorities included in this analysis.
7   Southport, which has become part of Sefton, metropolitan district. It is excluded from this analysis because the new authority cannot now be regarded predominantly as a 'resort' area.
8   Expenditure on education in 1974-5 is not comparable with previous years because local authorities no longer had to bear 90 per cent of the cost of mandatory awards to students.
9   Department of Environment, 'The Rate Support Grant', Cmnd. 5532, London, HMSO, January 1974.
10 Department of the Environment, 'The Future Shape of Local Government Finance', Cmnd. 4741, London, HMSO, 1971, p.40, para. 4.18.
11 Ibid., p.41, para. 4.21.
12 Department of Environment, 'The Rate Support Grants for 1975-6 for England and Wales', London, HMSO, 1975.
13 Wynne Godley and John Rhodes, The Rate Support Grant System, unpublished paper, Department of Applied Economics, University of Cambridge, 1972.
14 Op. cit., p.42, para. 4.26.
15 Department of the Environment, 'Rate Rebates in England and Wales, 1972-73', London, HMSO, 1974.
16 In all areas, further large proportions of elderly people have their rates paid by the Supplementary Benefits Commission.

CHAPTER 18   RETIREMENT TO THE SEASIDE: SUCCESS OR FAILURE?

1   E.g. Julian Mounter, Enter Holiday-makers; Exit Old People, 'The Times', 10 April 1967: 'The elderly come for the sea breeze, because "Aunt Jane lived here", because some son (I'm not sure where he lives now, but he will write soon; he always writes at Christmas) thinks it a suitable place to farm out a tiresome old mother.'

2 D.L. Spence, E.M. Feizenbaum, F. Fitzgerald and J. Roth, Medical Student Attitudes Toward the Geriatric Patient, 'Journal of the American Geriatric Society', vol.16, no.9, September 1968, p.979.
3 Simone de Beauvoir, 'Old Age', London, Andre Deutsch and Weidenfeld & Nicolson, 1972, p.265.
4 Ibid., p. 264.
5 C. Tibbitts, Retirement Problems in American Society, 'American Journal of Sociology', vol.59, no.4, January 1954, pp.305-6.
6 Anthony Whitehead, In the Service of Old Age, 'The Welfare of Psycho-geriatric Patients', Harmondsworth, Penguin Books, 1970, p.16.
7 See Chapter 2.
8 H.W. Mellor, Going to Live at the Seaside, 'Guardian', 20 May 1961.
9 In the report by the Countryside Commission, 'Coastal Recreation and Holidays, Special Study Reports', London, HMSO, 1969, retirement to the coast is mentioned only once in seven words on page 5.
10 Cf. British Tourist Authority, 'Visitors to Bexhill 1964' (unpublished). Quoted by kind permission of Bexhill Corporation.

APPENDIX 3   THE SAMPLING METHOD AND RESPONSE

1 A survey for the study by Amelia I. Harris, 'Social Welfare for the Elderly', Government Social Survey, HMSO, 1968. Thanks are due to Amelia Harris and the Government Social Survey for supplying unpublished material from this study.
2 It did emerge from the random sample that retired people were slightly more likely to live in the areas of more expensive housing, and to have omitted the other areas would have introduced very severe bias.

Selected bibliography

GENERAL REFERENCES ON OLD PEOPLE AND RETIREMENT

CUMMING, E. and HENRY, W. (1961), 'Growing Old: The Process of Disengagement', New York: Basic Books.
DONAHUE, W. (ed.) (1954), 'Housing the Aging', Ann Arbor: University of Michigan Press.
HAINES, K.J. and RAVEN, J. (1966), Old People: Study of Living Patterns, 'Architectural Journal', 26 October.
'JOURNAL OF SOCIAL ISSUES' (1958), vol.14, no.2; whole volume on different aspects of retirement.
LYNNE-SMITH, T. (ed.) (1951), 'Problems of America's Aging Population', Gainesville: University of Florida Press.
MARTIN, J. and DORAN, A. (1966), Evidence Concerning the Relationship between Health and Retirement, 'Sociological Review', vol.14, no.3, November.
ROSE, A.M. (1962),The Sub-culture of the Aging: A Topic for Sociological Research, 'The Gerontologist', vol.2, no.3, September.
ROSE, A.M. (1964), A Current Theoretical Issue in Social Gerontology, 'The Gerontologist', vol.4, no.1, May.
ROSE, A.M. and PETERSON, W.A. (eds) (1965), 'Older People and their Social World', Oxford: Blackwell Scientific Publication.
SHANAS, E. et al. (1968), 'Old People in Three Industrial Societies', London: Routledge & Kegan Paul.
SHENFIELD, B.E. (1957), 'Social Policies for Old Age', London: Routledge & Kegan Paul.
TIBBITTS, C. (1960), 'Handbook of Social Gerontology: Societal Aspects of Aging', University of Chicago Press.
TIBBITTS, C. and DONAHUE, W. (eds) (1962), 'Social and Psychological Aspects of Aging', New York: Columbia University Press.
TOWNSEND, P. (1957), 'The Family Life of Old People', London: Routledge & Kegan Paul.

TOWNSEND, P. and WEDDERBURN, D. (1965), 'The Aged in the Welfare State', London: Bell & Sons.
TUCKMAN, J. and LAVELL, M. (1957), Self-classification as Old or Not Old, 'Geriatrics', vol.12, pp.666-71.
TUNSTALL, J. (1966), 'Old and Alone', London: Routledge & Kegan Paul.
WILLMOTT, P. and YOUNG, M. (1960), 'Family and Class in a London Suburb', London: Routledge & Kegan Paul.
WILSON, R.L. (1960), 'Urban Living Qualities from the Vantage Point of the Elderly', Institute for Research in Social Science, University of W. Carolina.

RETIREMENT MIGRATION IN BRITAIN

BARR, J. (1965), For Old People Only, 'New Society', 25 November.
BELL, C.R. (1968), 'Middle Class Families, Social and Geographical Mobility', London: Routledge & Kegan Paul.
GILBERT, E.W. (1939), The Growth of Inland and Seaside Health Resorts in England, 'Scottish Geographical Magazine', vol.55.
GORDON, I.R. (1975), 'The Retirement Industry in the South West', London, Department of the Environment for the South West Economic Planning Council.
GREATER LONDON COUNCIL HOUSING DEPT, Seaside Bungalows Study, unpublished report in six parts.
HARRIS, A. (1966), 'Labour Mobility in Great Britain 1953-63', Government Social Survey, London: HMSO, Appendix VIII: Moving House by Elderly People.
JACKSON, J.A. (ed.) (1969), 'Migration', CUP Sociological Studies 2, Cambridge University Press.
LAW, C.M. and WARNES, A.M. (1973), The Movement of Retired People to Seaside Resorts: A Study of Morecombe and Llandudno, 'Town Planning Review', vol.44, no.4, October, p.373.
LEMON, A. (1973), Retirement and its Effect on Small Towns, 'Town Planning Review', vol.44, no.3, July, p.254.
MELLOR, H.W. (1962-3), Retirement to the Coast, 'Town Planning Review', no.34, April.
ROBINSON, L.P., MACKENZIE, L.M. and GREGORY, A.A. (1966), Problems of the Elderly in a Seaside Resort and Retirement Areas, unpublished paper to the Royal Society of Health Sessional Meeting, Southport, 1966.
SOUTH WEST ECONOMIC PLANNING COUNCIL (1975), 'Retirement to the Southwest', London, HMSO.
VICKERY, K.O.A. (1969), Post Retirement and Later Days, 'Royal Society of Health Journal', vol.89, no.4, July-August.

THE ECONOMIC CIRCUMSTANCES OF OLD PEOPLE

ATKINSON, A.B. (1969), 'Poverty in Britain and the Reform of Social Security', University of Cambridge Department of Applied Economics, Occasional Papers 18, Cambridge University Press.
COLE, D. and UTTING, J. (1962), 'The Economic Circumstances of Old People', Occasional Papers in Social Administration, no.4, Welwyn: Codicote Press.
MINISTRY OF PENSIONS AND NATIONAL INSURANCE (1954), 'Reasons for Retiring or Continuing at Work', London: HMSO.
MINISTRY OF PENSIONS AND NATIONAL INSURANCE (1966), 'Financial and Other Circumstances of Retirement Pensioners', London: HMSO.

HOUSING AND SOCIAL SERVICES FOR THE ELDERLY

CONSUMERS ASSOCIATION (1969), Arrangements for Old Age, 'Which', London.
DAVIES, B. (1968), 'Social Needs and Resources in Local Services', London: Michael Joseph.
HARRIS, A.I. (1968), 'Social Welfare of the Elderly', Government Social Survey, London: HMSO, vols. 1 and 2.
HOLE, W.V. and ALLEN, P.G. (1962), Dwellings for Old People, 'Architects Journal', vol.94, 9 May, pp. 1017-26.
HOLE, W.V. and ALLEN, P.G. (1964), Rehousing Old People, 'Architects Journal', vol. Aa3, 8 January, pp.75-82.
'HOUSING REVIEW' (1970), Housing Old People, reference sheet, 'Housing Review', vol.19, November-December, pp.159-60.
MELLOR, H., SMITH, R. and KARN, V. (1973), 'Housing in Retirement', London: NCCOP/Bedford Square Press.
PAGE, D. and MUIR, T. (1971), 'New Housing for the Elderly', London: Bedford Square Press or the National Corporation for the Care of Old People.
RICHARDSON, T.M. (1964), 'Age and Need, A Study of Older People in North Eastern Scotland', London: Livingstone.
ROBERTS, N. (1970), 'Our Future Selves', Services for the Elderly, London: Allen & Unwin.
SUMNER, G. and SMITH, R. (1969), 'Planning for Local Authority Services for the Elderly', University of Glasgow, Social and Economic Studies, no.17, London: Allen & Unwin.
TOWNSEND, P. (1962), 'The Last Refuge', London: Routledge & Kegan Paul.
WHITEHEAD, A. (1970), 'In the Service of Old Age: The Welfare of Psycho-Geriatric Patients', Harmondsworth: Penguin.

RETIREMENT MIGRATION IN THE USA

ALDRIDGE, G.J. (1959), Informal Social Relationships in a Retirement Community, 'Marriage and Family Living', no.21.

BARKER, M.B. (1966), 'California Retirement Communities', Berkeley: University of California.

BARR, P. (1968), Free Enterprise Aging, 'New Society', vol.12, no.313, 26 September.

BULTENA, G.L. and DOUGLAS, D.G. (1970), Family Patterns of Migrant and Non-Migrant Retirees, 'Journal of Marriage and the Family', vol.32, no.1.

BURGESS, E.W. (1954), Social Relations, Activities and Personal Adjustment, 'American Journal of Sociology', 1953-4, January.

BURGESS, E.W. (ed.) (1961), 'Retirement Villages', Ann Arbor: University of Michigan Press.

HARLAN, W.H. (1954), Community Adaptations to the Presence of Aged Persons: St Petersburg, Florida, 'American Journal of Sociology', 1953-4, January.

HOYT, G.C. (1954), The Life of the Retired in a Trailer Park, 'American Journal of Sociology', January.

KLEEMEIER, R.W. (1956), An Analysis of Patterns for Group Living for Older People, in I.L. Webber (ed.) 'Aging, A Current Appraisal', Gainesville: University of Florida Press.

KLEEMEIER, R.W. (ed.) (1961), 'Aging and Leisure', Oxford University Press.

LYNNE-SMITH, T. (ed.) (1952), 'Living in the Later Years', Gainesville: University of Florida Press.

MANLEY, C.R. (1954), The Migration of Older People, 'American Journal of Sociology', 1953-4, January.

WEBBER, I.L. (1954), The Organized Social Life of the Retired: Two Florida Communities, 'American Journal of Sociology', January.

Index

Chapters 3-13 are almost entirely concerned with elderly people in Bexhill and Clacton. The topics covered in these chapters are not therefore indexed under the town names but under the subjects concerned.

Abel-Smith, B. and Titmus, R., 368
Age, 66-9, 78, 79
    and children, 71, 75-6, 78
    differences of married couples, 67
    and health and social services, 103, 106, 231
    and income, 122-3
    and number of retirement moves, 157
    at retirement from work, 39, 40, 42, 89, 157; and ability to make new friends, 89; and number of moves, 157
Air pollution, 49-50
Anglesey, 17
Annuities, 153, 365
Atkinson, A.B., 363, 364
Attitudes
    to elderly people, 238-41
    of retired people: to living with other elderly people, 93-8, 360; to pre-retirement area and house, 46-8; to retirement from work, 38; to young people, 93-5
    to retirement resorts, 238-41

Bahamas, 4
Barker, M., 352
Bath, 11, 14
Beauvoir, Simone de, 238-9, 373
Bell, C.R., 359
Bexhill
    growth of, 6-7
    Housing Register, cases on, 141-4, 195
    local authority housing in, 194
    location of, 6
    origins of movers to, 27, 28-9
    Senior Citizens Club, 105, 115, 234, 362
    social class in, 7, 362
    tourist industry in, 7-8
Birmingham, 27, 187, 198, 199
Blackpool, 12, 19, 21, 25, 27, 69, 218
    health and social services

in, 195, 197, 203, 208,
209, 210, 213
Bognor Regis, 12, 14, 33,
189
Bournemouth, 12, 25, 69,
218
  health and social
    services in, 187, 195,
    197, 198, 204, 207, 208,
    209, 211, 212, 213
Bowls, 110
Breconshire, 17
Bridlington, 21
Brighton, 12, 14, 19, 25,
28, 218
  health and social
    services in, 194, 195,
    197, 198, 208, 209, 210,
    211, 212, 213
British Travel and Holidays
  Association (British
  Tourist Authority), 54,
  357, 373
Brothers and sisters, 76,
  78, 83, 100, 106
Budleigh Salterton, 33, 34
Bultena, G.L. and Marshall,
  D.G., 356, 359
Bungalows, 7, 46, 50, 51,
  53, 54, 56, 129, 130,
  149
  desire for, 151, 164,
    165
  prices of, 137-8
  rates of, 140
Bungalows-by-the-Sea Scheme
  (GLC), 2, 84, 107, 134,
  174, 176, 246, 360, 362,
  364, 366

Caermarthenshire, 17
Caernarvonshire, 17, 19
Cardiganshire, 17, 19
Car ownership, 109
Cartwright, A., 361
Change, desire for, 52, 55
Cheltenham, 11, 14
Cheyne, G. 22, 353

Chichester, 186, 187, 188,
189
Childlessness, 40-1, 42, 71,
78, 190
Children, small, attitude of
  elderly to living near,
  94; see also Sons and
  daughters
Chiropody, 102, 104, 235
Church attendance, 100, 112
Cinema attendance, 110
Clacton
  Darby and Joan club, 105
  growth of, 6-7
  location of, 6
  origins of movers to,
    28-9
  rate rebates in, 228
  social class in, 7, 362
  tourist industry in, 7-8
Climate, 12, 22, 49, 57,
  58-9, 166, 176
Club attendance, 108, 112-18,
  362
Coastal resorts, see Retirement resorts
Cole, D. and Utting, J., 363,
  364
Communities
  balanced, 96
  homogeneous, 96-8
  small, 86
Community care, 188, 190-2,
  206, 211, 212, 231-2
Community health and domiciliary services, see
  Health and social
  services
Commuting, 6, 38, 39
Conflicting interests in
  coastal areas, 247-8
Cornwall, 16, 21, 22, 210
Council housing, see Housing
Countryside, 19, 25, 160,
  175-6
Countryside Commission, 354,
  373
Cribier, F., 352
Cromer, 33

Daughters, 77; see also Sons and daughters
Davies, B., 367
Dawlish, 33
Death rates, 69
Denbighshire, 17
Devas, M.B. and Irvine, R.E., 367
Devon, 16, 19, 21, 22, 27, 33, 145
 health and social services in, 197, 210, 213
Dissatisfaction with retirement move, 172-3
 reasons for, 175-7
Doctors, see General practitioners
Dodd, P., 362
Domestic help, see Home helps
Domiciliary services, see Health and social services
Dorset, 16, 27, 196, 204
Droitwich, 14

East Anglia, 25, 26
Eastbourne, 8, 14, 19, 27, 28, 33, 56, 69, 148, 218
 health and social services in, 191-2, 194, 195, 197, 198, 205, 207, 208, 210, 212, 213,
 house prices in, 137-8, 150
East Coast, 22, 23
Education, expenditure on in resorts, 221-2
Emergencies, help in, 99-101
Employment
 of elderly people, 38-9, 42
 situation in resorts, 215
Environment
 of pre-retirement home, 47-8
 seaside, 49-50, 111, 174-5; cost of upkeep of, 224
Epsom, 11, 14
Essex, 19, 21, 22, 27, 28, 29, 32, 56, 177
 health and social services in, 196, 203, 204, 207, 210, 212
Evening classes, 112, 115
Exmouth, 27

Family Expenditure Survey, 123, 362, 364
Family type of retired people, 70-9; see also Household characteristics of retired people, Sons and daughters
Financial position of retired people, 120-8
Financial problems
 of hotel and nursing home charges, 147, 199-200
 of house and garden maintenance, 46, 50, 131-2, 158
Flats
 ground floor, rents of, 144, 150
 moves into, 164, 165
 ownership of, 129-30
 prices of, 137-8
 proportion of retired people living in, 129; converted and purpose-built, 129, 130, 154
 rates of, 140
Flintshire, 17, 19
France, 3
Friendliness in resorts, 86
Friends and relations
 contact with, 84-5
 dependence on, 96, 97, 106, 191
 encouraging to move, 84, 177-8
 help from, 99, 106

making new, 85-9
moving to join, 51, 57, 58, 159-60, 166
proximity of, 97, 175
Frinton, 21, 33, 204

Gans, H., 96, 215, 361
Gardening
contractors, 131
as leisure activity, 54, 55, 108, 157
problems of, 46, 131-4, 159, 165-6
Gardner, M.J., Crawford, M.O. and Morris, J.N., 353
General practitioners, 100, 101-3, 203-6, 213, 233-4
Geriatric beds, shortage of in resorts, 186-8
effect of, 186-8, 205, 211, 212, 236
Germany, 3
Gilbert, E.W., 353
Godley, W. and Rhodes, J., 372
Gordon, I., 366
Gould, P.R. and White, R.R., 353, 354
Grant
central government, 224
Rate Support, 217, 224, 225-8, 229-30
Greater London Council Bungalows-by-the-Sea Scheme, 2, 84, 107, 134, 174, 176, 360, 362, 364, 366
Ground rents, 139

Haines, K.J. and Raven, J., 360
Hampshire, 16, 27, 197
Harris, A., 211, 355, 356, 357, 361, 367
Harrogate, 11, 14

Hastings, 12, 13, 14, 28, 33, 69, 218, 227
health and social services in, 194, 195, 197, 198, 208, 211, 212
Health
and reasons for leaving work, 37
and reasons for moving, 49
of retired people in resorts, 89, 102, 116, 174, 176
Health and social services
expenditure on, 5, 218-21, 229
greater need for in resorts, 106
planning of, 235
provision of, 184-214, 233-7
reorganization of, 235-6
use of, 101-6
voluntarily provided, 234-5
see also individual services
Health visitors
provision of, 212-13, 234
visits by, 102, 105
Herne Bay, 19, 21, 27, 228
Hobbies, 108, 112-14; see also Gardening
Hole, W.V., 360
Holiday industry in resorts, 7-8, 34, 247
Holiday-makers, 28, 34
Holiday resorts, see Retirement resorts and under individual resorts
Holidays (seaside), 7, 12-13, 53-4, 59
decline of, 149, 154
identification with retirement, 53, 59
Home helps
provision of, 206-9, 213, 234

treatment of, 34
use of, 102, 104-5, 131;
private, 102, 105, 131
Home nurses
provision of, 211-12, 213, 234
visits by, 102, 105
Honeymoons in resorts, 55
Hospital facilities in resorts, 186-90, 233
effects of shortage of, 186-90, 205, 211, 236
unusual need for, 190-3
Hospital out-patients clinics, use of, 102, 105
Hospitals, discharges from, 198
Hotels and boarding houses, 4, 7, 13, 39, 149
as residential accommodation for the elderly, 145-50, 154, 199-201
House, attitude to location of, 47-8, 166, 177
Household characteristics of retired people, 70-9
and desire to move, 167
and tenure, 136
House prices
in London, 51, 138
in resorts, 34, 55, 56, 57, 124, 136-8, 150; and choice of resort, 137-8; and incomes of retired people, 136-7
House size, 130, 164, 165
attitudes to, 130-4, 149, 158
Housework, problems with, 46, 50, 131-3, 133, 165
Housing, 43-8, 129-55, 160, 194-6
attitudes to size and maintenance of, 43-4, 46, 130-4, 149, 158
local authority, 45, 141-5, 151, 194-6, 234; expenditure on, 219-20, 222

situation of private tenants, 141-5
tenure, 44-6, 135-6
tied, 44, 51
Housing associations, 2, 151-2, 234, 365
Housing Register
in Bexhill, 141-4
disqualification from, 142, 145, 151, 195
Hove, 12, 13, 14, 28, 69

Incomes of retired people, 90, 104, 109, 120-9, 136, 140-1, 144, 215, 216, 229, 232
and rates, 140-1, 216, 227-8
related to marital status and sex, 121-2
sources of, 126-7
and tenure, 136, 144
Institutional care, unusual need for in resorts, 190
Isle of Wight, 15, 16
health and social services in, 196, 197, 207, 208, 210
Isolation
of retired people, 34, 90; and club membership, 117-18; in country, 160; health and social services, 232; and loneliness, 90
types of, 81

Kay, D.W.K., Beamish, P. and Roth, M., 189, 368
Kent, 16, 21, 27, 28, 29, 32, 177, 207, 208
Kleemeier, R.W., 80, 119, 360

Lake District, 22
Lancashire, 19, 21, 22, 25, 27, 30, 31

health and social services in, 197, 362
Land in resorts, 7, 152, 154, 247
Leisure
activities of retired people in resorts, 107-19
facilities, dissatisfaction with, 176
Lincolnshire, 21
Lipset, S.M. and Bendix, R., 359
Littlehampton, 107
Living alone, 77, 78
and attitude to size of house, 130-1
club membership, 115
help in emergencies, 100
loneliness, 92
proximity of relations, 76
telephone ownership, 90
Loans, see Mortgages
Local authority housing, see Housing
Location of retirement areas, see Retirement areas
London, 22, 25, 26, 27, 28, 29, 30, 31, 43, 51, 56, 176, 218, 235
health and social services in, 197, 198
Loneliness, 90, 92
and attitude to moving, 159, 167-8, 173, 178; see also Isolation
Lowenthal, D., 354
Lyme Regis, 204
Lytham St Annes, 21, 27

Macpherson, R.K., Ofner, F. and Walsh, J.A., 353
Maintenance of house and garden, 43-4, 45, 46, 50, 55
attitudes towards, 130-4, 149, 158
cost of, 46, 50, 130-2, 158
relationship to income and marital status, 132
Malvern, 14
Margate, 12, 21
Marital status, 67-70
and ability to make new friends, 88
and age, 66-7
and childlessness, 71, 78
and contact with relations, 81, 83; proximity of, 73, 76
and encouraging friends to join them, 178
and help in emergencies, 100-1
and hospital referrals, 189-90, 191
and income, 121-3, 126
and leisure activities, 108, 110, 114, 115, 118
and living alone, 77, 78
and living in hotels, 146-7
and loneliness, 90-2
and maintenance of house, 132-3
and number of retirement moves, 156-7, 163
Married couples
age differences between, 66, 67
childlessness amongst, 71
family characteristics of, 70-9
isolation of, 101
proportions of in resorts, 67, 78
social life of, 88-9
see also Marital status
Meals services
provision of, 209-10, 213, 234; voluntary, 210, 235
use of, 102, 105
Media, attitudes towards retirement resorts, 238-41

Mediterranean resorts, 3, 4
Mellor, H., 352, 373
Melvyn Howe, G., 353
Mencher, S., 361
Merionethshire, 17
Merseyside, 25, 30, 198
Midlands, The, 21, 26, 28, 29, 30
Migration
  out of rural areas, 19
  rate to seaside areas, 16-19
  see also Moves, Retirement moves
Mobility, see Migration, Moves, Retirement moves
Montgomeryshire, 17
Morecombe, 228
Mortgages, 45, 138, 150
Mounter, J., 365, 372
Move
  desire to, 165
  expectation of further, 165
  inability to, 165, 171
  reasons for wanting to, 165-8
Move, the retirement, see Retirement moves
Moves, by elderly people, 24
  distance of, 24, 156, 157-8, 160
  frequency of, 24, 156-68
  out of cities, 30-31
  out of resorts, 66-9, 170-1
  pre-retirement, 43
  rapid, 160, 161-3
  reasons for, 49-57, 158-68
  see also Retirement moves
Moves, by young people from resorts and rural areas, 19

National Corporation for the Care of Old People, 352

National Parks Commission, 355
Natural increase in resorts, 19
Neighbours, help from, 99
Norfolk, 16, 22, 56
  health and social services in, 207, 210, 212
Nursing homes, 198-202, 234

Office of Health Economics, 361
Open space, lack of in cities, 47, 48, 50
Owner-occupiers (elderly)
  ability to move, 45
  financial problems of, 153, 154
  in flats, 45-6, 129-30
  lack of access to council housing, 145, 151
  maintenance problems for, 130-4
  and marital status, 135
  in pre-retirement home, 44-5
  proportions of in resorts, 135, 150
  reluctance to go into housing associations, 151
  sources of finance, 45, 138-9, 150

Page, D. and Muir, T., 360
Parks, use of, 110
Part III accommodation, 369; see also Residential homes for the elderly
Pensions, 15, 123, 126, 128, 363
Pimlott, J.A.R., 353
Poole, 204
Portugal, 3, 4
Preference
  for living with own age groups, 93
  for living with young people, 93-5; and desire to move, 173

Private homes for the elderly, see Residential homes for the elderly
Private patients, 103-4
Private provision of services, 106, 232-3
Private renting, 44, 45-6
Psychiatric beds, provision of in resorts, 188-92, 232, 235
Public expenditure
  cuts in, 217
  in resorts, 218-30;
  pressure to keep down, 222, 229
Public houses, use of, 110

Radio, use of, 109
Radnorshire, 17
Rail services, 12
Rateable values in resorts, 216, 227-9
Ratepayers associations, 222, 229
Rates, 50, 51, 139-41, 150, 217-18
  average for domestic property, 217-18
  and incomes, 140-1, 365
  in London, 51
  rebates, 217, 229, 230, 237
  worry over, 50, 51, 158
Rate Support Grant, see Grants, Rate Support
Relatives
  encouraging to move to resort, 84, 177-8
  help from, 100, 126
  moving to be with, 159, 160, 175
Rent allowances, 145, 147
Rents, 144
  ground, 139
Reorganization of local government and health services, 217, 221, 235-6

Residential homes for the elderly, 196-202, 233
  control of standards in, 200-1
  discharges from hospital into, 198-9
Residential preferences, surveys of, 22-3
Resorts, development of in nineteenth century, 11-13
Retirement
  age of, 15, 36
  ideas about, 52-6, 239-41
  reasons for, 15, 37-8
  usefulness in, 239-41
Retirement areas, distribution of, 15-23; see also Retirement resorts
Retirement communities, 1, 97
  abroad, 2-4
Retirement industry, 4
Retirement moves
  between resorts, 28, 29, 31
  directions of moves, 25-9
  effect on contact with relations and friends, 81-4
  international, 2-4
  number of, 156-68
  reasons for, 5, 49-57
  satisfaction with, 169-79
  scale of, 30-2
  subsequent, see number of
  timing of, 5, 39, 51
Retirement resorts
  abroad, 2-4
  choice of, 56-7, 137;
  reasons for, 57-61
  growth of, 11-15, 78-9
  location of, 2-4, 20-3;
  see also Retirement areas
Retirement 'specials', 2, 3
Retirement villages, 1, 2-3
Roberts, G., 11
Robinson, L.P., Mackenzie, L.M. and Gregory, A.A., 367

Rosow, I., 97, 98, 367
Royal Leamington Spa, 11, 14
Royal patronage of spas, 12
Royal Tunbridge Wells, 11, 14
Russell, Dr Richard, 11

Sainsbury, P., Costain, W.R. and Grad, J., 190, 368
St Leonards, 12
St Tropez, 12
Satisfaction with retirement move, 169-79
  reasons for, 174-5
Savings, 15, 125-8, 138-9, 141, 153
Scarborough, 11, 12, 21
Sea-bathing, 11
Sea-front, 110, 111, 119
Seaside, desire to live at, 52, 174
Seaton, 33, 34
Sex differences
  and church attendance, 112
  and club attendance, 114
  and housing maintenance problems, 132-3
  and income levels, 121-3
  and leisure activities, 108, 110
  and movers out of resorts, 66-9
  and private tenants and hotel residents, 141, 146
  see also Women
Shanas, E., 36, 37, 54, 355, 356, 357, 358, 360, 362, 363, 364
Sheltered housing, 151-2, 154, 195-6
Siblings, see Brothers and sisters
Sidmouth, 27, 33, 34, 69
Sillitoe, K.K., 362
Single people
  age of, 66-7; at time of move, 40
  attitudes to house, 131, 132, 133
  isolation of, 101
  leisure activities of, 108
  moves to be with relatives and friends, 58
  proportion of in resorts, 69-70
  relationship with brothers and sisters, 76, 83
  social class of, 70
  tenure, 135-6, 141
  see also Marital status
Snobbishness, 87, 362
Social activities, see Leisure, Social life of retired people
Social class
  and children, 41, 73, 74, 81-3
  and church and club attendance, 112, 114, 115
  and income, 121-2
  and marital status, 67, 70
  and number of moves, 163
  of population in resorts, 33-5
  and retirement age, 36-7
  and tenure, 44, 136
  and use of services, 104
Social life of retired people, 80-98, 107-19; see also Friends and relations, Sons and daughters, Clubs, etc.
  and satisfaction with move, 174, 176
Social services, see Health and social services, and under individual services
Somerset, 16, 19, 27
  health and social services in, 211, 212
Sons and daughters
  accompanying parents on move, 40, 42
  contact with, 81

help from, 100
  moving to live nearer,
    41, 75-6, 175
  numbers of, 40-1, 71
  proximity of, 71, 76,
    77, 78
Southampton, 21
South Coast, 19, 21, 22, 56,
    137, 149, 150
  health and social
    services on, 198, 206-7
South East of England, 25,
    26, 27, 28, 31, 183
Southend, 12, 21, 69, 218
  health and social
    services in, 195, 197,
    203, 207, 208, 209, 213
Southport, 12, 27, 227
  health and social
    services in, 194, 195,
    197, 198, 203, 204, 205,
    208, 209, 210, 211, 213
South West of England, 21,
    22, 25, 26, 31
Southwold, 33, 34
Spas, 11, 13-15
Spence, D.L., Feizenbaum,
    F.F. and Roth, J., 373
Sporting events, 110
Stairs, difficulty with,
    144, 150, 159, 165; see
    also Bungalows, Flats
Suburbia, 47, 57
Suffolk, 16, 56,
  health and social
    services in, 196, 210
Sumner, G. and Smith, R.,
    367
Superannuation, 44, 126;
    see also Pensions
Supplementary Benefits, 126,
    127, 140
Surrey, 27, 28, 29
Sussex, 15, 16, 21, 27, 28,
    29, 33, 56, 138, 145,
    177, 186
  health and social
    services in, 197, 198,
    205, 207, 208, 210, 212
Swanage, 34, 204

Teignmouth, 27, 33
Telephones, 90
Television, 108-9
Tenants, private, 141-5
Tenure
  changes of, 164
  and household type, 136
  and income, 136, 144
  and marital status, 135
  of the pre-retirement
    home, 44-6
  of the retirement home,
    135-6
  and social class, 136
Tibbitts, C., 361, 373
Tied housing, 44, 51
Torbay (Torquay), 27, 69
  health and social
    services in, 195, 197,
    198, 208, 212
Tourist attractions, expen-
    diture on, 224, 229
Townsend, P. and Wedderburn,
    D., 361
Traffic, 47, 50, 174

Unfriendliness in resorts,
    87, 88
Upper-class resorts, 33-4
USA, 2, 22, 356

Ventnor, 12
Vickery, K.O.A., 367
Voluntary work, 52, 234

Wales, 19, 22, 25, 26
Walpole, Horace, 11
Walton, 21, 33
Wells, 14
Welsh border country, 21, 22
West Country, 177
West Mersea, 33, 34
Westmorland, 16
Weston-Super-Mare, 27, 28
Weymouth, 12, 27
Whitby, 28
White, E., 362

Whitehead, A., 373
Whitstable, 21
Widows and widowers
　age at time of retirement move, 40
　attitudes to maintenance, 132-3
　children, returning to live with, 41
　contact with brothers and sisters, 83
　dissatisfaction with move, 172-3
　gardening problems, 132-3
　housework, problems with, 133
　leaving resorts, 68, 69, 78
　leisure activities of, 108
　moving to join friends and relations, 51, 58
　occupational pensions, loss of, 126, 128, 363
　proportion of in resorts, 67-9, 78
　see also Marital status
Williamson, J., 361

Willmott, P. and Young, M., 54, 55, 75, 76, 357, 359
Winter visits to resorts, 174
Women (in resorts)
　age of, 66-7
　incomes of, 121-3, 126; sources of, 126
　isolation and, 101
　leaving resorts, 66-9, 170
　leisure activities of, 108
　living in hotels, 146
　living together, 77, 78
　maintenance problems and, 132-3
　private renting and, 141
　savings of, 126
　single, 69-70, 78, 122
　widowed, 67-9, 78
Woolf, M., 356
Worthing, 2, 13, 14, 19, 27, 34, 69
　health and social services in, 186, 188, 194, 199

Yorkshire, 21, 22, 26, 30, 31, 56

Zimmer, B.G. and Hawley, A.H., 362

Routledge Social Science Series

Routledge & Kegan Paul   London and Boston
68–74 Carter Lane   London EC4V 5EL
9 Park Street   Boston   Mass 02108

Contents

International Library of Sociology 3
General Sociology 3
Foreign Classics of Sociology 4
Social Structure 4
Sociology and Politics 5
Foreign Affairs 5
Criminology 5
Social Psychology 6
Sociology of the Family 6
Social Services 7
Sociology of Education 8
Sociology of Culture 8
Sociology of Religion 9
Sociology of Art and Literature 9
Sociology of Knowledge 9
Urban Sociology 10
Rural Sociology 10
Sociology of Industry and Distribution 11
Documentary 11
Anthropology 11
Sociology and Philosophy 12
International Library of Anthropology 12
International Library of Social Policy 13
International Library of Welfare and Philosophy 13
Primary Socialization, Language and Education 13
Reports of the Institute of Community Studies 14
Reports of the Institute for Social Studies in Medical Care 14
Medicine, Illness and Society 15
Monographs in Social Theory 15
Routledge Social Science Journals 15

Authors wishing to submit manuscripts for any series in this catalogue should send them to the Social Science Editor, Routledge & Kegan Paul Ltd, 68–74 Carter Lane, London EC4V 5EL

●*Books so marked are available in paperback*
All books are in Metric Demy 8vo format (216 × 138mm approx.)

International Library of Sociology

General Editor John Rex

GENERAL SOCIOLOGY

Barnsley, J. H. The Social Reality of Ethics. *464 pp.*
Belshaw, Cyril. The Conditions of Social Performance. *An Exploratory Theory. 144 pp.*
Brown, Robert. Explanation in Social Science. *208 pp.*
● Rules and Laws in Sociology. *192 pp.*
Bruford, W. H. Chekhov and His Russia. *A Sociological Study. 244 pp.*
Cain, Maureen E. Society and the Policeman's Role. *326 pp.*
●**Fletcher, Colin.** Beneath the Surface. *An Account of Three Styles of Sociological Research. 221 pp.*
Gibson, Quentin. The Logic of Social Enquiry. *240 pp.*
Glucksmann, M. Structuralist Analysis in Contemporary Social Thought. *212 pp.*
Gurvitch, Georges. Sociology of Law. *Preface by Roscoe Pound. 264 pp.*
Hodge, H. A. Wilhelm Dilthey. *An Introduction. 184 pp.*
Homans, George C. Sentiments and Activities. *336 pp.*
Johnson, Harry M. Sociology: *a Systematic Introduction. Foreword by Robert K. Merton. 710 pp.*
●**Keat, Russell, and Urry, John.** Social Theory as Science. *278 pp.*
Mannheim, Karl. Essays on Sociology and Social Psychology. *Edited by Paul Keckskemeti. With Editorial Note by Adolph Lowe. 344 pp.*
Systematic Sociology: *An Introduction to the Study of Society. Edited by J. S. Erös and Professor W. A. C. Stewart. 220 pp.*
Martindale, Don. The Nature and Types of Sociological Theory. *292 pp.*
●**Maus, Heinz.** A Short History of Sociology. *234 pp.*
Mey, Harald. Field-Theory. *A Study of its Application in the Social Sciences. 352 pp.*
Myrdal, Gunnar. Value in Social Theory: *A Collection of Essays on Methodology. Edited by Paul Streeten. 332 pp.*
Ogburn, William F., and Nimkoff, Meyer F. A Handbook of Sociology. *Preface by Karl Mannheim. 656 pp. 46 figures. 35 tables.*
Parsons, Talcott, and Smelser, Neil J. Economy and Society: *A Study in the Integration of Economic and Social Theory. 362 pp.*
Podgórecki, Adam. Practical Social Sciences. *About 200 pp.*
●**Rex, John.** Key Problems of Sociological Theory. *220 pp.*
Discovering Sociology. *278 pp.*
Sociology and the Demystification of the Modern World. *282 pp.*
●**Rex, John** (Ed.) Approaches to Sociology. *Contributions by Peter Abell, Frank Bechhofer, Basil Bernstein, Ronald Fletcher, David Frisby, Miriam Glucksmann, Peter Lassman, Herminio Martins, John Rex, Roland Robertson, John Westergaard and Jock Young. 302 pp.*
Rigby, A. Alternative Realities. *352 pp.*

Roche, M. Phenomenology, Language and the Social Sciences. *374 pp.*
Sahay, A. Sociological Analysis. *220 pp.*
Strasser, Hermann. The Normative Structure of Sociology. *Conservative and Emancipatory Themes in Social Thought. About 340 pp.*
Urry, John. Reference Groups and the Theory of Revolution. *244 pp.*
Weinberg, E. Development of Sociology in the Soviet Union. *173 pp.*

FOREIGN CLASSICS OF SOCIOLOGY

●**Durkheim, Emile.** Suicide. *A Study in Sociology. Edited and with an Introduction by George Simpson. 404 pp.*
Professional Ethics and Civic Morals. *Translated by Cornelia Brookfield. 288 pp.*
●**Gerth, H. H.,** and **Mills, C. Wright.** From Max Weber: *Essays in Sociology. 502 pp.*
●**Tönnies, Ferdinand.** Community and Association. (*Gemeinschaft und Gesellschaft.*) *Translated and Supplemented by Charles P. Loomis. Foreword by Pitirim A. Sorokin. 334 pp.*

SOCIAL STRUCTURE

Andreski, Stanislav. Military Organization and Society. *Foreword by Professor A. R. Radcliffe-Brown. 226 pp. 1 folder.*
Coontz, Sydney H. Population Theories and the Economic Interpretation. *202 pp.*
Coser, Lewis. The Functions of Social Conflict. *204 pp.*
Dickie-Clark, H. F. Marginal Situation: *A Sociological Study of a Coloured Group. 240 pp. 11 tables.*
Glaser, Barney, and **Strauss, Anselm L.** Status Passage. *A Formal Theory. 208 pp.*
Glass, D. V. (Ed.) Social Mobility in Britain. *Contributions by J. Berent, T. Bottomore, R. C. Chambers, J. Floud, D. V. Glass, J. R. Hall, H. T. Himmelweit, R. K. Kelsall, F. M. Martin, C. A. Moser, R. Mukherjee, and W. Ziegel. 420 pp.*
Jones, Garth N. Planned Organizational Change: *An Exploratory Study Using an Empirical Approach. 268 pp.*
Kelsall, R. K. Higher Civil Servants in Britain: *From 1870 to the Present Day. 268 pp. 31 tables.*
König, René. The Community. *232 pp. Illustrated.*
●**Lawton, Denis.** Social Class, Language and Education. *192 pp.*
McLeish, John. The Theory of Social Change: *Four Views Considered. 128 pp.*
Marsh, David C. The Changing Social Structure of England and Wales, 1871-1961. *288 pp.*
●**Mouzelis, Nicos.** Organization and Bureaucracy. *An Analysis of Modern Theories. 240 pp.*
Mulkay, M. J. Functionalism, Exchange and Theoretical Strategy. *272 pp.*
Ossowski, Stanislaw. Class Structure in the Social Consciousness. *210 pp.*
●**Podgórecki, Adam.** Law and Society. *302 pp.*

SOCIOLOGY AND POLITICS

Acton, T. A. Gypsy Politics and Social Change. *316 pp.*
Clegg, Stuart. Power, Rule and Domination. *A Critical and Empirical Understanding of Power in Sociological Theory and Organisational Life. About 300 pp.*
Hechter, Michael. Internal Colonialism. *The Celtic Fringe in British National Development, 1536–1966. 361 pp.*
Hertz, Frederick. Nationality in History and Politics: *A Psychology and Sociology of National Sentiment and Nationalism. 432 pp.*
Kornhauser, William. The Politics of Mass Society. *272 pp. 20 tables.*
●**Kroes, R.** Soldiers and Students. *A Study of Right- and Left-wing Students. 174 pp.*
Laidler, Harry W. History of Socialism. *Social-Economic Movements: An Historical and Comparative Survey of Socialism, Communism, Co-operation, Utopianism; and other Systems of Reform and Reconstruction. 992 pp.*
Lasswell, H. D. Analysis of Political Behaviour. *324 pp.*
Mannheim, Karl. Freedom, Power and Democratic Planning. *Edited by Hans Gerth and Ernest K. Bramstedt. 424 pp.*
Mansur, Fatma. Process of Independence. *Foreword by A. H. Hanson. 208 pp.*
Martin, David A. Pacifism: *an Historical and Sociological Study. 262 pp.*
Myrdal, Gunnar. The Political Element in the Development of Economic Theory. *Translated from the German by Paul Streeten. 282 pp.*
Wootton, Graham. Workers, Unions and the State. *188 pp.*

FOREIGN AFFAIRS: THEIR SOCIAL, POLITICAL AND ECONOMIC FOUNDATIONS

Mayer, J. P. Political Thought in France from the Revolution to the Fifth Republic. *164 pp.*

CRIMINOLOGY

Ancel, Marc. Social Defence: *A Modern Approach to Criminal Problems. Foreword by Leon Radzinowicz. 240 pp.*
Cain, Maureen E. Society and the Policeman's Role. *326 pp.*
Cloward, Richard A., and **Ohlin, Lloyd E.** Delinquency and Opportunity: *A Theory of Delinquent Gangs. 248 pp.*
Downes, David M. The Delinquent Solution. *A Study in Subcultural Theory. 296 pp.*
Dunlop, A. B., and **McCabe, S.** Young Men in Detention Centres. *192 pp.*
Friedlander, Kate. The Psycho-Analytical Approach to Juvenile Delinquency: *Theory, Case Studies, Treatment. 320 pp.*
Glueck, Sheldon, and **Eleanor.** Family Environment and Delinquency. *With the statistical assistance of Rose W. Kneznek. 340 pp.*
Lopez-Rey, Manuel. Crime. *An Analytical Appraisal. 288 pp.*
Mannheim, Hermann. Comparative Criminology: *a Text Book. Two volumes. 442 pp. and 380 pp.*

Morris, Terence. The Criminal Area: *A Study in Social Ecology. Foreword by Hermann Mannheim. 232 pp. 25 tables. 4 maps.*
Rock, Paul. Making People Pay. *338 pp.*
●Taylor, Ian, Walton, Paul, and Young, Jock. The New Criminology. *For a Social Theory of Deviance. 325 pp.*
●Taylor, Ian, Walton, Paul, and Young, Jock (Eds). Critical Criminology. *268 pp.*

SOCIAL PSYCHOLOGY

Bagley, Christopher. The Social Psychology of the Epileptic Child. *320 pp.*
Barbu, Zevedei. Problems of Historical Psychology. *248 pp.*
Blackburn, Julian. Psychology and the Social Pattern. *184 pp.*
●Brittan, Arthur. Meanings and Situations. *224 pp.*
Carroll, J. Break-Out from the Crystal Palace. *200 pp.*
●Fleming, C. M. Adolescence: Its Social Psychology. *With an Introduction to recent findings from the fields of Anthropology, Physiology, Medicine, Psychometrics and Sociometry. 288 pp.*
● The Social Psychology of Education: *An Introduction and Guide to Its Study. 136 pp.*
●Homans, George C. The Human Group. *Foreword by Bernard DeVoto. Introduction by Robert K. Merton. 526 pp.*
● Social Behaviour: *its Elementary Forms. 416 pp.*
●Klein, Josephine. The Study of Groups. *226 pp. 31 figures. 5 tables.*
Linton, Ralph. The Cultural Background of Personality. *132 pp.*
●Mayo, Elton. The Social Problems of an Industrial Civilization. *With an appendix on the Political Problem. 180 pp.*
Ottaway, A. K. C. Learning Through Group Experience. *176 pp.*
Plummer, Ken. Sexual Stigma. *An Interactionist Account. 254 pp.*
Ridder, J. C. de. The Personality of the Urban African in South Africa. *A Thematic Apperception Test Study. 196 pp. 12 plates.*
●Rose, Arnold M. (Ed.) Human Behaviour and Social Processes: *an Interactionist Approach. Contributions by Arnold M. Rose, Ralph H. Turner, Anselm Strauss, Everett C. Hughes, E. Franklin Frazier, Howard S. Becker, et al. 696 pp.*
Smelser, Neil J. Theory of Collective Behaviour. *448 pp.*
Stephenson, Geoffrey M. The Development of Conscience. *128 pp.*
Young, Kimball. Handbook of Social Psychology. *658 pp. 16 figures. 10 tables.*

SOCIOLOGY OF THE FAMILY

Banks, J. A. Prosperity and Parenthood: *A Study of Family Planning among The Victorian Middle Classes. 262 pp.*
Bell, Colin R. Middle Class Families: *Social and Geographical Mobility. 224 pp.*
Burton, Lindy. Vulnerable Children. *272 pp.*
Gavron, Hannah. The Captive Wife: *Conflicts of Household Mothers. 190 pp.*

George, Victor, and **Wilding, Paul.** Motherless Families. *248 pp.*
Klein, Josephine. Samples from English Cultures.
  1. Three Preliminary Studies and Aspects of Adult Life in England. *447 pp.*
  2. Child-Rearing Practices and Index. *247 pp.*
Klein, Viola. Britain's Married Women Workers. *180 pp.*
  The Feminine Character. *History of an Ideology. 244 pp.*
McWhinnie, Alexina M. Adopted Children. *How They Grow Up. 304 pp.*
● **Morgan, D. H. J.** Social Theory and the Family. *About 320 pp.*
● **Myrdal, Alva,** and **Klein, Viola.** Women's Two Roles: *Home and Work. 238 pp. 27 tables.*
Parsons, Talcott, and **Bales, Robert F.** Family: Socialization and Interaction Process. *In collaboration with James Olds, Morris Zelditch and Philip E. Slater. 456 pp. 50 figures and tables.*

SOCIAL SERVICES

Bastide, Roger. The Sociology of Mental Disorder. *Translated from the French by Jean McNeil. 260 pp.*
Carlebach, Julius. Caring For Children in Trouble. *266 pp.*
George, Victor. Foster Care. *Theory and Practice. 234 pp.*
  Social Security: *Beveridge and After. 258 pp.*
George, V., and **Wilding, P.** Motherless Families. *248 pp.*
● **Goetschius, George W.** Working with Community Groups. *256 pp.*
Goetschius, George W., and **Tash, Joan.** Working with Unattached Youth. *416 pp.*
Hall, M. P., and **Howes, I. V.** The Church in Social Work. *A Study of Moral Welfare Work undertaken by the Church of England. 320 pp.*
Heywood, Jean S. Children in Care: *the Development of the Service for the Deprived Child. 264 pp.*
Hoenig, J., and **Hamilton, Marian W.** The De-Segregation of the Mentally Ill. *284 pp.*
Jones, Kathleen. Mental Health and Social Policy, 1845-1959. *264 pp.*
King, Roy D., Raynes, Norma V., and **Tizard, Jack.** Patterns of Residential Care. *356 pp.*
Leigh, John. Young People and Leisure. *256 pp.*
● **Mays, John.** (Ed.) Penelope Hall's Social Services of England and Wales. *About 324 pp.*
Morris, Mary. Voluntary Work and the Welfare State. *300 pp.*
Morris, Pauline. Put Away: *A Sociological Study of Institutions for the Mentally Retarded. 364 pp.*
Nokes, P. L. The Professional Task in Welfare Practice. *152 pp.*
Timms, Noel. Psychiatric Social Work in Great Britain (1939-1962). *280 pp.*
●   Social Casework: *Principles and Practice. 256 pp.*
Young, A. F. Social Services in British Industry. *272 pp.*
Young, A. F., and **Ashton, E. T.** British Social Work in the Nineteenth Century. *288 pp.*

SOCIOLOGY OF EDUCATION

Banks, Olive. Parity and Prestige in English Secondary Education: a Study in Educational Sociology. *272 pp.*

Bentwich, Joseph. Education in Israel. *224 pp. 8 pp. plates.*

●**Blyth, W. A. L.** English Primary Education. *A Sociological Description.*
  1. Schools. *232 pp.*
  2. Background. *168 pp.*

Collier, K. G. The Social Purposes of Education: *Personal and Social Values in Education. 268 pp.*

Dale, R. R., and **Griffith, S.** Down Stream: *Failure in the Grammar School. 108 pp.*

Dore, R. P. Education in Tokugawa Japan. *356 pp. 9 pp. plates.*

Evans, K. M. Sociometry and Education. *158 pp.*

●**Ford, Julienne.** Social Class and the Comprehensive School. *192 pp.*

Foster, P. J. Education and Social Change in Ghana. *336 pp. 3 maps.*

Fraser, W. R. Education and Society in Modern France. *150 pp.*

Grace, Gerald R. Role Conflict and the Teacher. *150 pp.*

Hans, Nicholas. New Trends in Education in the Eighteenth Century. *278 pp. 19 tables.*

● Comparative Education: *A Study of Educational Factors and Traditions. 360 pp.*

●**Hargreaves, David.** Interpersonal Relations and Education. *432 pp.*
● Social Relations in a Secondary School. *240 pp.*

Holmes, Brian. Problems in Education. *A Comparative Approach. 336 pp.*

King, Ronald. Values and Involvement in a Grammar School. *164 pp.*
  School Organization and Pupil Involvement. *A Study of Secondary Schools.*

●**Mannheim, Karl,** and **Stewart, W. A. C.** An Introduction to the Sociology of Education. *206 pp.*

Morris, Raymond N. The Sixth Form and College Entrance. *231 pp.*

●**Musgrove, F.** Youth and the Social Order. *176 pp.*

●**Ottaway, A. K. C.** Education and Society: An Introduction to the Sociology of Education. *With an Introduction by W. O. Lester Smith. 212 pp.*

Peers, Robert. Adult Education: *A Comparative Study. 398 pp.*

Pritchard, D. G. Education and the Handicapped: *1760 to 1960. 258 pp.*

Richardson, Helen. Adolescent Girls in Approved Schools. *308 pp.*

Stratta, Erica. The Education of Borstal Boys. *A Study of their Educational Experiences prior to, and during, Borstal Training. 256 pp.*

Taylor, P. H., Reid, W. A., and **Holley, B. J.** The English Sixth Form. *A Case Study in Curriculum Research. 200 pp.*

SOCIOLOGY OF CULTURE

Eppel, E. M., and **M.** Adolescents and Morality: *A Study of some Moral Values and Dilemmas of Working Adolescents in the Context of a changing Climate of Opinion. Foreword by W. J. H. Sprott. 268 pp. 39 tables.*

● **Fromm, Erich.** The Fear of Freedom. *286 pp.*
● The Sane Society. *400 pp.*
Mannheim, Karl. Essays on the Sociology of Culture. *Edited by Ernst Mannheim in co-operation with Paul Kecskemeti. Editorial Note by Adolph Lowe.* 280 pp.
Weber, Alfred. Farewell to European History: *or The Conquest of Nihilism. Translated from the German by R. F. C. Hull.* 224 pp.

SOCIOLOGY OF RELIGION

Argyle, Michael and **Beit-Hallahmi, Benjamin.** The Social Psychology of Religion. *About 256 pp.*
Nelson, G. K. Spiritualism and Society. *313 pp.*
Stark, Werner. The Sociology of Religion. *A Study of Christendom.*
 Volume I. *Established Religion. 248 pp.*
 Volume II. *Sectarian Religion. 368 pp.*
 Volume III. *The Universal Church. 464 pp.*
 Volume IV. *Types of Religious Man. 352 pp.*
 Volume V. *Types of Religious Culture. 464 pp.*
Turner, B. S. Weber and Islam. *216 pp.*
Watt, W. Montgomery. Islam and the Integration of Society. *320 pp.*

SOCIOLOGY OF ART AND LITERATURE

Jarvie, Ian C. Towards a Sociology of the Cinema. *A Comparative Essay on the Structure and Functioning of a Major Entertainment Industry. 405 pp.*
Rust, Frances S. Dance in Society. *An Analysis of the Relationships between the Social Dance and Society in England from the Middle Ages to the Present Day. 256 pp. 8 pp. of plates.*
Schücking, L. L. The Sociology of Literary Taste. *112 pp.*
Wolff, Janet. Hermeneutic Philosophy and the Sociology of Art. *150 pp.*

SOCIOLOGY OF KNOWLEDGE

Diesing, P. Patterns of Discovery in the Social Sciences. *262 pp.*
● **Douglas, J. D.** (Ed.) Understanding Everyday Life. *370 pp.*
● **Hamilton, P.** Knowledge and Social Structure. *174 pp.*
Jarvie, I. C. Concepts and Society. *232 pp.*
Mannheim, Karl. Essays on the Sociology of Knowledge. *Edited by Paul Kecskemeti. Editorial Note by Adolph Lowe.* 353 pp.
Remmling, Gunter W. The Sociology of Karl Mannheim. *With a Bibliographical Guide to the Sociology of Knowledge, Ideological Analysis, and Social Planning.* 255 pp.

Remmling, Gunter W. (Ed.) Towards the Sociology of Knowledge. *Origin and Development of a Sociological Thought Style. 463 pp.*
Stark, Werner. The Sociology of Knowledge: *An Essay in Aid of a Deeper Understanding of the History of Ideas. 384 pp.*

URBAN SOCIOLOGY

Ashworth, William. The Genesis of Modern British Town Planning: *A Study in Economic and Social History of the Nineteenth and Twentieth Centuries. 288 pp.*
Cullingworth, J. B. Housing Needs and Planning Policy: *A Restatement of the Problems of Housing Need and 'Overspill' in England and Wales. 232 pp. 44 tables. 8 maps.*
Dickinson, Robert E. City and Region: *A Geographical Interpretation 608 pp. 125 figures.*
   The West European City: *A Geographical Interpretation. 600 pp. 129 maps. 29 plates.*
● The City Region in Western Europe. *320 pp. Maps.*
Humphreys, Alexander J. New Dubliners: *Urbanization and the Irish Family. Foreword by George C. Homans. 304 pp.*
Jackson, Brian. Working Class Community: *Some General Notions raised by a Series of Studies in Northern England. 192 pp.*
Jennings, Hilda. Societies in the Making: *a Study of Development and Redevelopment within a County Borough. Foreword by D. A. Clark. 286 pp.*
●**Mann, P. H.** An Approach to Urban Sociology. *240 pp.*
Morris, R. N., and **Mogey, J.** The Sociology of Housing. *Studies at Berinsfield. 232 pp. 4 pp. plates.*
Rosser, C., and **Harris, C.** The Family and Social Change. *A Study of Family and Kinship in a South Wales Town. 352 pp. 8 maps.*
●**Stacey, Margaret, Batsone, Eric, Bell, Colin,** and **Thurcott, Anne.** Power, Persistence and Change. *A Second Study of Banbury. 196 pp.*

RURAL SOCIOLOGY

Chambers, R. J. H. Settlement Schemes in Tropical Africa: *A Selective Study. 268 pp.*
Haswell, M. R. The Economics of Development in Village India. *120 pp.*
Littlejohn, James. Westrigg: *the Sociology of a Cheviot Parish. 172 pp. 5 figures.*
Mayer, Adrian C. Peasants in the Pacific. *A Study of Fiji Indian Rural Society. 248 pp. 20 plates.*
Williams, W. M. The Sociology of an English Village: *Gosforth. 272 pp. 12 figures. 13 tables.*

SOCIOLOGY OF INDUSTRY AND DISTRIBUTION

Anderson, Nels. Work and Leisure. *280 pp.*
● **Blau, Peter M.,** and **Scott, W. Richard.** Formal Organizations: *a Comparative approach. Introduction and Additional Bibliography by J. H. Smith. 326 pp.*
Dunkerley, David. The Foreman. *Aspects of Task and Structure. 192 pp.*
Eldridge, J. E. T. Industrial Disputes. *Essays in the Sociology of Industrial Relations. 288 pp.*
Hetzler, Stanley. Applied Measures for Promoting Technological Growth. *352 pp.*
   Technological Growth and Social Change. *Achieving Modernization. 269 pp.*
Hollowell, Peter G. The Lorry Driver. *272 pp.*
Jefferys, Margot, *with the assistance of Winifred Moss.* Mobility in the Labour Market: *Employment Changes in Battersea and Dagenham. Preface by Barbara Wootton. 186 pp. 51 tables.*
Millerson, Geoffrey. The Qualifying Associations: *a Study in Professionalization. 320 pp.*
● **Oxaal, I., Barnett, T.,** and **Booth, D.** (Eds). Beyond the Sociology of Development. *Economy and Society in Latin America and Africa. 295 pp.*
Smelser, Neil J. Social Change in the Industrial Revolution: *An Application of Theory to the Lancashire Cotton Industry, 1770–1840. 468 pp. 12 figures. 14 tables.*
Williams, Gertrude. Recruitment to Skilled Trades. *240 pp.*
Young, A. F. Industrial Injuries Insurance: *an Examination of British Policy. 192 pp.*

DOCUMENTARY

Schlesinger, Rudolf (Ed.) Changing Attitudes in Soviet Russia.
   2. The Nationalities Problem and Soviet Administration. *Selected Readings on the Development of Soviet Nationalities Policies. Introduced by the editor. Translated by W. W. Gottlieb. 324 pp.*

ANTHROPOLOGY

Ammar, Hamed. Growing up in an Egyptian Village: *Silwa, Province of Aswan. 336 pp.*
Brandel-Syrier, Mia. Reeftown Elite. *A Study of Social Mobility in a Modern African Community on the Reef. 376 pp.*
Crook, David, and **Isabel.** Revolution in a Chinese Village: *Ten Mile Inn. 230 pp. 8 plates. 1 map.*
Dickie-Clark, H. F. The Marginal Situation. *A Sociological Study of a Coloured Group. 236 pp.*
Dube, S. C. Indian Village. *Foreword by Morris Edward Opler. 276 pp. 4 plates.*

India's Changing Villages: *Human Factors in Community Development.* 260 pp. 8 plates. 1 map.
Firth, Raymond. Malay Fishermen. *Their Peasant Economy.* 420 pp. 17 pp. plates.
Firth, R., Hubert, J., and Forge, A. Families and their Relatives. *Kinship in a Middle-Class Sector of London: An Anthropological Study.* 456 pp.
Gulliver, P. H. Social Control in an African Society: a Study of the Arusha, Agricultural Masai of Northern Tanganyika. *320 pp. 8 plates. 10 figures.*
Family Herds. *288 pp.*
Ishwaran, K. Shivapur. *A South Indian Village.* 216 pp.
Tradition and Economy in Village India: *An Interactionist Approach.* Foreword by Conrad Arensburg. 176 pp.
Jarvie, Ian C. The Revolution in Anthropology. *268 pp.*
Little, Kenneth L. Mende of Sierra Leone. *308 pp. and folder.*
Negroes in Britain. *With a New Introduction and Contemporary Study by Leonard Bloom.* 320 pp.
Lowie, Robert H. Social Organization. *494 pp.*
Peasants in the Pacific. *A Study of Fiji Indian Rural Society.* 248 pp.
Smith, Raymond T. The Negro Family in British Guiana: *Family Structure and Social Status in the Villages. With a Foreword by Meyer Fortes.* 314 pp. 8 plates. 1 figure. 4 maps.

SOCIOLOGY AND PHILOSOPHY

Barnsley, John H. The Social Reality of Ethics. *A Comparative Analysis of Moral Codes.* 448 pp.
Diesing, Paul. Patterns of Discovery in the Social Sciences. *362 pp.*
●**Douglas, Jack D.** (Ed.) Understanding Everyday Life. *Toward the Reconstruction of Sociological Knowledge. Contributions by Alan F. Blum. Aaron W. Cicourel, Norman K. Denzin, Jack D. Douglas, John Heeren, Peter McHugh, Peter K. Manning, Melvin Power, Matthew Speier, Roy Turner, D. Lawrence Wieder, Thomas P. Wilson and Don H. Zimmerman.* 370 pp.
Jarvie, Ian C. Concepts and Society. *216 pp.*
●**Pelz, Werner.** The Scope of Understanding in Sociology. *Towards a more radical reorientation in the social humanistic sciences.* 283 pp.
Roche, Maurice. Phenomenology, Language and the Social Sciences. *371 pp.*
Sahay, Arun. Sociological Analysis. *212 pp.*
Sklair, Leslie. The Sociology of Progress. *320 pp.*

International Library of Anthropology

General Editor Adam Kuper

Brown, Paula. The Chimbu. *A Study of Change in the New Guinea Highlands.* 151 pp.

Hamnett, Ian. Chieftainship and Legitimacy. *An Anthropological Study of Executive Law in Lesotho.* 163 pp.
Hanson, F. Allan. Meaning in Culture. *127 pp.*
Lloyd, P. C. Power and Independence. *Urban Africans' Perception of Social Inequality.* 264 pp.
Pettigrew, Joyce. Robber Noblemen. *A Study of the Political System of the Sikh Jats.* 284 pp.
Street, Brian V. The Savage in Literature. *Representations of 'Primitive' Society in English Fiction, 1858–1920.* 207 pp.
Van Den Berghe, Pierre L. Power and Privilege at an African University. *278 pp.*

International Library of Social Policy

General Editor Kathleen Jones

Bayley, M. Mental Handicap and Community Care. *426 pp.*
Butler, J. R. Family Doctors and Public Policy. *208 pp.*
Davies, Martin. Prisoners of Society. *Attitudes and Aftercare.* 204 pp.
Holman, Robert. Trading in Children. *A Study of Private Fostering.* 355 pp.
Jones, Kathleen. History of the Mental Health Service. *428 pp.*
  Opening the Door. *A Study of New Policies for the Mentally Handicapped.* 260 pp.
Thomas, J. E. The English Prison Officer since 1850: *A Study in Conflict.* 258 pp.
Walton, R. G. Women in Social Work. *303 pp.*
Woodward, J. To Do the Sick No Harm. *A Study of the British Voluntary Hospital System to 1875.* 221 pp.

International Library of Welfare and Philosophy

General Editors Noel Timms and David Watson

● Plant, Raymond. Community and Ideology. *104 pp.*

Primary Socialization, Language and Education

General Editor Basil Bernstein

Bernstein, Basil. Class, Codes and Control. *3 volumes.*
  1. *Theoretical Studies Towards a Sociology of Language.* 254 pp.
  2. *Applied Studies Towards a Sociology of Language.* 377 pp.
  3. *Towards a Theory of Educational Transmission.* 167 pp.
Brandis, W., and Bernstein, B. Selection and Control. *176 pp.*
Brandis, Walter, and Henderson, Dorothy. Social Class, Language and Communication. *288 pp.*

Cook-Gumperz, Jenny. Social Control and Socialization. *A Study of Class Differences in the Language of Maternal Control. 290 pp.*
● Gahagan, D. M., and G. A. Talk Reform. *Exploration in Language for Infant School Children. 160 pp.*
Robinson, W. P., and Rackstraw, Susan D. A. A Question of Answers. *2 volumes. 192 pp. and 180 pp.*
Turner, Geoffrey J., and Mohan, Bernard A. A Linguistic Description and Computer Programme for Children's Speech. *208 pp.*

Reports of the Institute of Community Studies

Cartwright, Ann. Human Relations and Hospital Care. *272 pp.*
●   Parents and Family Planning Services. *306 pp.*
Patients and their Doctors. *A Study of General Practice. 304 pp.*
Dench, Geoff. Maltese in London. *A Case-study in the Erosion of Ethnic Consciousness. 302 pp.*
● Jackson, Brian. Streaming: *an Education System in Miniature. 168 pp.*
Jackson, Brian, and Marsden, Dennis. Education and the Working Class: *Some General Themes raised by a Study of 88 Working-class Children in a Northern Industrial City. 268 pp. 2 folders.*
Marris, Peter. The Experience of Higher Education. *232 pp. 27 tables.*
Loss and Change. *192 pp.*
Marris, Peter, and Rein, Martin. Dilemmas of Social Reform. *Poverty and Community Action in the United States. 256 pp.*
Marris, Peter, and Somerset, Anthony. African Businessmen. *A Study of Entrepreneurship and Development in Kenya. 256 pp.*
Mills, Richard. Young Outsiders: *a Study in Alternative Communities. 216 pp.*
Runciman, W. G. Relative Deprivation and Social Justice. *A Study of Attitudes to Social Inequality in Twentieth-Century England. 352 pp.*
Willmott, Peter. Adolescent Boys in East London. *230 pp.*
Willmott, Peter, and Young, Michael. Family and Class in a London Suburb. *202 pp. 47 tables.*
Young, Michael. Innovation and Research in Education. *192 pp.*
● Young, Michael, and McGeeney, Patrick. Learning Begins at Home. *A Study of a Junior School and its Parents. 128 pp.*
Young, Michael, and Willmott, Peter. Family and Kinship in East London. *Foreword by Richard M. Titmuss. 252 pp. 39 tables.*
The Symmetrical Family. *410 pp.*

Reports of the Institute for Social Studies in Medical Care

Cartwright, Ann, Hockey, Lisbeth, and Anderson, John L. Life Before Death. *310 pp.*
Dunnell, Karen, and Cartwright, Ann. Medicine Takers, Prescribers and Hoarders. *190 pp.*

Medicine, Illness and Society
General Editor W. M. Williams

Robinson, David. The Process of Becoming Ill. *142 pp.*
Stacey, Margaret, *et al.* Hospitals, Children and Their Families. *The Report of a Pilot Study. 202 pp.*
Stimson, G. V., and **Webb, B.** Going to See the Doctor. *The Consultation Process in General Practice. 155 pp.*

Monographs in Social Theory
General Editor Arthur Brittan

●**Barnes, B.** Scientific Knowledge and Sociological Theory. *192 pp.*
Bauman, Zygmunt. Culture as Praxis. *204 pp.*
●**Dixon, Keith.** Sociological Theory. *Pretence and Possibility. 142 pp.*
Meltzer, B. N., Petras, J. W., and **Reynolds, L. T.** Symbolic Interactionism. *Genesis, Varieties and Criticisms. 144 pp.*
●**Smith, Anthony D.** The Concept of Social Change. *A Critique of the Functionalist Theory of Social Change. 208 pp.*

Routledge Social Science Journals

The British Journal of Sociology. *Managing Editor – Angus Stewart; Associate Editor – Michael Hill. Vol. 1, No. 1 – March 1950 and Quarterly. Roy. 8vo. All back issues available. An international journal publishing original papers in the field of sociology and related areas.*
Community Work. *Edited by David Jones and Marjorie Mayo. 1973. Published annually.*
Economy and Society. *Vol. 1, No. 1. February 1972 and Quarterly. Metric Roy. 8vo. A journal for all social scientists covering sociology, philosophy, anthropology, economics and history. Back numbers available.*
Religion. Journal of Religion and Religions. *Chairman of Editorial Board, Ninian Smart. Vol. 1, No. 1, Spring 1971. A journal with an interdisciplinary approach to the study of the phenomena of religion.*
Year Book of Social Policy in Britain, The. *Edited by Kathleen Jones. 1971. Published annually.*

Printed in Great Britain by Unwin Brothers Limited
The Gresham Press Old Woking Surrey
A member of the Staples Printing Group   June 1975